A MONOGRAPH
OF THE WORKS OF
McKIM
MEAD &
WHITE
1879-1915

A MONOGRAPH OF THE WORKS OF

McKIM MEAD & WHITE 1879-1915

NEW EDITION FOUR VOLS. IN ONE
WITH AN ESSAY BY LELAND ROTH
BENJAMIN BLOM NEW YORK 1973

ARNO PRESS

NEW YORK • 1977

First published New York, 1915
Reissued 1973 by Benjamin Blom, Inc.
with a new essay and notes on the plates
by Leland M. Roth

Reprint Edition 1977 by Arno Press, Inc.

Printed in the United States of America
Noble Offset Printers, Inc. New York, NY 10003

Library of Congress Cataloging In Publication Data

McKim, Mead & White.
    A monograph of the works of McKim, Mead & White
1879-1915.

    Includes bibliographical references.
    1. McKim, Mead & White. 2. Architecture, Modern—
19th century—United States. 3. Architecture, Modern—
20th century—United States. I. Title.
NA737.M4A5   1973   720'.6'57471   72-152624

INTRODUCTION

by Benjamin Blom

Mᴏʀᴇ ᴛʜᴀɴ ꜰɪᴠᴇ ᴅᴇᴄᴀᴅᴇꜱ after the systematic denigration of McKim, Mead & White enough of their work has been destroyed, truncated, and vandalized to force a second look by those once most adamant in their claims that M M & W, and other classicists, were mere copycats; worse, responsible for stifling and setting back for decades the development of a genuine, vernacular, indigenous, and above all original American architecture. That judgment is now part of the historical record, to be found with themes and variations in every book by every historian who upheld Richardson, Sullivan, and Frank Lloyd Wright as the *only* and *true* modern American architects, the progenitors of the Bauhaus, International style, and other modern styles which, unlike that of the classicists', so it was said, married function (as they defined it) to form. Those others—McKim, Mead & White among them—may have been brilliant antiquarians and archaeologists, copying styles and ornaments to suit and/or placate the nouveau-riche taste of the super nouveau riche, but originality was hardly their forte. "Rich men's architects" was the epithet, one outstanding historian going so far as to disclaim completely the architect label, relegating the classicists to the role of engineers and craftsmen. Such was the well-nigh universal viewpoint of the movers and shakers of society, promulgated from classroom to classroom, school to school, book to book, with only the stridency varying in degrees. So looked at, the classicists' buildings took on a special characteristic: Dispensable. The climate had been nurtured; the wreckers' balls followed, one building after another pulverized without too much or any protest. If the classicists were indeed the dead weight all these architects, cityplanners, historians, and others claimed they were, why would anyone care?

The more that was torn down, the more the nonspecialists became disturbed, the volume and vehemence of the protest movement increasing with each new assault upon still another of those allegedly "copyist" buildings. An outstanding historian of the culture of cities said of one such building, still extant, "Light, air, space, and silence . . . were all forfeited in this inept design," the reference being to the 42nd Street New York Public Library. A few specialists, Henry Hope Reed and Ada Louise Huxtable among them, had other thoughts, putting into words the feeling of those disturbed by the gap left in the cityscape when such "inept" buildings landed in New Jersey's marshes. The Vanderbilt Mansion, Pennsylvania Railroad Station, and other exemplars of Rich Men's Architecture scattered throughout New York began to be seen as more than the expression of power and as imperialist facades; their color, ornamentation, style, and their very opulence provided a study in contrast and diversity that gave the city its sparkle, its visual excitement, in part its grandeur, now enjoyable to Everyperson.

That McKim, Mead & White were quite capable of developing American idioms—the shingle style among them—the *Monograph* and other works make explicitly clear. Stylistically they reversed their earlier course by choice, mainly because of a special set of circumstances, uniquely American, that begged for a "classical" solution. Some of the work of the "modernists" was equally exciting to many—contributions to the cityscape (in Chicago especially) that in turn heightened the diversity and visual stimulation that make cities the never-ending works-in-progress of the human mind. The classicists, responding to a set of historical circumstances, gave our cities an opulence and grandeur; the modernists experimented with new technics and forms to blaze the way for later developments. Few indeed today would advocate the sterility of going back to that earlier classicism, but more and more today see it as a major contribution to our cityscape, stylistically and in terms of the placement of its buildings.

Decades after the death of American classicism, and well after the almost total triumph of the "moderns," the denigration of the works of M M & W, Carrère & Hastings, Post, Flagg, and others continued full blast, and not only in the books and classrooms. Walter Gropius, the founder of the Bauhaus School, for example, played a major role in designing the Pan-Am Building which, aesthetics aside (and few indeed are enamored with that structure), is an affront to the classicists' carefully wrought cityscape; the new building overwhelmed Grand Central Terminal, lording loud and boisterously over Park Avenue south and north. Gropius's colleague, Marcel Breuer, now advocates placing an elephantine structure atop Grand Central airspace, a visual *coup de grâce* to its exterior setting. Washington Square, its character in large measure still delineated by Stanford White's Washington Arch and Judson Memorial Church, is now subjected to a Philip Johnson fortress-like building that is completely out of character with the delicate fabric of that historic square. To create the climate in which such things can operate one has first to adopt the stance of contempt for the classicists.

The age of classicism may have passed, but the more some "modernists" build, the greater the appreciation of that earlier style. Too many of the glass-faced creations currently lining Manhattan's avenues have proved to be far less than the heralds of a new American humanist architecture, their windswept plazas and bank-lined street fronts dulling the cityscape, their look-alike styles injecting gray monotony. Whereas the classicists' structures reflected the tastes of identifiable individuals, some of these new structures seem to mirror the consensus of the faceless directors that run corporate boards; in the field of housing the Le Corbusier inspired "projects," from Stuyvesant Town to its latter day descendants (Pruitt-Igoe in St. Louis, for example), also appear less and less inspiring as more and more crop up all over the cityscape.

In the academic world an interesting development occurred, unwittingly undermining the "copycat" charge leveled at the classicists and throwing new light on the originality of the modernists. The more these academics looked into the origins and genesis of the modern styles, the more they traced earlier, then still earlier, then still earlier prototypes.

How brilliant these adaptations, they said, how truly American and original the juxtapositions! Few would dispute their judgment although some might ask why these standards cannot in any way be applied to the classicists.

The staggering number of outstanding classic and Renaissance buildings destroyed in the past few decades is hinted at by Nathan Silver in *Lost New York*. Most went down with little or no protest despite the evident adaptability of many to contemporary use, the availability of ample space elsewhere for entirely new buildings, and the aesthetic worth of these structures to large masses of people, especially those who recognize that cities are attractive to the degree they stimulate diverse tastes.

Recently, however, the heightened violation of the city-dweller's right to an architectural heritage, and the vandalism, have aroused a protest that is loud and clear although, regrettably, still too frequently limited to famous buildings. The value judgments and thinking processes that permitted entire neighborhoods first to be neglected, then destroyed (the "start from the ground up" bulldozer mentality) are the value judgments and thinking processes that ultimately made possible the destruction of McKim, Mead & White's Madison Square Garden and Penn Station. In the past historic monuments have been neglected, razed, or radically altered because of alleged economic necessity, obsolescence, or the need for "improvement." Now crime prevention is advanced as the reason why Oscar Newman, Director of New York University's Institute of Planning and Housing, advocates placing a seven-foot-high picket fence around one of New York's most renowned open spaces — Washington Square — with Stanford White's Washington Arch within its northern boundaries and McKim, Mead & White's Judson Memorial Church to the south. That picket fence is to discourage "winos" and down-and-outers from invading the park and to reduce the incidence of crime and vandalism, attributed to "a few characters" (*Village Voice*, April 12, 1973). That the roots of crime and criminality may be traced to sources other than "a few characters," that racism, sexism, low wages, or the horrors of the South Bronx's countless abandoned and garbage-filled buildings — to cite a few specifics — could play a part in the city's malaise appears to have been overlooked.

The proposed fence represents still another gross assault on a New York landmark. It is possible to conceive of the proposal as a palatable means of coping with a major social problem that admittedly exists in the square if it is seen as the only viable solution, and then only if it may reasonably be expected to work. But if the winos are free to move into this area now via the limited access roads leading to the square, will eight unattended gates present a more formidable obstacle? How will those gates alter the notorious lack of police surveillance and action in the region? Moreover, what is to stop muggers, purse-snatchers, and the like from operating near the unattended gates? If criminality and vandalism are to be contained by such means, can barbed wire around White's Washington Arch be far behind? And if that fails, why not issue a private seven-foot-high picket fence cage, mobile and on roller skates, to any individual desirous of entering such dangerous grounds?

The distorted social value judgments and the dubious practicality of the proposal aside, it is clear that before hundreds of thousands of dollars are spent on a fence that will offend many, please few, the City of New York should restore essential services and reverse the well-nigh criminal neglect by its departments of parks, sanitation, and police that prepared the ground for the vandalism against people, space, and buildings long before the winos entered the park.

The city's problems are real, clear for all to see. Too often Experts, some living in the suburbs or farther away, rivet their attention only on the decay, writing off the city as disease-ridden and doomed. But to the millions who live in New York the paradoxes and contradictions are clear; to them daily life is not a constant source of terror and frustration. And among the pleasures is a plethora of buildings and spaces that are visually stimulating and provide services in quantity and quality unique to a city. Now that the put-down of American classic architecture is being challenged by increasing numbers of people, the extant buildings by McKim, Mead & White have a better chance to survive and continue to play their role in the cityscape. The aesthetic and socially distorted value judgments that have caused the neglect and destruction of so much of our heritage have not succeeded in turning New York into Necropolis, the City of Death; it need not happen unless by failing to exercise our options and assuming responsibility we make it so.

Spring 1973
New York

The views expressed in the introduction are those of the publisher, Benjamin Blom, and are not necessarily those of others.

McKIM, MEAD & WHITE REAPPRAISED

by Leland Roth

The period between the Reconstruction and the out-break of the First World War was a time of vigorous urban growth in the United States.[1] During the first half of those so-called confident years the passion to build cities manifested itself in a brashness and boldness entirely appropriate to the national character; yet vigor and individuality soon led to a tangle of visual confusion and disorder. The prevalent High Victorian and Second Empire styles that architects in the United States were shaping into truly national idioms often resulted in distinct masterpieces of plastic invention; unfortunately, designs by those less skilled proliferated at a much higher rate as builders strove to accommodate an urban population that was doubling approximately every twenty years.[2] For each urban dweller in 1870 there were almost five by 1915, causing a veritable explosion of buildings and services. The results somehow miraculously worked, although the sense of order and grace that most sensitive Americans saw in Europe was lacking. In the slums, it must be said, little progress of any kind was made, and for great numbers of urban poor the success of the development of American cities in the late nineteenth century was dubious at best. The depth of poverty the urban poor were required to endure was well documented by Jacob A. Riis in "How the Other Half Lives" (1890).[3] That edition contained only drawings made from Riis's original photographs, and although the drawings failed to convey the true measure of the problem, they were sufficient to help awaken reform.

Some encouraging signs began to appear: challenged by the success of Frederick Law Olmsted in creating areas of refreshment through landscape and parklands in the cities of the United States, business leaders returned

from travels in Paris and Venice longing to create in their own country the architectural pleasures that had captivated them abroad. They wanted color and texture such as they had seen in Italy, a style that was at once inventive and yet obeyed discreet rules and formed harmonious townscapes. They wanted a style of architecture that reaffirmed the Vitruvian traditions, buildings that gave equal consideration to functional arrangement, structural soundness and visual pleasure; they wanted "commodity, firmness and delight."[4] And they demanded of their architects that all three considerations of design be brought into balance, with none sacrificed, least of all visual delight.

The architects themselves, especially those in the increasingly crowded eastern cities, began to sense the architectural dilemma by the time of the 1876 centennial, although none seemed ready to propose a clear solution to the problem of congested urban centers. Some, however, began to venture suggestions as to what course urban architecture might take. One of them, Robert S. Peabody, wrote in 1877 that architects should not become overly concerned with historical accuracy; rather, they should concentrate on another aspect:

the artist's clever art in harmonizing whatever his fancy leads him to with itself and its surroundings. From this point of view, whatever the attractions of other sources, from no field can suggestions be drawn by an artist more charming and more fitted to our usage than from the Georgian mansions of New England.[5]

In the coordination of parts and the congenial inter-relationships of the New England Georgian buildings Peabody indicated a point of departure for contemporary architects.

The attention focused on America's past during the centennial years resulted in a renewed examination of Georgian precedents for urban structures; yet the scale of this style seemed too diminutive, scarcely able to provide those qualities of scale and assuredness that were more and more desired in the exploding cities. Then in 1882 a group of palatial houses designed by

Grateful thanks are offered to Wilson G. Duprey, Curator of the Map and Print Room of the New-York Historical Society, New York, and the White family of Saint James, New York, all of whom graciously made material available for study. Acknowledgment is also due to Benjamin Blom who had data collected on the present state of much of the firm's work and to A. E. Santaniello who offered helpful criticism and edited the text.

McKim, Mead and White for the railroad entrepreneur Henry Villard began to take shape on Madison Avenue in New York; many architects of the eastern seaboard saw in this Renaissance design an intimation of how clarity and order might be brought to their cities. With the example of the Villard houses and with the aid of the many publications of Renaissance and classic architecture made available at the end of the nineteenth century, American architects returned to a classicism whose appeal had never entirely faded in this country,[6] a tradition reaching as far back as Thomas Jefferson. Nearly a century earlier Jefferson had written of the value of classic models, especially in the creation of public buildings, pointing out that "every new edifice is an actual and permanent acquisition to the State, adding to its value as well as to its ornament."[7] If Jefferson could find the proper sources for an American architecture in Vitruvius, Palladio and the Maison Carree in Nimes, then nineteenth-century architects were justified in evoking Bramante, Peruzzi and Vignola for renewed inspiration. The promise of the Villard houses was reaffirmed in the design for McKim, Mead and White's Boston Public Library, published in 1888; it was fulfilled beyond expectation when the building was opened in 1895.[8] Here all the resources of the architecture of the past were gathered together, fused with modern construction techniques and embellished with the finest works of art. Its interior was a virtual palace and the exterior drew together and gave final definition to the vast open space of Copley Square, showing that the civic responsibilities of a building could be coordinated with its internal functions. The library also demonstrated the kind of public splendor that could be achieved when architects, painters and sculptors worked in concert. Here was a building which demonstrated that in America, as in Europe, the city could be a work of art.

The Villard houses and the Boston Public Library persuaded a growing number of architects of the viability of Renaissance classicism. The use of such classicism for civic, public, commercial, residential and industrial buildings spread until, by the time of Mead's death in 1928, there was virtually no village or town in the United States that could not boast of a bank or courthouse in some variant of this classic theme. During the early years of the twentieth century the influence of the firm extended even to England, where a number of architects studied the designs of McKim, Mead and White as an alternative to the revived Queen Anne mode then so prevalent. The first published evaluation of this influence came as a surprise to many architects in the United States, who had been unaware of the extent of the firm's transatlantic influence. In 1924 a critical essay on the firm was published by the English architectural historian and teacher Charles Herbert Reilly, who attested to the high regard in which the firm's designs were held by many architects abroad. Reilly writes that "the work of McKim, Mead and White will be found, I think, to be one of the great determining forces of the architecture of our time . . . . [It] sums up the finest aspirations of a great people at a great epoch."[9]

The architectural designs of McKim, Mead and White satisfied a pervasive need for clear architectural authority and adherence to tradition as well as a desire for sumptuous detail, qualities that attracted many Americans during this period of social and cultural transition. The extraordinarily large number of commissions given to the firm—some 784 significant commissions actually designed by either McKim, Mead or White between 1872 and 1909—testifies to its success. Actually, in the period covered by the Monograph, 1879 to 1915, some 875 major commissions were received by the office as evidenced by the bill books and other records of the firm at the New-York Historical Society. (All these records were systematically examined by the author during the four-year period from 1967 to 1971.) The firm's commissions were spread across the entire continent from the Atlantic to the Pacific and from Texas to Montreal. In addition to the effect of the buildings on their immediate environs, their influence was magnified through the extensive publication of the firm's work in professional journals.

The influence of the firm was also apparent in the great number of young architects who obtained their training in the office. There were few architectural schools in the United States in the 1880s, and the increasing recognition given to the firm persuaded many aspiring young architects to seek positions as draftsmen for McKim, Mead and White as the best possible training. Literally hundreds of men passed through the office, as the list of names in Charles Moore's biography of McKim indicates.[10]

Both McKim and White, but especially McKim, took the responsibility for educating future architects very seriously, and they inculcated their concern in the men who succeeded them in the office after McKim's death in 1909. Indeed, the commitment to architectural education led the successors in the firm to accept the offer to publish the "Monograph of the Work of McKim, Mead and White" in 1914. The decision to publish the work of McKim, Mead and White may have been strengthened by Reilly's request in 1910 for drawings and photographs to be used by his architectural students at the University of Liverpool. Through the Monograph the best designs of the firm could be placed in the hands of young architects to be used as a guide and reference, much as the plates of Rome by Letarouilly had served McKim and White earlier.[11] Thus the publication of the Monograph became the third factor in the firm's influence.

Much of the character of the firm's work was the direct result of a fortunate collaboration of harmoniously contrasting personalities. McKim has been described as a methodical scholar, with a slow, painstaking method of arriving at the best solution. He consulted book after book and had his assistants spend hours looking up data for him, particularly in Letarouilly. He would stand over his assistants' tables altering the position of a line a fraction of an inch, first in one direction and then another, until the exact balance and proportions for the design had been achieved. The designs seemed to take forever, and yet somehow they were completed. White, on the other hand, worked at a feverish pace and handled many more commissions than either McKim or Mead. He would burst into the office, firing off instructions to his assistants, making rapid sketches on sheet after sheet of paper to show what he wanted. Then he would disappear, leaving the draughtsmen to decipher it all. White was always ready to experiment with new plan arrangement, materials and color, if they could achieve the impact and vitality he desired. It then became Mead's job to bring a balance between the two opposing forces, for he was the governor of the engine, deliberate, shrewd and levelheaded. While McKim and White obtained their own commissions and saw them through the office, the designs were always subject to criticism from all the partners. In the evening, when the office was closed and the draughtsmen gone, the three could be found together, enjoying their cigars, going over each other's designs. White's son, Lawrence Grant White, described their relationship:

The new firm was a singularly happy combination of men of radically different temperaments. McKim was a calm, deliberate scholar—shy, cautious, with a quiet way of speaking which, however, masked a strong will, so that he usually carried his point in an argument. Each building which he produced was an architectural event. He built decidedly in the grand manner, even to the point of austerity; and his work has a noble, intellectual quality, a sober perfection which is completely satisfying.

White's character was in many respects the opposite of McKim's. He was exuberant, restless, a skyrocket of vitality. He worked at terrific pressure and produced a great many buildings, which are graceful and charming rather than imposing, and often profusely ornamented. He was always striving for new effects, and never hesitated to be architecturally incorrect in order to solve a problem. Once a draughtsman came to him in despair because the axis of a scheme which he had indicated could not be maintained. "Damn it all, bend the axis," was the reply.

"Vogue la Galere" was the motto of the firm; and if McKim was the hull and White the sails of the ship, Mead was both rudder and anchor; for it was his sound judgement, often lacking in the make-up of the other two men, which steered them safely through the shoals, and enabled them to weather the storms. There is a story in which Mead is quoted as saying that it took all his time to keep his partners from "making damn fools of themselves"; and St. Gaudens once drew an amusing caricature of Mead struggling to fly two kites, labeled White and McKim, which were pulling in different directions. But, besides his business judgement, Mead's extraordinary grasp of architectural planning was of incalculable value to the firm. He possessed that instinctive sense of scale and proportion which makes the development of the elevations follow naturally and logically from the plan. Although he gave less of his time to actual designing than his partners, he often not only conceived the scheme which was the basis of the whole design, but gave timely criticism which had vital bearing upon the finished work.[12]

William Rutherford Mead (Fig. 1), the oldest of the three, was born August 20, 1846, the son of a prosperous lawyer of Brattleboro, Vermont. A small rural community, Brattleboro nevertheless enjoyed some fame as a health resort and attracted notable visitors who took the water cure. Mead's older brother, Larkin, was a sculptor whose early commissions included two

Figure 1. William Rutherford Mead. From "Notable New Yorkers of 1896-1899," edited by Moses King.

large marble figures for the state capitol located in Montpelier: "Vermont" for the dome (1857) and "Ethan Allen" for the interior (1861). It may have been with Larkin, or perhaps on his own, that Mead first saw the Vermont State Capitol, a notable Greek Revival building that he later said probably influenced his decision to study architecture.

Little else is known of Mead's home life. He attended Norwich Academy, Northfield, Vermont, and was graduated from Amherst College in 1867. The following year he worked for an engineer whose name is unknown.[13] In July 1868 he entered the office of the New York architect Russell Sturgis[14] as a paid student, staying until he left for Italy in 1871. He settled in Florence, where his brother had established a studio, and pursued his architectural studies at the Academia delle Belle Arti, where his knowledge of and sympathy for Italian Renaissance architecture was nurtured. Returning to the United States in the autumn of 1872 after a short tour of Europe, Mead called at the Sturgis office hoping to regain his position. But business was very slack and in a casual inquiry at the office of a young architect in the same building Mead met McKim for the first time. At the moment McKim was laboring to finish a number of residences, and the prospect of Mead's assistance was welcome. The two worked together thereafter, obtaining their own work individually but sharing a common office and coming to each other's aid.[15]

Charles Follen McKim (Fig. 2), who was one year Mead's junior, was born August 24, 1847, in rural Chester County, Pennsylvania, the son of markedly dissimilar parents. His father, an active, vocal and dedicated advocate of abolition during his entire life, devoted his energies to the education of freedmen after the Civil War; his soft-spoken mother was a resolute Quaker.[16] McKim's boyhood was spent in Germantown, outside Philadelphia, and many of his later architectural preferences can be understood when it is remembered that he came of conservative, cultivated Philadelphia ancestry and had been brought up to observe and retain the forms and traditions of an established society.[17]

McKim had received his early education at a boarding school run by the abolitionist Theodore D. Weld at Perth Amboy, New Jersey, and in public schools in Philadelphia. In September 1866 he entered the Lawrence Scientific School of Harvard University, having chosen mining engineering as his career. During his freshman year McKim asked his parents' permission to complete his studies at the School of Mines in Paris and was persuaded by his father to reconsider such a decisive step and to spend the summer working for Russell Sturgis, an acquaintance of the elder McKim. In late spring of that year McKim altered his decision in favor of an architectural career but was still determined to finish his training in Paris. He spent the summer in Sturgis's office, absorbing the strict Ruskinian doctrine that Sturgis espoused: honest expression of materials, clear indication of function, sound construction and adherence to the Gothic in all things. (Curiously, McKim left the office shortly before Mead arrived.)

In September 1867 McKim arrived in Paris and prepared to take the entrance examinations for the Ecole des Beaux-Arts. Following his admission he spent almost three years at the Ecole, using the opportunity to travel on the Continent and in England. He did not always rigorously follow the program of the bimonthly design problems—the projets—but he thoroughly absorbed the basic principles taught at the Ecole: logical planning, careful articulation of the parts of the design in plan and elevation and generosity of scale.

Figure 2. Charles Follen McKim. From "Notable New Yorkers of 1896-1899," edited by Moses King.

This is not to suggest, however, that during these years the Ecole advocated the inherent superiority of one historic style over any other. On the contrary, the principle that McKim was taught was that the style of a design should be developed to suit the use and function of the particular building. Thus the Ecole design problems focused on individual buildings, and even as late as the turn of the century larger questions of urban interrelationships and urban planning were ignored. Historically, of course, it must be said that few practicing architects in McKim's years of professional schooling viewed such broad urban problems as their proper sphere of activity. Nevertheless, individual students, among them McKim, were aware of the relationship between architecture and the urban environment and went on to discover how to extend the Ecole's lessons of planning and its over-all architectural principles to the city as a whole.

When the Franco-Prussian War broke out in 1870 McKim quickly returned home along with many of his countrymen. During his years in Paris he had witnessed the rebuilding of the city; he had seen the armies of Baron Haussmann's workers cutting broad swathes through the ancient city, laying down stately avenues bordered with full-grown trees. Whatever sense of loss he might have felt at the destruction of the old city's weathered Gothic buildings, he carried back to America the conviction that literally anything was possible in shaping a new urban order if one had the necessary determination.

Following his arrival in New York in late summer McKim sought a position in the office of the architect Henry Hobson Richardson, who had at one time been a student at the Ecole and possibly had been recommended by McKim's father's friend, Frederick Law Olmsted. Despite a temporary lull in office work Richardson hired McKim as draftsman, perhaps because of the uniqueness of his training. At the time of McKim's return in 1870 no more than thirteen Americans had attended the Ecole, some of whom had attended only briefly and had made no impression on their return.[18] Richardson may also have realized the value of McKim's recent observation of contemporary European buildings.

Soon after McKim's entry into the office a new geometric tautness began to emerge in Richardson's designs, the result of McKim's Ecole drafting technique. The influence can be detected in the design for the Brattle Square Church, which was completed just after McKim came into the office. As Henry-Russell Hitchcock has observed, "it is somewhat strange . . . that the admirers of Charles F. McKim have never claimed that the crystallization of Richardson's style in this church was due, at least in part, to the influence of this young assistant who entered Richardson's office in June . . . ."[19] It seems clear that both men learned much from their association.

In July 1872 Richardson won the competition for the design of Trinity Church, Boston. McKim assisted in the development of the design of the church but then, as he obtained commissions of his own, began to reduce his work load in the Richardson office.[20] Since the first Trinity design had to be thoroughly restudied because of financial and structural problems, the work was given over in part to a new draftsman who had recently come into Richardson's office that same summer—the young Stanford White.

Stanford White (Fig. 3) was born November 9, 1853, in New York, the son of a well-known literary and music critic and Shakespearean scholar, Richard Grant White. In his Tenth Street home young Stanford met some of the most famous figures of American letters and must have seen the correspondence arriving for his father bearing the names Emerson, Lowell, Dickens and Browning. The New York architect Calvert Vaux was acquainted with White's father, as was also his associate, the landscape architect Frederick Law Olmsted.

From childhood Stanford White demonstrated a genuine talent for drawing and water colors. His pencil or brush was seldom idle during the family trips to Fort Hamilton, New York, or Newburgh on the Hudson, where his aunt lived. To become a painter was the young White's ambition, but there were practical considerations: however respected his father's writing may have been, it was definitely not lucrative, and the cost of a painter's training was beyond the family's means. John La Farge, a friend of his father's, warned Stanford that a painter's position was very precarious and the financial rewards slight. White's father sought the advice of Olmsted, who suggested that the boy be apprenticed to the architect Henry Hobson Richardson.[21] So it was that in the late summer of 1872 Stanford White began his career in the office of Richardson.

During the next few years as the Trinity Church design was brought to its final stage, McKim and White became well acquainted, though McKim was increasingly absorbed in his own practice. By the time Richardson removed his office to Boston in 1874 McKim was well established in his own practice, sharing the office with Mead. It was in the same year that McKim and Mead collaborated for the first time, on a design entered in the competition for the new city hall in Providence, Rhode Island.[22] White, meanwhile, moved to the Brookline office in Boston with Richardson and was given a large measure of responsibility for the William Watts Sherman house commission, which came into the office that year. With this design a second influence can be observed in Richardson's work. McKim had brought a new emphasis on geometric severity; White's influence led to an emphasis on surface patterns and texture. As developed by Richardson, concern for the skin of the building resulted in an architecture in which the surface became a continuous dominating feature—the Shingle Style. During the next four years White's responsibility in the Richardson office broadened to include coordinating exterior surface details and designing interior appointments. By 1878 White had saved some money for a trip to Europe, planning to stay until his funds gave out. When he sailed early in July 1878 he was joined by his friend McKim, whose wife had suddenly and unexpectedly sued for divorce. The repercussions of this unhappy event would soon affect the professional careers of both men.

In 1874, when he had begun independent practice, McKim had married Annie Bigelow of New York. During this time Annie's brother, William B. Bigelow, had begun to assist McKim and Mead. Bigelow had studied for a short time in 1873 and 1874 at the Ecole and was a very accomplished draftsman, able to do with facility and vivacity what McKim or Mead could only do painstakingly. Then in 1877 McKim, Mead and Bigelow were joined by White for a walking tour of colonial New England buildings that were then attracting attention in the professional journals.[23] Sketching their way along the coasts of Massachusetts and New Hampshire, they seemed to be searching for a national heritage on which to build an American architecture. They stored away these sketches of an earlier architecture of simple clarity and reasoned order, to draw on them in future years. Early in 1878 it was decided that since their work had become so intertwined, the partnership of McKim, Mead and Bigelow should be formed. With the sudden suit for divorce, however, the friendship between McKim and Bigelow began to deteriorate and a few months later Bigelow retired from the firm. It was at this point that McKim joined White for a jaunt in Europe, back to the Paris of more carefree days. It should be noted that the entire episode of the divorce has remained a hushed event in the life of McKim, with no clear reasons ever set forth. Following the divorce McKim was separated from his three-year-old daughter Margaret to whom he was deeply attached. It was not until 1899 that father and daughter were reunited, re-establishing an intimacy that would endure for the remainder of their lives.

Figure 3. Stanford White. From "Notable New Yorkers of 1896-1899," edited by Moses King.

McKim and White spent some six weeks together in France visiting various buildings and finally persuading their friend Saint-Gaudens, then living in Paris, to take a quick trip down the Rhone River. When McKim returned to New York in September White stayed on, living with Saint-Gaudens and his family and frequenting the studio in Paris which Saint-Gaudens had set up to work on his Farragut statue. The work on this statue marked the beginning of the careers of both men, for White worked closely with Saint-Gaudens designing the base. In later years McKim, White and Saint-Gaudens collaborated many times on some of the most successful sculptural and architectural ensembles ever created in the United States, a few of which are discussed below.[24] While in France in 1878 and 1879 White made the Saint-Gaudens home his headquarters for numerous sketching excursions. During the summer of 1879 White's savings began to dwindle, and he was forced to sail home in August.

White first intended to return to Richardson's office, but McKim let him know that Bigelow's position in the firm was now vacant. Mead may have hesitated, perhaps out of his New England conservatism, at taking on a third partner after the difficulties caused by Bigelow's departure. White's exuberance, of course, was the very antithesis of Mead's own personality. But McKim defended White, pointing out that although he lacked formal training he was exceptionally adept at drawing. Since McKim and Mead had just lost their delineator in Bigelow, here was the opportunity to obtain another, and White's drawings for Richardson amply proved he was as capable as Bigelow.[25]

Thus early in September 1879 the firm of McKim, Mead and White was formed. Each partner brought his own unique abilities to the firm: McKim, who sought first clarity in plan, translating that into elevation and then section, in the tradition of the Ecole; White, who was primarily concerned with color, followed by form and texture, proportion afterward and plan last of all; and Mead, whose common sense effected the daily compromises that kept the office running smoothly.[26] This complex combination of personalities and abilities would eventually produce an architecture as varied in building type and configuration as the designers themselves were varied in temperament. The astounding range of their interests meant that little occurred in commerce, transportation, society, finance, city planning or any other facet of American culture at the time in which one of the three partners was not interested and involved. It is, therefore, no surprise that the firm of McKim, Mead and White was called on to design almost every kind of building known to the profession.

The fullest record of this remarkably varied and creative architectural production is found in the plates of "A Monograph of the Work of McKim, Mead and White," and it is to these volumes that one must turn to discover not only the individual achievement of single

buildings but also the evolution of a style of urban architecture and the slow unfolding of a concept of environmental planning. But a word of caution is in order for the reader who approaches the Monograph for the first time: the arrangement of the plates may suggest that the firm followed a very meandering path in the selection of the styles used in their designs, changing from Norman and French Romanesque to Francois Ier and Italian Renaissance. This apparent confusion exists because buildings are shown in chronological order according to their dates of completion: the date at which the designs were actually conceived may be anywhere from two to ten years prior to that. The most striking example of this contradiction is the Boston Public Library, actually designed in the autumn of 1887 but not completed until eleven years later. The correct dates for each design, determined by careful examination of the firm archives, are given in the notes to the plates that have been added to this edition of the Monograph. Since the content of the Monograph is so rich and so seemingly disorganized, it seems advisable to sketch out the major groups of buildings that the firm designed, discussing briefly designs illustrated in the Monograph that are representative of each group.

The firm of McKim, Mead and White first became known through the planning of summer houses in the Shingle Style. In these highly inventive creations each partner's qualities were given full play. McKim's commissions showed a characteristic all-embracing geometrical order that organized the entire composition; White's designs displayed a sensitive balance of dissimilar picturesque elements. When both partners combined their best efforts in a single design the result was particularly striking, as in the summer house for Cyrus McCormick at Richfield Springs, New York (Fig. 4).[27] Here the hand of McKim can be traced in the monumental gable of the facade and in the broad masonry platform on which the entire house is placed, while White's contribution can be seen in the juxtaposition of projecting veranda and voids cut into the block of the house, as well as in the shingle patterns and panels of stucco containing designs in bits of colored glass which enrich the entire surface of the house.

The McCormick house, begun in the autumn of 1880 and finished in 1882, is only one of many such summer homes designed in these early years of the firm. These houses, and others by the firm's contemporaries, helped establish the Shingle Style and create a new American idiom. Whether in rural New York State or along Boston's North Shore or in the summer colony of Newport, these shingled houses were meant to exploit their playful individualism in isolated natural settings. They were informal environments for the casual life enjoyed by summer refugees from the city. These houses had no need to acknowledge civic responsibilities or duties to fellow citizens; they could be whatever the imagination of the architect and his client might conceive.

Such fierce individualism, however intriguing, probably accounts for the exclusion of the shingled houses from the Monograph. When the plates for the volumes were selected in 1914 the major problem confronting most architects was the judicious coordination of urban buildings into a harmonious cityscape. The bravura enjoyed in the woods of New York was far from the architectural decorum needed on Fifth Avenue, and so the often magnificent Shingle Style buildings were passed by in favor of urban buildings.[28]

Despite the reluctance to admit the virtues of the Shingle Style, the first plate is in fact an urban building with a shingle skin. The Newport Casino incorporated many of the characteristics of the Shingle Style, at the same time displaying an early concern for the environment of the street.[29] Designed in late 1879 to provide recreational facilities for the growing summer colony at Newport, the Casino posed a unique problem: a design that could incorporate housing, shops for rental income, offices for the Casino, restaurant facilities and tennis courts. The solution adopted was ingenious; at the rear, within the enclosure of the building, the design is free and airy, and the court facade balances large dormers on one side against the tower on the other side of the central archway. Here, within the enclosed court, freedom

is exploited, but on the street side, playfulness is curbed by the geometry of a symmetrical arrangement. On the Bellevue Avenue front are eight small shops, four on either side of the central entrance arch, each with a similar front to the street. Windows and broad gables above the shop fronts are balanced about the center, creating one comprehensive geometrical envelope. Although the view down the street is varied by slight projections back and forth, and the shingled surfaces are enlivened by various patterns, the dominant horizontal lines remain unbroken, and the street is preserved, even strengthened. Nascent in the design of the Newport Casino are the qualities that would make famous the later work of the firm, especially the sensitive balance between exterior responsibilities to the street and the interior necessities of the building itself.

Another building combining the picturesque qualities of the Shingle Style with the needs of the road was the Narragansett Pier Casino begun in 1883 (Plate 6).[30] In a much more adventurous spirit the building itself comes out to bridge the road, forming the entrance to the Casino. This portion of the building, with its towers, candle-snuffer roofs and arch, was built of rough-faced masonry, and the remainder of the building, which stretched out to the sea, was of wood. Hurricanes and

Figure 4. Cyrus H. McCormick Residence, Richfield Springs, N.Y., 1880-82.
A summer house that is one of the earliest, most picturesque of the firm's shingled works.

fires have swept this portion away, but the arch still commands the shore road.

It has been noted that the Bellevue Avenue facade of the Newport Casino was developed as a decidedly formal composition. In pursuing and developing the possibilities of formal order it was perhaps natural that McKim should return to the sketches made on what Mead called the "famous trip" of 1877, souvenirs of an eighteenth century heritage that contained ripe suggestions of a new geometrical clarity. It is significant that the only summer house published in the Monograph, the most formal of them all, is one based most closely on these studies of 1877–the H. A. C. Taylor house of Newport, Rhode Island (Plate 16). The design is perhaps earlier than usually thought, since the work was initiated in 1882, preliminary studies were prepared in the autumn of 1883 and construction was started in September 1884.[31] The house is conceived as a clearly de-

fined cube, discreet and cool, its breadth of scale marking it a product of McKim but with details drawn from eighteenth century Newport and the Brothers Adam. Its significance in American architecture is that it marked the beginning of the "Colonial Revival," which has continued with varying degrees of "correctness" and generosity of spirit to the present day. Equally important, it marks the emergence of a clear formal order in American domestic architecture in urban as well as rural dwellings.

One of the earliest opportunities to confront the problem of the town house[32] was offered by the Charles A. Whittier house in Boston, Massachusetts, 1881-83 (Plate 3). This was an unusual commission in that it constituted only part of a double house, the other half of which was the F. L. Higginson house by H. H. Richardson (Fig. 5).[33] The house was located in the recently opened Back Bay section of Boston, on land

Figure 5. Charles A. Whittier and F. L. Higginson Double House, Boston, 1881-83. A very early, successful example of collaboration among American architects. Photo, "American Architect and Building News," 14 (November 24, 1883), pl. 413.

reclaimed from tidal marshes where new houses were being erected by some of Boston's most notable citizens. McKim, Mead and White and Richardson established a common roof line and used similar materials for their houses. The disposition of the basic formal elements is roughly symmetrical, and yet each half is distinctly different without attacking its neighbor. McKim, Mead and White selected Francois Ier details for their portion of the design, perhaps because this style was close to the Italian Renaissance, whose rational order they sought to recapture, and at the same time was just one step away, so to speak, from the manner in which Richardson worked. The double residence was a particular success, with McKim, Mead and White faring a little better by comparison, as Hitchcock has observed. (The degree of this success cannot be properly adjudged from the plate in the Monograph, however, since it shows only the McKim, Mead and White portion of the block.)

When Henry Villard gave McKim the commission in April 1882 for six houses to be built on a large lot on Madison Avenue, it was immediately evident that each house had to function as part of a unified whole and at the same time retain an individual character. McKim, perhaps with Villard's assistance, worked out the main features of a plan that grouped the houses around a central court. But before he was able to develop the design further, McKim had to go to Oregon to examine the sites for several commissions Villard had given for a number of buildings for the Northern Pacific Railroad.[34] The sketches for the Villard houses were turned over to White to develop, but before he could complete them he too had to leave New York. The still unfinished detailing of the houses was given to White's assistant, Joseph Morrill Wells, who agreed on the condition that he be given a free hand in the choice of details. As a result the Romanesque character that White may have initially intended was replaced with elements that Wells based on the Cancelleria in Rome, believed at the time to be a design of Donato Bramante.

Joseph Morrill Wells is an enigmatic figure in the history of the firm. He came into the office almost at the same time as White, perhaps slightly later, in September 1879. Wells had been born near Boston, studied architecture with Clarence Luce and worked for Peabody and Stearns. He then moved to New York where he was a draftsman for Richard Morris Hunt. Wells was an ardent enthusiast of the Italian Renaissance even before McKim and White began to use it extensively; while working for Peabody and Stearns, for example, Wells prepared careful renderings of the Cancelleria and the Palazzo Farnese, buildings he called "true architecture." From July 1880 to January 1881 Wells toured England, Italy and France (it is possible that he left Paris through the Gare de l'Est, whose court resembles that of the Villard houses). From Florence he wrote to White that "Italian architecture is great and grand and dignified." It is also possible that while in Italy Wells saw the Palazzo Cervini in

Montepulciano, whose small court on the street and plain unpilastered walls also anticipate the Villard houses. Little more than a year after his return Wells would begin work on the project that may be said to have established the Renaissance style in America.[35]

In the Villard design Wells crystallized McKim and White's Italianate tendencies into a coherent office style with the restrained, assured urbanity so wanted in the visually disorganized nineteenth century city (Plates 7-11). Through the device of the court and the unobtrusive detailing, six individual houses were deftly articulated and yet the complex as a whole had a single identity and a unified force. And it was undeniably grand. On this theme of restrained and ordered calm, of grandeur in austerity rather than sumptuousness, the firm worked many variations during the next twenty-eight years. The later plans all belong to a basic generic type, and although the type was often varied to suit the nature of the particular client all the firm's designs subscribed to basic rules of architectural decorum in the street fronts, whether the particular details came from the Italian Renaissance or American Georgian. Some examples of these town houses are found in the Monograph, such as the H. A. C. Taylor houses in New York City (Plates 80-82 and 121), the James J. Goodwin house (Plates 120-121), the Charles Dana Gibson house (Plates 191-192) and the more richly decorated Payne Whitney house (Plates 289-292).

The Villard houses and the Boston Public Library brought the firm of McKim, Mead and White to the attention of their professional colleagues and those concerned with architecture. For us today perhaps the Boston Library is the most famous of the many civic and public buildings the firm designed, and rightly so, for it is the most commanding and beautifully finished of the firm's extant buildings. The commission for the library, given to McKim in 1887, was complexity itself. Boston had been trying to replace its old Boylston Street building for eight years, with success forestalled by political machinations and an unclear conception of what a large free municipal library should be; there was no precedent in the United States for a library of that size and function. The Copley Square site given to the city by the state legislature was magnificent but enclosed on all sides by a collection of buildings that could hardly have been more varied. The square itself, an immense open space comparable in size to the Piazza di San Marco in Venice, somehow had to be brought together by the new library. Walter Muir Whitehill, in his history of the library, describes the problem the architect faced:

The Romanesque masses of Richardson's Trinity Church dominated Copley Square from its commanding position at the east. To the north, an unobtrusive block of brick and brownstone houses, broken by the low facade of the Second Church—an academic exercise in the revival of English Gothic—fronted on Boylston Street, while at the far corner, beyond Dartmouth Street, the north Italian Gothic campanile of Cummings and Sears' new Old South Church supplied a vertical accent that could not be ignored. Across the way Sturgis and Brigham had housed the new

Museum of Fine Arts in one of those unhappy red brick and yellow terra cotta approximations of Gothic that make one wish that John Ruskin had never gone to Italy, while at the corner of Dartmouth Street and Huntington Avenue, S. S. Pierce and Company sold their excellent groceries in a building that at once parodied Richardson's style and sought to recreate the picturesque roof tiles of old Nuremberg. Truly it was no easy matter to fill the vacant lot to the west with a structure that would have architectural quality of its own and still not swear at its motley and aggressive neighbors, while simultaneously creating for the first time in America "an ideal library" . . . .[36]

In the very early studies for the library done in the autumn of 1887, McKim developed the basic organization of the Copley Square facade, an arcade above a high basement (Plates 100-109). As the design was studied and restudied, the arcade was made deeper and stronger, after the example of the Colosseum in Rome and perhaps Alberti's church of San Francesco in Rimini.[37] McKim realized that Richardson's craggy and massive Trinity Church should be balanced by firm horizontal lines—a decision reached, ironically enough, by a clue given by Richardson himself. In the continuous powerful arcade McKim was pursuing, essentially, a line of development that Richardson had taken up during his last years.[38] The tall tower of the new Old South Church would also be heightened by this harmonious contrast. And through the device of the long arcade, the large reading room stretching across the entire front of the building could be expressed externally. At the same time the broad expanse of the library could embrace the whole of Copley Square and make it comprehensible as an urban space.

From the beginning the trustees under the leadership of Samuel A. B. Abbott felt that the library should be a monumental building, worthy of the city of Boston, "a palace for the people" as they wrote in the annual report in 1888.[39] As the work on the library continued the conception grew in scope, and McKim and the trustees persuaded the city government to raise the necessary additional funds so that the finest artistic talent and materials could be obtained. To this end the sculptor Augustus Saint-Gaudens was to have created groups of figures for either side of the entrance. Unfortunately Saint-Gaudens was unable to complete them, but he did execute the panels over the entrance representing the seals of Massachusetts, Boston and the library. Daniel Chester French was engaged to execute the doors of the entrance, and in the grand stair hall Saint-Gaudens's brother, Louis, carved the two large lions.

In 1890 McKim and White, aided by Saint-Gaudens, approached Edwin Austin Abbey with the suggestion that he do a series of murals for the book delivery room of the library. John Singer Sargent too was asked to paint a series of murals in the upper hallway. Both Abbey and Sargent were anxious to try their hands at large-scale work, and by 1891 they were both busy at Abbey's large studio at Morgan Hall, Gloustershire, England. During 1891 McKim also called on Puvis de Chavannes in Paris, offering him the commission to paint

murals for the grand stair hall. In addition, McKim spoke with James McNeill Whistler about working on murals, but because of lack of funds these were never done; John La Farge's proposed paintings for Bates Hall were never realized because of the artist's procrastinations.

When at last the building was opened to the public in 1895 there was revealed an orchestration of fine marbles, sculpture, mosaics, painting, color and light that no one had expected to find on this side of the Atlantic. In the vestibule and grand stair hall the finest marbles gathered from quarries in Europe and America were carefully combined to create subtle effects of color. The Boston Public Library exulted in a public splendor that enriched the spirit of anyone who ascended the grand staircase; it was indeed "a palace for the people."

Although the Boston Public Library is the largest library built by the firm, its workmanship and interior appointments are rivaled by the Morgan Library, the last of four related buildings that belong to the large body of public buildings raised in the United States around the turn of the century to glorify the arts and learning. The first two buildings in the group were designed in 1891 within a few months of each other. The Walker Art Gallery, Bowdoin College, Brunswick, Maine, was begun in September (Plates 45-46), and the Whittemore Memorial Library, Naugatuck, Connecticut, was begun in November 1891. Although all four buildings had similar functional requirements and hence similar T-shaped plans—consisting of a central octagonal or square room opening to flanking primary rooms and a subsidiary wing to the rear—there are important differences among them. Both the Walker Art Gallery and the Whittemore Library have a dome over the central room. The dome of the Whittemore Library is very low and is set on a low drum, while that of the Walker Art Gallery is fuller and placed on a higher drum. The portico of the Whittemore Library consists simply of two Ionic columns in antis (if the term is stretched somewhat) supporting a low pediment. The plasticity of the Walker Art Gallery's Palladian entrance contrasts strongly with the broad blank surfaces of the flanking brick walls, and this contrast is heightened by the planar quality of the brick walls and the hollow of the entrance loggia behind the Palladian arch. This juxtaposition of blank wall and shaded Palladian entrance was later restudied in the design for the Morgan Library.

The third building in the series was the Free Public Library of the Oranges, Orange, New Jersey, begun in March 1900. In this the main block resembles that of the Whittemore Library with its low gable roof, while the full dome looks more like that of the Walker Art Gallery, though it is raised on an octagonal drum that breaks through the roof. The entrance is strongly marked by a freestanding Ionic portico of four columns carrying a pediment filled with low relief carving.

Whatever perfection of proportion may have been undeveloped in the Orange Free Library was certainly achieved in the Morgan Library, New York, begun in September 1902 (Plates 241-49).[40] This was a design to which McKim devoted a great deal of time and energy, making certain that all the elements were carefully balanced. The entire facade (Plate 243) is based on elements divided by three: the three nearly equal bays, with shallow reveals between them, are divided into three sub-units in the same relationship as the major bays' elements. The attic story is divided into recessed panels whose surrounding frames carry up the lines of the pilasters below. The walls of the library are of marble blocks whose surfaces were so carefully cut and ground that the blocks were perfectly laid with dry joints, the technique used in the Erechtheum on the Athenian Acropolis. The interiors of the library, though much smaller and more intimate than those of the Boston Public Library, are perhaps even more carefully wrought. The ceiling paintings in the vestibule and in the East Room are by H. Siddons Mowbray. Morgan's private room to the west has a ceiling from the Aldobrandini Palace in Venice. As in the Boston Library, the finest and rarest of marbles were fitted together to create a subtle play of colors. To McKim's contemporaries of the classical persuasion the Morgan Library appeared to be perfection itself.[41] Although we may not embrace its classicism so wholeheartedly, the Morgan Library nevertheless represents standards of careful study, attention to details and painstaking craftsmanship that embarrass us because so often we lack the will to do as well. Set among the anonymous towers of midtown Manhattan like a precious jewel box, the Morgan Library teaches a lesson in scale and urban decorum that should continue to challenge us as long as our cities last.

Besides the summer houses, urban houses and public buildings, the firm of McKim, Mead and White is known for designs for park furniture and architectural settings for sculpture, an area of work little represented in the Monograph. In 1889 the firm began work on a number of designs for entrances, balustrades, shelters and miscellaneous structures for Prospect Park in Brooklyn (Plates 20-21). Here McKim and White reflected the influence of Olmsted, which they had felt from their youth, helping to bring to completion a great undertaking begun nearly thirty years earlier when Olmsted and Vaux had first laid out this gracious urban park.

In addition to their sensitivity toward landscape, McKim and White paid tribute to Olmsted's influence in their persistent efforts to combine and integrate their design with the work of other artists. A striking example of this is the close collaboration between Saint-Gaudens and Stanford White in the Farragut Memorial (Plate 15). As early as 1875 Saint-Gaudens began working on a design for the statue, and White made several sketches for a base that would incorporate seating in its curving wings. The design was made final in 1879, with Saint-Gaudens's relief sculpture on the base. At every stage of the evolution of the design the artists offered critical

opinions on each other's work so that when the memorial was finally erected and the finished work unveiled in Madison Square in 1881, there appeared a fusion of sculpture and architecture seldom before seen in this country. Fittingly, Olmsted himself had been consulted by White on the choice of sites for the ensemble.

The same close collaboration occurred later in the Robert Gould Shaw Memorial on which Saint-Gaudens worked with McKim (Plates 164-165). In 1880 Saint-Gaudens began the preliminary work—a freestanding equestrian figure placed before a high bronze screen on which was modeled a tree and a long inscription. When McKim became involved in the design of the architectural setting almost a decade later, Saint-Gaudens had changed the sculptural design greatly. Since the screen had now become a relief showing Colonel Shaw's troops, McKim and Saint-Gaudens incorporated a setting of living trees on either side of the bronze figure of the Colonel and the enframing screen. Sculpture, architecture and landscape were thus combined in one organic design.

The Deacon Chapin Memorial for Springfield, Massachusetts, begun by Saint-Gaudens and White in 1884, was to utilize even more of the natural setting. Saint-Gaudens's figure, to be placed in Stearns Park, was a huge bronze of Deacon Samuel Chapin, who had settled the Connecticut River valley in 1642. In the finished design Chapin strides forward, his cape billowing around him in sweeping curves, which White's broad swelling circular base picks up and reinforces. When White examined Stearns Park he suggested building a complete park setting of statue, granite bench, fountain, shrubs and trees (Fig. 6).

The Chapin family liked this expanded proposal; plans were drawn, Saint-Gaudens's bronze completed and the elaborate complex unveiled in 1887.[42] The twelve-foot figure of Deacon Chapin and its expansive base were framed by a semicircular screen of trimmed tall hedges. Before the statue stretched a rectangular area enclosed by a low pine hedge, with a row of white birches on each side of the enclosure. At the far end of the rectangle was a circular fountain, recalling the broad circular base of the statue, and in the center a pink granite bench completed the design.

This pleasant little park was, unfortunately, located in an area of the city marked for substantial redevelopment. Between the destruction of the old surroundings and the building of the new, the park was thoroughly vandalized. The bronze and its circular base were removed to a position in front of the Springfield public library, and the granite bench and fountain were sent to other city parks.

The most complete of these sculpture-architecture-and-landscape ensembles designed by Saint-Gaudens and White is the Adams Memorial in Rock Creek Cemetery, Washington, D.C. (Figs. 7 and 8), begun in 1887 and completed in 1891. For this commission, from the historian Henry Adams as a memorial to his wife who had taken her own life, Saint-Gaudens modeled a solitary robed figure seated in front of a plain pink granite slab designed by White. The figure was placed at one side of a hexagonal enclosure whose three facing sides held seats of pink granite. This hexagonal area was set inside a rectangular bed of holly trees and cedars. The figure, never intended as a portrait of Mrs. Adams, was meant to symbolize timelessness, peace or perhaps the concept of Nirvana. Saint-Gaudens later called it the "Mystery of the Hereafter," beyond pain and joy. Seated within the evergreen holly and cedar (now grown into an enveloping bower), the figure muses, hand raised to cheek, silent, in an eternal reverie, giving assuagement to those who come to sit quietly under the enclosing branches. The Shaw, Chapin and Adams memorials were conceived as living things changing from season to season, becoming more complete with each passing year, as organic as Olmsted's parks.

There is one major area of McKim, Mead and White's achievement that is given virtually no coverage in the Monograph—large-scale projects such as in the design of multidwelling units, groups of houses and the planning

of communities. This is unfortunate not only because it is an area of particular importance today, but also because it is an area in which McKim, Mead and White made significant contributions. We should not be surprised to discover that they were not simply the designers of plush Italianate houses for the rich. Rather, they saw the design of a single building as part of the neighborhood or community in which it was to play a role. Two of the firm's earliest commissions in 1879 were, in fact, concerned with the actual creation of a new community. While White was still in Europe in the summer of 1879, McKim and Mead were engaged by Stewart Hartshorn to design several buildings for a suburban community he was developing at Short Hills, New Jersey. Hartshorn, who had made a fortune with the spring-loaded window-shade roller he patented in 1864,[43] had withdrawn from active participation in his business and had moved his family to a farm in Millburn Township, New Jersey, because he was so impressed by the natural beauty of the area. In the 1870s the rolling hills were still well wooded, and the few inhabitants were clustered in the old village of Millburn through which ran a branch of the Erie and Lackawanna Railroad. Here in this woodland Hartshorn decided to carry out his boy-

Figure 6. Deacon Chapin Memorial, Springfield, Mass., 1884. Sketch by White showing the entire ensemble. From L. G. White, "Sketches and Designs by Stanford White," pl. 28.

Figure 7 (Left). Adams Memorial, Rock Creek Cemetery, Washington, D.C., 1888-91. View of Saint-Gaudens's figure.

Figure 8 (Below). Adams Memorial, Rock Creek Cemetery, Washington, D.C., 1888-91. View of the complete ensemble showing White's granite bench at the right, now covered over with the holly and cedar planted around it.

hood ambition of creating an "ideal" community, to be called Short Hills because of its topography. Acquiring some 1,763 acres, Hartshorn laid out streets following the contours of the land and planted additional trees. The quarry and sawmill he opened were to provide building materials for the new homes. Hartshorn then asked McKim to furnish drawings for a model house to be built in the new town, apparently as a speculative venture to start the project. For the community to thrive, however, it needed some visual focus, a sign of communal identity; thus Hartshorn next asked the firm (in November 1879) to design a community hall. This was perhaps one of the first commissions given to White, who had just assumed his place in the office. The building, known locally as the "music hall" and elsewhere as the Short Hills Casino, was completed in the summer of 1880 (Fig. 9).[44] White drew upon the memory of his recent travels in Brittany in his design, portions of which are said to be based on the Chateau de Plecis Mace near Angers. The building provided several meeting rooms on the ground floor, with a large auditorium on the floor above. Besides providing for recreational activities, and the popular Gilbert and Sullivan productions, the "music hall" served as the first home of the Short Hills school. Later it provided for the first meetings of the Short Hills Episcopal church, and for ten years was the site of the town meetings. The Short Hills Casino provided the necessary social amenities for the village, an attraction for new residents in its first crucial years.

In the summer of 1881, almost a year after the Casino opened, a group of New Yorkers commissioned the firm to lay out a small resort community on Montauk, Long Island.[45] The seven men, who called themselves the Montauk Association, had purchased a large block of land at the very end of the island. The firm was asked to design a shingled fishing cottage for each of the members, a common stable and laundry, and a common Association Hall at the center with recreational facilities. Each house is distinctly different from the others, each is given a different orientation, and yet the group possesses a communal identity through the use of a com-

Figure 9. Short Hills Casino, Short Hills, N.J., 1879-80. From G. W. Sheldon, "Artistic Country Seats," vol. 1, 116.

mon shingle design idiom. The Association Hall burned during the 1930s, but six houses remain, facing toward the sea on gentle rises in the scrub-covered sand.

Another facet of this frequently overlooked aspect of the firm's work are designs they made for speculative builders for commerical structures and housing complexes. The firm built a large number of buildings for Ogden and Robert Goelet, and they also provided designs for the builders Michael Reid and David H. King, Jr. One design made for King is especially beautiful and is beginning to receive some much deserved attention, the so-called Striver's Row, in New York City (Figs. 10,11).[46] This block-long housing complex, called "the best large row-house development in New York" in a recent guide to the architecture of the city, was commissioned by King in September 1891. King built houses on the north side of 138th Street and on both sides of 139th Street, between Seventh and Eighth Avenues, following designs by James Brown Lord, Bruce Price, and McKim, Mead and White, with the designs by the latter only on the north side of 139th Street. The townhouses, intended for professionals and businessmen of moderate incomes who desired to move uptown into fashionable Harlem, were laid out on such a scale as to "create a neighborhood," as a brochure of 1891 states. The general plan called for three long rows of houses with a wide areaway between the houses on 138th and 139th Streets. Wide transverse passages in turn divide the long rows into three nearly equal blocks. The entrances to these passages were ornamented by high wrought iron gates. The ends of the blocks on Seventh and Eighth Avenues were given an additional story, with the ground floors of the apartment buildings given over to shops.

Each of the salient points in the McKim, Mead and White design—the end of the block, the transverse walkways and the centermost houses—was subtly and precisely articulated by slight projections of the walls and by detailing in the brickwork. The material throughout the firm's portion of the development is a tawny terracotta-colored glazed brick. The choice of material, the restraint and studied proportions of the design (indicating the contribution of McKim), and the careful execution make this group of houses one of the best works of the firm.

By the time the King model houses were ready for occupancy in the summer of 1893 McKim, Mead and White were busy with another commission for a small residential community. In 1892 Edward Dean Adams retained the firm to design a group of buildings to house the new electric generating station at Niagara Falls, New York. As the scope of the undertaking widened, the company building the generating plant decided to construct a small residential village to house the workers at the station. Consequently in February 1893 McKim, Mead and White were engaged to design the nucleus of a

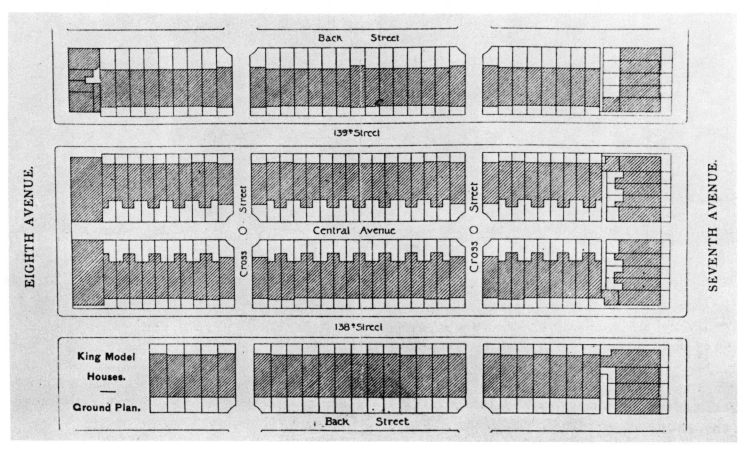

Figure 10. King Model Houses, New York, 1891-92. Plan.

Figure 11. King Model Houses, New York, 1891-92. Careful detailing and
sound construction are evident in this recently cleaned house at 259 W.
139th Street. Photo, Leland Roth.

village that was given the name "Echota" from an Indian word meaning "place of refuge." One contemporary, John Bogart, described the results: "An unattractive expanse of poor meadowland has become a model town, with inviting residences at very moderate expense for the families of all who may have to do with the busy industries called into action by the wonderful power drawn from the Falls."[47] White planned sixty-seven free-standing houses and duplexes for 112 families (Figs. 12,13). By using a few basic plan arrangements for these two- and four-bedroom houses and by inverting the plans, White achieved a maximum of differentiation among the houses, although they all clearly belong to the same family. A simple wood frame vernacular style was used throughout; all the houses are sheathed in shingles and clapboard, painted yellow with white trim, and highlighted with a few classical details. The village school and waterworks were designed by others, but the firm designed the community house with ground-floor general store and meeting rooms and baths on the upper floor. Today the houses and community hall still exist, though somewhat worn, within the limits of Niagara Falls.

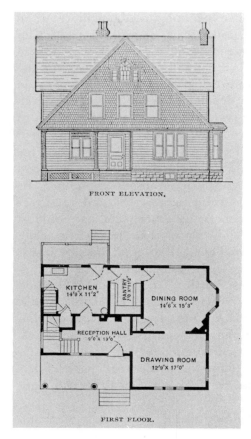

FRONT ELEVATION.

FIRST FLOOR.

Figure 13. Plan and Elevation of one of the houses at Echota, designed by White. From J. Bogart, "The Industrial Village of Echota at Niagara," Cassier Magazine, 1895, 318.

Figure 12. Plan of Echota, Niagara Falls, N.Y., 1893-95. Figures in black show the nucleus of the houses designed by White. From J. Bogart, "The Industrial Village of Echota at Niagara," Cassier Magazine, 1895, 318.

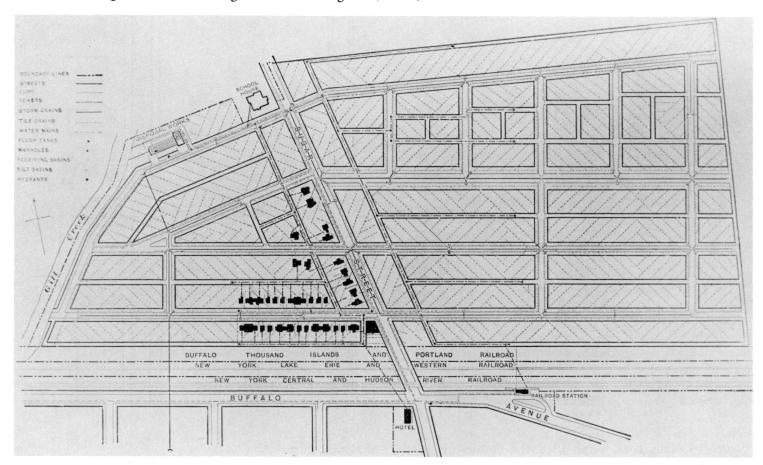

What comprehensive planning could achieve when carried out on a regional scale was shown to McKim very early in his career, when in 1882 Henry Villard engaged him to design a number of buildings for the Northern Pacific Railroad. Villard felt that success in any kind of building depended on the integrated development of the entire region in which the building was to play a part, however small. This philosophy governed Villard's development of the whole Oregon territory, for he understood that if the Northern Pacific Railroad were to prosper, the subsidiary transportation lines, the farmlands and the development of natural resources must all be made to function smoothly and harmoniously together; the well-being of one was intrinsically bound up with the well-being of all the others.[48] It was as a part of this integrated master plan for the development of the northwest territory that McKim, Mead and White designed the "Portland House" hotel and the terminal station in Portland, Oregon; a station and hotel in Tacoma, Washington; another station in Mandan; a hospital for Northern Pacific employees at Brainerd, Minnesota; and even the interiors of the steam packets that ran between Tacoma, Portland and San Francisco, California.

When in 1887 the firm was given the first of eleven commissions by John Howard Whittemore, they encountered a similar concern for over-all regional development. In this case the region was that around Whittemore's home in Naugatuck, Connecticut, an archetypal

New England mill town,[49] where he had built a prosperous business manufacturing small malleable iron parts. Whittemore chose to remain in Naugatuck, a town of only 6000 people, and to create for it the advantages of more populous cities. Fortunately Whittemore's paternalism was a good deal more relaxed and adaptive than that of his contemporary George Pullman, who had built an entire factory town for his railroad car works and his employees in Illinois.

The first commission was for a large house for Whittemore's own use at the edge of Naugatuck overlooking the iron works on the Naugatuck River. In 1891 Whittemore turned his attention to urban amenities for the small town, beginning the design for a small but richly ornamented public library in memory of his son. With the library Whittemore and McKim, Mead and White began the architectural definition of the town green. The library was one of the first public buildings placed around the common, defining the open space (Figs. 14,15). Within the year the firm designed a small bank (Whittemore was one of its directors) to be built immediately to the south of the library. The urban qualities that could be added to the still ill-defined green became evident when in September 1892 Whittemore gave the firm the commission for a public school to be built directly west of the green at the foot of a hill. The school, a gift to the city by Whittemore, was placed directly in line with a Civil War column in the middle of the green. In the winter of 1894-95 Whittemore had the

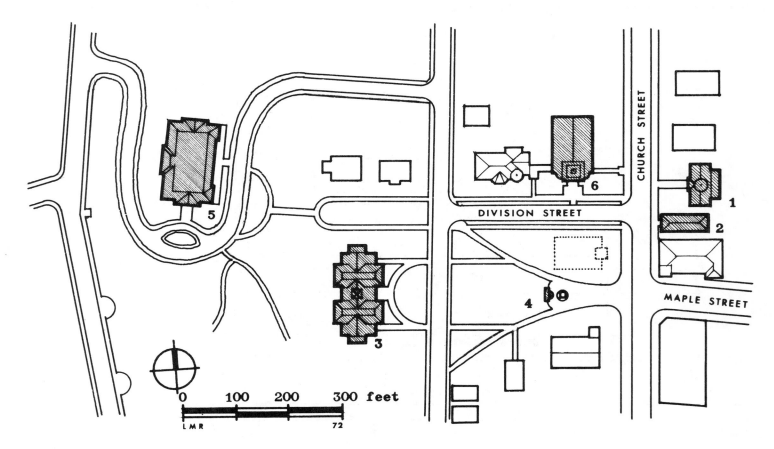

Figure 14. Naugatuck, Conn. Plan of buildings designed by McKim, Mead and White, 1891-1901. Drawing by Leland Roth.

Figure 15. Naugatuck, Conn. Aerial photo of area around town green. Courtesy Whittemore Memorial Library, Naugatuck, Conn.

firm plan a network of walks in the town common, focusing on and radiating out from the central Civil War column. At this newly defined center a public fountain was incorporated into the design of the walks (Fig. 16).

The landscaping and furnishing of the Naugatuck green was only a portion of a much larger enterprise. In Middlebury, some seven miles northeast of Naugatuck, Whittemore had accumulated a large estate that he planned to connect to Naugatuck by a landscaped corridor leading all the way to the green. For this work he engaged the landscape architect Charles Eliot.[50] In 1894 on a hilltop in Middlebury McKim, Mead and White designed a summer house that is a small masterwork in the tradition of the Shingle Style (Fig. 17) with a carefully controlled geometrical envelope unifying the entire structure. Built on a ridge overlooking Lake Quassapaug, the summer house commands a view of the rolling wooded hills that stretch away to the northeast.

Upon completion of the library, bank, grammar school and the landscaping of the green, the center of

Naugatuck had been given a definite focus. The town, now with some 8000 inhabitants, soon felt the need for additional educational facilities, and in 1901 Whittemore engaged the firm to design a public high school. In the earlier phase of their work in Naugatuck McKim, Mead and White had utilized all the available sites around the green, yet this new and necessarily large structure had to be integrated into the planned arrangement already begun. The solution was to place the high school on a terrace in the hillside, just behind and north of the grammar school, using it to close off an axis that ran from the library and bank at the opposite end of Division Street. A view of the high school looking down this axis toward the library and bank in the distance is shown in Plate 221.

Shortly after the designs for the high school were begun the firm received a commission for a Congregational church in Naugatuck (Plates 220-221), an assignment due, no doubt, to Whittemore's presence on the church's building committee. (Whittemore had also

Figure 16. Fountain, Naugatuck, Conn., 1895. The Salem Elementary School
can be seen behind the fountain on the left. In the background on the right,
where the trees obscure the view, is the site where the high school was later
built.

donated the site for the new church next to the existing
parish house, north of the green.) McKim, Mead and
White based their design closely on the old church on
the green itself, but because the white frame building
had badly deteriorated, the new church was designed in
more permanent brick and limestone. By placing the
new church so that it was directly opposite the center of
the common, marked by the Civil War column and fountain, a minor perpendicular axis was created, binding
together the two parallel axes.

McKim, Mead and White built three houses in or near
Naugatuck for Whittemore, in addition to six commissions carried out in the center of town. Thus after four-
teen years of growth and development Naugatuck possessed a town center both ordered in plan and picturesque in appearance, markedly contrasted to the blind
expansion of nearly every industrialized city in the same
years. The work of McKim, Mead and White, carried out
under the enlightened patronage of Whittemore, acted
as a stimulus to the town. After Whittemore's death in
1910 a memorial bridge across the Naugatuck River was
constructed through public subscription. During the
next several years the Neary Building was built east of
the green, making complete its enclosure on that side,
and a new post office and two new banks were added
along Church Street, north of the library. All these
buildings are small, and in their respect for the scale and
varied activities of the street they continue in the spirit
of civic awareness begun by McKim, Mead and White.

Related to this kind of city planning is the laying out
of large institutional complexes, an aspect of the firm's
work shown in the Monograph. The most well-known
example of this kind of planning is Columbia University,
New York. In the spring of 1892 the university began to
make plans to move to a large tract of open land in
Morningside Heights, far from the increasing clutter and
confusion of the existing downtown facility. McKim
was asked to join with Richard Morris Hunt, Charles C.
Haight and William Robert Ware to form a committee to
study the site and recommend a plan for the new buildings.[51] During the next year the committee examined
models of the proposed site and drew up suggestions for

its development. An impasse was reached when Hunt insisted the complex look west, out toward the Palisades, and Haight preferred east. McKim felt convinced that it should face south, toward the city that was slowly spreading up Manhattan. In his eyes the university was to be itself a miniature city set on a hill facing the distant heart of New York. The university officials agreed with McKim, and the commission for Columbia University was given to the firm on November 4, 1893.

The Columbia University plan worked out by McKim during 1893 and 1894 resembles in some ways the arrangement of the University of Virginia created by Thomas Jefferson (Plates 47 and 110). The similarities were perhaps inevitable; not only was McKim an ardent believer in the architectural principles of Jefferson and an admirer of his work, but the University of Virginia was at that time the only planned educational complex in the country. Following Jefferson's example, McKim placed his library at the head of a group of buildings; with all other units subordinated to it, it became the visual as well as the scholarly focus of the ensemble. To make this focus clear, the Low Library was built entirely of limestone, while all the other surrounding structures were of deep red brick with limestone trim. And as at Charlottesville, the ground in front of the library was carried down in a series of terraces, although at Columbia they are precisely and monumentally differentiated by substantial retaining walls, staircases and paved piazzas. Instead of placing the classroom buildings in two rows facing each other, as Jefferson had done, McKim arranged these buildings and living quarters in four groups of six buildings each, forming a series of small courts in the vicinity of the library, and framing one large court to the south of the library. This court was to be closed off by a large building on West 114th Street, directly opposite the library.

The master plan for Columbia was never completely carried through, and only the buildings at the perimeter were finished—large open expanses having replaced closed intimate courts in popularity during the 1930s. The small centrally planned buildings on either side of the library were built, but only one of the interior units was erected, the Avery Building housing the school of architecture and the Avery architectural library. Thus if one wishes to see the Columbia campus as the urban environment in miniature it was meant to be, he must walk to the courtyard between Avery and Fayerweather Halls; there he can sense the close, intimate scale that McKim had in mind. The barren expanses that oppress the visitor today are not what McKim wished for Columbia, neither would he have chosen the group of ill-defined buildings at the southwest corner. All the carefully calculated space and enclosure, that special sense of place generated by the library and its surrounding classroom buildings, is there allowed to seep ineffectually away.

In 1892-93, while McKim was occupied with Columbia, a commission came into the office for the develop-

Figure 17. John Howard Whittemore Residence, Middlebury, Conn., 1895.
Courtesy New-York Historical Society, New York.

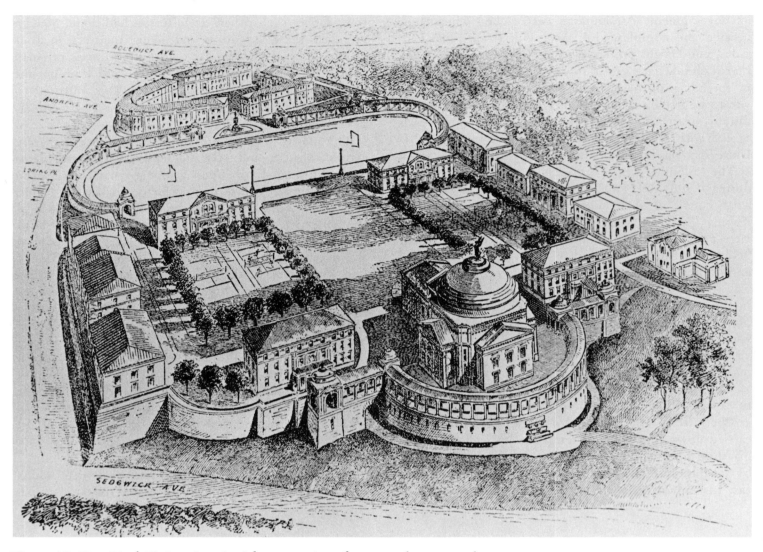

Figure 18. New York University. Aerial perspective of proposed campus plan.
Designed 1893-94. Plate 74 of the Monograph shows the plan of the buildings
in the foreground. From J. L. Chamberlain, "New York University," 187.

ment of a series of new buildings for New York University at the new University Heights campus in the Bronx section of New York City. White was engaged by two members of the college council to design a chemistry laboratory and a lecture hall. The gift of the large library by Helen Miller Gould in 1895 created the central group—the library flanked by the Hall of Languages and a projected Hall of Philosophy—shown in Plate 74. White's over-all scheme for the NYU campus appears to have been much more extensive (Fig. 18).[52] He envisaged a large court with rows of trees directly in front of the library. Parallel lines of buildings were to enclose the court at the far northern and southern extremities and two additional buildings were to face the two "Halls" from the other side of the large court. Beyond this court was the Ohio athletic field; White oriented his entire complex of buildings so as to create an arrangement into which the field would fit integrally. Accordingly the axis of the library bisected the field. Beyond the field to the east White planned an informal group of dormitory buildings, the first of which was built through the gener-

osity of Helen Gould. Although this dormitory was arranged to follow the line of the site, that is, at an angle to the more formal group of academic buildings on the other side of the field, it is so placed that its northernmost entrance is directly on the axis of the library at the other end of the campus. Unfortunately this subtle relationship was destroyed when the recent Gould Student Center totally blocked the view. Little suggestion of such a comprehensive plan is given by the Monograph plate, which shows only the central group of flanking buildings. It should be noted that the library was pushed to the far edge of the University Heights plateau in order to provide as much room as possible for subsequent campus building. Raised on a massive basement, the library and its Hall of Fame command a view of the Harlem River below and a glimpse of the Palisades in the distance.[53]

In the New York University library White followed his prototype, the Jefferson library Rotunda at the University of Virginia, more closely than had McKim in the Columbia library. It would appear from the firm archives that White crystallized the NYU library design during 1894 or 1895 and began construction in June 1896, at the same time that he became involved in restoring the Jeffersonian rotunda itself in Charlottesville, Virginia. Since this restoration and the additions made by the firm to Jefferson's original campus have received much criticism, a careful examination of the events is perhaps necessary.[54] On October 27, 1895, a fire started in the far corner of the annex that had been added to the rear of Jefferson's library Rotunda.[55] The fire spread southward into the Rotunda itself, gutting the interior and destroying the wooden dome that had marked the heart of the University of Virginia. After some immediate emergency measures by a local architect, the Visitors (i.e. Trustees) of the university selected White as the architect for the restoration in January 1896. By this time the faculty had carefully weighed many possible solutions and had decided on a general university development plan that included the restoration of the Rotunda: At the time of the fire the university was in need of expanding its teaching facilities, especially in the sciences. Even before the fire there was a general desire to pull down the annex because it detracted from Jefferson's original building. Now this difficult problem was solved; the annex was gone and new facilities were mandatory. After much discussion the faculty reported to the Rector and Visitors on October 31, 1895, suggesting that a competent architect be engaged to restore the Rotunda as faithfully as possible and to erect a portico on the north side of the Rotunda with steps leading down to an esplanade on the site of the old annex. The interior of the Rotunda was to be opened up from the dome down to the portico floor, replacing the two floors Jefferson had used to house the various agencies originally in the building. To replace the annex lecture rooms the architect was to design an "Academical Building" with a central horseshoe-shaped auditorium. He was also to design a physics laboratory and an engineering building with a separate power house. The faculty proposal located the sites of the academic building and the two science buildings at the southern end of Jefferson's original Lawn, thus closing the quadrangle. The faculty concluded its report by saying that they were—

deeply impressed with the propriety of following in these buildings classical types of design and of locating them so as to create a harmonious combination with the original Jeffersonian group. As we examine the additions made to this system by Jefferson's successors, we are forced to confess with a certain shame, that not one of them has added in the least degree to the harmony and beauty and magnificence of the original composition. We recommend, therefore, that the Visitors select as their professional advisor, a man not of local repute only, but of broad and national consideration, that he be instructed to consider in his designs not merely the convenience and elegance of the simple structure, but its effect as a member of our general architectural system, and that he submit to your Board a comprehensive scheme which shall embody his advice on the location not only of the buildings recommended in this report, but also of such additional dormitories, hospital buildings, official quarters, and so on as the Visitors

may contemplate. The study of our grounds as a problem of landscape gardening should at the same time receive some attention.[56]

White apparently closely followed the locations selected by the faculty in their report, although he did try in several ways to make the new buildings less intrusive (Plates 110-112A). The buildings themselves were designed in a very reserved manner, so as not to detract from the Rotunda at the other end of the Lawn. Then they were placed on a fourth terrace several feet lower than the original three terrace levels, so that the view was still open over the roofs of the new buildings. In addition the three new structures were connected by open pergolas, through which one could still see the valley below. Unfortunately the valley, so pastoral and verdant in Jefferson's time, is now crowded by the urban growth of Charlottesville; those who protest the closing of the Lawn plead for a landscape that can exist now only in our imagination, a romanticism destroyed by modern technology.

In the earlier discussion of the firm's work on the David H. King Model House complex, it was noted that McKim, Mead and White also made designs for speculative office buildings. Although none of these early designs is represented in the Monograph, McKim, Mead and White actually gained a local reputation for their New York office buildings of the 1880s, creating what could be called a "New York style," analagous to the Chicago office building with its steel skeleton, "Chicago windows" and structurally expressive exterior skin. This New York idiom can be seen in three particularly representative buildings: the American Safe Deposit Company and Columbia Bank of 1882, the Phillips and Lloyd Phoenix residence of 1882 and the Goelet Building of 1886 (Figs. 19, 20, 21). The bank building and the Phoenix residence, long since demolished, once stood at the corner of Fifth Avenue and 42nd Street and at 23 E. 33rd Street, respectively. The Goelet Building, now with four additional upper stories, happily still stands at Broadway and 20th Street. In these New York buildings a smooth ashlar basement story supports upper walls of brick. Each of the two basement floors of the bank building houses one of the co-owner institutions, while the lower floors of the Goelet Building are opened up by means of a large arcade to provide show windows. The Phoenix residence, perhaps the best of the three, has a restrained and very simple basement story.

The most significant feature of all the buildings, however, is the grouping of upper floor windows into vertical strips, with the brick walls between expressed as solid piers. The vertical window strips are surrounded by frames of continuous bands of brick or terra cotta ornament. The spandrels between the windows of the various floors are filled with panels of either terra cotta, as in the Phoenix residence, or panels of cut brick, as in the other two buildings. These panels are given distinct-

Figure 19. American Safe Deposit Company and Columbia Bank, New York,
1882. Courtesy Museum of the City of New York.

Figure 20. Phillips and Lloyd Phoenix Residence, New York, 1882.
From "American Architect and Building News," 87 (February 4,
1905), pl. 1519.

Figure 21. Goelet Building, New York, 1886. Courtesy Museum of the City
of New York.

ly different designs at each floor level. The attic stories of the buildings, particularly the bank and the Phoenix residence, are clearly marked by ornamental patterns laid up in the brickwork.

The rationale is obvious: these buildings are based on an architecture of the wall. No structural frame is suggested since these are bearing wall structures, adapted to the solid foundation conditions of Manhattan, just as the Chicago type, with its frame, caisson foundations and exterior expression derived in part from its skeleton, was well suited to the spongy subsoil conditions of that city.

These early buildings, with their expression derived directly from use and construction material, were for some reason excluded from the Monograph in 1914. Their influence, already felt in Philadelphia and Washington, D.C., might otherwise have been much more extensive and might possibly have established a true "New York School."

The Monograph does, however, include the later commercial and residential architecture, buildings designed in the 1890s and the early 1900s, and these works are consequently much more widely known. The firm became particularly noted for commercial buildings and banks during the later years, one good example of which is the Knickerbocker Trust Company of New York (Plates 208-12), a building sometimes credited (or blamed) with initiating the practice of designing banks to look like Roman temples.[57] Among the many banks that drew inspiration from the Knickerbocker model are the First National Bank of Champaign, Illinois, by Mundie and Jensen and the Detroit Trust Company by Albert Kahn. Hundreds of other derivatives can be found across the country.[58] One reason for the widespread influence of the Knickerbocker bank was, perhaps, the highly favorable discussion of it by the architectural critic Montgomery Schuyler, whose penetrating articles on American bridges and skyscrapers examined their uniquely modern significance and national character.[59] Schuyler saw in the Knickerbocker bank the reconciliation of modern building techniques with a rational theory of classical design. The orders, truly colossal in size, are appropriately used to carry a single roof element covering four enclosed floors. The individual floors themselves are articulated by much more diminutive dark bronze members set well back from the visually supportive columns. The columns therefore are not compromised. As a further detail the banking room, with its need for security, is indicated by the bronze grillage on the first floor. The Knickerbocker Trust Company building was short-lived, however, because its small size was uneconomical in an area of Manhattan even then populated by tall buildings. Even the Knickerbocker bank was to have been a skyscraper of thirteen stories, but financial problems encountered by the tenants who were to build the upper portion cut short those plans; only the lower four floors were constructed. The lower portion, built according to the original

plans, was capable of carrying the upper nine floors, however. But a developer never came forward, the vertical expansion was never carried out, and eventually the bank had to come down.[60] Since the completed portion of the Knickerbocker bank was designed as the basement element of a much taller building, the extremely rich and vigorous Corinthian capitals and the frieze above are perfectly logical; as part of a much larger whole they would not have been unduly assertive. Yet even in its truncated state, the Knickerbocker Trust Company building was a feast for the eyes of Fifth Avenue strollers.

Another especially interesting bank commission, one that again underscores McKim's concern with preserving valued local traditions and forms, was for the Bank of Montreal, Montreal, Canada (Plates 213-216a). The original building on St. James Street (Plate 213) dated from 1845 and was based directly on David Rhind's Commercial Bank of Scotland in Edinburgh. The Montreal architect responsible for the building, John Wells, made one significant addition to Rhind's design, a low wooden dome behind the pediment. With the growth of the bank's business the original building proved too crowded and inconvenient, and ravages of weather forced the removal of the dome.[61] McKim, Mead and White were thus called upon to remodel the existing building and to create a harmonious addition.

Since it was impossible to expand the bank on either side on St. James Street, the only alternative was to add to the rear, but a complication arose in that the ground fell away some twenty-five feet between St. James Street and Craig Street, the next street parallel to St. James. Fortification Lane, a narrow alley between the two streets, could not be closed off, even for so eminent a taxpayer as the Bank of Montreal. McKim overcame these problems by creating a large new banking room along Craig Street, raised on a high basement and joined to the original building by a hall bridging Fortification Lane (Plate 215). Behind the original portico on St. James Street was a recessed section of the porch framed by four columns that McKim selected as the module to be used throughout his addition. The module forms the width of the hall bridging the lane and is repeated in the four columns framing the center bay of the new banking room. The flanking bays of the banking room are identical in size, with piers between the bays providing the necessary dimensions so that the entire lot could be filled without changing the size of the basic module. Although it was natural to place the banking room perpendicular to the line of the original building and the connecting hall, the angle at which Craig Street ran forced McKim to use a device that the firm had employed earlier in the Bowery Savings Bank in New York— a room within a room. (See the Bowery Bank, Plate 66.) Beyond the interior wall, formed by the module columns, lies an outer wall running along Craig Street, with the distance between the walls varying from one end of the building to the other. In the interstice various minor offices are arranged. On the exterior of the Craig Street wall the module of the interior is matched by a similar module of colossal Tuscan pilasters (Plate 216). The observer walking around the building thus sees the Corinthian order of the older St. James Street facade carried straight through the building to become the massive Tuscan pilaster group triplicated on the Craig Street side.

Once the Craig Street building was completed, and banking operations moved to the new room, the interior of the old building was removed and completely rearranged to house the necessary offices and conference rooms, while above the walls were reinforced to carry a restoration of Wells's original dome, this time constructed as a monolithic Guastavino vault.[62]

The work for the Bank of Montreal is representative of McKim's designs at their best. One notes the very careful attention to the proportions of the component parts, the modular organization and the precise articulation of the elements of the design. Similar attention to careful organization can be observed in such designs as the Agricultural Building at the Columbian Exposition (Plates 41-42) and in the Army War College, Washington, D.C. (Plates 265-267). As impressive is McKim's deliberate and sensitive awareness of a valued architectural heritage in the restoration of the dome that had long been a landmark of Montreal.

McKim, Mead and White believed that buildings of the same basic type and use can still adapt to a particular environment and place. An illustration of this is the series of branch libraries designed for the New York Public Library system between 1902 and 1914 (Plates 196-199). The individual buildings were to be scattered about the city within easy reach of all citizens. The plans for each of these branch libraries were nearly identical to that shown in Plate 196, yet each building is an imaginative variation on a common theme. The designs have a sense of balance, one might even say erudition, that seems suitable for a library. Each design is so varied as to be quickly distinguished from the others, making each library unique to its particular neighborhood.

McKim, Mead and White also used this device of variations on a theme for the series of New York clubhouses they designed for a widely divergent group of organizations. The Century Club, designed in 1889 (Plates 27-29), was the home of a group of artists, art critics and those interested in the arts. White conceived the building as a distant relative of the palaces of Verona, appropriately bathed in a wealth of plastic ornamentation, an echo of the spirit of the early Italian Renaissance. In contrast, McKim's design for the New York Harvard Club, located only one block away, refers not to Italy but, in its deep-red-brick-and-white-limestone trim, to the straightforward simplicity and sobriety of Georgian Boston and the Harvard Yard. It speaks the architectural language of Charles Bulfinch. In

a third example, McKim's University Club of New York, designed to house an organization of graduates of America's oldest colleges and universities, the basic motifs again come from Renaissance Italy, but the reference here is not as much to the Italy of the visual arts as the place where humanistic learning and discourse were revived. Elements from the Palazzo Spannochi, Siena, and the Palazzo Albergati, Bologna, are freely quoted.[63]

Though McKim, Mead and White are perhaps best known today for their design for Pennsylvania Station, New York, it was only one of a number of commissions for transportation and industrial facilities. Included with such work were several powerhouses, the first of which the firm designed for Niagara Falls in 1892 (Fig. 22). Here the firm used the kind of heavy masonry characteristic of their mentor, H. H. Richardson, perhaps in an effort to symbolize the great power of the Falls now being harnessed for the first time. All but one of the buildings of the Niagara Falls generating station have been destroyed; the transformer house still stands, and the central bay of the main powerhouse has been re-erected on Goat Island as a memorial to the men and machinery that first generated and transmitted alternating electricity on a commercial basis.[64]

The Niagara complex was followed in 1902 by the design of the exterior of the Interborough Rapid Transit powerhouse on 59th Street in New York (Plate 207). The internal arrangement of the generating machinery as planned by the engineers of the subway system consisted of two very long parallel sections, with a long boiler house on the south and a long generating building on the north. Each section was divided into six self-sufficient stations, with a boiler room half and a generating room half, served by its own chimney. The two parallel sections were 83 and 117 feet wide and the length of all six stations was 694 feet.[65] White collaborated with the company engineers in developing an exterior bay unit for both short and long sides of the building. Three bays on the long sides mark one generating station, with the bays so arranged that the dividing line falls in the middle of the arches. In this way the chimney for each station falls in line with the solid pier of the arcade below. Although now soiled with grime and partially despoiled of its ornament, the IRT powerhouse exterior was originally light in tone with basement walls of pink granite supporting buff brick walls with buff terra cotta ornamentation.

Pennsylvania Station was, of course, the culmination of this industrial work. McKim made the initial designs in April 1902 (Plates 300-310) but the preparation for the station, the largest building erected in modern times in one continuous operation, required years of effort.[66] Construction was finally begun in 1905, and the building was completed in 1911 after McKim's death. Pennsylvania Station was the fruition of long years of planning by the Pennsylvania Railroad in its competition with the New York Central for traffic to the west. It was only after the development of powerful electric

Figure 22. Niagara Falls Power Station, Niagara Falls, N.Y., 1892. Courtesy
Niagara Mohawk Power Corp.

locomotives that the Pennsylvania could proceed with definite plans for tunneling under the supposedly unbridgeable Hudson River. Through these tunnels trains could run directly from Jersey City into the heart of Manhattan; passengers no longer had to board a ferry to cross the Hudson. Heretofore, the Central had the advantage because it ran directly to 42nd Street, only slightly uptown and a short carriage ride to the commercial and financial centers of New York. Now the Pennsylvania trains, drawn by the new electric locomotives, could burrow beneath the Hudson, then cross Manhattan, Long Island, and perhaps even press on into New England. But this subsurface travel posed a problem for McKim: somehow the power and image of the railroad, the symbols of progress of the nineteenth century, had to be expressed in the design even though the trains themselves would not be visible. The problem was compounded when the Pennsylvania acquired control of the Long Island Railroad and decided to bring the two roads together at the new station. The volume of traffic would be tremendous, for not only would there be through passengers to and from points south, but also the daily hoard of commuters pulsing through the station twice a day, funneling in from Long Island and New Jersey in the morning and fanning out again in the evening. These commuters needed a direct connection with the planned rapid transit stations below grade at both ends of Penn Station. With the expansiveness characteristic of the firm's work, McKim provided for

all this multifarious activity, making Penn Station not only a functional but a majestic portal of New York.

The basic plan as conceived by McKim was to be contained within a massive wall-like outer ring whose uniformity would bind together the tremendous expanse of the building. To preserve and heighten the solidity and muscularity of this perimeter McKim used Tuscan columns and pilasters, drawing inspiration from Bernini's Tuscan colonnade surrounding the Piazza of St. Peter's, Rome. Both architects used this simplest, most massive order because both had the same problem of organizing and controlling great distances through their designs. The colonnade of Penn Station was to be three blocks long on Seventh Avenue. To counter this long horizontal march of column and pilaster McKim raised up the huge clerestory of the waiting room, whose distant eaves could be glimpsed from sidewalk level. To assure that the soaring reaches of the waiting room interior would have apprehensible scale McKim modeled this huge room on the Baths of Caracalla.

In addition to the formal elements of the exterior and interior, and the solemn majesty they engendered, the smooth functioning of the station was guaranteed by a series of floor levels and ramps. The tracks of the Pennsylvania road were to be at the lowest level, with the Long Island tracks the southernmost of the subterranean train-yard. These tracks were to lie below the tubes of the planned subways to the east and west of the station. The subway stops at each end of the station were then connected by a long concourse that also led directly to stairs down to the Pennsylvania and Long Island trains. Above this subway concourse was the main waiting room floor, itself still one story below street grade. Passengers could, however, be delivered directly to this level by vehicular ramps running down from Seventh Avenue. Baggage could likewise be handled at the waiting room level before vehicles went back up the ramp to the street. From every direction pedestrians could enter the station and descend to the waiting room level on special staircases. Each of the component parts of the traffic—subway passengers, commuters, passengers arriving by carriage or automobile, pedestrians and baggage—had its own flow pattern, which was merged with the others only at the point of train boarding.

If, through almost deliberate misuse over the last twenty years of its existence, Penn Station was virtually *made* to fail, the logic and clarity of McKim's original design was not at fault. It is symptomatic of our age that as the function and pattern of use of the station changed, that imaginative and sympathetic use of the station did not change with it. The almost criminal neglect and abuse of Penn Station, coupled with changing values, caused us to lose sight of the wonderful spatial release from the increasingly more crowded streets of the city the station provided. We gradually lost the ability even to perceive its public grandeur, to enjoy its civic excess. It is not to be wondered that when it fell into jeopardy we could not stir ourselves— we had sneered too long at what it had become, and once a pattern of disrespect is established it persists. Nor have we been able to bring ourselves to build its better. As Vincent Scully has observed, "through it one entered the city like a god. Perhaps it was really too much. One scuttles in now like a rat."[67]

The classical forms that McKim had evoked in his design for Penn Station had originally lent the building authority; in the building's declining years the very same forms made it suspect. McKim, White and most other architects of their period looked to the architecture of the ancients and the Renaissance for the assurance of authority they felt desirable in a building. For urban buildings, especially, these sources seemed to express qualities of intellect and imagination, of good order, proportion, balance and urbanity. The phenomenon is not restricted to Americans: in England Sir Charles Barry and Decimus Burton had paraphrased the Palazzo Farnese in their London clubhouses built in the 1830s and 1840s. And when American architects began to draw heavily on the Italian Renaissance in the 1890s, many Italian architects themselves began to investigate their own architectural heritage. The most accomplished Italian architect working in this vein was Gaetano Koch (1849-1910). Relying almost exclusively on the Palazzo Farnese as his model, Koch designed several still impressive buildings in Rome, among them the Banca d'Italia of 1885 and the Palazzo Margherita of 1886, now the American embassy.[68]

Because McKim, Mead and White drew on ancient and Renaissance sources it is said that they did not produce an American architecture. In the act of adaptation, however, they expressed characteristics that can be identified as American, even in their more Italianate designs. Invariably the firm strengthened horizontal lines, regularized and reduced the number of parts and emphasized the relation to the ground. These and other transformations can be easily identified in the three general classes to which the firm's more derivative designs belong. First, buildings based directly on individual identifiable models (although often erroneously considered copies, these derivative designs are always much changed from the originals). Second, buildings combining features from several recognizable prototypes. Third, buildings which, although stylistically of the Italian Renaissance or some other period, are entirely original creations. The characteristic changes that occurred whenever a European source was followed can be most readily observed in the buildings of the first group of so-called copies: the New York State Building at the Columbian Exposition, the New York Herald Building, the Joseph Pulitzer residence, the Tiffany Building, the H. A. C. Taylor house in New York and the Butler Institute of American Art in Youngstown, Ohio.

The New York State Building at the World's Columbian Exposition enjoyed a particularly significant site directly across from Charles B. Atwood's Art Building (Plates 43-44). Designed in April 1892, it was to be "a convenient and comfortable club house for New Yorkers, where they might rest, obtain information, entertain their friends. . . ."[69] When it was completed it was immediately recognized as being derived from the Villa Medici, Rome, by Annibale Lippi, 1544 (Fig. 23). In essence this is true, but many changes were made. In the garden facade of the Villa Medici the center element is recessed behind the side wings, and the roof heights, string courses and all other horizontal lines of the villa are discontinuous from the side wings to the center block. In the New York State Building, on the other hand, all the horizontal lines are continuous, running completely around the building. The roof lines and the cornice are made particularly prominent. Although some of the relief sculpture of the villa is absent to allow for more windows, an entirely new band of sculpture is introduced as a frieze below the cornice, containing within it small square windows. This richly modeled frieze further emphasizes the horizontal line of the cornice. Instead of the tall tower projections of the villa's facade and its sloping tile roofs, in the New York State Building the small belvederes were placed on the flat roof terraces, which provided elevated views of the fair grounds. Semicircular porches were added at both ends, while at the front the villa's constricted staircase was replaced by a broad terrace and a wide fan of stairs; this was a public building to which access had to be easy and generous.

The firm's New York Herald Building was also derived from an Italian source (Plates 62-64A). James

Figure 23. Villa Medici, Rome. Annibale Lippi, 1544. Courtesy Yale Art Library.

Gordon Bennett, the headstrong publisher of the paper, decided in 1891 to leave Park Row in lower Manhattan, the home of all the other newspapers in the city, and to blaze a path in New York journalism by locating his new building in the heart of the theater district. And he had definite ideas about the building. It was not to be a forbidding tower like the one Joseph Pulitzer had just built for the "World," but much more accessible, low and more human. Work on the building began in May 1892 on a narrow trapezoid site just north of the intersection of Broadway and Sixth Avenue, an area directly in the steady stream of increasingly heavy midtown traffic. Bennett instructed White that his building was to be a replica of the Palace of the Doges in Venice. Braving Bennett's wrath (Bennett was famous for tolerating absolutely no interference) White argued against the ornateness of the Venetian model (in any case, New York already had a copy—the National Academy of Design by Peter B. Wight, built 1863-65), suggesting instead the somewhat more chaste Palazzo del Consiglio in Verona, to which Bennett gave his consent (Fig. 24). The Consiglio is essentially a frontal building, with only a facade on the town's piazza (it does have one open side, but it is not exposed to full view). The facade,

designed to create a complex of overlaid rhythms, has on the lower floor an arcade of eight openings, with pilasters framing the ends and bisecting the arcade in the middle. Above, however, are four identical bays (no center bisector) containing a bifoil window in the center of each bay. The wall surfaces around the windows are decorated with fresco designs. Leading up to two openings of the arcade are short flights of steps which, in their spacing, add yet another pattern to the system of rhythm and counterrhythm created in the facade.

In adapting this design for the Herald Building, White felt it necessary to eliminate many of the complicated rhythms which, although effective in a short frontal facade, would be distracting in a large trapezoidal building on a site surrounded on all sides by city streets. By making the bays identical, he was able to run continuous arcades along the long Broadway and Sixth Avenue sides as well as along the northern 35th Street side. He called attention to the short 34th Street facade by altering the bay design, thus emphasizing the main entrance to the building on the ground floor and Mr. Bennett's suite of rooms directly above. This side was further enhanced by the sculptural group on the roof, the only portions of the building remaining on the site

Figure 24. Palazzo del Consiglio, Verona. Fra Giacondo, 1476. Courtesy Yale
Art Library.

today. Supervised by Minerva, who stands at the center, the smaller male figures continue to strike out the hours on Herald Square in New York. White re-created the fading fresco designs of the Consiglio in Verona in more permanent low relief terra cotta panels. Along the eaves of the building owls with electrically lighted eyes blinked down on Herald Square; Bennett considered the bird his personal talisman and demanded that its image be about him constantly.[70]

Both the New York State and the Herald buildings were based on single sources, but in the Joseph Pulitzer house of 1900 (Plates 180-82), two specific Venetian palazzi were used as the basis of the design. This might seem to suggest that this design belongs in the second group of derivative designs, but in this case the Venetian models are by the same architect and are extremely close in appearance, so that it can be said that there is essentially one source. The varied rhythms of the upper floors of the Pulitzer house are taken from the Palazzo Pesaro in Venice by Baldassare Longhena, 1676 (Fig. 25) but in the McKim, Mead and White design the broken entablature of the Palazzo Pesaro is stretched

into a continuous horizontal element. Like the Palazzo Pesaro, the Pulitzer house has carefully articulated corners marking the end of the enclosing walls. The rusticated ground floor of the Pulitzer house is taken from Longhena's Palazzo Rezzonico in Venice of 1667, though the central entrance of the Pulitzer house breaks forward slightly. It is particularly significant that White, who was in charge of this design, severely reduced the extremely plastic figures in the spandrels and keystones of Longhena's very Baroque design. All the details are made sharper and crisper than the more expansive forms of Longhena.

The plasticity of design, here more pronounced than in much of the firm's work, has been in part attributed to Pulitzer's loss of sight; he demanded that the architects bring him plaster models to study by touch, judging the elements in relief by how clearly he could feel them. With advancing years and increasing loss of sight, Pulitzer's eccentricities became more exacerbated, particularly his obsession for silence. Close study of the plans of the house will reveal double wall construction in Pulitzer's personal rooms. Even this effort to reduce external noise was not sufficient for Pulitzer, who later added a separate addition to the rear of the house with even more elaborate precautions.[71]

In June 1903 White began studies for a large new store for Tiffany and Company in New York (Plates 261-64). His design was based on the Palazzo Grimani in Venice by Michele Sanmicheli, 1556 (Fig. 26) but again many changes occurred. As with the Veronese and Venetian palazzi mentioned earlier, Sanmicheli's varied rhythms are reduced to a single bay type. In the Palazzo Grimani the end bays have paired columns and the center bays have single columns; the openings of the bays are alternately round-headed and square-headed. White placed an arched window in each bay and framed it with pairs of columns, but his bays are framed by single columns in the center of the 37th Street side of the building; Sanmicheli's figural keystones and the fluting of the pilasters and columns were also eliminated. In a further departure the spandrels of the second floor of the Tiffany building are glazed, opening up the wall to still more light and making the wall itself simply a grid. Along with the large expanses of glass on the first floor,

this device serves to reveal the steel frame supporting the store.

In the H. A. C. Taylor house in New York, begun in May 1894 (Plate 81), a Florentine model was followed with several modifications. The Palazzo Bartolini-Salembeni by Baccio d'Agnolo (Fig. 27), the source of the design, has three stories, while the Taylor house had four stories plus attic. The basic frame and three bays of the d'Agnolo model were observed, and the second and third floors of the model emulated. But in the Taylor house the rusticated ground floor was compressed, the third floor and attic story simply invented, and engaged Ionic columns substituted on the second floor for d'Agnolo's pilasters.

A final example of the firm's use of Italian sources is the Butler Institute of American Art in Youngstown, Ohio, begun in February 1917 (Plates 394-94A). It should be specifically noted that this design was begun long after both McKim and White were dead and Mead had virtually retired from the firm—thus the dependence on the model is much more marked than in the designs by White or McKim. The design is entirely the creation

Figure 25. Palazzo Pesaro, Venice. Baldassare Longhena, 1676.

Figure 26. Palazzo Grimani, Venice. Michele Sanmicheli, 1556.

of William Mitchel Kendall, who had assumed McKim's position in the firm. Kendall rendered in cut stone the garden casino of the Villa Farnese at Caprarola, presumably designed by Vignola about 1550 (Fig. 28). The solid outer portions of the casino were expanded to create three nearly equal divisions of the facade, similar to the Morgan Library, and the windows of the casino became niches. The Farnese casino was of brick covered with stucco, but since the art gallery was to be of stone, the details could be made much crisper. And where the casino had a small constricted staircase leading up to the central arch, the art gallery was given a broad flight of stairs with the entire width of the arcade opened up. It is interesting to note that this McKim, Mead and White building later served, in turn, as the inspiration for the William L. Clements Library in Ann Arbor, Michigan, designed by Albert Kahn in 1923.[72]

Even this short discussion of buildings based on clearly recognizable Italian models indicates the scope of the changes made by the architects when adapting such prototypes to their own ends. Similar observations can be made of the more original designs based on Renaissance

Figure 27. Palazzo Bartolini-Salembeni, Florence. Baccio d'Agnolo, 1517-20.

sources: the Henry Villard houses, the Boston Public Library, the Century Club and the Morgan Library. One can also note the characteristic use of generally Italianate sources for such buildings as the Metropolitan and University Clubs, the Second National Bank in New York, and the Racquet and Tennis Club, all illustrated in the Monograph. If one compares the Madison Square Garden tower to the Giralda of Seville, Spain, or the doors of St. Bartholomew's Church, New York, to the entrance of St.-Gilles-du-Gard, France, several basic changes can be found paralleling those in the more derivative designs. In sum, these changes involve the following: The horizontal lines are strongly emphasized, multiplied or otherwise stressed, binding the whole design together, as in the New York State Building. The model is regularized, complex rhythms are simplified and variations made uniform, so that the design as a whole is more easily comprehended and given greater apparent unity, as in the Herald Building. The number of elements or components found in the model is reduced, simplifying the composition. Details become harder, sharper, crisper, and the entire building becomes

Figure 28. Garden Casino, Villa Farnese, Caprarola. Vignola, c.1552.

tauter. The building's relationship to the ground is
strengthened by the use of broad podiums, terraces, fans
of stairs and similar devices. An additional word should
perhaps be said concerning ornament: one finds it most
often confined to distinct areas where it approaches the
point of saturation, setting up a sharp contrast between
the blank wall surfaces and the enlivened zones of ornamentation. This balance of rich ornamented areas with
broad plain areas is especially indicative of the work of
White.[73]

The underlying themes of strong horizontality, clear
statement of component parts, tautness and strong relationship to the ground we can observe in McKim, Mead
and White are also characteristics of the architecture of
Frank Lloyd Wright. Moreover, they are qualities that
have been identified as uniquely American in feeling,
marking our architecture from the first translations of
English Georgian architecture on this side of the Atlantic. The same changes toward simplification and tautness that appear in McKim, Mead and White's work also
appear in the work of our first architects, such as

Richard Munday, Peter Harrison and later Charles
Bulfinch.[74] These characteristic changes in the Georgian
buildings make them distinctly American and reveal a
unique and identifiable national spirit. The same
is true of the Renaissance buildings of McKim, Mead
and White. Curiously Europeans usually perceive this
much more readily than we. Le Corbusier, for example,
marveled at the vitality of America and her skyscrapers,
and although he warned against the deadening effect of
servile attachment to the past, he confessed that "in
New York . . . I learn to appreciate the Italian Renaissance. It is so well done that you could believe it to be
genuine. It even has a strange, new firmness which is not
Italian but American."[75]

The architecture of McKim, Mead and White is strongly
expressive of the attitudes and values of its own time
and place; it is an architecture, moreover, that displays
an acute awareness of the nature and the potential of

urban life. The Boston Public Library and the Herald Building in particular illustrate a sensitivity to the urban condition; both were located in crowded centers of daily activity and both not only proved successful in meeting the challenge of their sites but did so in a uniquely individual manner. Most important of all, both buildings enhanced the quality of life around them and made their cities more rewarding places in which to live (Fig. 29).

It is important to remember that McKim, his partners and his fellow architects were quick to respond to the external civic responsibilities of a building, viewing this aspect as equal to the internal functional requirements. For instance, in the initial design of the Boston Public Library shown to the trustees, McKim had used a single square-headed door set close to the surface of the wall. When one of the trustees observed that the door seemed more to keep people out than to invite them in, McKim immediately designed a more generous entrance. In sub-sequent studies the design incorporated a triple-arched opening, echoing the arcade above and leading to an entrance loggia with groups of sculpture in front of the door, an invitation for people in turn to fill the space before the library. The entrance was even further developed by large lamp clusters cantilevered over the arches, creating an open canopy over the doors. One was now welcomed, urged to enter the library and enjoy the treasures within (Plate 100).

In the discussion of the Herald Building it was noted that White enlarged the Veronese town hall to fill a trapezoidal lot, and to join the energy and vivacity of the Consiglio with the electric and tumultuous life of New York's most crowded thoroughfare (Fig. 30). This was, of course, the very problem, for the new Herald Building was set in the midst of a clamorous theater district; any building intended to survive in this environment had to be as brazen and colorful as the surroundings themselves. In meeting Broadway on its own terms the Herald Building succeeded by becoming a theatrical spectacle itself. The long arcades on the Broadway and Sixth Avenue sides were opened up, creating long shaded loggias offering escape from the crush of the street. But once inside the long gallery along Broadway, the pedestrian could look down through large plate glass windows of the inner arcade onto the Herald's press room and watch the thunderous machines weaving their ribbon of pulp, the news of the world taking palpable form before his eyes.

McKim, Mead and White always endeavored to enrich and improve the urban environment, but at the same time they were sensitive to established patterns and traditions of the place in which they built. Two houses built by the firm in Boston show how they responded to the traditional bowed front characteristic of Beacon Hill since the early nineteenth century. In their house for John F. Andrews, begun in 1883 (Plate 17), McKim, Mead and White recalled the Georgian brick and dou-ble-bowed facade of the Women's Club of 1818 by Alexander Parris. And in the George A. Nickerson house

begun in 1895 (Plate 97), the firm echoed the austere granite facade and single bay of Parris's equally reserved Sears house of 1816. Both houses are related in their details and materials to the Italian classicism of the Vil-lard houses, and yet in their configuration they belong very much to Boston and they contribute to the special sense of place that has always been such an integral part of that city's appeal. Similarly McKim had referred to the eighteenth century heritage of Newport when he built the H. A. C. Taylor house there, for in the library he installed a reproduction of a local eighteenth century room.[76] When McKim was later given the commission for the Johnston Memorial gate at Harvard (Plates 19-19A), he took pains to find clinker bricks that dupli-cated the texture and color of those used in buildings on either side of the gate, Massachusetts Hall, 1718, and Harvard Hall, 1764. McKim continued to use this brick for the other gates around Harvard Yard that he was subsequently asked to design (Plates 152-154). In the discussion of the Bank of Montreal it was noted that McKim rebuilt the original dome in more permanent materials. When White replaced the destroyed wooden dome of the rotunda of the University of Virginia with a fireproof dome of Guastavino tile, and removed certain accretions to Jefferson's original design, he actually re-stored Jefferson's Rotunda to its original external appearance, thus re-emphasizing even more its resem-blance to its prototype, the Pantheon of Hadrian in Rome.

McKim, Mead and White based their design for the new Congregational Church in Naugatuck, Connecticut, closely on the previous church, whose attenuated white steeple had been a landmark of the town for half a century and meant much to the members of the congre-gation.[77] The new Naugatuck church is a typical eight-eenth century New England meetinghouse, incorpo-rating features of specific buildings, such as the Park Street church in Boston. In the elements of the spire McKim, Mead and White went back to the ultimate source of these meetinghouses, to James Gibbs's Saint-Martin's-in-the-Fields, London, but, characteristically, they telescoped the stages of the spire and varied their arrangement. In scores of such instances, McKim, Mead and White sought to reinforce a special sense of place in American towns and cities.

From what was in essence a restricted stylistic vocab-ulary, McKim, Mead and White were able to select modes appropriate to the nature of many widely dif-ferent buildings, always choosing a style that would make clear the use of the buildings. The more plastic, ebullient and visually complex motifs that recalled northern Italy and Spain were used for places of in-formal, lighthearted activity, such as Madison Square Garden (Plates 30-37). White was nearly always in charge of designs of this nature. More sober and austere expressions based on the High Renaissance and ancient Rome were for places of a more restrained, formal and conservative character where the gravity of the occasion called for a more controlled environment, such as the

48

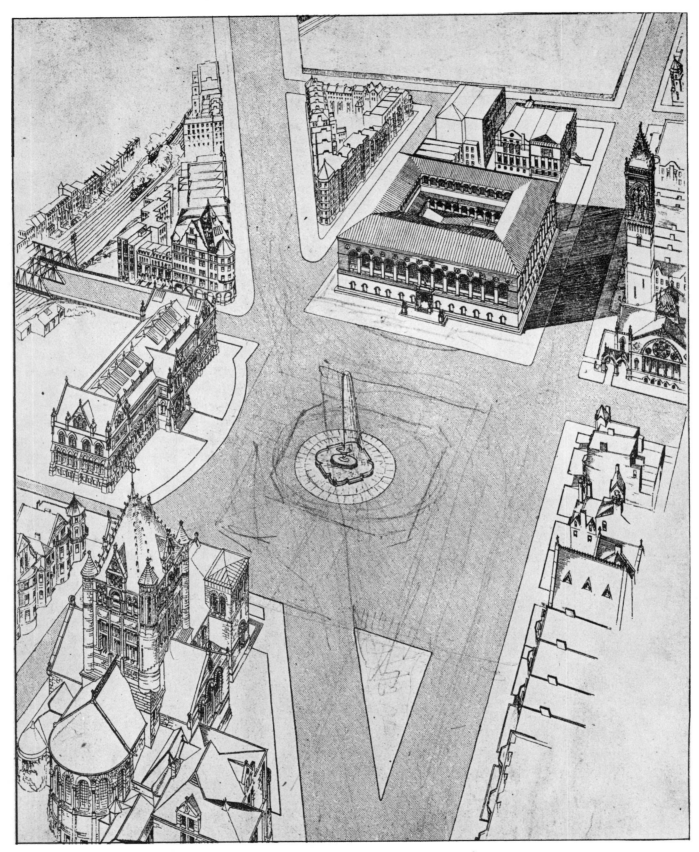

Figure 29. Boston Public Library, Boston, 1887-98. Aerial perspective of
Copley Square. The heterogeneous architectural environment of Copley
Square shows well in this drawing, a record of the degree to which McKim
wished to integrate his design into the square. The sketches over the fountain
at the center are by one of the members of the firm and show some study of
the completion of the square. From the MM&W Archives, New-York Historical Society, New York.

Figure 30. New York Herald Building, New York, 1892-95. This contemporary view illustrates the pulsating atmosphere in which the Herald Building maintained its own strong identity. Courtesy New-York Historical Society, New York.

Rhode Island State Capitol (Fig. 31 and Plates 183-190). These are usually McKim's designs. For buildings of domestic or educational use, the Georgian mode was reserved. The dark red brick with white wooden or limestone trim had come to connote erudition because of its use in the eighteenth century buildings of Harvard and Yale. Hence, McKim used nearly identical styles for his Harvard gates, the Harvard Union and the New York Harvard Club and its later additions, creating a family of related buildings. It was, obviously, to the classic modes that the firm returned again and again. In 1883 the small church of St. Paul's, Stockbridge, Massachusetts, was designed as a Norman chapel, with the porch inspired by a staircase at Canterbury (Plate 4). In 1886 the church of St. Peter's, Morristown, New Jersey (Plate 23), was designed as an Early English Gothic parish church like that of St. Cuthbert's in Wells, England. Both churches, it may be noted, are Episcopalian, and the styles selected were ecclesiastically correct. The later churches of the firm were designed along Italian Renaissance lines or, as in the case of the Madison Square Presbyterian Church begun in 1903, Italian Rennaissance tempered with Byzantine elements (Plates 251-257).

By what process of thought a particular stylistic decision was reached in the daily activity of the firm has never been determined. McKim did write that the most exemplary buildings were the Theater of Marcellus, Hadrian's Villa, the Baths of Diocletian and the works of Bramante, Peruzzi, San Gallo and Vignola. He also recommended the study of the landscape architecture of the Villas around Rome. His classical preferences were clear. But why the firm adopted a particular style was never set forth: they issued no tracts or manifestoes. Yet, even though the three architects wrote and spoke little on details of architectural theory, such stylistic preferences were so fully understood and shared by the young men who succeeded in the office that the specific point at which the stylistic manner of the original office ceases and the successor firm begins is difficult to locate precisely. As the attributions given in the plate captions prepared by the author for the present edition of the Monograph indicate, between 1895 and 1905 the junior members of the firm were given more and more responsibility; a number of these commissions must be regarded as largely the work of the younger men, especially in the details of buildings.

William Rutherford Mead outlived both his partners, but after McKim's death in 1909 he acted almost solely as adviser and consultant to the younger members of the firm. He was made president of the American Academy in Rome and spent most of his remaining years in Europe. The successor firm was made up of five men: William Mitchel Kendall, Burt Leslie Fenner, William Symmes Richardson, Lawrence Grant White, and Teunis J. Van der Bent. To do justice to these men and to view

the Monograph equitably, it is necessary to discuss briefly these successors in the firm: they were responsible for the Monograph's publication, and they designed almost a quarter of the buildings displayed in it.

William Mitchel Kendall (1865-1951) was graduated from Harvard in 1876, studied architecture two years at the Massachusetts Institute of Technology and finished his training with a year and a half of independent study in France and Italy. He came into the office in October 1882 and soon became closely associated with McKim. When McKim was later obliged to spend much of his time out of the office because of his work on the Chicago World's Fair and the replanning of Washington, D.C., his office work was placed in Kendall's hands.

Burt Leslie Fenner (1869-1926) was a student at the University of Rochester and MIT from 1887 to 1891. Perhaps because Fenner's father had been a classmate of Mead's at Amherst, Fenner was given a place in the office as Mead's associate immediately after his graduation from MIT.

William Symmes Richardson (1873-1931) was born in Massachusetts but soon moved with his family to California, where he entered the University of California in 1890, leaving after two years to continue his architectural studies at MIT. In 1894 he traveled in Europe while studying for a short time at the Ecole des Beaux-Arts in Paris; on his return to the United States in 1895 he was admitted to the office. Although he often worked with McKim, he was chiefly White's assistant.

On January 1, 1906, Kendall, Fenner and Richardson were made full partners in the firm; this was only six months before Stanford White was assassinated on the roof garden of his own Madison Square Garden and McKim began to fail rapidly in health.

Lawrence Grant White (1888-1956), the only son of Stanford White, was graduated from Harvard in 1907 and entered the Ecole des Beaux-Arts the following year. He entered the office in 1914, becoming a partner in 1919. The fifth member, Teunis J. Van der Bent (1863-1936) was a native of the Netherlands and a graduate of the University of Delft, 1885. He joined the office in 1887 and was made a partner in 1909, specializing in engineering and construction planning.[78]

All the buildings in the fourth volume except one—Pennsylvania Station—were conceived and carried out by these younger men. Neither McKim nor White had any connection with these buildings, and whatever contribution Mead may have made was very slight since he had virtually withdrawn from office affairs. Some of these later works, such as the Municipal Building, the apartment house at 998 Fifth Avenue and the Racquet and Tennis Club, are often and erroneously discussed as the work of McKim. (The attribution of the Municipal Building is particularly ironic: McKim wanted little to do with the design of skyscrapers and felt them impossible to make beautiful.) Careful examination will reveal that these later designs are simpler in conception and have sparce ornamentation. The sudden absence of

White's exuberant detail and ornament is very apparent, and it is possible to follow in the later plates the gradual relaxation of McKim's organizational logic. Fortunately, however, in 1920 Kendall compiled a list of attributions for the late work of the firm which makes clear the division of responsibility among the successors. The information contained in this list is found in the notes to the plates.

The work of McKim, Mead and White has been lauded and condemned in equal measure. During the lifetime of McKim and White it was broadly attacked by Russell Sturgis and at times supported by Montgomery Schuyler. This roughly even-handed justice gave way to a less-sympathetic critique. During the period from 1920 to 1960, when an alternative architectural philosophy of pragmatic utility was advanced by Bauhaus enthusiasts, the architecture of McKim, Mead and White went into eclipse. The criticism was, in part, valid: the generations of academic architects who followed McKim, Mead and White had learned the forms better than the principles of the classical heritage and initiated a period of slow ossification. Thus the widespread influence of the firm was slowly forgotten and even erased altogether as, one by one, columnar facades came down to make way for conveniently packaged glass boxes.

In recent years a new appreciation of the architecture of McKim, Mead and White has begun to appear. This reexamination has appeared in the studies of such art historians and architectural critics as Vincent Scully, Henry-Russell Hitchcock, Carroll L. V. Meeks and Ada Louise Huxtable.[79] Recently George Heard Hamilton, writing about buildings such as those by McKim, Mead and White, stated that they "were sensitively designed and have become valued civic monuments, providing continuity as well as dignity in our changing urban environments. Such would have been true of Pennsylvania Station . . . ."[80]

Figure 31. Rhode Island State Capitol, Providence, R.I., 1891-1904.

The reexamination that began with the shingled country houses now has extended to many classical urban buildings as well. This renewed sensitivity has sparked the battle for the preservation of what remains of the firm's work. Recently the Villard houses, for example, were saved from destruction and their future made somewhat more secure. Perhaps it was necessary to lose Penn Station to shake us out of our lethargy, to make us realize just how much we have to lose if we continue to procrastinate.

As our urban centers have atrophied, we have come to realize that it was the variety of the center city that made it live, that classic facades of stone and marble were an important visual part of this variety. These buildings are to some a threat because they represent an alternate mode of perception and a different set of priorities; now we see that they added incalculable value to our cities. As the English architectural critic Theo Crosby recently wrote, "this multitude of experiences intricately and subconsciously overlaid is the very stuff of cities, and the product of a rich mix of uses and associations . . . . It is the rewarding end product of complexity (and it has also a very real cash value)."[81] Crosby suggests that our older classical buildings should be allowed to play an ameliorative role in our cities; that we change our image of these buildings as white elephants to cultural and architectural gadflies.

We once had little use for such buildings, lacking the ability to evaluate ornament, embellishment, the large and serene vision of classic order; now we are beginning to see the value in these same qualities. Perhaps we have come to sense the underlying truth in Hannah Arendt's observation that when utility is taken as the basic meaning of human interaction, the result approaches meaninglessness.[82]

McKim, Mead and White built unashamedly in a monumental manner. They and their clients believed it proper to build in this way, knowing well that one has to pay for the public life, for to build truly monumentally one must be committed to it. Lewis Mumford summed up this attitude when he wrote that "most ages, to make the monument possible have (in Ruskin's terms) lighted the lamp of sacrifice, giving to the temple or the buildings of state, not their surplus, but their very lifeblood, that which should have gone into the bare decencies of life for the common man." Mumford recognizes that "an age that has deflated its values and lost sight of its purposes will not, accordingly, produce convincing monuments."[83] The work of McKim, Mead and White exposes the emptiness of much recent urban renewal and tells us that we are not really committed to building according to patterns of human interaction or for the spiritual as well as physical comfort of men. If commitment is taken as the criterion, our most telling monument may well be footprints on the moon.

McKim, Mead and White made their buildings monuments in the sense that Mumford used the term—"buildings of permanent value, enriching the eye, sustaining the spirit"—for to them this was what all architecture should be. It is therefore impossible to evaluate such architecture by a cash-nexus alone; they do not yield their promise to this kind of thinking nor do they fit with our current esthetic of disposability. The preservation and care of such monumental architecture finds justification not through arguments of present necessity, popular demand or pure utility but through the belief that they offer alternative suggestions to our concept of building and living in cities—the belief that part of the mandate given to architects is that our urban environment should be made visually and spiritually rewarding.

THE ORIGINAL EDITION

In 1914 the Architectural Book Publishing Company approached the firm of McKim, Mead and White and inquired about the possibility of publishing a monograph of the work of the firm. Because the Monograph was to be an educational and reference volume for practicing architects, the buildings selected were naturally those that the firm felt most representative and most germain to current problems. As a result, much of the very early picturesque shingled work was omitted in favor of the later urban work. For the same reasons a large number of drawings of detail were specially prepared, since it was felt that this was information of value to the student.

Not only drawings but most of the photographs were actually made specifically for the Monograph. Naturally, many of the photographs do not show the buildings in their original, often low-scaled, surroundings. Even as the last volume was in preparation, the Madison Square Presbyterian Church was lost, its small size having made

it a financial anomaly in a new New York. The Herald Building soon followed.

In 1915 installments of the Monograph began to appear in lots of twenty plates each. These plates were not issued in numerical order, and because of the substitutions of plates a discontinuous numbering of the plates resulted. By 1917 three of the four planned volumes of one hundred plates each had been published, but the mounting war effort impeded progress; most of the office draftsmen had been conscripted to work on defense drawings, and quotas on paper had affected the quality of the printing. The last section of twenty plates was eventually published in 1920.

Five years after the last number of the Monograph appeared, an abridged Students Edition was published. This consisted of two volumes, 136 plates in all, of drawings selected from the original edition. No photographs were reproduced, possibly in an effort to keep down the cost.

NOTES

1. Among the many books on the growth of American cities during the period, two good studies are Arthur M. Schlesinger, *The Rise of the City*, New York, 1933; and Charles N. Glaab and A. Theodore Brown, *A History of Urban America*, New York, 1967, which has a good bibliography. The statistics of American urban growth may be found in Adna Ferrin Weber, *The Growth of Cities in the Nineteenth Century*, New York, 1899. (Paperback, 1967)

2. For a comprehensive discussion of the Second Empire and High Victorian modes in the United States, see Henry-Russell Hitchcock, *Architecture, Nineteenth and Twentieth Centuries*, 3rd ed., Baltimore, 1968, specifically pp. 152-253. Bibliography. (Paperback, 1971)

3. Riis's photographs were published in the 1901 edition of *How the Other Half Lives*. A new edition containing 100 photographs was issued 1970.

4. Paraphrase of Vitruvius by Sir Henry Wotton in *The Elements of Architecture*, London, 1624. Referring to book 1, chapter 3 of Vitruvius, *On Architecture,* Wotton writes, "Well building hath three Conditions. Commoditie, Firmenes and Delight." An enthusiast of architecture, Wotton helped in the popularization of the English Renaissance of Inigo Jones.

5. Robert S. Peabody, "Georgian Homes of New England," *American Architect*, vol. 2 (1877), pp. 338-39. Quoted by Vincent Scully, *Shingle Style*, New Haven, 1955, p. 45.

6. The architectural publication of the middle of the nineteenth century is discussed in Henry-Russell Hitchcock, *Architecture of H. H. Richardson and His Times*, New York, 1936 (MIT paper, 1966, with bibliography), passim.

7. For Jefferson's ideas on the use of classic models see his description of architecture in Virginia in Notes on Virginia, 1779, and letter to James Madison, Paris, September 20, 1785, reprinted in A. Koch and W. Peden, ed., *The Life and Selected Writings of Thomas Jefferson*, New York, 1944, pp. 271, 381.

8. The design of the Boston Public Library was published in *American Architect*, vol. 23 (May 26, 1888), p. 246, pl. 650. Through such publication the Boston Public Library became the model for a design for a post office by Bailey and Truscott, published in *American Architect*, vol. 61 (July 16, 1898), pl. 1177.

9. Charles Herbert Reilly, *McKim, Mead and White*, London, 1924 (reprinted 1972), pp. 7, 24. This is the only discussion to date of the work of the firm considered *in toto*. Reilly (1874-1948) was an English architect who later became head of the School of Architecture of the University of Liverpool. In 1909 he wrote an extremely complimentary article on American architecture, which he had just had the opportunity to see: "The Modern Renaissance in American Architecture," *Royal Institute of British Architects-Journal*, vol. 17 (1909-10), pp. 630-35. Shortly afterward Reilly corresponded with the McKim, Mead and White office to obtain photographs and drawings to be used as references and examples for his architectural students at the University of Liverpool, according to letters in the McKim, Mead and White Archives, New-York Historical Society, New York (hereafter cited as NYHS).

10. To this date the fullest biographies of the two principals of the firm are Charles Moore, *The Life and Times of Charles Follen McKim*, Boston, 1929, and Charles C. Baldwin, *Stanford White*, New York, 1931. Both have very informative appendices.

11. P. M. Letarouilly (1795-1855) was the author of *Edifices de Rome moderne,* 3 volumes, 1840-57, whose plates showing Italian Renaissance buildings served as a bible for young academic architects in Europe and in the United States.

12. Lawrence Grant White, *Sketches and Designs by Stanford White*, New York, 1920, contains valuable biographical information and a wealth of illustrations showing White's versatility. A very intimate view of the office and the principals is given by H. Van Buren Magonigle, "A Half Century of Architecture," *Pencil Points*, vol. 13, pp. 115-18, 223-26.

13. Moore, . . . *McKim*, p. 40. Mead's first employer was probably the equivalent of today's civil engineer.

14. Russell Sturgis (1836-1909), a relatively successful architect in New York, began reducing his practice during the 1880s in order to concentrate on writing. He then became better known as an architectural critic and writer. The majority of his articles appeared in the *Architectural Record*. See Peter Bonnet Wight, "Reminiscences of Russell Sturgis," *Architectural Record*, vol. 26 (August 1909), pp. 122-31.

15. See Moore, . . . *McKim*, pp. 40-42, and *Dictionary of American Biography*, vol. 12, p. 473.

16. See *D.A.B.*, vol. 12, pp. 103-04.

17. See Alfred Hoyt Granger, *Charles Follen McKim*, Boston, 1913, pp. 28-29 for this observation.

18. The first American to study architecture at the Ecole was Richard Morris Hunt, who attended the school from 1846 to 1853. See James Philip Noffsinger, *The Influence of the Ecole des Beaux-Arts on the Architects of the United States*, Washington, D.C., 1955.

19. Hitchcock, *Richardson . . .* , MIT Press, p. 116.

20. For material on McKim see Moore, . . . *McKim*, pp. 3-42 and *D.A.B.*, vol. 12, pp. 99-102.

21. From a letter dated April 9, 1885, from F. L.

Olmsted to Stanford White on the occasion of his father's death. In the Manuscript Division, NYHS. It is evident that both McKim and White knew Olmsted from their youth and that this early acquaintance bred a love and respect for the natural world. In *Stanford White* (p. 5), Baldwin relates the incident in which White came upon a farmer on Long Island about to cut down a number of fine oaks for firewood. White protested, and finally the farmer agreed that $50.00 each would be a generous price for the trees as wood. White paid him the money on condition that the trees be allowed to stand.

22. Published in the *New York Sketch Book of Architecture*, vol. 2, no. 6 (December 1874).

23. The Peabody article referred to in note 5 above is one of a number of similar articles and is a particularly good example.

24. For a discussion of four of these ensembles see pp. 21-22. Information regarding the collaboration of these artists can be found in Augustus Saint-Gaudens, *The Reminiscences of Augustus Saint-Gaudens*, 2 vols., New York, 1913; Baldwin, *Stanford White*; Moore, . . . *McKim*; and Louise Hall Tharp, *Saint-Gaudens and the Gilded Era*, Boston, 1969, passim.

25. See the renderings of the Cheney residence, *American Architect*, vol. 3, no. 126 (May 25, 1878), and of the Sherman residence, *New York Sketch Book of Architecture*, vol. 2, no. 5 (May 1875).

26. The order of White's priorities is given by Philip Sawyer, "Stanford White as those trained in his office knew him," *Brickbuilder*, vol. 15 (December 1906), p. 247.

27. The now destroyed Cyrus McCormick house is illustrated and discussed by Scully, *Shingle Style*, pp. 136-37, fig. 122. Scully analyzes the domestic work of the firm with great insight, sympathy and poetry.

28. Some architects today believe that the shingled houses have as much to teach as the formal urban buildings. The accommodation of the exterior to the varied and contrasting internal uses is an example of the complexity of which the architect Robert Venturi writes in *Complexity and Contradiction in Architecture*, New York, 1966, p. 75.

29. See Scully, *Shingle Style*, pp. 131-33, fig. 111-115.

30. See Scully, *Shingle Style*, p. 134. Scully writes that the Narragansett Pier Casino was begun as early as 1881. The records of the firm at the NYHS do not support this date. The bill books, containing daily records of all bills sent out by the office for services rendered, are complete from 1878 beyond 1920, and according to them work on the Narragansett Pier Casino was begun in October 1883, when the recording of travel expenses started.

31. The bill books of the firm record the following information: Travel expenses for the H. A. C. Taylor commission began July 1882. Preliminary studies for a stone house to cost $67,300 were completed by December 1883, but during the spring and summer of 1884 the design was changed to that of a frame house costing $46,800 with a stable costing $11,000. Construction began in February 1885 and was substantially complete by January 1886. The cost including interior finishing was $65,782.50. The change from masonry to frame construction may help account for the somewhat severe appearance of the H. A. C. Taylor house.

32. *Townhouse* is used here in the sense of an urban dwelling on a long narrow contiguous lot, often with common party walls, and with a small yard at the rear. Usually, as in New York, the main floor is raised one-half story above sidewalk level and is entered by means of a high stoop, while a service entrance to the kitchen and pantries is one-half story below sidewalk grade.

33. See Hitchcock, *Richardson . . .*, MIT Press, pp. 218-22, pl. 69.

34. As president of the Northern Pacific Railroad from 1881 to 1884 Villard commissioned McKim, Mead and White to design several stations and other structures connected with the railway.

35. For the details of the design development of the Villard houses see Moore, . . . *McKim*, pp. 47-49. For Wells's drawings for the Martin Brimmer residence by Richard Morris Hunt, see *American Architect*, vol. 2, no. 57 (January 27, 1877). Wells's letters to White from Europe are reprinted in Baldwin, *Stanford White*, pp. 364-67; the manuscript originals are in the Manuscript Division, NYHS. For further information on Wells see Moore, . . . *McKim*, pp. 42, 48-49; Baldwin, *Stanford White*, pp. 357-68, portrait; C. Howard Walker, "Joseph Wells, Architect, 1853-1890," *Architectural Record*, vol. 66 (July 1929), pp. 15-18, portrait.

36. Walter Muir Whitehill, *Boston Public Library, A Centennial History*, Cambridge, Mass., 1956, pp. 141-42. For the story of the library design and the creation of its embellishments see Moore, . . . *McKim*, pp. 62-94.

37. William T. Partridge relates that one evening while McKim was looking at a photograph of the Colosseum, he was suddenly impressed by the strength of its arcade and decided to emulate its severity (Partridge manuscript material, Avery Library, Columbia University, New York). That the final library design also resembles Labrouste's Bibliotheque Sainte-Genevieve, Paris, is not mere coincidence. Undoubtedly McKim was influenced unconsciously by the Labrouste design since the Bibliotheque was a well-established and frequently imitated paradigm among Ecole students during the years McKim was there. I owe this information to Neal Levine.

38. This very interesting observation is made by Hitchcock, *Architecture . . .*, 3rd ed., pp. 229-30.

39. Archives of the Boston Public Library, Boston, Massachusetts.

40. For details concerning the Morgan Library see Moore, . . . *McKim*, pp. 278-83.

41. Particularly Royal Cortissoz. See his "Some Critical Reflections on the Architectural Genius of Charles F. McKim," *Brickbuilder*, vol. 19 (February 1910), pp. 23-37. The Morgan Library is "the bed rock of pure architecture . . . the bones of the design, so to say, are faultlessly articulated . . . ."

42.   White's design sketch for the Chapin memorial is shown in Lawrence Grant White, *Sketches and Designs . . .*, pl. 28. See Tharp, *Saint-Gaudens . . .*, p.210.

43.   For Hartshorn, see *National Cyclopedia of American Biography*, vol. 36, p. 480. For the history of the development of Short Hills, see Cora L. Hartshorn, "A Little History of the Short Hills section of Millburn Township, N. J., developed by Stewart Hartshorn." Mimeograph dated July 31, 1946, in the Millburn Public Library. Published in the Millburn *Item*, July 8, 1954.

44.   The Short Hills Casino is discussed and illustrated in Scully, *Shingle Style*, p. 133, pl. 116.

45.   The seven clients were Dr. Cornelius Agnew, William L. Andrews, A. W. Benson, Alfred Hoyt, Alexander E. Orr, Henry Sanger, and Henry G. deForest. They also engaged F.L. Olmsted to advise on the grounds.

46.   Recently noted in Norval White and Elliot Willensky, ed., *A.I.A. Guide to New York City*, New York, 1967, p. 165, illus. Of particular interest is the booklet at the Avery Library, *The King Model Dwellings, situated on 138th and 139th Streets, Seventh and Eighth Avenues,* New York (1891?). This is an illustrated realtor's brochure advertising the new development.

47.   John Bogart, "The Industrial Village of Echota at Niagara," *The Cassier Magazine*, 1895, pp. 307-21, illus. See also Edward Dean Adams, *Niagara Power*, 2 vols., privately printed for the Niagara Falls Power Co., 1927. Especially vol. 1, pp. 328-30, illus.

48.   Villard himself gave this analysis of his thinking about the development of the Northern Pacific territory in *The Early History of Transportation in Oregon*, written in 1900, published by the University of Oregon, 1944. See also James B. Hedges, *Henry Villard and the Railways of the Northwest*, New Haven, 1930.

49.   For information on J. H. Whittemore and Naugatuck, see Constance McLaughlin Green, *History of Naugatuck, Connecticut,* Naugatuck, Conn., and New Haven, 1948. This material is condensed in one chapter of C. M. Green, *American Cities in the Growth of the Nation,* London, 1957 (Harper Colophon paperback, 1965). The series of buildings by the firm in Naugatuck was discussed by A. C. David, "An Architectural Oasis," *Architectural Record,* vol. 19 (February 1906), pp. 135-44, illus.
Whittemore commissioned a total of eleven buildings by McKim, Mead and White. Nine of these were built in Naugatuck: three houses, a public library, bank, grammar school, landscaping of the green, high school, and the Congregational Church. Two buildings were erected in nearby Waterbury, Conn., and both are illustrated in the *Monograph*: the Buckingham Building, 1903, plate 323; and the Waterbury Railroad Station, 1907, plate

311 (Whittemore was a director of the railroad).
It appears that Whittemore planned to build two additional buildings in Naugatuck, making the reorganization of the town center even more complete. Among the firm's records at the Avery Library, New York, are photographs of two designs for a new bank and a large classical town hall to replace the High Victorian Gothic building across from the green. Both designs are dated 1906.

50.   Concerning Whittemore's conservation and landscaping of the Middlebury region, see *Encyclopedia of Connecticut Biography*, Boston, 1917, vol. 1, p. 282.

51.   The date is from a letter from the office of President Seth Low of Columbia University to McKim, dated May 17, 1892 (Correspondence of C. F. McKim, Manuscript Division, Library of Congress, Washington, D.C.). Other dates used for Columbia are from the same correspondence. For additional information on the Columbia University design see Moore, . . . *McKim*, pp. 264-72.

52.   Views of the NYU complex are reproduced in Joshua L. Chamberlain, *New York University, Its History, Influence, Equipment and Characteristics*, Boston, 1901. Shown are the aerial perspective drawing of the comprehensive plan, Hall of Chemistry, Gould Dormitory. The aerial perspective was also published in *Architects and Builders Magazine*, vol. 3 (1901-02), p. 167.

53.   That is, until 1964 when Marcel Breuer's Julius Silver Residence Center compromised the library's focal position.

54.   For example, Hitchcock, in his *Architecture . . .*, 3rd ed., 1968, p. 445, note 7, writes, "The fact that McKim, Mead and White blocked the view at the bottom of Jefferson's layout with a new building in the twentieth [*sic*] century is curious evidence of the lack of understanding of the essential qualities of the architecture and planning of this period on the part of even the most sophisticated 'traditional' architects—men who professed the greatest admiration for the work of such predecessors as Jefferson and yet proceeded to destroy its essence whenever the opportunity arose."
Besides the fact that the building sites were selected by the faculty and Visitors, it should be borne in mind that Jefferson and McKim, Mead and White acted on the basis of two different architectural philosophies. Jefferson's was romantic and envisaged open composition while McKim, Mead and White adhered to a more Roman point of view which sought to create series of enclosed spaces.

55.   The Rotunda, closely modeled on the Pantheon, Rome, consisted of a tall cylindrical drum capped by a low saucer dome; a hexastyle Corinthian portico faced the Lawn. In the mid-nineteenth century a rectangular annex was added to the rear of the Rotunda, compromising the clarity of the drum and changing the plan of the building into the shape of a keyhole.

56.   Faculty Report to the Rector and Visitors, October 31, 1895. Typescript in the University of Virginia Archives, Alderman Library, University of Virginia, Charlottesville, Virginia.

57.   See John Burchard and Albert Bush-Brown, *The Architecture of America, A Social and Cultural History*, Boston, 1961, p. 264. This extremely comprehensive work documents well, if unsympathetically, the influence of the firm and especially McKim, during the years 1890-1910.

58.   For the First National Bank of Champaign, Illinois, see *Architectural Record*, vol. 38 (July 1915), pp. 184-85. For the Detroit Trust Company, see Ferry W. Hawkins, *The Buildings of Detroit*, Detroit, 1968, p. 226. This book is an excellent study of the topography of the city and how its various phases of development reflect the course of architecture in the country. The influence of the firm is well documented by Hawkins. It appears very probable that Albert Kahn was affected by the design of the Municipal Building, New York, in his General Motors Building of 1922.

59.   See Montgomery Schuyler, "A 'Modern Classic,'" *Architectural Record*, vol. 15 (May 1904), pp. 431-44, illus. Reprinted in a collection of Schuyler's essays, *American Architecture and Other Writings*, William H. Jordy and Ralph Coe, ed., Cambridge, Mass., 1961.

60.   The information concerning the planned upper floors is found in the office correspondence, MM&W Archives, NYHS.

61.   For a comprehensive history of the Bank of Montreal see Merrill Dennison, *Canada's First Bank*, 2 vols., New York, 1967. Especially vol. 1, pp. 285-88, 337-38.

62.   The Guastavino vault was a method of construction developed by Raphael Guastavino from Catalan methods such as those used by Antoni Gaudi. The Guastavino vault was made up of flat tiles laid in an extremely tenacious mortar. Several layers of these tiles with joints overlapped formed a shell which was structurally monolithic and performed very much in the manner of present thin concrete shells. McKim, Mead and White were the first architects to use this technique of fireproof construction extensively, beginning with the Boston Public Library in 1887. For Guastavino and his vaulting techniques see George Collins, "The Transfer of Thin Masonry Vaulting from Spain to America," *Society of Architectural Historians Journal*, vol. 3 (October 1968), pp. 176-201, illus.

63.   For the University Club see Moore, . . . *McKim*, pp. 255-63.

64.   See Adams, *Niagara Power*, vol. 1, pp. 65-75, illus.

65.   See *Interborough Rapid Transit: The New York Subway, Its Construction and Equipment*, New York, 1904, pp. 65-89. Reprinted 1971.

66.   See Moore, . . . *McKim*, pp. 273-77. Plans, elevations, and sections were published, *American Architect*, vol. 89 (May 26, 1906), pp. 175 and 180, pl. 1587. The history of the building and of the railroad is found in George H. Burgess and Miles C. Kennedy, *Centennial History of the Pennsylvania Railroad Company*, Philadelphia, 1949.

67.   Vincent Scully, *American Architecture and Urbanism*, New York, 1969, p. 143.

68.   Italian architecture of this period is discussed well by the late Caroll L. V. Meeks, *Italian Architecture: 1750-1914*. New Haven, 1966, especially pp. 337, 376-86, illus.

69.   For the history and design of the New York State Building see *Report of the Board of General Managers of the Exhibit of the State of New York at the World's Columbian Exposition*, Albany, 1894, pp. 92-103, illus.

70.   See Baldwin, *Stanford White*, pp. 218-220, especially the Birch Burdette Long rendering facing page 218. For James Gordon Bennett see Richard O'Connor, *The Scandalous Mr. Bennett*, Garden City, N.Y., 1962.

71.   See Don Carlos Seitz, *Joseph Pulitzer*, New York, 1924, pp. 13-14, 252-53.

72.   Kahn himself felt this to be the best of his buildings. See Ferry Hawkins, *Buildings of Detroit*, p. 215, illus.

73.   White's love of rich detail and surface pattern can be seen in his earliest drawings and sketches published by Lawrence Grant White in *Sketches and Designs* . . . . .

74.   Similar characteristic transformations are identified and discussed by Vincent Scully in *American Architecture and Urbanism*, New York, 1969.

75.   Le Corbusier, *Quand les cathedrals etaient blanches,* 1937. (*When the Cathedrals Were White*, New York, 1964, p. 60).

76.   Mentioned by George William Sheldon, *Artistic Country Seats*, 2 vols., New York, 1886-87. See vol. 1, p. 9.

77.   Frank Warren, "History of the Naugatuck Congregational Church," manuscript in the archives of the Congregational Church, Naugatuck, Connecticut.

78.   Briefly, the later history of the firm is: W. S. Richardson retired in 1921 following an accident. James Kellum Smith entered the office in 1924 and became a partner in 1929. The firm continued under the direction of L. G. White and J. K. Smith, retaining the original name until, with the deaths of L. G. White in 1956 and Smith in 1961, the firm came to an end.

79.   See Scully's *Shingle Style* and *American Architecture and Urbanism*. In Hitchcock's recent editions of . . . *Richardson*, pejorative passages concerning McKim, Mead and White have been toned down, and also in his *Architecture* . . . , 3rd ed., pp. 398-402. Before his death Carroll L. V. Meeks began to give eclectic American architecture the sympathetic critical study it had been so long denied. His convincing observations are put forward in three articles: "Picturesque Eclecticism," *Art Bulletin*, vol. 32 (September 1950), pp. 226-35; "Creative Eclecticism," *Society of Architectural Historians Journal*, vol. 11 (December 1953), pp. 15-18; "Wright's Eastern Seaboard Contemporaries: Creative Eclecticism

in the United States Around 1900," *Studies in Western Art*, The Acts of the Twentieth International Congress of the History of Art, vol. 4, Princeton, 1963. All three articles probe the extremely knotty questions of this period; in them Meeks proposes a stylistic rationale and discipline seldom before granted to such eclectic architecture.

80. George Heard Hamilton, *Nineteenth and Twentieth Century Art*, New York, 1970, p. 157.

81. Theo Crosby, *The Necessary Monument, Its Future in the Civilized City*, Greenwich, Conn., 1970. In this short but provocative book Crosby discusses how the Paris Opera has been preserved, how London's Tower Bridge could be made a focal point in the contemporary city, and how the unique and tremendous potential to do likewise with Penn Station can now never be realized.

82. Hannah Arendt, *The Human Condition*, Chicago, 1958, pp. 153-54.

83. This and subsequent references to Lewis Mumford refer to his "Monumentalism, Symbolism and Style," *Architectural Review*, vol. 105 (April 1949), pp. 173-80, a little-known article revealing a seldom observed side of Mumford.

BIBLIOGRAPHY

ARCHIVAL SOURCES

Archives, McKim, Mead and White Office, New-York Historical Society, New York.

Letter Collection, McKim Office Day Books, Manuscript Division, Library of Congress, Washington, D.C.

White Family Collection, Saint James, L. I., N. Y.

SELECTED SOURCES

ANDREWS, WAYNE Architecture, Ambition and Americans: A Social History of American Architecture. New York: 1964.

———"McKim, Mead and White: New York's Own Architects," New-York Historical Society Quarterly, XXXV (January 1951), 87-96.

BACON, HENRY "Charles Follen McKim—A Character Sketch," Brickbuilder, XIX (February 1910), 38-47.

BALDWIN, CHARLES C. Stanford White. New York: 1931. [Review: Architectural Forum, LV (December 1931), sup. 8]

BROWN, GLENN "Personal Reminiscences of Charles Follen McKim," Architectural Record, XXXVIII-XXXIX (November 1915-February 1916). Four articles entitled: McKim and The American Institute of Architects, McKim and the Park Commission, McKim and the White House, McKim's Way.

BURCHARD, JOHN, and BUSH-BROWN, ALBERT The Architecture of America: A Social and Cultural History. Boston: 1961.

CHAPMAN, JOHN JAY "McKim, Mead and White," Vanity Fair, XIII (September 1919), 37, 102, 104.

CORTISSOZ, ROYAL American Artists. New York: 1923.

———Art and Common Sense. New York: 1913.

———"Some Critical Reflections on the Architectural Genius of Charles F. McKim," Brickbuilder, XIX (February 1910), 23-37.

DAVID, A. C. "An Architectural Oasis," Architectural Record, XIX (February 1906), 135-44.

DAVIS, RICHARD HARDING "Stanford White," Collier's (August 4, 1906), 17.

DESMOND, HENRY W., and CROLY, HERBERT "The Work of Messrs. McKim, Mead & White," Architectural Record, XX (September 1906), 153-246.

DOWNING, ANTOINETTE F., and SCULLY, VINCENT J. The Architectural Heritage of Newport, Rhode Island. 2nd ed. New York: 1967.

GRANGER, ALFRED H. Charles Follen McKim: A Study of His Life and Work. Boston: 1913. [Review: "A Great Imaginative Interpreter of the Renaissance Traditions. Charles Follen McKim, A Study of His Life and Work," Architectural Record, XXV (May 1914), 463-65.]

HEWLETT, J. MONROE "Stanford White, As Those Trained in His Office Knew Him," Brickbuilder, XV (December 1906), 245-46.

HILL, FREDERICK PARSELL Charles F. McKim, the Man. Francestown, N. H.: 1950.

HITCHCOCK, HENRY-RUSSELL Architecture: Nineteenth and Twentieth Centuries. 3rd ed. Harmondsworth: 1968.

———The Architecture of H. H. Richardson and His Times. New York: 1936.

———"Frank Lloyd Wright and the Academic Tradition of the Early Eighteen-Nineties," Warburg and Courtauld Institute Journal, VII (1944), 46-63.

MAGONIGLE, H. VAN BUREN "A Half Century of Architecture," Pencil Points (March, May 1934), 115-18, 223-26.

MEEKS, CARROLL L. V. "Wright's Eastern Seaboard Contemporaries: Creative Eclecticism in the United States Around 1900," Acts of the Twentieth International Congress of the History of Art. 4 vols. Princeton: 1963. IV, 64-77.

MOORE, CHARLES Daniel H. Burnham, Architect, Planner of Cities. 2 vols. Boston: 1921.

———The Life and Times of Charles Follen McKim. Boston: 1929. [Reviews: American Magazine of Art, XXI (March 1930), 178; International Studio, XCV (April 1930), 70; Apollo, XII (July 1930), 60]

PEABODY, ROBERT S. "A Tribute," Brickbuilder, XIX (February 1910), 55-56.

RAMSEY, STANLEY C. "The Work of McKim, Mead and White," Royal Institute of British Architects—Journal, XXV, 3rd series (November 5, 1917), 25-29.

REILLY, CHARLES HERBERT McKim, Mead and White. London: 1924.   Reprinted 1973 by Benjamin Blom, Inc.

ROSS, ALBERT RANDOLPH "Stanford White As Those Trained in His Office Knew Him," Brickbuilder, XV (December 1906), 246.

SAINT-GAUDENS, AUGUSTUS The Reminiscences of Augustus Saint-Gaudens. 2 vols. New York: 1913.

SAINT-GAUDENS, HOMER "Intimate Letters of Stanford White, Correspondence with His Friend & Coworker Augustus Saint-Gaudens," Architectural Record, XXX (August-October 1911), 107-16, 283-98, 399-406.

SAWYER, PHILIP "Stanford White As Those Trained in His Office Knew Him," Brickbuilder, XV (December 1906), 247.

SCHUYLER, MONTGOMERY American Architecture and Other Writings. Edited by W. H. Jordy and R. Coe. 2 vols. Cambridge, Mass.: 1961.

———"Charles Follen McKim," Architectural Record, XXVI (November 1909), 381-82.

SCULLY, VINCENT American Architecture and Urbanism. New York: 1969.

———The Shingle Style. New Haven: 1955.

STURGIS, RUSSELL "McKim, Mead and White," Architectural Record, Great American Architects Series, I (May 1895).

SWALES, FRANCIS S. "Master Draftsmen, Part I. Stanford White," Pencil Points, V (April 1924), 59-64.

THARP, LOUISE HALL Saint-Gaudens and the Gilded Era. Boston: 1969.

WALKER, C. HOWARD "The Influence of McKim," Brickbuilder, XIX (February 1910), 48-53.

———"Joseph Wells, Architect, 1853-1890," Architectural Record, LXVI (July 1929), 14-18.

———"Stanford White—His Work," Brickbuilder, XV (December 1906), 243-44.

WHITE, LAWRENCE GRANT Sketches and Designs by Stanford White. New York: 1920.

WIGHT, PETER BONNETT "Reminiscences of Russell Sturgis," Architectural Record, XXVI (August 1909), 123-31.

NOTES ON THE PLATES

DATES

The dates used in this edition of the Monograph have been extracted from the bill books in the McKim, Mead and White Archives, New-York Historical Society, New York, which contain day-to-day copies of all bills rendered to clients. Where bills include travel and miscellaneous expenses prior to the date of construction, this has been assumed to indicate when serious design began. When construction began very early in the spring, the design is assumed to have been made during the previous autumn and winter, as in the case of the Newport Casino. The dates of actual construction are taken from the periodic bills for portions of work certified to be completed by the various contractors.

ATTRIBUTIONS

The partners in charge are attributed on the basis of information in the biographies of McKim and White by Moore and Baldwin listed in the Bibliography. Both writers obtained information from members of the families and from later firm members, such as Lawrence Grant White. An additional list of attributions by William Mitchell Kendall, prepared around 1920, provided much of the information incorporated here. The Kendall list is found in the MM&W archives, New-York Historical Society. It should be remembered, however, that all designs were a joint effort by all the partners, who freely received and offered suggestions and criticism. If it were not for the Kendall list, it would be nearly impossible to attribute the firm's designs on the basis of internal artistic evidence alone. Generally the attributions are meant to indicate who supervised the job rather than who had sole artistic control.

COST

The cost is given as a relative index. In virtually all cases the figures are those finally submitted by the contractors and used by the firm in computing their commissions—5% for the structure and 10% for interior finishing and detailing. Consequently, these figures do not include the cost of land or any subsequent furnishings installed by the owner. Where known, in a few cases, total costs are given.

1. Newport Casino, 194 Bellevue Avenue, Newport, R.I. Designed 1879 for James Gordon Bennett; constructed 1880-81; White in charge. Cost: *c.* $125,000. According to tradition, Bennett decided to build his own club when his membership in the Newport Reading Room was canceled, and hired White to draw up the design. Extant, now the National Lawn Tennis Hall of Fame. In 1953 fire destroyed the upper floors on the north side of the court. Partially restored.

2. Ross Winans Residence, 1217 St. Paul St., Baltimore, Md. Designed 1881; constructed 1882-83; White in charge. Attribution: Baldwin. Cost: $164,187. Design influence: Francois Ier in detail. Extant, now dentists' offices; minor interior changes, date uncertain.

3. Charles A. Whittier Residence, 270 Beacon St., Boston, Mass. Designed 1881; constructed 1882-83; McKim in charge. Attribution: Kendall. Cost: $153,180. Design influence: Francois Ier in detail. Demolished, date uncertain; replaced by an apartment house.

4. St. Paul's Church, Main and Church St., Stockbridge, Mass. Designed 1883; constructed 1884-85; McKim in charge. Attribution: Moore, Kendall. Cost: unrecorded—no fee charged. Built by Charles Butler in memory of his wife, Susan Ridley Sedgwick Butler. Design influence: Norman in inspiration; the porch from a staircase at Canterbury Cathedral. Extant; in excellent condition.

5-5a. Charles L. Tiffany Residence, 19 E. 72 St., New York, N.Y. Designed 1882; constructed 1883-85; White in charge. Attribution: Baldwin, Kendall. Cost: unrecorded, *c.* $100,000. Destroyed 1936. This was a triple house. The lower floors were for Charles L. Tiffany, the third floor for his daughter, and the floors within the roof for his son, Louis C. Tiffany. The younger Tiffany provided White with a sketch of the upper area showing it as he wished to have it built. See Robert Kock, *Louis C. Tiffany* (New York, 1964), pp. 62-63.

6. Narragansett Casino, Ocean Rd., Narragansett Pier, R.I. Designed 1883; constructed 1884-86; McKim in charge. Attribution: Kendall. Cost: $65,900, total. The wooden portions have been destroyed by successive fires and hurricanes. The stone arch, somewhat altered, still bridges Ocean Rd.

7-11. Henry Villard Residences, 451-457 Madison Ave., New York, N.Y. Designed 1882; constructed 1883-85; McKim, White, & Wells in charge. Attribution: Moore, Baldwin, & Kendall. Cost: $587,134 for Villard house alone; *c.* $750,000 total for all four houses. Design influence: details derived from the Cancelleria, Rome.

The original tenants were Edward Dean Adams, 455 Madison; Artemas H. Holmes, 453 Madison; and Harris C. Fahnestock, 457 Madison. The commission was given by Villard to McKim, but since McKim was then preoccupied with other commissions for Villard for the Northern Pacific Railroad, White took on the planning of the group of houses. After making the initial plans, White had to leave the office on other business, and Wells was given charge of completing the design and its detailing. See Moore, . . . *McKim,* pp. 47-48. Purchased by Whitelaw Reid from Villard in 1886. Extant, now the offices of the Archdiocese of New York (see Plate 358 arrd caption for alterations).

12-13, 14. Charles J. Osborn Residence, South Barry Ave., Mamaroneck, N.Y. Designed 1883; constructed 1884-85; White in charge. Attribution: Baldwin, Kendall. Cost: $181,310. Charles Osborn, the confidential broker of Jay Gould, built this country house on the shore of Long Island Sound. It is now the home of the Mamaroneck Beach, Cabana and Yacht Club. Burned May, 1971. Partial restoration is proposed.

14 [Top]. Commodore William Edgar Residence, 29 Old Beach Rd., Newport, R.I. Designed 1884; constructed 1885-86; McKim in charge. Attribution: Kendall. Cost: $42,870. The house is constructed of flat buff-colored Roman brick. Extant, residence.

15 [Left]. David Glasgow Farragut Monument, Madison Square, New York, N.Y. Designed 1879-80; constructed 1880-81; statue, Augustus Saint-Gaudens; base, White. Cost: unrecorded. Extant; Saint-Gaudens's bronze has a new base, a replica of the original now at the Saint-Gaudens Studio, Cornish, New Hampshire. Originally facing Fifth Ave., at 25th St., the ensemble was moved to the interior of the square during the 1930s. The design commemorates one of the most famous naval officers of the Civil War.

15 [Right]. Peter Cooper Monument, Cooper Square, 7th St. & Third Ave., New York, N.Y. Designed 1894; constructed 1897; figure by Augustus Saint-Gaudens; base by White. Cost: unrecorded. In memory of the founder of The Cooper Union, established as a philanthropic school of art and technology. Extant.

16. H. A. C. Taylor Residence, Annandale Rd., Newport, R.I. Designed for Henry Augustus Coit Taylor 1882-84 (see p. 54, note 31); constructed 1885-86; McKim in charge. Attribution: Kendall. Cost: $65,782.50. This design initiated the Adamesque colonial revival that continued through the Second World War and, in an abridged fashion, survives to the present. Demolished 1952.

17. **John F. Andrews Residence,** Commonwealth Ave. & Hereford St., Boston, Mass. Designed 1883; constructed 1885-88; McKim in charge. Attribution: Kendall. Cost: $135,362. Extant.

18 [Left]. **Russell and Erwin Building,** 35 West Main St., New Britain, Conn. Designed 1883-84 for H. E. Russell and C. B. Erwin; constructed 1884-85; Joseph Wells in charge. Attribution: Kendall et al. Cost: $105,533. This is the single example of a design carried out entirely by Joseph Morrill Wells, an associate in the office. The building was designed as a small hotel, with shops on the ground floor. Altered 1907-09 by the firm to house the New Britain City Hall. Extant.

18 [Right]. **Algonquin Club,** 217 Commonwealth Ave., Boston, Mass. Designed 1886; constructed 1887-89; McKim in charge. Attribution: Kendall, Moore. Cost: $197,121. Extant; minor interior modernization.

19-19A. **Johnston Gates,** Harvard University, Massachusetts Ave., Cambridge, Mass. Gift of Samuel Johnston (Class of 1885). Designed 1889; constructed 1890; McKim in charge. Attribution: Moore, Kendall. Cost: $9,972. McKim selected clinker brick, which was unfashionable at the time, to simulate the texture and color of adjacent Harvard and Massachusetts Halls (see caption for Plates 152-54). Extant.

20-21. **Entrances to Prospect Park,** Prospect Park, Brooklyn, N.Y. Designed 1889; constructed 1889-95, 1907-08; White in charge. Attribution: Kendall, Baldwin. Cost: approximately $331,853. During the years 1889-1907 McKim, Mead & White designed a number of entrances to Prospect Park being developed in Brooklyn. Besides major entrances at the Grand Army Plaza, Ocean Ave. and Parkside, Coney Island Ave. and Parkside, and at 9th St. and Prospect Park West, the firm designed other pieces of park furniture and ornament for the interior of the park. Extant.

22. **New York Life Insurance Building,** 20 West 9th St. Kansas City, Mo. Designed 1887; constructed 1888-90; Mead and White in charge. Attribution: Kendall. Cost: $1,134,875. Interior modernized in 1933 and during the 1960s. Built on an H-shaped plan. This is one of the very few tall buildings designed by the firm, especially noteworthy because of its early date. Extant.

23. **Saint Peter's Church,** Miller Rd. and South St., Morristown, N.J. Designed 1886; constructed 1887-90, 1890-92; McKim in charge. Attribution: Kendall. Cost: $125,949. Design influence: English parish churches, such as St. Cuthbert's, Wells. Extant.

24-26. **Germantown Cricket Club,** Manheim and Morris Sts., Philadelphia, Pa. Designed 1889; constructed 1890-91; McKim in charge. Attribution: Kendall. Cost: c. $78,500. Extant.

27-29. **Century Club,** 7 West 43rd St., New York, N.Y. Designed 1889; constructed 1890-91; McKim and White in charge. Attribution: Kendall, Baldwin. Cost: $212,908. Extant.

30-37. **Madison Square Garden,** 26th to 27th Sts., from Madison to Park Ave. South, New York, N.Y. Designed 1887; constructed 1889-91; White in charge. Attribution: Kendall, Baldwin. Cost: $1,170,604. Design influence: the tower was based on the Giralda (Seville, 1159-1568). A complex multipurpose building, Madison Square Garden combined two theatres, amphitheatre, restaurant, and all the necessary auxiliary facilities, including stables for 400 horses below the amphitheatre. Destroyed 1925. New York Life Insurance Building now occupies the site.

38. **Edwin D. Morgan Residence,** "Beacon Rock," Harrison Ave., Newport, R.I. Designed 1888; constructed 1889-91; McKim, White in charge. Attribution: Kendall, Baldwin. Cost: $228,338. Extant.

39-40. **Washington Arch,** Washington Square, New York, N.Y. Designed 1889; constructed 1891-92; White in charge. Attribution: Baldwin. Cost: c. $128,000. Originally White designed an arch in wood for the end of Fifth Ave. as a street ornament for the celebration of the centennial of Washington's inauguration in New York, April 30, 1789. The design proved so popular that a revised version in marble was erected within Washington Square through public subscription. Extant.

41-42. **Agricultural Building,** World's Columbian Exposition, Jackson Park, Chicago, Ill. Designed 1891; constructed 1892-93; McKim in charge. Attribution: Kendall, Moore. Cost: $699,317. This lath and plaster shell, surrounding a steel frame shed, was designed as one of a group of buildings organized around the expansive malls and the Court of Honor. Destroyed 1894, after the closing of the exposition.

43-44. **New York State Building,** World's Columbian Exposition, Jackson Park, Chicago, Ill. Designed 1892; constructed 1893; McKim in charge. Attribution: Kendall, Moore. Cost: $150,560. Design influence: Villa Medici, Rome. Destroyed 1894, after the closing of the exposition.

45-46. **Walker Art Gallery,** Bowdoin College, Brunswick, Maine. Designed for Mary S. and Harriet S. Walker 1891; constructed 1892-94; McKim in charge. Attribution: Kendall. Cost: $109,843. Built in memory of Theophilus Walker by his nieces. In the four tympana below the central dome are murals by the most well-known American mural painters of the time: Abbott Thayer ("Florence" 1893); Kenyon Cox ("Venice" 1893); Elihu Vedder ("Rome" 1893); and John La Farge ("Athens" 1893), the best of the group. This is probably the most representative cross-section of 19th century American mural painting.

47. Columbia University, West 116th St. & Broadway, New York, N.Y. Designed 1893-94; constructed 1895-1913 and later; McKim in charge. Attribution: Kendall, Moore. Cost: $5,000 for development of the master plan. Extant.

48-54. Low Library, Columbia University, West 116th St. and Broadway, New York, N.Y. Designed 1893-94; constructed 1895-98; McKim, Kendall in charge. Attribution: Kendall, Moore. Cost: $1,106,729. Named for Seth Low, Mayor of Brooklyn, New York, and President of Columbia University. Extant.

55-56. Judson Memorial Church, 55 Washington Square South, New York, N.Y. Designed for Berean Baptist Church of Christ, 1888; constructed 1890-93, addition at 54 Washington Square South 1895-96; White in charge. Attribution: Kendall, Baldwin. Cost: $240,578. Named in honor of Adiniram Judson, the first Baptist foreign missionary to Burma. Extant, deteriorating.

57-61. Metropolitan Club, 1 East 60th St. at Fifth Ave., New York, N.Y. Designed 1891; constructed 1892-94; White in charge. Attribution: Kendall, Baldwin. Cost: $1,062,800. Extant.

62-64A. New York Herald Building, Broadway and 35th St., New York, N.Y. Designed for James Gordon Bennett 1892; constructed 1892-95; White in charge. Attribution: Baldwin. Cost: $559,815. Design influence: Palazzo del Consiglio, Verona. Destroyed 1921; replaced by a skyscraper.

66-68. Bowery Savings Bank, Bowery and Grand St., New York, N.Y. Designed 1893; constructed 1893-95; White in charge. Attribution: Kendall, Baldwin. Cost: $519,664. Extant.

69-71. Elliott F. Shepard Residence, Scarborough, N.Y. Designed 1890-92; constructed 1892-95; Mead in charge. Attribution: Kendall. Cost: $808,764. Extant.

72. Garden City Hotel, 7th St. and Park Ave., Garden City, Long Island, N.Y. Designed 1894; constructed 1895-96, 1899-1901; White in charge. Attribution: Kendall, Baldwin. Cost: $122,473; $231,405 for rebuilding after fire. Design influence: Independence Hall, Philadelphia, Pa. (1731-52), for the tower at the center. Rebuilt after a fire, 1899-1901. The center tower was added at this time. Demolished 1973; to be replaced by a hotel-and-condominium complex.

73. Battle Monument, Thayer and Washington Rd., United States Military Academy, West Point, N.Y. Designed 1891; constructed 1896-97; White in charge. Attribution: Kendall, Baldwin. Cost: $56,752. Raised in memory of the troops and officers of the Regular Army killed in the Civil War. Extant.

74-77. Gould Library, New York University, University Ave. and W. 181st St., New York, N.Y. Designed 1892-95; constructed 1896-1903; White in charge. Attribution: Kendall, Baldwin. Cost: $692,368. Extant; the ground floor was damaged by fire in 1969 and is under restoration.

Hall of Languages, New York University. Designed 1892-94; constructed 1894-95. Cost: $68,628. Extant.

79. Robert W. Cumming Residence, 368 Mount Prospect Ave., Newark, N.J. Designed 1894; constructed 1895-96; McKim in charge. Attribution: Moore. Cost: $70,789.

80-82. H. A. C. Taylor Residence, 3 East 71st St., New York, N.Y. Designed for Henry Augustus Coit Taylor 1894; constructed 1894-96, 1907; McKim in charge. Attribution: Kendall. Cost: $275,733. Remodeled by the firm in 1907. Design influence: Palazzo Bartolini-Salembeni, Florence. Destroyed c. 1932.

83-84. Frederick W. Vanderbilt Residence, Hyde Park, N.Y. Designed 1895; constructed 1896-99; McKim, Mead in charge. Attribution: Kendall, Moore. Cost: $521,466. Extant, now the Vanderbilt Mansion National Historic Site, a public museum.

85-91. Brooklyn Institute of Arts and Sciences, Eastern Pky. and Washington Ave., Brooklyn, N.Y. Designed 1893; constructed 1895-1907, 1913-15, and later; McKim in charge. Attribution: Kendall. Cost: c. $1,800,000. The building, now called the Brooklyn Museum, was built in six stages; the entire structure, however, was never completed as planned by the firm. The sculptural figures on the facade are by Daniel Chester French et al. Extant. During the 1930s the lobby was moved to the ground floor and the grand staircase on the exterior removed.

93. New York Life Insurance Company, 346 Broadway, New York, N.Y. Remodeling of existing building. Designed 1896; constructed 1896-99; White in charge. Attribution: Kendall, Baldwin. Cost: $1,775,454 for remodeling the entire building. Extant; the Board of Directors' Room was removed to the present New York Life Insurance building in 1929.

94-95. Thomas Nelson Page Residence, 1759 R St., NW, Washington, D. C. Designed 1896; constructed 1896-97; White in charge. Attribution: Kendall, Baldwin. Cost: $72,890. Extant, now part of the French Legation in Washington, D.C.

96 [Right]. **Double House for Francis Amory and Richard Olney,** 413-415 Commonwealth Ave., Boston, Mass. Designed 1890; constructed 1890-92; McKim in charge. Attribution: Kendall. Cost, $97,381. Extant.

96, 97. George A. Nickerson Residence, 303 Commonwealth Ave., Boston, Mass. Designed 1895; constructed 1895-97; McKim in charge. Attribution: Kendall. Cost: $97,711. Extant.

98-99. Sherry's Hotel, 522 Fifth Ave., at 44th St., New York, N.Y. Designed for Louis Sherry 1896; constructed 1897-98; White in charge. Attribution: Kendall, Baldwin. Cost: $1,322,611. Destroyed c. 1930.

100-109. Boston Public Library, Copley Square, Boylston and Dartmouth Sts., Boston, Mass. Designed 1887; constructed 1888-1898; McKim in charge. Attribution: Kendall, Moore. Cost: $2,743,285, total. Design influence: Colosseum, Rome (70-80 A.D.); San Francesco, Rimini (Alberti, 1446). Extant. An addition by Philip Johnson is currently being built to the rear of the original building. The addition will almost double the space of the library, allowing the heavy daily traffic to be diverted to the new portion. The original building will then be restored to its original character. The original McKim, Mead & White building has recently been cleaned, revealing the light-pink Milford granite. This stone will also be used to face the Johnson addition.

110-112A. University of Virginia, Charlottesville, Va. Buildings designed 1896; constructed 1896-98; White in charge. Attribution: Kendall, Baldwin. **Mechanical Laboratory (Cocke Hall):** cost, $39,460; extant. **Academic Building (Cabell Hall):** cost, $78,484; extant. **Rotunda:** cost, $109,058; extant.

113-115. Casino, Rhinebeck, N.Y. Designed for John Jacob Astor 1902; constructed 1902-04; White in charge. Attribution: Kendall, Baldwin. Cost: $238,126. Design influence: Grand Trianon, Versailles (Jules Hardouin Mansart, 1687).

116-119. The Cullum Memorial, United States Military Academy, West Point, N.Y. Designed 1893-95; constructed 1896-98; White in charge. Attribution: Kendall, Baldwin. Cost: $217,273. Built through the gift of Maj. Gen. George W. Cullum, class of 1833, as a recreational facility for the cadets.

120. James J. Goodwin Residences, 15-17 West 54th St., New York, N.Y. Designed 1896; constructed 1896-98; Mead and White in charge. Attribution: Kendall. Cost: $152,770. Extant, now the Rhodes School.

121. H. A. C. Taylor Residences, 2-4 East 72nd St., New York, N.Y. Designed 1894; constructed 1894-96; McKim in charge. Attribution: Roth. Cost: $84,528. Destroyed c. 1935.

122-123. Radcliffe College Gymnasium, Radcliffe College, Garden and Mason Sts., Cambridge, Mass. Designed 1897; constructed 1898-99; McKim in charge. Attribution: Kendall, Moore. Cost: $58,438. Extant.

124-126. State Savings Bank, Fort and Shelby Sts., Detroit, Mich. Designed 1898; constructed 1898-1900; White in charge. Attribution: Kendall, Baldwin. Cost: $291,290. Extant, now houses the Manufacturers National Bank of Detroit.

130-140C. The University Club, 1 West 54th St., at Fifth Ave., New York, N.Y. Designed 1896; constructed 1897-1900; McKim in charge. Attribution: Kendall, Moore. Cost: $1,108,541 for the building; $2,043,757, total. Design influence: Palazzo Spannochi, Siena, and the Palazzo Albergati, Bologna. Addition by the firm, 1916-20. The ceiling paintings in the library by H. Siddons Mowbray are based in style and color on those by Pinturicchio in the Borgia Apartments in the Vatican. On the exterior, the shields incorporated in the walls carry the emblems of eighteen colleges. Extant.

141-143. Boston Symphony Music Hall, Huntington and Massachusetts Ave., Boston, Mass. Designed for Henry L. Higginson 1892-98; constructed 1899-1901; McKim in charge. Attribution: Kendall, Moore. Cost: $457,460 for the building; c. $750,000 total, including land. Extant; still the home of the Boston Symphony.

144-145. William C. Whitney Residence (interiors), 871 Fifth Ave., at 69th St., New York, N.Y. Designed 1897; constructed 1898-1902; White in charge. Attribution: Kendall, Baldwin. Cost: c. $156,100. White directed the elaborate redecorating of the Whitney house, leaving the original brownstone front virtually untouched. The house had been built in 1880 for Robert L. Stuart, following designs by William

Schicknel. Whitney purchased the house in 1896. Destroyed November, 1942.

146. Alfred Atmore Pope Residence, "Hill Stead," 671 Farmington Ave., Farmington, Conn. Designed 1898; constructed 1899-1901; White in charge. Attribution: Kendall. Cost: *c.* $50,000. The character of the design—a version of Washington's Mount Vernon—was determined by Mr. Pope and his daughter Theodate, who was an architect. Because of this decision and the large amount of work Miss Pope did on the design, White reduced his usual fee. Extant, now a museum.

147-151. Edwin D. Morgan Estate, "Wheatley Hills," Wheatley Rd., Wheatley, Long Island, N.Y. Designed 1890; constructed 1890, 1898-1900; McKim in charge. Attribution: Kendall. Cost: *c.* $96,000. Built in two stages. The first stage, begun in 1890, included the central unit of the main house, the portion shown in the upper half of Plate 151. The extensive service buildings and the grounds were completed in the second stage from 1898 to 1900. Partially extant (?), in ruins.

152-154. Memorial Gateways, Harvard University, Cambridge, Mass. The gates illustrated in the *Monograph* are part of a series of 16 gates and connecting fences that completely enclose Harvard Yard. The first gate, designed by McKim in 1889, was the **Johnston Gate** (Plates 19-19A). The **Meyer Gate** (Plate 158) followed in the winter of 1889, and the **Porcellian Gate** (Plates 152-154) was begun soon after in the spring of 1890. Since these 3 gates were free-standing, McKim suggested to the Harvard Corporation that a continuous enclosure around the yard be planned, providing a number of gate sites. Enthusiasm for the project grew and funds were solicited, until by 1899 a definite program of building could be started. A group of 12 gates was designed by McKim and Kendall during 1899-1900 and constructed over the next 6 years. All are extant.

Porcellian Gate: designed 1890; constructed 1891; cost, unrecorded.

Gates for the Classes of 1870, 1875, 1877, and 1890: designed 1899; constructed 1900; costs, $3,905 (1870), $4,162 (1875), $12,916 (1877), and $4,195 (1890).

Gates for the Classes of 1857 and 1880: designed 1900-01; constructed 1902; costs, $5,525 (1857), $16,174 (1880).

Gate for the Classes of 1887 and 1888: designed 1900; constructed 1905-06; cost, $13,049.

155-156. Henry W. Poore Residence (interiors), 1 Lexington Ave. at 21st St., New York, N.Y. Designed 1899; constructed 1899-1901; White in charge. Attribution: Baldwin. Cost: $137,844. Destroyed *c.* 1930. White carried out extensive interior remodeling

for Henry W. Poore, a friend. The commission also included stables and a squash court at 134 E. 22nd St.

157. Cornell University Medical School, First Ave. and 28th St., New York, N.Y. Designed for Oliver H. Payne 1898; constructed 1899-1901; White in charge. Attribution: Kendall, Baldwin. Cost: $736,199. Destroyed 1968.

158. Gate for the Class of 1879 ("Meyer Gate"), Harvard University, Cambridge, Mass. (See note 152-154 above.) Designed 1889; constructed 1890-91; McKim, Kendall in charge. Attribution: Kendall. Cost: unrecorded. Extant, still in use.

158-161. Harvard Union, Harvard University, Prescott and Harvard Sts., Cambridge, Mass. Designed for Henry L. Higginson 1899; constructed 1900-01; McKim in charge. Attribution: Kendall, Moore. Cost: $238,972. Extant, still in use.

162-163. Philip A. Rollins Residence, 28 E. 78th St., near Madison Ave., New York, N.Y. Designed 1899-1900; constructed 1900-03; Mead and McKim in charge. Attribution: Kendall. Cost: $102,759. Extant, now the New York branch office of the American Automobile Association.

162 [Right]. Thomas B. Clarke Residence, 22 E. 35th St., New York, N.Y. Designed 1902; constructed 1902; White in charge. Attribution: Roth. Cost: unrecorded. Design influence: Based on such work of Richard Norman Shaw as his New Zealand Chambers, London (1872-73), or his own home, Ellerdale Road, London (1875). Clarke was a well-known art collector at the turn of the century and a personal friend of the architect's. Stanford White designed this new house for Clarke, but its construction was not supervised by the office; hence there are very few records of this, one of the finest and most intimately scaled of White's designs. Extant, now the Collectors Club.

164-165. Robert Gould Shaw Memorial, Boston Commons, Boston, Mass. Designed 1891; constructed 1896-97 (construction of the setting continued until 1902); McKim in charge. Attribution: Kendall. Cost: $23,113. The commission was given to Augustus Saint-Gaudens in 1881, but the sculpture was not completed for 14 years. Both the location in the Commons (across from the State House) and the architectural setting incorporating trees were worked out by McKim. Col. Robert Gould Shaw was a young Bostonian who died in the Civil War at the head of a regiment of Negro volunteers he had recruited. Extant.

166-170. Clarence H. Mackay Residence, "Harbor Hill," Roslyn Rd. and Harbor Hill Rd., Roslyn, Long Island, N.Y. Designed for John Mackay, father of Clarence H. Mackay, 1899; constructed 1900-02, 1906; White in charge. Attribution: Kendall, Baldwin. Cost: $781,483, including work on the grounds and out-buildings. Design influence: Chateau Maisons-Lafitte, outside Paris (Francois Mansart, 1642-46). The model was dictated to White by Mrs. Katherine Duer Mackay, wife of Clarence Mackay. Destroyed c. 1945; now a suburban housing development. The only remaining portion is the gatehouse at Roslyn Rd. and Harbor Hill Rd., now the clubhouse for a swimming club.

171-174. Herman Oelrichs Residence, "Rosecliff," Bellevue Ave., Newport, R.I. Designed 1897; constructed 1899-1902; White in charge. Attribution: Kendall, Baldwin. Cost: $298,043. Design influence: Grand Trianon, Versailles (Jules Hardouin Mansart, 1687). Extant.

175-178. White House (renovation and alterations and Executive Offices wing) 1600 Pennsylvania Ave., Washington, D. C. Designed 1902; constructed 1902-03; McKim in charge. Attribution: Kendall, Moore. Cost: White House, $429,061; Executive Offices wing, $55,925. Extant, still in use. During Theodore Roosevelt's administration, the White House was restored and the Executive Offices moved from the White House to a new wing. The restrained Federalist classicism replaced Victorian accretions to the original building (designed by James Hoban, 1791-92). Office activities were finally removed from the President's residence and housed in a "temporary" west wing which was designed to incorporate early terraces planned by Thomas Jefferson. Additional alterations are as follows: In 1909 the offices were expanded; in 1927 a third floor was added under the roof of the White House; in 1929 a fire necessitated reconstruction of the Executive Offices; in 1942 the East Wing was constructed; in 1948-52 the entire interior of the White House was removed and stored while new foundations and steel framing were installed. The only major change in the McKim, Mead & White renovation has been the painting of the paneled dining room and the gilding of the trim in 1961. The "temporary" Executive Offices in the West Wing now appear to have become permanent.

180-182. Joseph Pulitzer Residence, 7-11 E. 73rd St., New York, N.Y. Designed 1900; constructed 1901-03; White in charge. Attribution: Kendall, Baldwin. Cost: $369,310. Design influence: Palazzo Pesaro (Baldassare Longhena, 1676), Palazzo Rezzonico (Longhena, 1667) and Palazzo Labia, all in Venice. Extant, now divided into apartments.

183-190. Rhode Island State Capitol, Providence, R.I. Designed 1891; constructed 1895-1904; Mead and McKim in charge. Attribution: Kendall, Moore. Cost: $2,368,714 for the building; $3,018,417, total. Design influence: United States Capitol. Extant. The entire building, including the dome, is built of white marble. The dome is the second largest of 4 such marble domes in the world, those of St. Peter's, Rome; the Taj Mahal, India; and the Minnesota Capitol, St. Paul. The building is placed in a 14-acre hilltop setting which dominates the city of Providence.

191-192. Charles Dana Gibson Residence, 127 E. 73rd St., New York, N.Y. Designed 1902; constructed 1902-03; White in charge. Attribution: Baldwin. Cost: $49,734. Built as the home of the creator of the "Gibson Girl," Charles Dana Gibson, a good friend of White's. Gutted and altered to accommodate offices, c. 1950. Extant, now the American Scandinavian Association.

193-195. St. Bartholomew's Church, Porch, Park Ave. and 51st St., New York, N.Y. Designed for Mrs. Cornelius Vanderbilt 1901; constructed 1901-03; White in charge. Attribution: Kendall, Baldwin. Cost: $133,996. Design influence: St. Gilles-du-Gard, France. The Romanesque porch by White is decorated by three prominent American sculptors. The north portal contains the work of Herbert Adams; the center portal contains sculpture by Daniel Chester French assisted by Andrew O'Connor, who carved the frieze; the south portal contains the work of Philip Martiny. The porch and doors are in memory of Cornelius Vanderbilt, Warden of St. Bartholomew's, presented by his wife and children. Extant; in 1918 the porch was removed from the church at Madison Ave. and 44th St. (shown in these plates) and rebuilt at the current location of the church on Park Ave. by Bertram G. Goodhue.

196-199. New York Public Library, Branch Buildings. Designed by McKim and Kendall beginning late 1901. Altogether 11 branch buildings, 8 of which are reproduced in the *Monograph*, were designed by the firm, all based on a basic plan.

St. Gabriel's Branch, 303 E. 36th St., New York, N.Y. Constructed 1906-08; cost, $81,541. Demolished(?).

Chatham Square Branch, 31 E. Broadway, New York, N.Y. Constructed 1902-03; cost, $72,314. Extant.

115th Street Branch, 203 W. 115th St., New York, N.Y. Constructed 1907-09; cost, $79,219. Extant.

125th Street Branch, 224 E. 125th St., New York, N.Y. Constructed 1903-04; cost, $68,078. Extant.

Thompkins Square Branch, 331 E. 10th St., New York, N.Y. Constructed 1903-05; cost, $75,141. Extant.

Woodstock Branch, 759 E. 160th St., New York, N.Y. Constructed 1912-14; cost, $104,823. Extant(?).

Mt. Morris, Harlem, Branch, 9 W. 124th St., New York, N.Y. Constructed 1907-09; cost, $84,582. Extant.

Hamilton Grange Branch, Amsterdam Ave. and W. 145th St., New York, N.Y. Constructed 1905-06; cost, $99,459. Extant.

200-203. Columbia University, New York, N.Y. **Earl Hall (Plates 200, 202)**: designed *c.* 1894-95; constructed 1901-02; McKim in charge. Attribution: Kendall. Cost: $155,870. Extant; still in use. **Furnald Hall (Plate 201)**: designed *c.* 1895; constructed 1912-14; McKim and Kendall in charge. Attribution: Kendall. Cost: $315,512. Extant; still in use. **Fountains, South Court, and South Terrace (Plates 200, 201, 203)**: designed 1893-95; constructed 1895-98; McKim in charge. Attribution: Kendall, Moore. Cost: *c.* $358,000. Extant, still in use.

204-206.   Harvard University, Cambridge, Mass. **Memorial Gateway, Class of 1885 (Plate 204)**: designed 1900-01; constructed 1901-04; McKim and Kendall in charge. Attribution: Kendall. Cost: $7,501. Extant, still in use. **Robinson Hall (Plates 204,205,206)**: designed 1899; constructed 1900-02; McKim and Kendall in charge. Gift of Mr. and Mrs. Nelson Robinson of New York. Attribution: Kendall, Moore. Cost: $132,524. Extant, in use as Graduate School of Design.

207.   Interborough Rapid Transit Company Power House, 59th St. and Eleventh Ave., New York, N.Y. Designed 1902; constructed 1903-04; White in charge. Attribution: Kendall, Baldwin. Cost: unrecorded. White provided only the design of the masonry shell of the power house. The interior was planned by I. R. T. engineers who also supervised the construction. Some of the original smokestacks have been removed and a single tall chimney built, *c.* 1960. The cornice has also been removed. Extant, still in use.

208-212.   Knickerbocker Trust Company, 358 Fifth Ave. (34th St. & Fifth Ave.), New York, N.Y. Designed 1901; constructed 1902-04; White in charge. Attribution: Kendall, Baldwin. Cost: $618,255. Design influence: Corinthian order, Temple of Mars Ultor, Rome. The building was originally planned to be 13 stories high. Only the lowest 4 floors, the base element of the design, were constructed, although all preparations were made for the eventual addition of the upper 9 stories. Demolished *c.* 1910-25.

213-216A.   Bank of Montreal, St. James and Craig Sts., Montreal, Quebec, Canada. Designed 1900; constructed 1901-05; McKim in charge. Attribution: Kendall. Cost: $1,448,376. Extant, still in use.

217.   Four Mausoleums, Woodlawn Cemetery, New York, N.Y. **Charles J. Osborn Mausoleum**: designed and constructed 1909; Kendall or W. S. Richardson in charge; cost, $3,900. Extant. **Henry Augustus Coit Taylor Mausoleum**: designed and constructed 1900-01; White [Baldwin] in charge; cost, $137,040. Extant. **Robert and Ogden Goelet Mausoleum**: designed and constructed 1899; White(?) in charge; cost, $52,000. Extant. **Henry E. Russell Mausoleum**: designed and constructed 1894; White(?) in charge; cost, $25,532. Extant.

219, 221.   Naugatuck High School, Hillside Ave., Naugatuck, Conn. Designed for John Howard Whittemore 1901; constructed 1902-05; Van der Bent, Mead and Kendall in charge. Attribution: Kendall. Cost: $247,875. Interior destroyed by fire in 1961. Completely restored and the exterior cleaned in 1961-63. Cost: $525,000. Whittemore originally established a trust fund of $40,000 to provide for maintenance of the school in 1905. By the time of the fire in 1961 the fund no longer existed and the school was rebuilt through insurance payments and local levies. Extant, now the Naugatuck Junior High School.

220-221.   Congregational Church, Division and Church Sts., Naugatuck, Conn. Designed 1901; constructed 1901-03; Mead and McKim in charge. Attribution: Kendall. Cost: $98,320. Design influence: tower adapted from St. Martin-in-the-Fields, London (James Gibbs, 1722-26). Extant, still in use.

222-224.   Thomas Jefferson Coolidge, Jr., Residence, Manchester, Mass. Designed 1902; constructed 1903-04; McKim in charge. Attribution: Kendall. Cost: $183,514. Design influence: purportedly, the design refers to "Monticello," the home of Coolidge's ancestor, Thomas Jefferson. Demolished *c.* 1965.

225-226.   Lambs' Club, 128 W. 44th St., New York, N.Y. A club for actors, named after Charles and Mary Lamb. Designed 1903; constructed 1904-05; White in charge. Attribution: Baldwin, Kendall. Cost: $169,098. Expanded and doubled in size. Extant, still in use.

227.   Women's Building, University of Illinois, Wright St., Urbana, Ill. Designed 1903; constructed 1904-05; McKim and Fenner in charge. Attribution: Kendall. Cost: $70,739. Much enlarged and expanded to the east in 1913 and 1923-24. Extant, now known as the English Building.

228-229.   Harmonie Club, 4 E. 60th St., New York, N.Y. Designed 1904; constructed 1904-07; White in charge. Attribution. Baldwin, Kendall. Cost: $463,718. Extant, still in use.

230-231. New England Trust Company, Devonshire and Milk Sts., Boston, Mass. Designed 1904; constructed 1905-07; McKim in charge. Attribution: Kendall. Cost: $443,833. Extant, but not in use.

232. Buckingham Building, Grand and Bank Sts., Waterbury, Conn. Designed for John Howard Whittemore 1903-04; constructed 1905-06; Kendall and Van der Bent in charge. Attribution: Kendall. Cost: $179,835. Originally built by Whittemore to provide rental income for the Waterbury Hospital. Four stories of offices were wrapped around a large central auditorium used for public performances and meetings. Demolished 1969; replaced by a multilevel parking garage.

234-240. Gorham Company Building, 390 Fifth Ave. at 36th St., New York, N.Y. Designed 1903; constructed 1904-06; White in charge. Attribution: Kendall, Baldwin. Cost: *c.* $950,000. For a time the building housed "Russeks" and was known by that name. It is now an office building. The Fifth Ave. ground floor facade has been modernized. The large copper cornice was once enameled with several colors but the polychromy has been lost. Extant, still in use.

241-249. Morgan Library, 33 E. 36th St., New York N.Y. Designed for J. Pierpont Morgan 1902; constructed 1903-07; McKim in charge. Attribution: Kendall, Moore. Cost: $1,154,669. Design influence: based on the attic story of the Nymphaeum, Villa Papa Giulia, Rome, attributed to Ammanati, *c.* 1555. An annex was erected at 29 E. 36th St. in 1928 (Benjamin W. Morris, architect). Plate 241: The panels of low relief sculpture in the attic are by Andrew O'Connor. Plate 242: The reclining lionesses flanking the entrance stair are by Edward Clark Potter. Plate 242A: The bronze doors are 16th-century Italian, artist unknown. Plate 246: The lunettes in the vestibule were painted by H. Siddons Mowbray. Plates 247-248: The ceiling panels in the East Room were painted by H. Siddons Mowbray.

Built of carefully laid marble blocks with no mortar in the classic Greek manner. The library was designed as the repository of Morgan's extensive collection of manuscripts, ivories, incunabula, and art objects. Extant; it is now a research library and public museum.

251-257. Madison Square Presbyterian Church, Madison Ave. and 24th St., New York, N.Y. Designed 1903; constructed 1904-06; White in charge. Attribution: Baldwin, Kendall. Cost: $306,022. An exercise in subtle polychromy, much of the terra cotta of this building was glazed in light colors. Destroyed 1919. The green granite columns and the entrance portion of the church were preserved and incorporated by Donn Barber in his building for the *Hartford Times,* Hartford, Conn., which still stands. Other portions of the building went to the Brooklyn Museum and the Metropolitan Museum of

Art. The pediment relief sculpture (Plate 253) was designed by H. Siddons Mowbray and modeled by Adolph A. Weinman.

259-260. Mrs. William Kissam Vanderbilt, Jr., Residence, 666 Fifth Ave., New York, N.Y. Designed 1904; constructed 1905-07; White in charge. Attribution: Baldwin, Kendall. Cost: $399,055. Design influence: based on the Francois Ier style of the Richard Morris Hunt design for the adjoining W. K. Vanderbilt house of 1879. Demolished *c.* 1925.

261-264. Tiffany & Co., 409 Fifth Ave. at 37th St., New York, N.Y. Designed 1903; constructed 1903-06; White in charge. Attribution: Kendall, Baldwin. Cost: $1,970,951. Design influence: Palazzo Grimani, Venice (Sanmicheli, 1556). Extant; interior entirely renovated.

265-267. Army War College, Fort McNair, 4th and P Sts., SW, Washington, D.C. Designed 1902-03; constructed 1904-08; McKim and Kendall in charge. Attribution: Kendall, Moore. Cost: unrecorded. McKim was engaged to replan the entire military base. Only the War College itself is shown in the photograph in the *Monograph,* but other buildings were completed including, among those shown on the plan (Plate 265), the Officers Mess (D), Officers Houses (F), Field Officers Houses (G), Non-Com Officers Houses (H), Barracks (L), Engineer Store House (M), Commissary (N), Mess Halls (O), and others; see legend, Plate 265. Extant, still in use.

268-271. James L. Breese Residence, Southampton, Long Island, N.Y. Designed 1898-1904; constructed 1905-07; White in charge. Attribution: Baldwin. Cost: $54,269. Extant, now an economics study center of Amherst College.

274-276. Bellevue Hospital, 26th to 29th Sts. and First Ave., New York, N.Y. Designed 1903-06; McKim, Kendall, and Van der Bent in charge. Attribution: Kendall. Portions carried out by the firm 1906 to 1920: Pavilions A and B constructed 1906-11; Pathological Wing constructed 1907-11; Boiler House and Coaling Station constructed 1908-11; Laundry constructed 1909-11; Pavilions L and M constructed 1911-15; Pavilions I and K constructed 1912-16. Extant.

275X, 277-279. Metropolitan Museum of Art, Fifth Ave., between 80th and 84th Sts., New York, N.Y. Designed 1904-06; constructed 1906-26; McKim, Kendall, and W. S. Richardson in charge. Attribution: Kendall. In 1904 the firm was engaged to prepare a comprehensive plan for expansion of the museum. Portions were completed, beginning in 1906 and continuing through 1926. Thereafter the master plan was revised. As the key to

Plate 279 indicates, the McKim, Mead and White additions were built along Fifth Ave. Extant.

280-282. Colony Club, 120 Madison Ave., near 30th St., New York, N.Y. Designed 1904; constructed 1905-08; White in charge. Attribution: Kendall, Baldwin. Cost: $289,176. Designed as a club for "venerably connected and socially prominent ladies," hence, perhaps, the delicate and diminutive details. Extant, now the American Academy of Dramatic Arts.

283-284. Memorial Gateways, Princeton University, Nassau St., Princeton, N.J. Designed 1904; constructed 1904-05; McKim and Kendall in charge. Attribution: Kendall. Cost: $17,636 (Nassau Street Gates); $35,740 (Athletic Field Gates). Designed and built while Woodrow Wilson was president of Princeton University. The Nassau St. Gate was given by Augustus Van Wickle in memory of an ancestor, Nathaniel FitzRandolph, donor of Princeton's original campus property in the mid-18th century. The Gates, now known as the FitzRandolph Gateway, frame the entrance to the campus from Nassau St., the main thoroughfare of Princeton. The Athletic Field Gates, given by Ferris S. Thompson, were designed by W. S. Richardson and built in 1910-13. Extant.

285-288. John Innes Kane Residence, 610 Fifth Ave., New York, N.Y. Designed 1904; constructed 1904-08; McKim and W. S. Richardson in charge. Attribution: Kendall. Cost: $511,473. Design influence (ground floor): Palazzo Massimi alle Colonne, Rome (Peruzzi, 1535). Demolished c. 1930.

289-292. Payne Whitney Residence, 972 Fifth Ave., New York, N.Y. Commissioned by Oliver H. Payne, uncle of Payne Whitney, 1902; constructed 1902-06, interiors finished 1909; White in charge. Attribution: Kendall, Baldwin. Cost: $1,061,846. This house was the southern half of a double house (the northern half was built for the J. C. Lyons Co., realtors, in 1902-05). Major renovations have been made in the interior. Purchased by the French Government in 1952. Extant, now the Press and Information Office of the French Embassy, New York.

293-293A. University Cottage Club, Princeton University, Princeton, N.J. Designed 1904; constructed 1904-06, interiors finished 1908; McKim in charge. Attribution: Kendall. Cost: $119,793. The gallery, library, and writing rooms were given by Stephen S. Palmer. Extant.

294. Trinity Church and Parish House, Northern Blvd., Roslyn, Long Island, N.Y. Designed for Mrs. Clarence H. Mackay 1905; constructed 1906-07; White and W. S. Richardson in charge. Attribution: Baldwin and Kendall. Cost: $58,197 (both church and parish house). Extant, still in use.

295-299A. National City Bank, 55 Wall St., New York, N.Y. Designed 1905-07; constructed 1908-10, interiors finished 1914; McKim and W. S. Richardson in charge. Attribution: Kendall. Cost: $2,290,315. The commission was for the remodeling of the United States Customs House designed in 1842 by Isaiah Rogers. When the Customs House moved from this building in 1907 the National City Bank had the firm enlarge the original 3-story Ionic building, gutting the interior to provide the necessary large banking room and superimposing a 3-story Corinthian stage above Roger's Ionic portion. The skylight has been covered over. Extant, still in use (now called the First National City Bank).

300-310. Pennsylvania Station, 31st-33rd Sts. between Seventh and Eighth Aves., New York, N.Y. Designed 1902-05; constructed 1905-11; McKim and W. S. Richardson in charge. Attribution: Kendall, Moore. Cost: $10,568,191. The basic design was laid out by McKim before ill health curtailed his office responsibilities; the details were entirely Richardson's creation. Design influence: The external colonnades owed some inspiration to those of Soane's Bank of England (1795-1805) and Bernini's colonnade enclosing the Piazza di San Pietro, Rome (1657-66). The majestic general waiting room was based on the central hall of the Baths of Caracalla, Rome. At the upper level of the waiting room were 6 large murals by Jules Guerin (Plate 306) showing the areas served by the Pennsylvania and Long Island Railroads. The station was demolished 1963-64 to make way for the new Madison Square Garden and an office building. Some of the original staircases remain in the "renovated" subterranean station.

311. Waterbury Station, New Haven Railroad, Grand and Bank Sts., Waterbury, Conn. Designed 1906-07; constructed 1907-09; W. S. Richardson in charge. Attribution: Kendall. Cost: $268,859. Built while John Howard Whittemore was a director of the company. Design influence: The tower is based on the tower of the Palazzo Pubblico, Siena (1288-1309). Extant, now houses a railway station and offices of the Waterbury *Republican* newspaper. During the 1950s the major part of the station was converted for use by the newspaper. No major damage was done to the original fabric of the structure.

313-319. Buildings for Columbia University, New York, N.Y. All 5 buildings shown in this group were designed during 1900-05 by William Mitchell Kendall, according to the list of attributions prepared by Kendall.

Hamilton Hall (Plate 313): constructed 1905-09; cost, $435,376. Extant.

School of Journalism (Plates 313, 316). Both the school and the building were established through the provisions of the will of Joseph Pulitzer. Constructed 1912-13; cost, $450,583. Extant.

Avery Hall, School of Architecture (Plates 314, 315, 317): constructed 1911-12; cost, $315,423. Extant.

Kent Hall, School of Law (Plates 314, 315, 316, 319): designed 1907-09; constructed 1909-11; cost, $427,332. Extant.

Philosophy Building (Plates 317-318): constructed 1910-11; cost, $307,578. Extant.

320-327. Municipal Building, Center and Chambers Sts., New York, N.Y. Designed for the City of New York 1907-08; constructed 1909-13, interiors finished 1916; Kendall and Van der Bent in charge. Attribution: Kendall. Cost: $5,932,175 for exterior; $3,122,129 for interiors. The commission was won in competition in 1908. The program of the competition stipulated that the building was to straddle Chambers St. and to incorporate a large subway station threaded through its foundations. The building houses the many offices of New York city government and is surmounted by a figure of Civic Fame by Adolph Alexander Weinman. McKim had very little to do with this design; his failing health required him to leave the office. Extant.

329-331. Girard Trust Company, Broad and Chestnut Sts., Philadelphia, Pa. Designed 1904; constructed 1905-09; W. S. Richardson, Furness, Evans and Co., Associated Architects, in charge. Attribution: Kendall. Cost: unrecorded. Extant.

333-335. Knickerbocker Trust Company—Downtown Building (later, Columbia Trust Company), 60 Broadway, New York, N.Y. Designed 1906-07; constructed 1908-12; White and W. S. Richardson in charge. Attribution: Baldwin, Kendall. Cost: $1,951,003. Destroyed c. 1965(?).

336-337. Edward T. Blair Residence, 1516 Lake Shore Dr., Chicago, Ill. Designed 1912; constructed 1912-14; Kendall in charge. Attribution: Kendall. Cost: $156,245. Extant, now owned by the International College of Physicians and Surgeons.

338-339. Second National Bank, 250 Fifth Ave., New York, N.Y. Designed 1907; constructed 1908; W. S. Richardson in charge. Attribution: Kendall. Cost: $262,885. Extant, now a branch of the First National City Bank.

340-345. Harvard Club of New York City, 27 W. 44th St., New York, N.Y. McKim and Kendall in charge. Attribution: Moore. Built in three stages. First stage: the 3-story element on 44th St. Designed by McKim in 1893; constructed 1894-95. Second stage: Harvard Hall, to the rear of the first stage, on 45th St. Designed by McKim in 1900-02; constructed 1902-05; cost, $362,524. Third stage: a 6-story element on 44th St. and expansion on 45th St. Designed by Kendall in 1913; constructed 1913-16; cost, $476,985. Extant, still in use.

346-347. 998 Fifth Avenue Apartment House, 998 Fifth Ave. at 81st St., New York, N.Y. Designed for Century Holding Company 1910; constructed 1911-15; W. S. Richardson in charge. Attribution: Kendall. Cost: $806,909. Extant, still in use.

348. P. H. B. Frelinghuysen Residence, Normandy Heights Rd. and Columbia Rd., Morristown, N.J. Designed 1909; constructed 1910-13; W. S. Richardson in charge. Attribution: Kendall. Cost: $108,461. Addition, 1970. Extant, now Morris Museum of Arts and Sciences.

349-351A. Percy R. Pyne Residence, 680 Park Ave., New York, N.Y. Designed 1906-07; constructed 1910-12; Kendall in charge. Attribution: Kendall. Cost: $348,899. Extant, now the Center for Inter-American Relations, formerly the home of the Russian Delegation to the United Nations.

352-353. President's House, Columbia University, 60 Morningside Drive at 116th St., New York, N.Y. Designed 1910; constructed 1911-12; Kendall in charge. Attribution: Kendall. Cost: $165,656. Extant, still in use.

354. Elon H. Hooker Residence (alterations), Greenwich, Conn. Designed 1911; constructed 1911-12; Fenner in charge. Attribution: Kendall. Cost: $90,056. Extant(?).

355-356A. Bank of Montreal, Winnipeg Branch, Portage and Main Sts., Winnipeg, Manitoba, Canada. Designed 1909; constructed 1910-12; W. S. Richardson in charge. Attribution: Kendall. Cost: $1,175,411. Extant.

357. Additions to the New York Post Graduate Hospital, Second Ave. and 20th St., New York, N.Y. Designed 1910; constructed 1910-12; Kendall and Van der Bent in charge. Attribution: Kendall. Cost: $878,184. Through repetition of basic units and extension of string courses and cornices, the addition was made to appear a part of the original building, seen to the left. Demolished, date unknown.

358. Library for Whitelaw Reid, 451 Madison Ave., New York, N.Y. Designed 1909; constructed 1910; Kendall in charge. Attribution: Roth. Cost: $438,244 for interiors and remodeling. The library was only one part of an extensive remodeling and renovation program carried out by Reid, who had purchased the house from Henry Villard in 1886. Extant, now the offices of the Archdiocese of New York.

360-364A. U. S. Post Office, New York City, 31st to 33rd Sts. between Eighth and Ninth Aves., New York, N.Y. Designed 1908; constructed 1909-18; Kendall in charge. Attribution: Kendall. Cost: $4,257,695. Addition at rear, 1935. Extant. Situated directly above the Pennsylvania Railroad tracks to facilitate mail handling. The 3-block-long colonnade echoed that of Penn Station, which once stood across the street. In the frieze of the long colonnade runs an inscription chosen by the architects, now famous as the motto of the postal service: "Neither snow, nor rain, nor heat, nor gloom of night stays these couriers from the swift completion of their appointed rounds." (Herodotus *Histories* 8. 100.)

365-366. Royal Trust and Realty Co., 105 St. James St., Montreal, Quebec, Canada. Designed 1911; constructed 1912-14; W. S. Richardson in charge. Attribution: Kendall. Cost: $901,605. The Royal Trust Company adjoins the Bank of Montreal. The original domed building of the bank can be seen to the left in the photograph, Plate 365. Extant (?).

367-368. Students' Building, Vassar College, Poughkeepsie, N.Y. Designed 1912; constructed 1912-14; Mead and Kendall in charge. Attribution: Kendall. Cost: $168,223. Extant.

369-370. Minneapolis Museum of Fine Arts, 201 E. 24th St., Minneapolis, Minn. Designed 1911; constructed 1911-14; W. S. Richardson in charge. Attribution: Kendall. Cost: $459,783. Additions, 1926. Extant, now known as The Minneapolis Institute of Arts. To be renovated, restored, and expanded with an addition by Kenzo Tange scheduled for completion by 1975.

372-375. American Academy in Rome, Via Angelo Masina 5, Rome, Italy. Designed *c.* 1910; constructed 1912-14; Kendall in charge. Attribution: Kendall. Cost: unrecorded. A complex that provides residential, studio, and library facilities for the fellows of the Academy working in architecture, painting, sculpture, music, art history, classical studies, and related subjects. Extant, still in use.

376. Clark Memorial (Pan Fountain) and Memorial Gate, Class of 1891, Columbia University, New York, N.Y.

Clark Memorial: designed by Kendall; constructed 1907-08; cost, $11,740. Extant. Originally placed at the far northeastern corner of the Columbia property, at Amsterdam Ave. and 120th St. (see Plate 47). The bronze by G. G. Barnard is now in the courtyard between Avery and Fayerweather Halls.

Memorial Gate, Class of 1891: constructed 1917; cost, $6,801. Located behind Earl Hall on Broadway. Extant.

377-379. Botanical Museum of the Brooklyn Institute of Arts and Sciences, 1000 Washington Ave., Brooklyn, N.Y. Designed 1913; constructed 1914-16; Kendall in charge. Attribution: Kendall. Extant; the administration building for the Brooklyn Botanic Gardens.

380-383. Burke Foundation Hospital for Convalescents, Mamaroneck Ave., White Plains, N.Y. Designed for Winnifred Masterson Burke Relief Foundation 1912; constructed 1912-15. Cost: $1,237,018. Extant.

384-387. Court of the Universe, Panama-Pacific Exposition, nr. Marina Blvd., San Francisco, Calif. Designed 1912-14; constructed 1914-15; W. S. Richardson in charge. Attribution: Roth. Cost: unrecorded. The exposition celebrated the opening of the Panama Canal. The Court of the Universe was the large central court shown in the block plan (Plate 384). The large arch shown in Plate 386 is the Arch of the Rising Sun, surmounted by the sculptural group, Nations of the East, by A. Stirling Calder, Leo Lentelli, and Frederick G. R. Roth. The figures atop the free-standing columns of the arch are of the Guardian Angel by Leo Lentelli. The Fountain of the Rising Sun (Plates 386 and 387) is by Adolph A. Weinman. The figure repeated above the colonnade is Star by A. Stirling Calder. The Column of Progress (Plate 387) combines bas relief panels by Isidore Konti at the base with the figure at the top, Adventurous Archer, by Herman A. MacNeil. In the distance, behind the Column of Progress, can be seen the Tower of Jewels, by Carrere and Hastings. Demolished 1915.

388-390. National McKinley Birthplace Memorial, 40 N. Main St., Niles, Ohio. Designed 1915; constructed 1915-18; Kendall in charge. Attribution: Roth. Cost $278,840. The firm's first use of the Greek Doric order occurs in this design. Extant.

392-393. Double House for Geraldyn Redmond and the Countess de Laugier Villars, 701-03 Park Ave., New York, N.Y. Designed 1912; constructed 1913-15;

Kendall in charge. Attribution: Kendall. Cost: $350,041 for both houses. Demolished; date unknown.

394-394A. Butler Art Gallery, 524 Wick Ave., Youngstown, Ohio. Designed for Joseph G. Butler 1917; constructed 1917-20; Kendall in charge. Attribution: Roth. Cost: $165,736. Design influence: Garden Casino, Villa Farnese, Caprarola, Italy (Vignola, *c.* 1550). Additions made 1931, 1952. The building houses a notable collection, begun by Joseph G. Butler, of works representing a broad range of American artistic endeavor. Extant, still in use.

395-396. Franklin National Bank, Chestnut St., Philadelphia, Pa. Designed 1915; constructed 1915-17; W. S.

Richardson in charge. Attribution: Roth. Cost: $768,443. Demolished, date uncertain.

397-397A. Thomas Newbold Residence, 15 E. 79th St., New York, N.Y. Designed 1916; constructed 1916-18. Cost: $147,819. Extant.

398-399A. Racquet and Tennis Club, 370 Park Ave., New York, N.Y. Designed 1916; constructed 1916-19; W. S. Richardson in charge. Attribution: Roth. Cost: $1,105,547. Design influence: Reflects the severity of the Palazzo Antinori, Florence. The Racquet and Tennis Club and Mies van der Rohe's Seagram Building, across the street, are excellent foils for one another. Extant, still in use.

LIST OF PLATES*

*The Table of Contents for the four volumes of the original 1915 edition of the Monograph are reprinted here in reduced size.

LIST OF PLATES

LIST OF PLATES

LIST OF PLATES

THE PLATES

PLATE 1

MCKIM, MEAD & WHITE

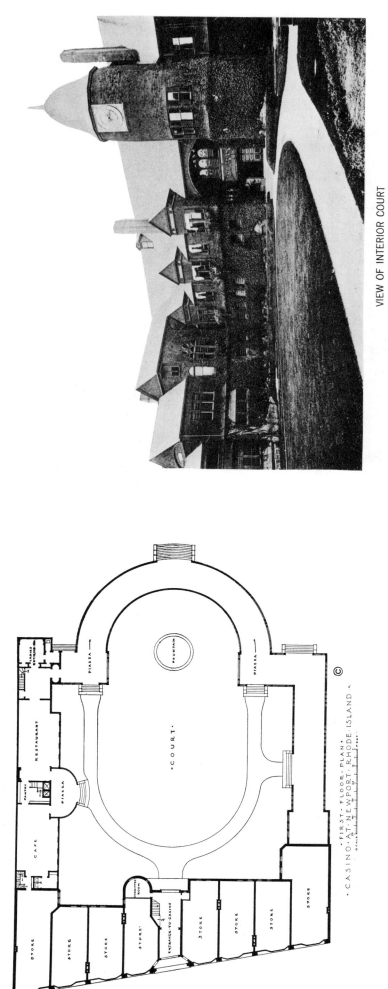

VIEW OF INTERIOR COURT

· FIRST · FLOOR · PLAN ·
· CASINO · AT · NEWPORT · RHODE · ISLAND ·

· CASINO · AT · NEWPORT · RHODE · ISLAND ·

SCALE   FEET

1881

ROSS WINANS, RESIDENCE, BALTIMORE, M. D.

ENTRANCE DETAIL

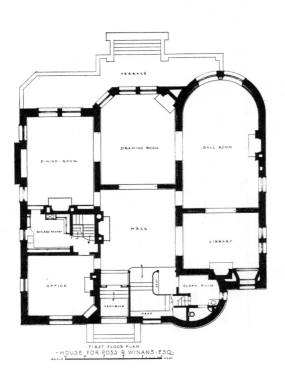

1882

PLATE 3

MCKIM, MEAD & WHITE

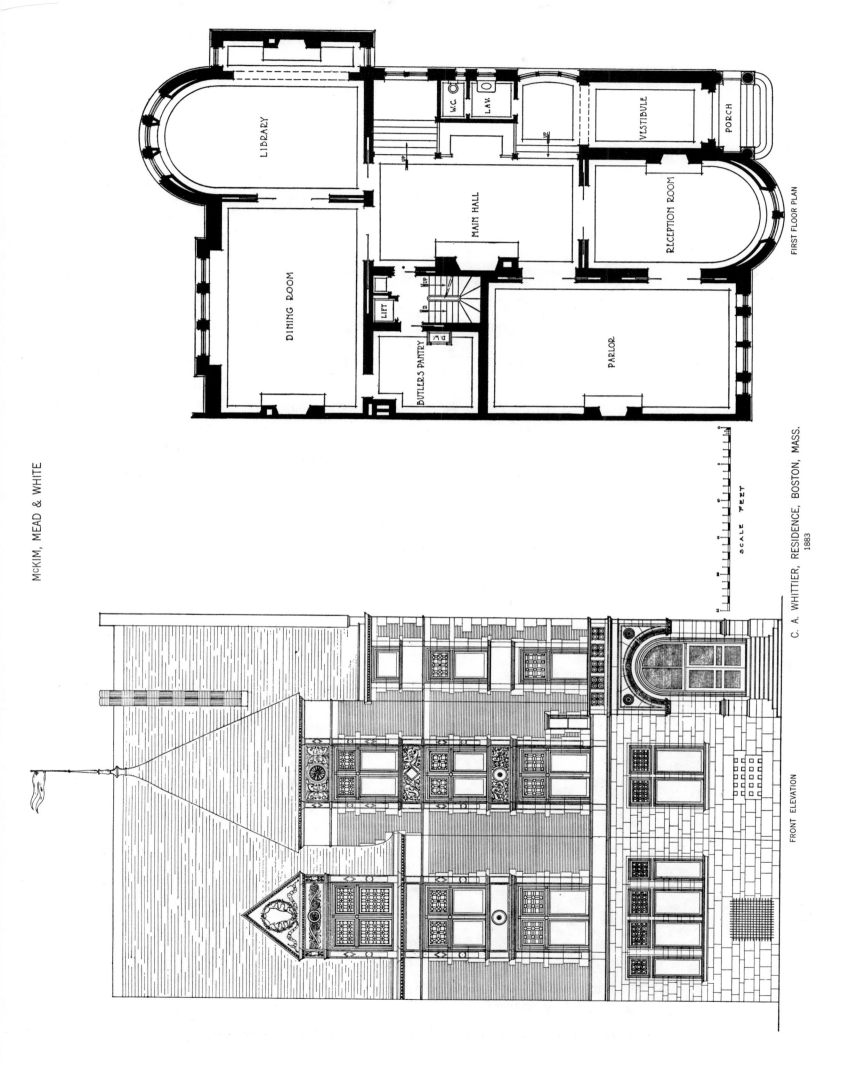

LIBRARY

DINING ROOM

W.C.

LAV.

MAIN HALL

VESTIBULE

LIFT

BUTLER'S PANTRY

RECEPTION ROOM

PARLOR

PORCH

FIRST FLOOR PLAN

SCALE FEET

FRONT ELEVATION

C. A. WHITTIER, RESIDENCE, BOSTON, MASS.
1883

ST·PAUL'S·CHURCH··STOCKBRIDGE·MASS·

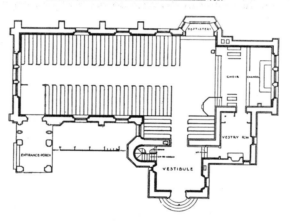

ST. PAUL'S CHURCH - STOCKBRIDGE, MASS.
1883

CHARLES L. TIFFANY, RESIDENCE, NEW YORK CITY.
1884

McKIM, MEAD & WHITE

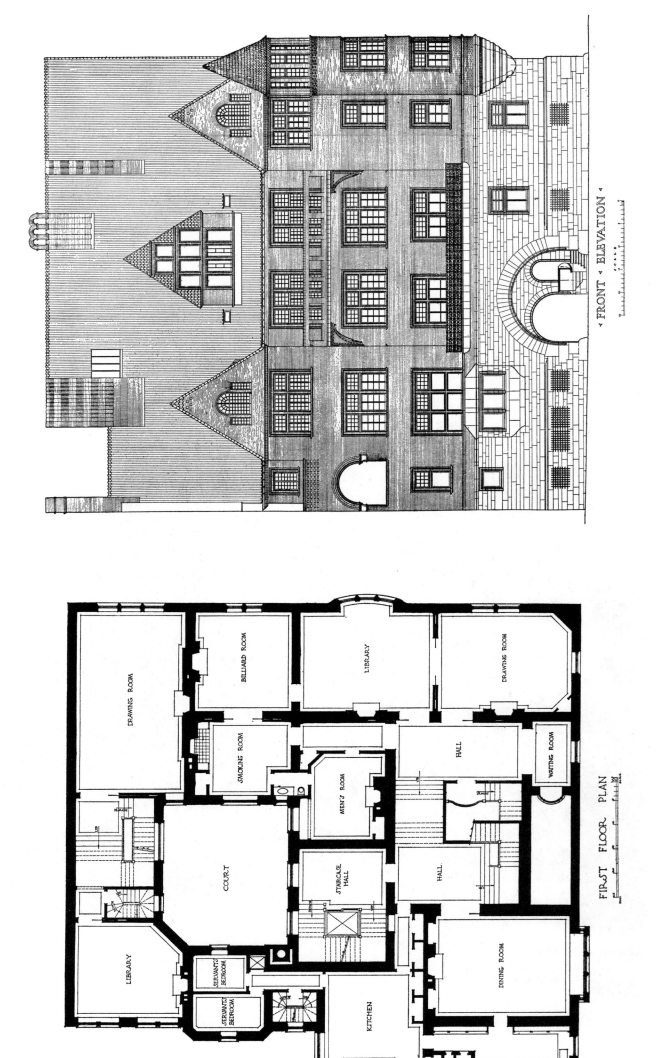

· FRONT · ELEVATION ·

FIRST FLOOR PLAN

CHARLES L. TIFFANY, RESIDENCE, NEW YORK CITY.
1884

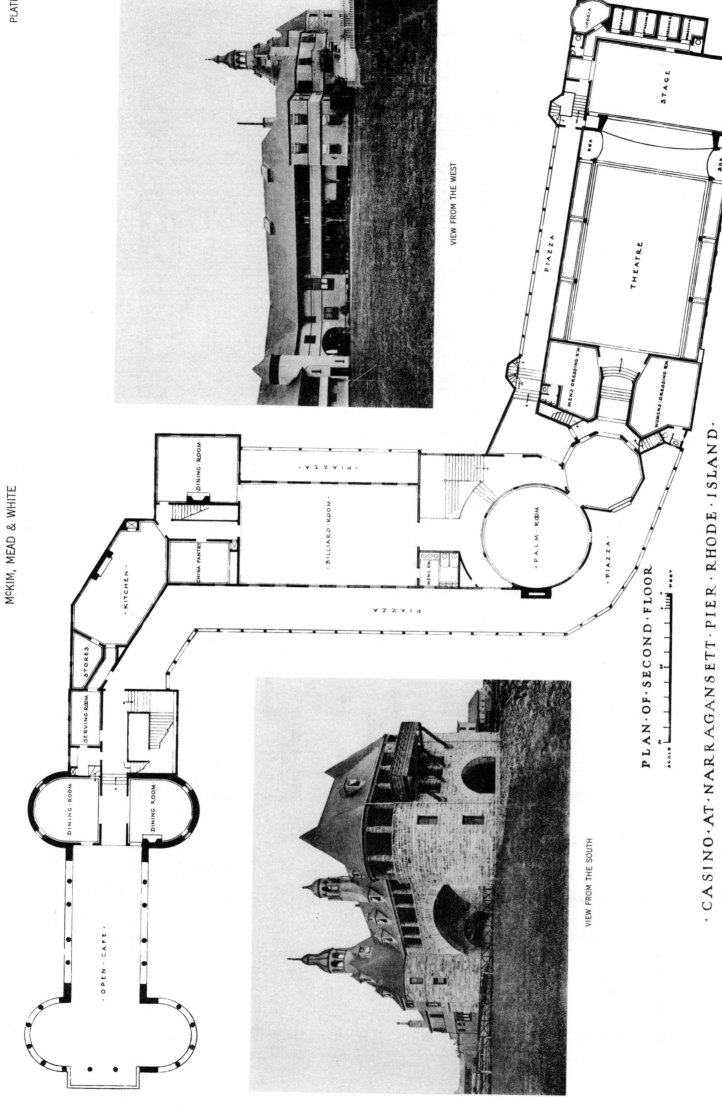

PLATE 6

McKIM, MEAD & WHITE

VIEW FROM THE WEST

VIEW FROM THE SOUTH

PLAN·OF·SECOND·FLOOR

SCALE

1884

·CASINO·AT·NARRAGANSETT·PIER·RHODE·ISLAND·

STAGE

THEATRE

PIAZZA

BOX

BOX

LOGGIA

MENS·DRESSING·RM

WOMENS·DRESSING·RM

·PALM·ROOM

·PIAZZA·

PIAZZA

·PIAZZA·

·BILLIARD·ROOM·

MENS RM

·CHINA·PANTRY·

·KITCHEN·

STORES

SERVING·ROOM

·DINING·ROOM

DINING·ROOM

DINING·ROOM

·OPEN·CAFE·

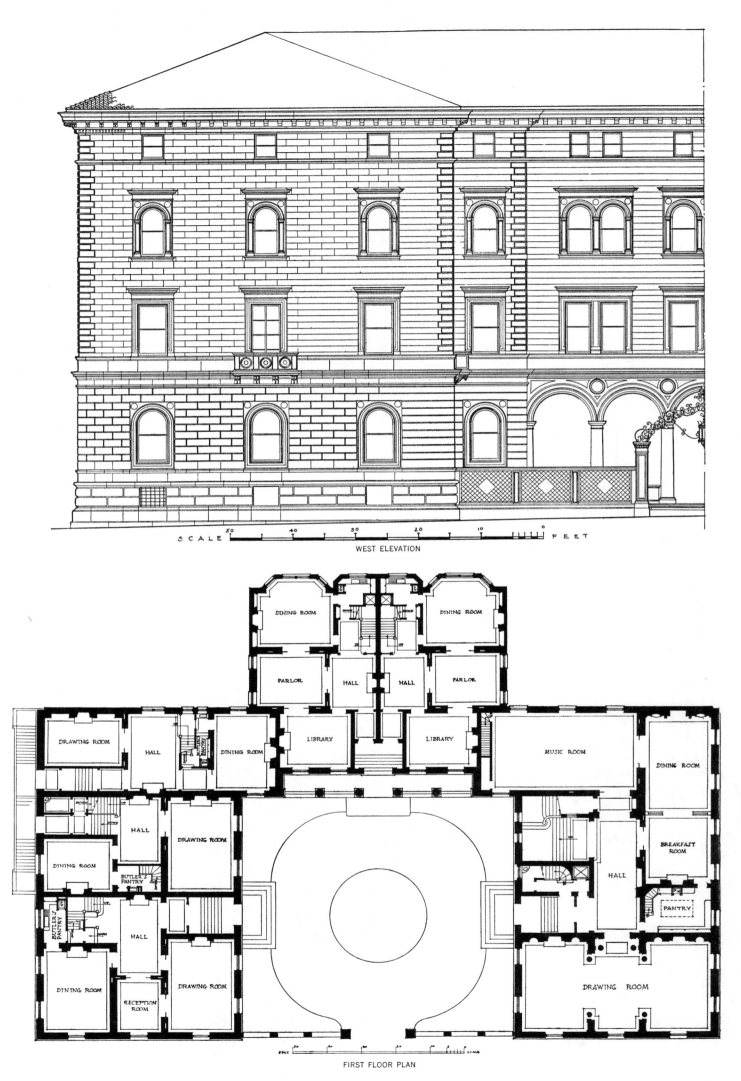

SCALE 50 40 30 20 10 0 FEET

WEST ELEVATION

FIRST FLOOR PLAN

HENRY VILLARD, RESIDENCE, NEW YORK CITY.
1885

MADISON AVENUE FACADE

ENTRANCE GATEWAY

HENRY VILLARD, RESIDENCE, NEW YORK CITY.
1885

PLATE 9

McKIM MEAD & WHITE

DOOR TO DINING ROOM

MANTEL IN ENTRANCE HALL

HENRY VILLARD, RESIDENCE, NEW YORK CITY.
1885

LUNETTE OVER MANTEL

ENTRANCE HALL

HENRY VILLARD, RESIDENCE, NEW YORK CITY.
1885

PLATE 11

McKIM MEAD & WHITE

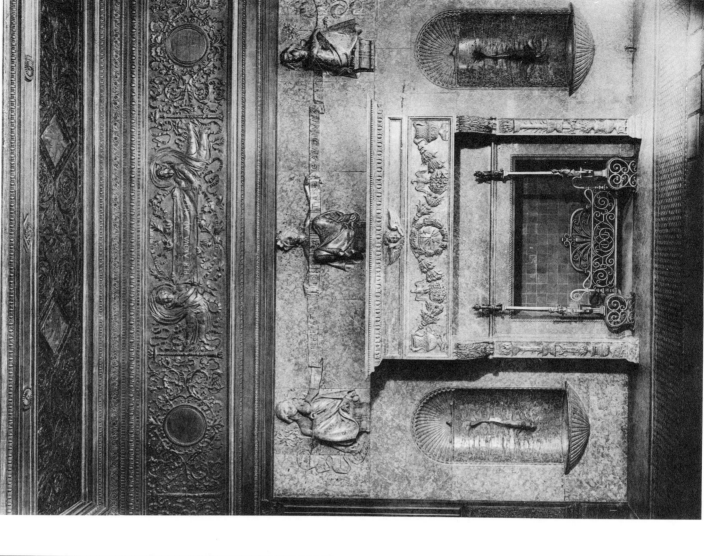

MANTEL IN DINING ROOM

HENRY VILLARD, RESIDENCE, NEW YORK CITY.
1885

DINING ROOM

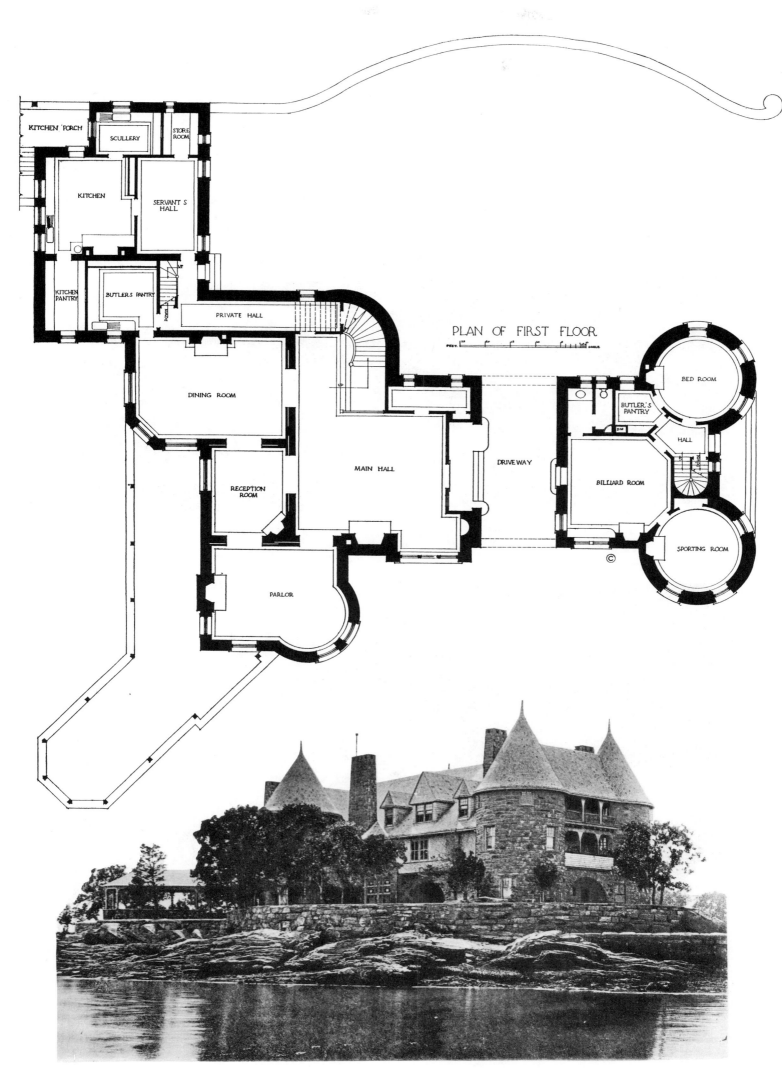

KITCHEN PORCH

SCULLERY

STORE ROOM

KITCHEN

SERVANT'S HALL

KITCHEN PANTRY

BUTLER'S PANTRY

PRIVATE HALL

PLAN OF FIRST FLOOR

DINING ROOM

RECEPTION ROOM

MAIN HALL

DRIVEWAY

BED ROOM

BUTLER'S PANTRY

HALL

BILLIARD ROOM

PARLOR

SPORTING ROOM

RESIDENCE OF CHARLES J. OSBORN, MAMARONECK, N. Y.
1885

RESIDENCE OF CHARLES J. OSBORN, MAMARONECK, N. Y.
1885

CHARLES J. OSBORN, MAMARONECK. N. Y. - GATE LODGE.
1885

RESIDENCE OF MRS. WILLIAM EDGAR, NEWPORT, R. I.
1886

CHARLES J. OSBORN, MAMARONECK, N. Y. - THE STABLE.
1885

PLATE 15

McKIM, MEAD & WHITE

PETER COOPER MONUMENT
1897

SCULPTURE BY AUGUSTUS ST. GAUDENS

DAVID GLASGOW FARRAGUT MONUMENT
1881

H. A. C. TAYLOR, RESIDENCE, NEWPORT, R. I.

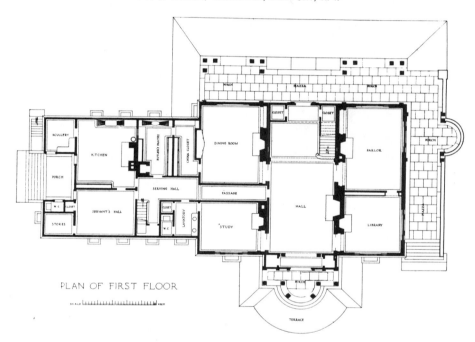

PLAN OF FIRST FLOOR

H. A. C. TAYLOR, RESIDENCE, NEWPORT, R. I.
1886

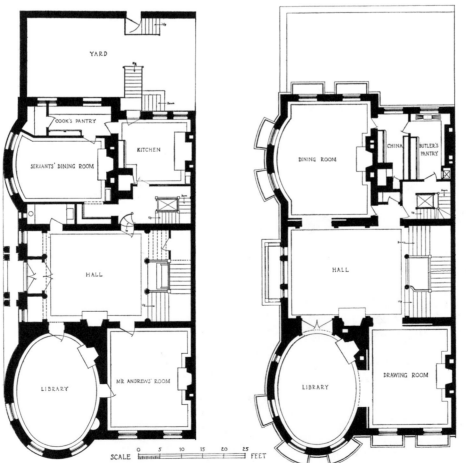

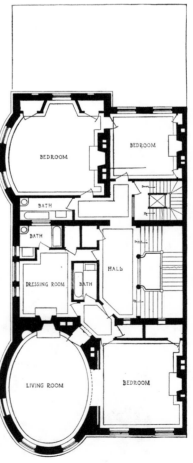

GROUND FLOOR PLAN

SCALE 0 5 10 15 20 25 FEET

FIRST FLOOR PLAN

SECOND FLOOR PLAN

JOHN F. ANDREWS, RESIDENCE, BOSTON, MASS.
1886

PLATE 18

MCKIM, MEAD & WHITE

ALGONQUIN CLUB, BOSTON, MASS.
1889

RUSSELL AND ERWIN BUILDING, NEW BRITAIN, CONN.
1885

PLATE 19

McKIM, MEAD & WHITE

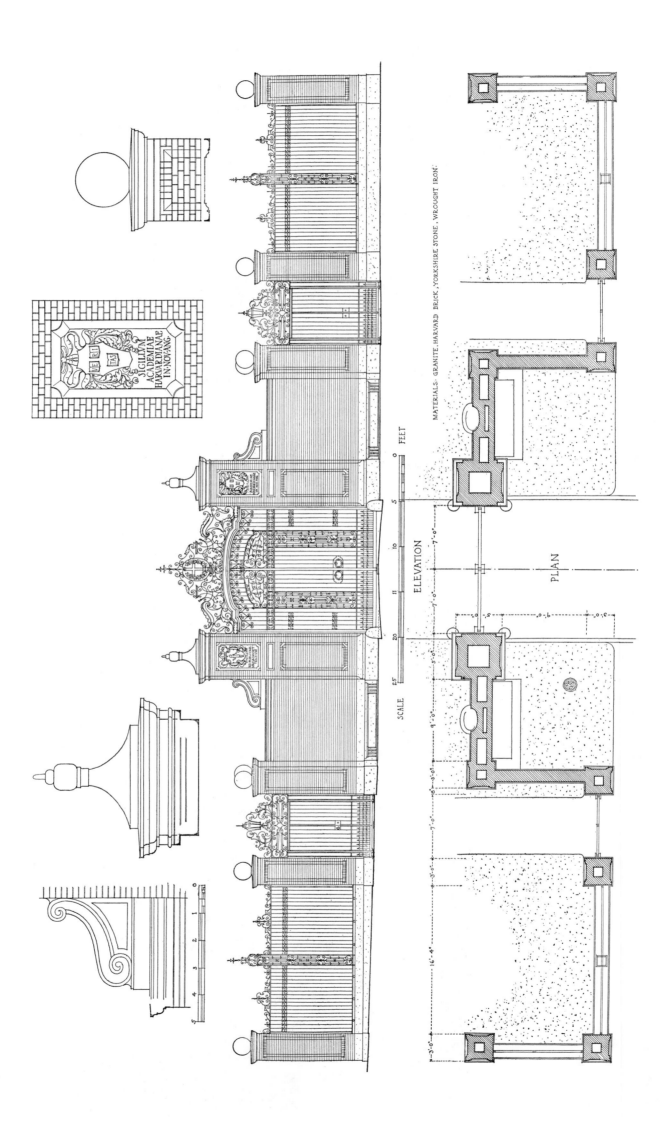

SIGILLVM
ACADEMIAE
HARVARDIANAE
IN·NOV·ANG·

MATERIALS:- GRANITE, HARVARD BRICK, YORKSHIRE STONE, WROUGHT IRON.

ELEVATION

PLAN

SCALE   FEET

JOHNSTON GATES, MAIN ENTRANCE HARVARD UNIVERSITY, CAMBRIDGE MASS.
1894

MCKIM, MEAD & WHITE

JOHNSTON GATES, HARVARD UNIVERSITY, CAMBRIDGE MASS.
1890

SHELTER AT CONEY ISLAND AVENUE ENTRANCE

SHELTER AT EASTERN PARKWAY ENTRANCE

ENTRANCES TO PROSPECT PARK, BROOKLYN, N. Y.
1890 - 1894

PLATE 21

McKIM, MEAD & WHITE

PERGOLA AT 15 TH ST. ENTRANCE.

DETAIL AT CONEY ISLAND AVENUE ENTRANCE

PEDESTAL AND SEAT AT CONEY ISLAND AVENUE ENTRANCE, BRONZE GROUP BY FREDERICK MAC MONNIES.

ENTRANCES TO PROSPECT PARK BROOKLYN, N. Y.
1890

ELEVATION
NEW YORK LIFE INSURANCE COMPANY, BUILDING, KANSAS CITY, MO.
1890

CHANCEL AND CHOIR SCREEN

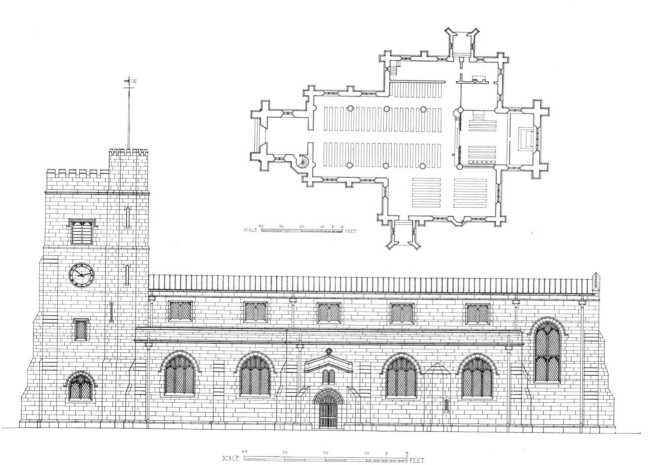

PLAN AND ELEVATION OF ORIGINAL SCHEME

ST. PETER'S CHURCH, MORRISTOWN, N. J.
1890

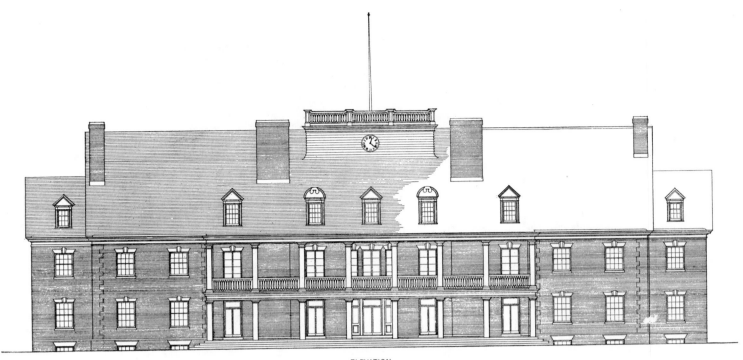

ELEVATION

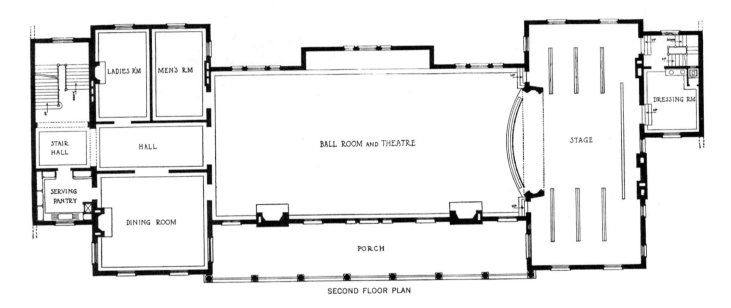

SECOND FLOOR PLAN

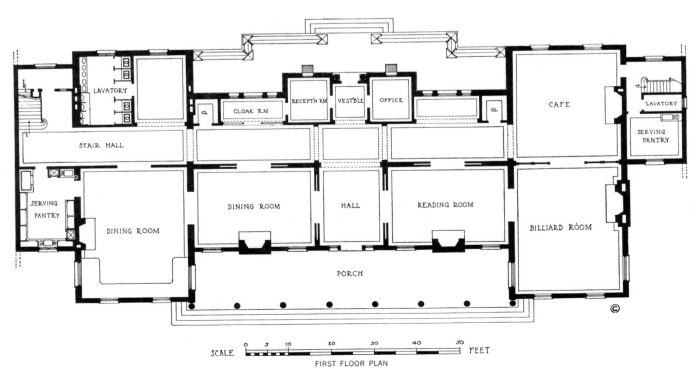

FIRST FLOOR PLAN

GERMANTOWN CRICKET CLUB, PHILADELPHIA, PA.
1891

FACADE TOWARD PLAYING FIELD

MAIN ENTRANCE GATES

GERMANTOWN CRICKET CLUB, PHILADELPHIA, PA.
1891

PLATE 26

McKIM, MEAD & WHITE

DETAIL OF ENTRANCE

GERMANTOWN CRICKET CLUB, PHILADELPHIA, PA.
1891

MANTEL IN DINING ROOM

PLATE 27

MCKIM, MEAD & WHITE

CENTURY CLUB, NEW YORK CITY.
1891

PLATE 28

McKIM, MEAD & WHITE

·FRONT·ELEVATION·

SCALE

FEET

CENTURY CLUB, NEW YORK CITY.
1889

MDCCCLXXXIX

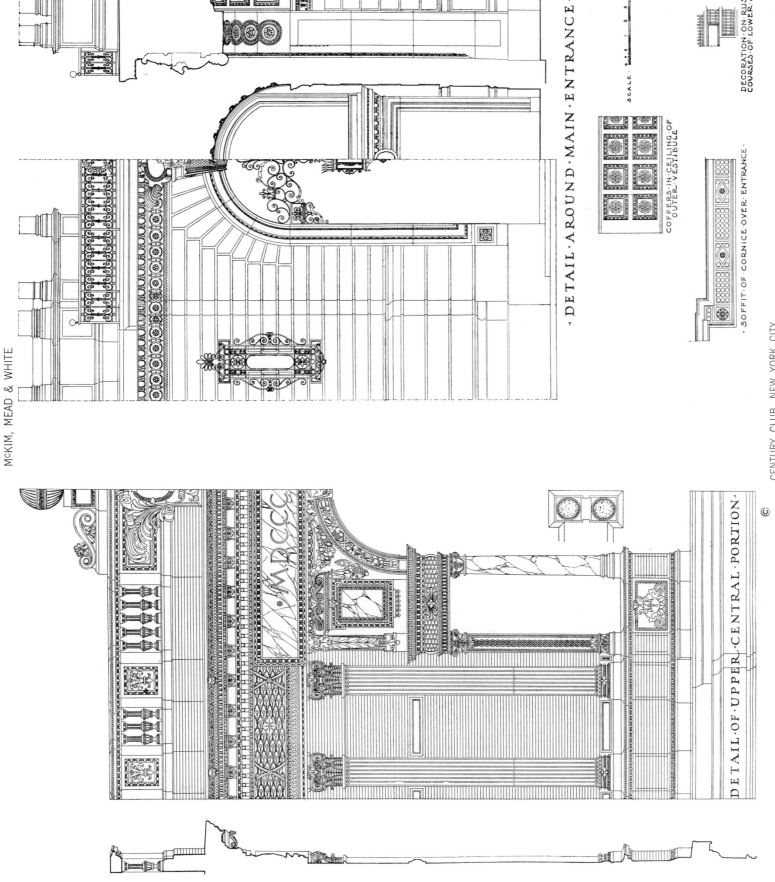

PLATE 29

McKIM, MEAD & WHITE

· DETAIL · AROUND · MAIN · ENTRANCE ·

· DETAIL · OF · UPPER · CENTRAL · PORTION ·

COFFERS · IN · CEILING · OF
OUTER · VESTIBULE

· SOFFIT · OF · CORNICE · OVER · ENTRANCE ·

DECORATION · ON · RUSTICATED
COURSES · OF · LOWER · STORIES

SCALE.

FEET

CENTURY CLUB, NEW YORK CITY.

1889

MDCCC

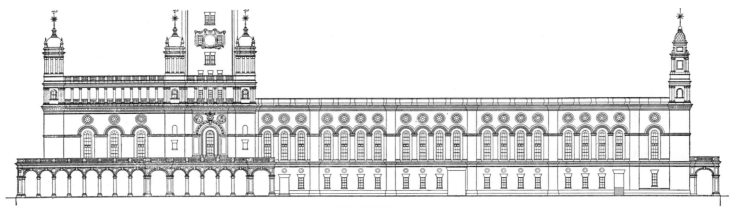

TWENTY-SIXTH STREET ELEVATION

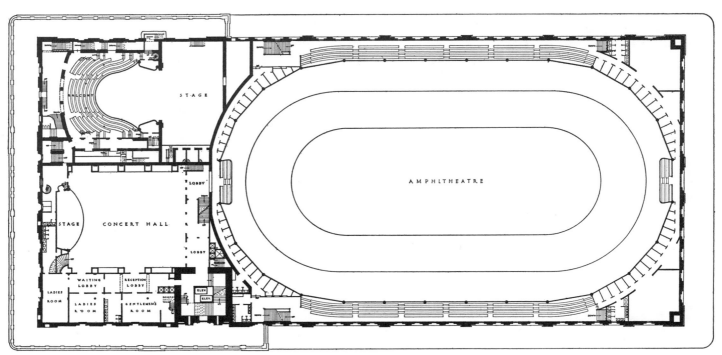

BALCONY FLOOR PLAN

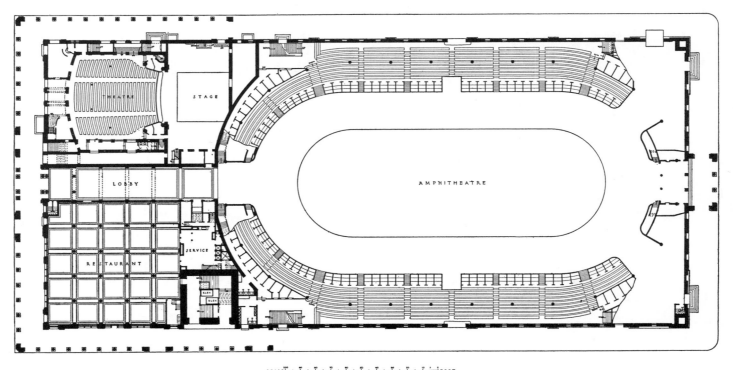

SCALE _____ IN FEET

GROUND FLOOR PLAN

MADISON SQUARE GARDEN, NEW YORK CITY.

1891

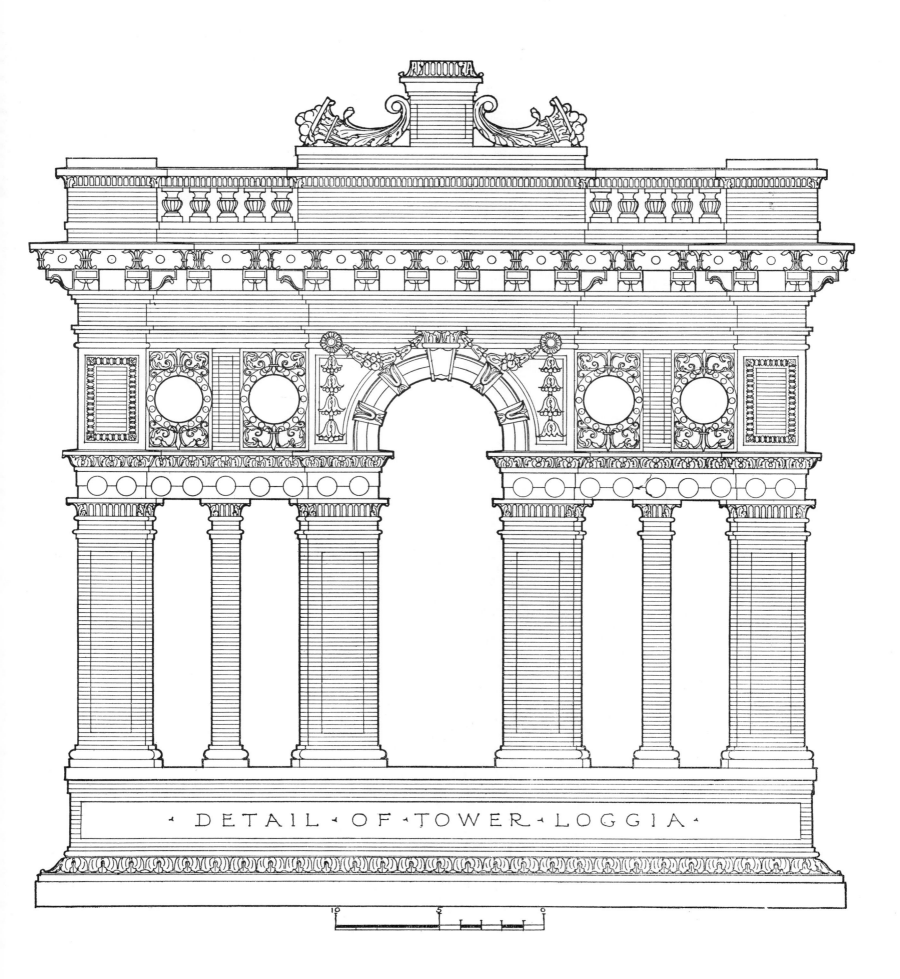

· D E T A I L · O F · T O W E R · L O G G I A ·

PLATE 31 - 31 A

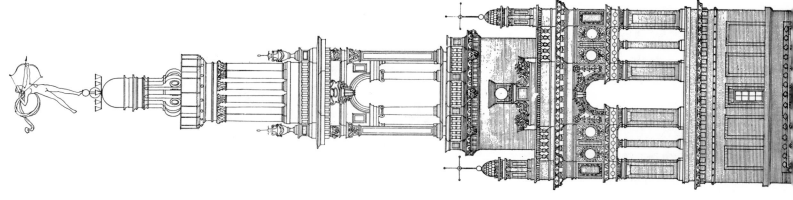

MCKIM, MEAD & WHITE

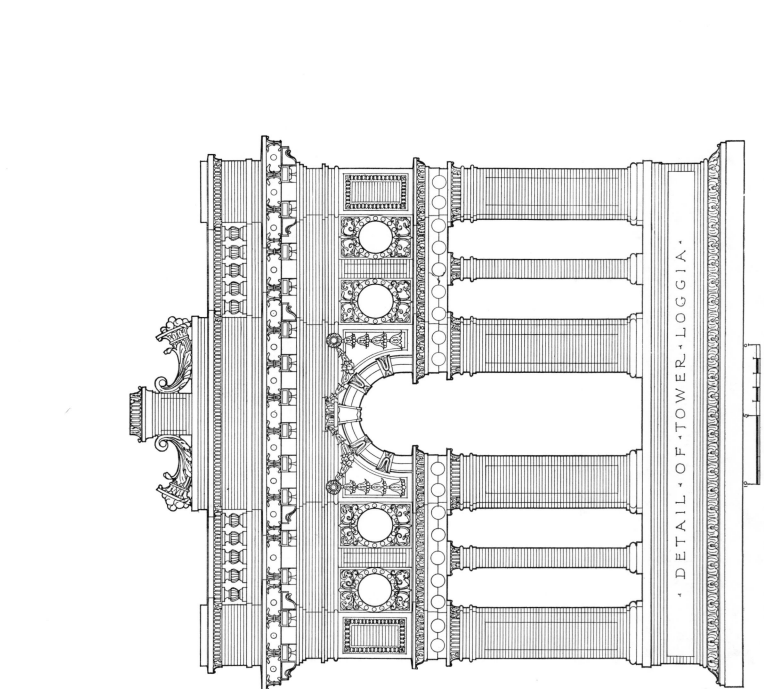

· DETAIL · OF · TOWER · LOGGIA ·

SCALE

FEET

MADISON AVENUE ELEVATION
MADISON SQUARE GARDEN, NEW YORK CITY.
1891

SOUTHWEST ANGLE FROM MADISON SQUARE
MADISON SQUARE GARDEN, NEW YORK CITY.
1891

PLATE 33

McKIM, MEAD & WHITE

ARCADE AT MAIN ENTRANCE

MADISON SQUARE GARDEN, NEW YORK CITY.

CENTRAL MOTIVE ON MADISON AVENUE ABOVE ENTRANCE

TERRA COTTA DETAILS OF LOWER ARCADE

MADISON SQUARE GARDEN, NEW YORK CITY.
1891

PLATE 35

McKIM, MEAD & WHITE

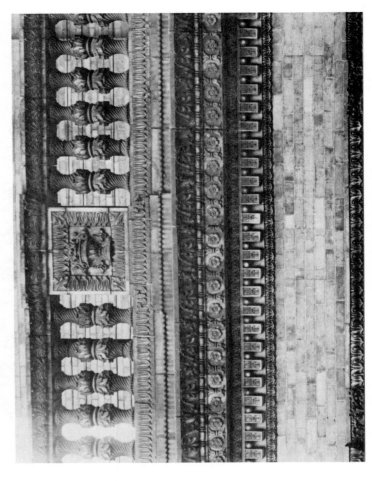

DETAILS OF LOWER ARCADE

MADISON SQUARE GARDEN, NEW YORK CITY.
1891

LOWER ARCADE

PLATE 36

McKIM, MEAD & WHITE

COLONNADE OF ROOF GARDEN

UPPER PART OF TOWER

MADISON SQUARE GARDEN, NEW YORK CITY.
1891

DETAILS OF TERRA COTTA AND BRICKWORK ON TOWER

MADISON SQUARE GARDEN, NEW YORK CITY.
1891

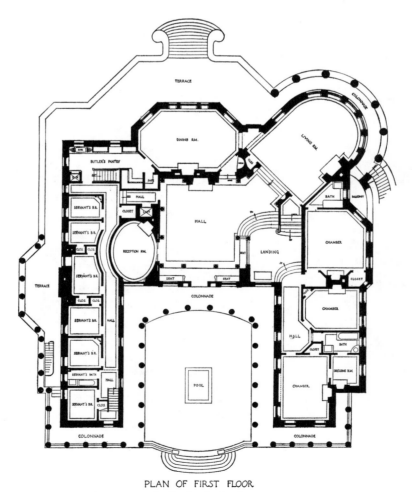

PLAN OF FIRST FLOOR

E. D. MORGAN RESIDENCE, NEWPORT, R. I.
1891

THE WASHINGTON ARCH, NEW YORK CITY.
1892

PLATE 40

MCKIM, MEAD & WHITE

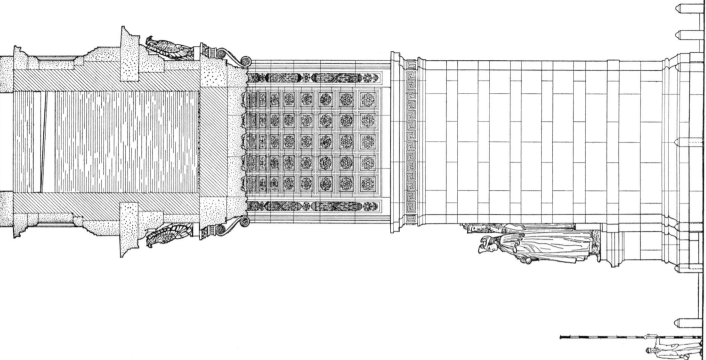

TO COMMEMORATE THE ONE HUNDREDTH ANNIVERSARY
OF THE INAUGURATION OF GEORGE WASHINGTON
AS FIRST PRESIDENT OF THE UNITED STATES

ERECTED BY THE PEOPLE OF THE CITY OF NEW YORK

SECTION

NORTH ELEVATION

THE WASHINGTON ARCH, NEW YORK CITY.

1892

PLATE 41-42

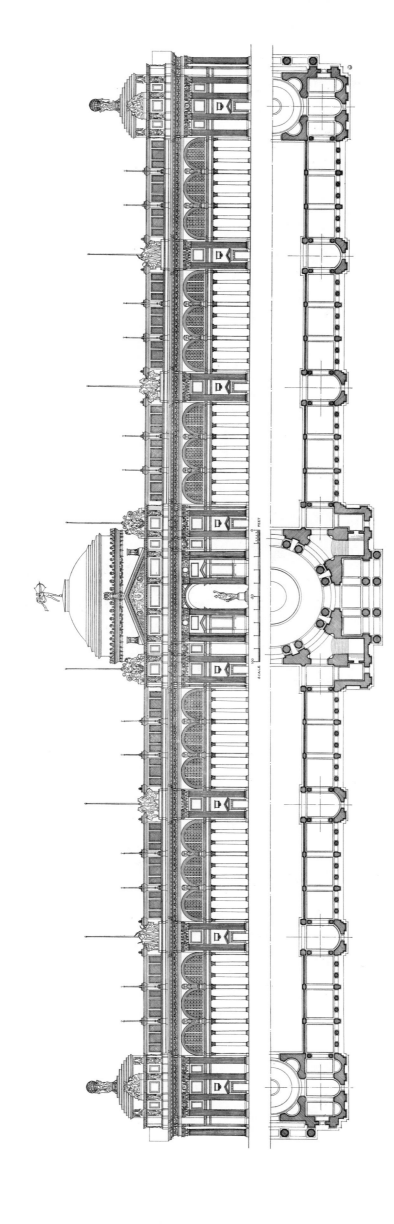

McKIM, MEAD & WHITE

AGRICULTURAL BUILDING, WORLD'S COLUMBIAN EXPOSITION, CHICAGO, ILLINOIS.
1893

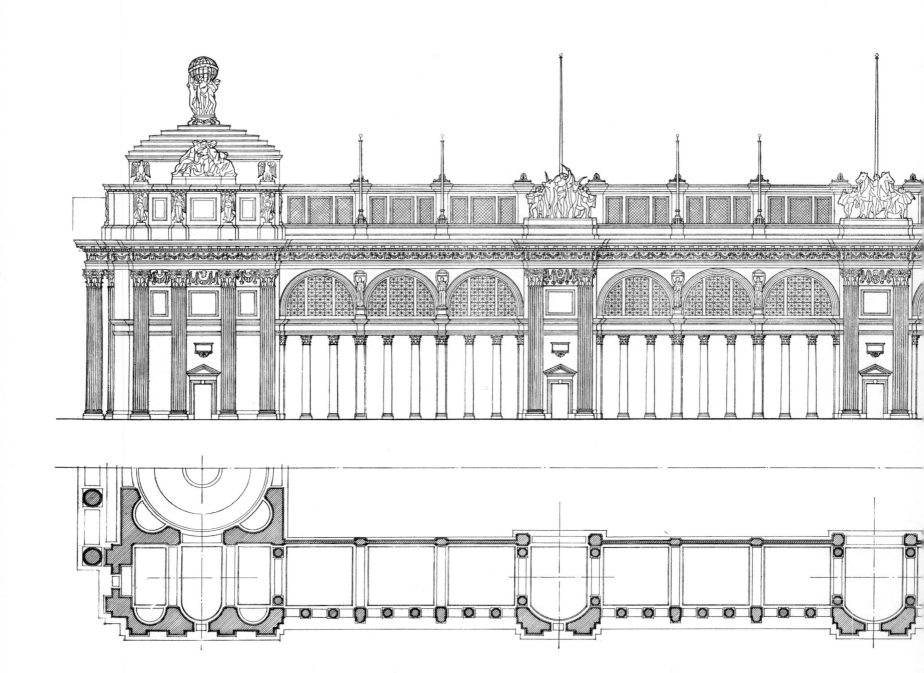

PLATE 41-42

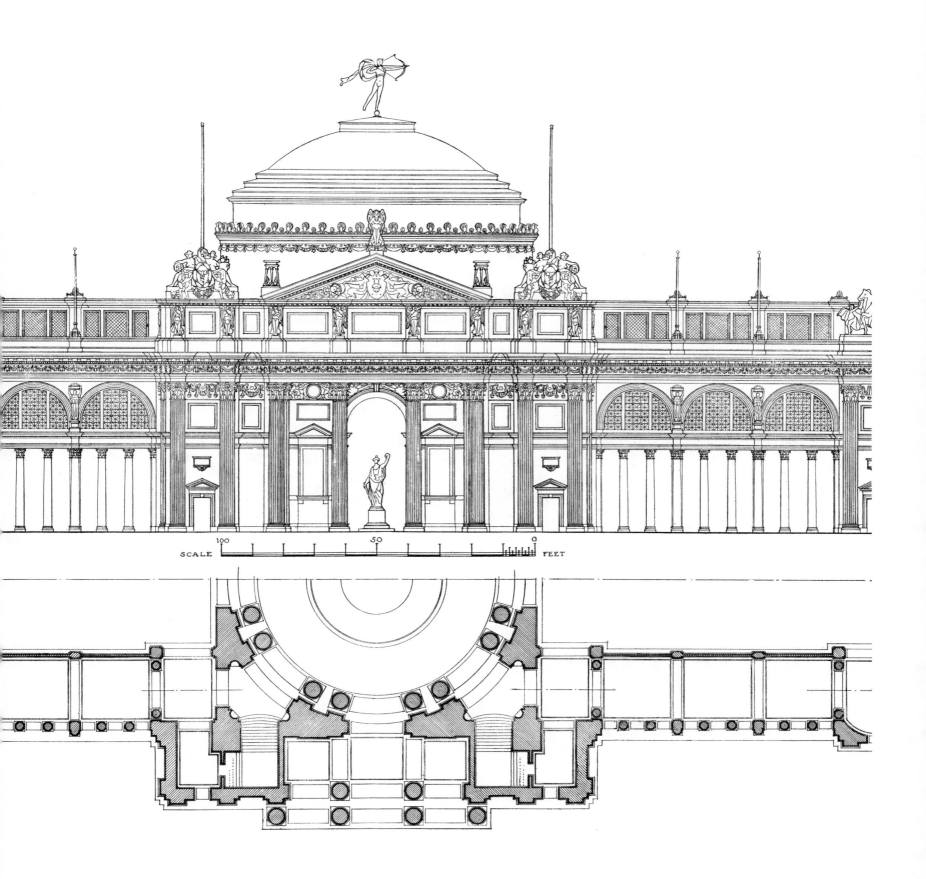

SCALE 100 50 0 FEET

PLATE 41-42

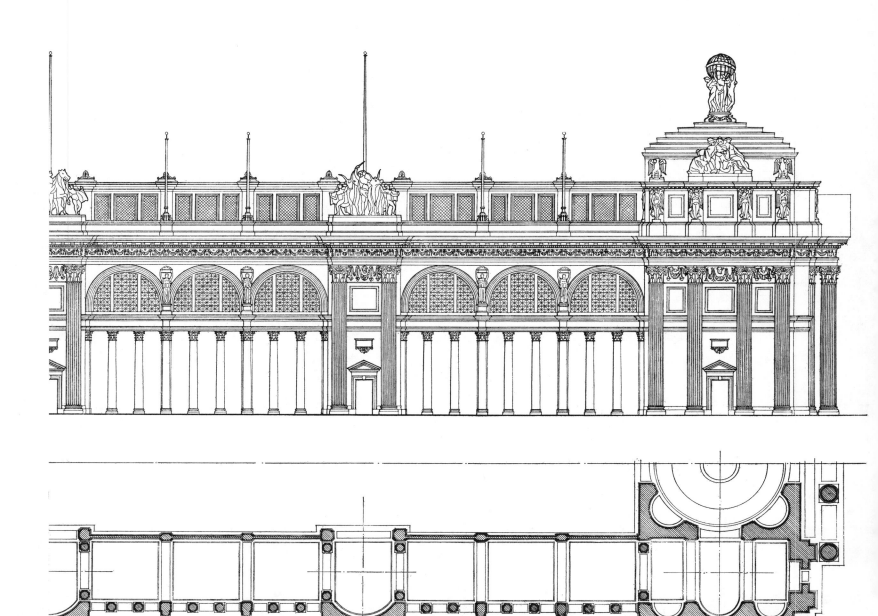

PLATE 43

McKIM, MEAD & WHITE

NEW YORK STATE BUILDING, WORLD'S COLUMBIAN EXPOSITION, CHICAGO, ILLINOIS.
1893

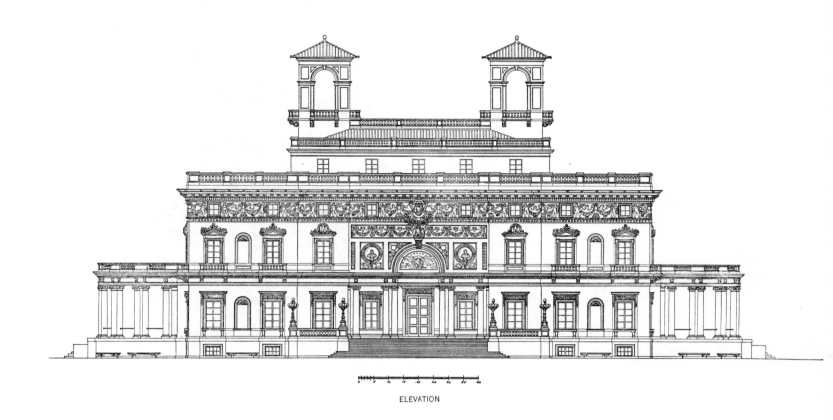

ELEVATION

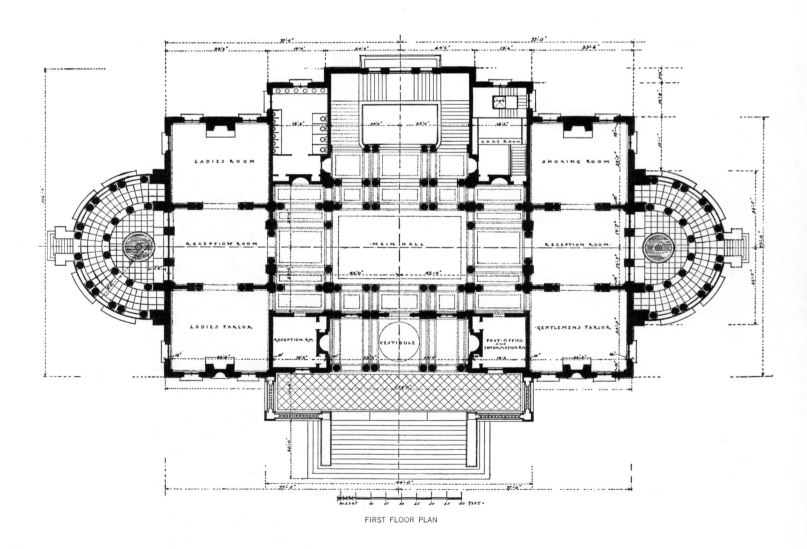

FIRST FLOOR PLAN

NEW YORK STATE BUILDING, WORLD'S FAIR, CHICAGO, ILLINOIS.
1893

WALKER ART BUILDING BOWDOIN COLLEGE, BRUNSWICK, ME.
1893

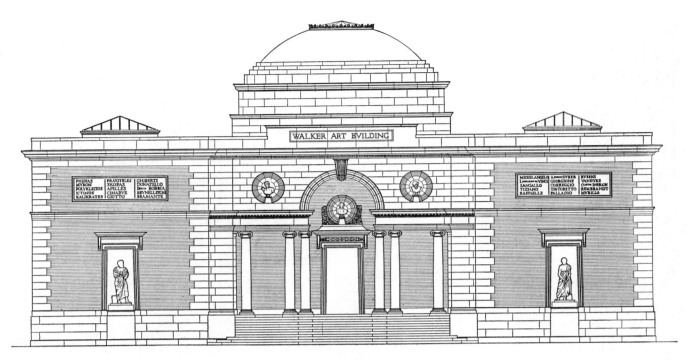

WALKER ART BVILDING

| PHIDIAS MYRON POLYKLEITOS ICTINOS KALIKRATES | PRAXITELES SKOPAS APELLES CIMABVE GIOTTO | GHIBERTI DONATELLO DELLA ROBBIA BRVNELLESCHI BRAMANTE |

| MICHELANGELO LIONARDO da VINCI SANZIO TIZIANO RAFFAELLE | A. DVRER GIORGIONE CORREGIO TINTORETTO PALLADIO | RVBENS VANDYKE CLAVDE LORRAIN REMBRANDT MVRILLO |

SCALE FEET

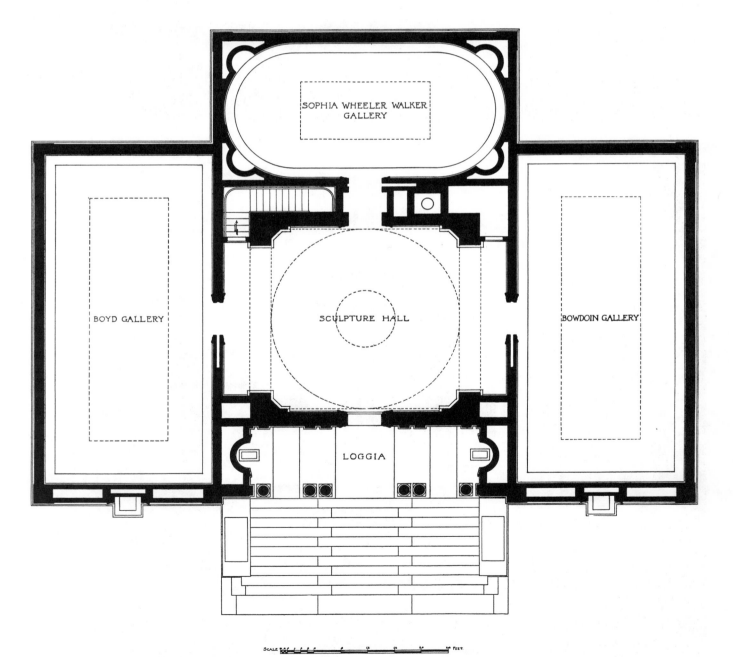

SOPHIA WHEELER WALKER GALLERY

BOYD GALLERY

SCULPTURE HALL

BOWDOIN GALLERY

LOGGIA

SCALE FEET

WALKER ART GALLERY, BOWDOIN COLLEGE, BRUNSWICK, MAINE.
1893

PLATE 47

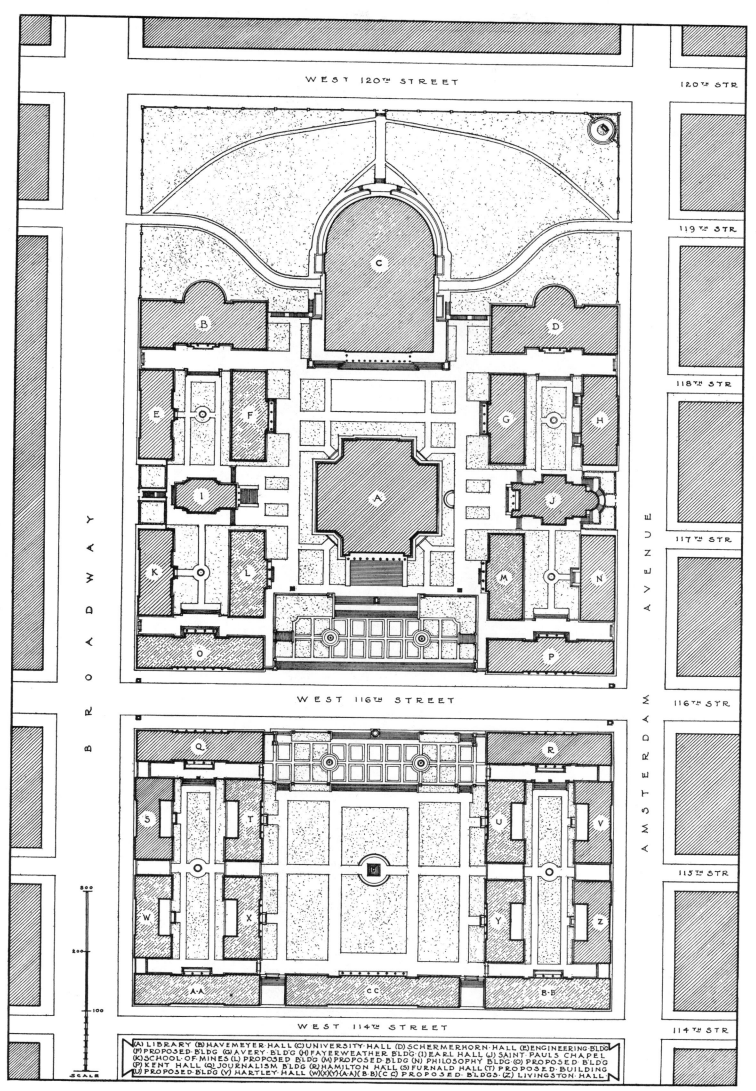

BLOCK PLAN
COLUMBIA UNIVERSITY, NEW YORK CITY.
1893

PLATE 48

MCKIM, MEAD & WHITE

COLUMBIA UNIVERSITY LIBRARY, NEW YORK CITY.
1893

PLATE 49

McKIM, MEAD & WHITE

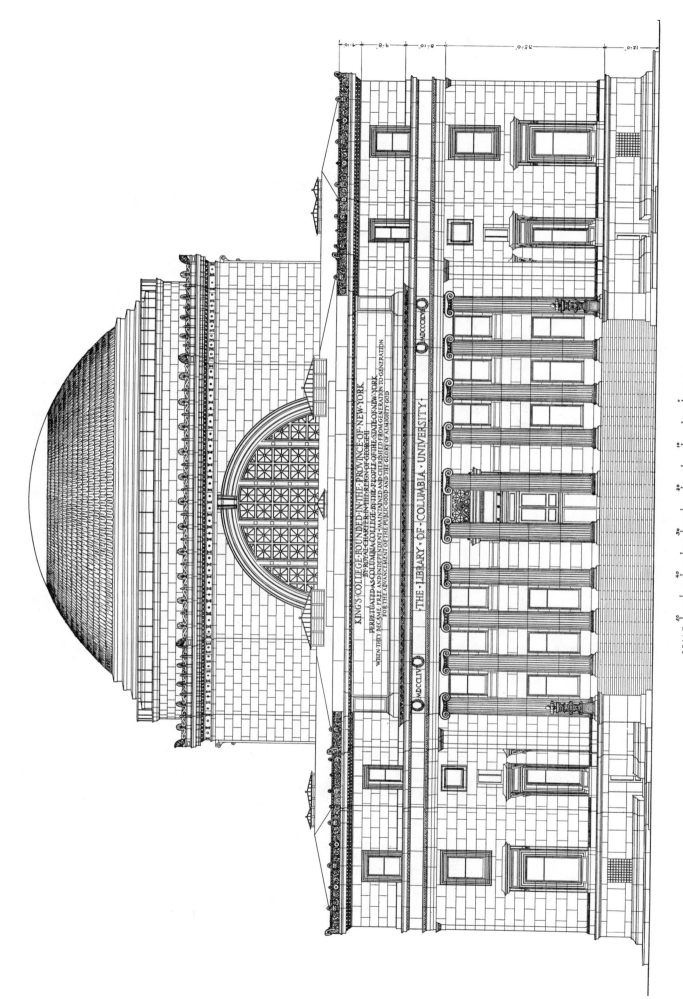

KING'S·COLLEGE·FOUNDED·IN·THE·PROVINCE·OF·NEW·YORK
BY·ROYAL·CHARTER·IN·THE·REIGN·OF·GEORGE·II·
PERPETUATED·AS·COLUMBIA·COLLEGE·BY·THE·PEOPLE·OF·THE·STATE·OF·NEW·YORK
WHEN·THEY·BECAME·FREE·AND·INDEPENDENT·MAINTAINED·AND·CHERISHED·FROM·GENERATION·TO·GENERATION
FOR·THE·ADVANCEMENT·OF·THE·PUBLIC·GOOD·AND·THE·GLORY·OF·ALMIGHTY·GOD

·THE·LIBRARY·OF·COLUMBIA·UNIVERSITY·

SCALE

SOUTH ELEVATION

FEET

COLUMBIA UNIVERSITY LIBRARY, NEW YORK CITY.
1893

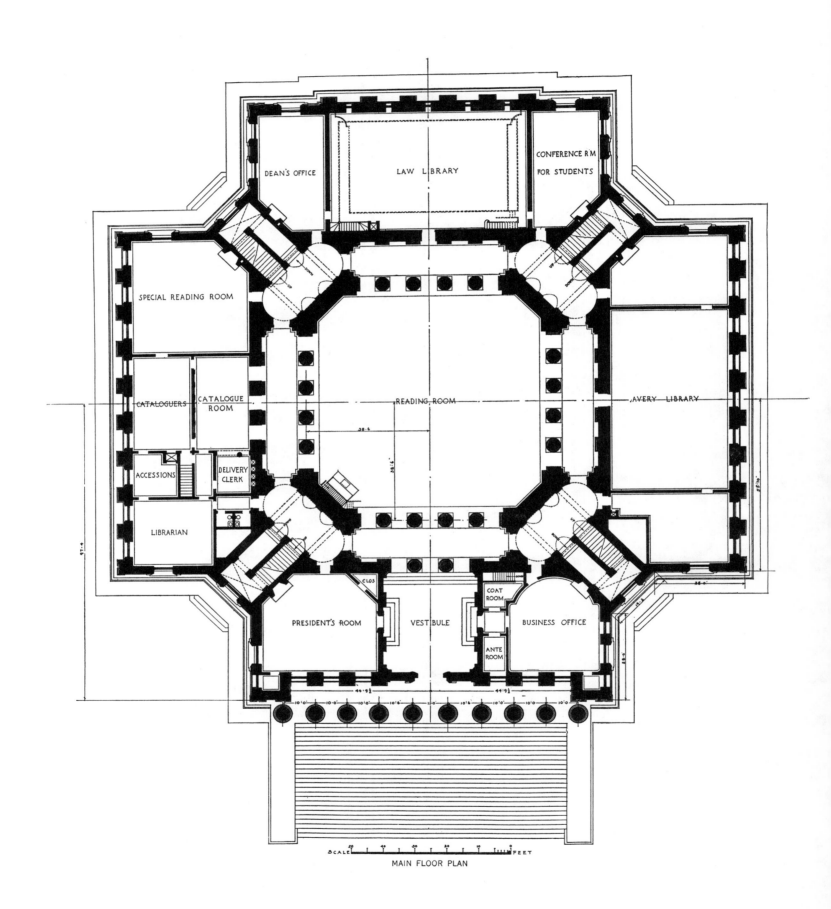

DEAN'S OFFICE

LAW LIBRARY

CONFERENCE R'M FOR STUDENTS

SPECIAL READING ROOM

CATALOGUERS

CATALOGUE ROOM

READING ROOM

AVERY LIBRARY

ACCESSIONS

DELIVERY CLERK

LIBRARIAN

CLOS.

COAT ROOM

PRESIDENT'S ROOM

VESTIBULE

BUSINESS OFFICE

ANTE ROOM

SCALE FEET

MAIN FLOOR PLAN

COLUMBIA UNIVERSITY LIBRARY, NEW YORK CITY.
1893

UPPER·CHENEAU

MDCCL

DETAILS
OF·THE
SOUTH
PORTICO

SIDE·WINDOWS
FIRST·STORY

PLATE 52

McKIM, MEAD & WHITE

VESTIBULE

GENERAL VIEW READING ROOM

COLUMBIA UNIVERSITY LIBRARY, NEW YORK CITY.
1893

McKIM, MEAD & WHITE

PLATE 53

DETAIL IN READING ROOM

TRUSTEES ROOM

COLUMBIA UNIVERSITY LIBRARY, NEW YORK CITY.
1893

BRONZE CAPITALS

ASCUTNEY·GREEN·GRANITE·SHAFTS

OPEN

ORNAMENT →

← ORNAMENT →

← ORNAMENT

LIMESTONE

BELGIAN BLACK MARBLE BASE

BROWN·NUMIDIAN·MARBLE

WROUGHT IRON GATES

CONTINUE →

OPEN

CENTRE OF ROOM

FLOOR LINE

FEET

DETAILS OF READING ROOM
COLUMBIA UNIVERSITY LIBRARY. NEW YORK CITY.
1893

ENTRANCE DOORWAY

JUDSON MEMORIAL CHURCH, WASHINGTON SQUARE, NEW YORK CITY.
1893

‹ DETAIL OF MAIN ENTRANCE ‹

‹ SECTION ‹

SCALE |⊢⊢⊢⊢⊢⊢⊢⊢⊢⊢⊢⊢⊢| FEET

JUDSON MEMORIAL CHURCH, WASHINGTON SQUARE, NEW YORK CITY.
1893

PLATE 57

MCKIM, MEAD & WHITE

THE METROPOLITAN CLUB, NEW YORK CITY.
1894

PLATE 58

MCKIM, MEAD & WHITE

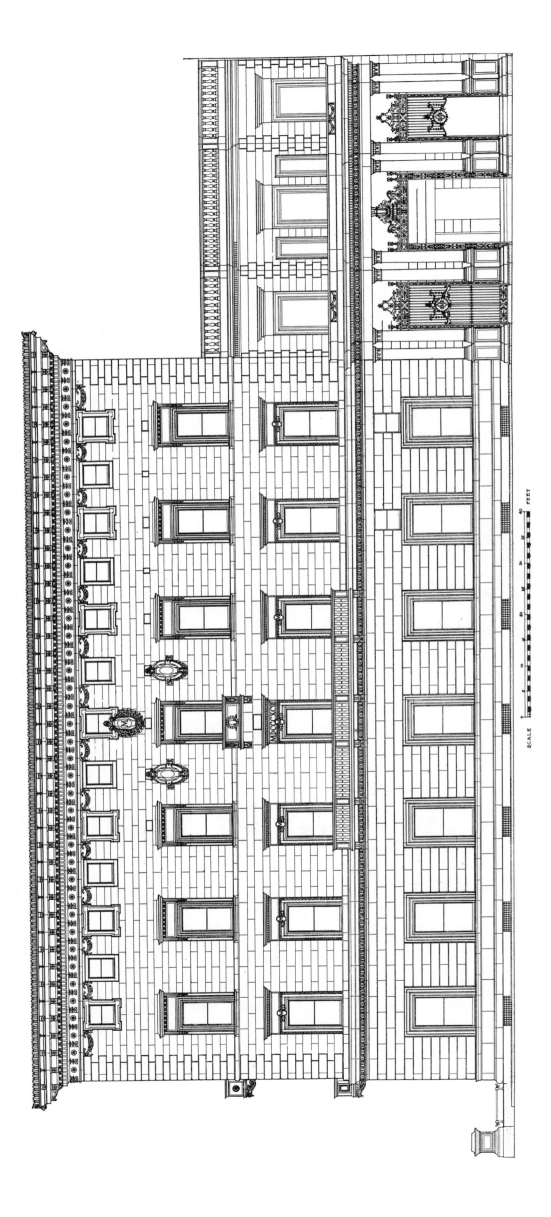

SCALE

FEET

SIXTIETH STREET ELEVATION

METROPOLITAN CLUB, NEW YORK CITY.
1894

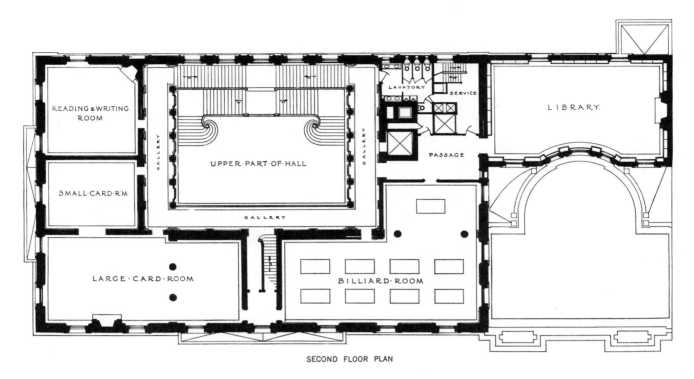

SECOND FLOOR PLAN

METROPOLITAN CLUB NEW YORK CITY.

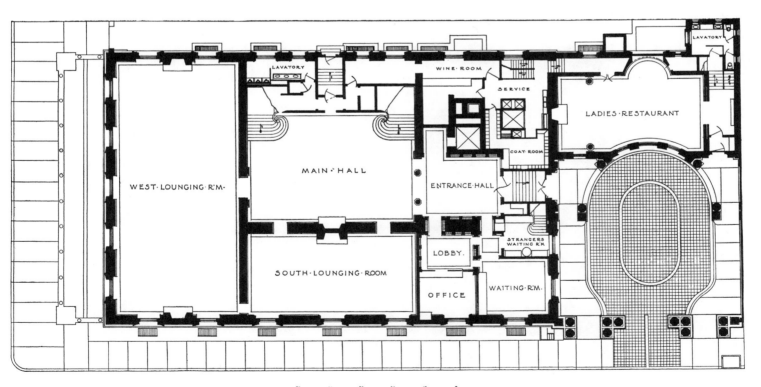

FIRST FLOOR PLAN

METROPOLITAN CLUB, NEW YORK CITY.
1894

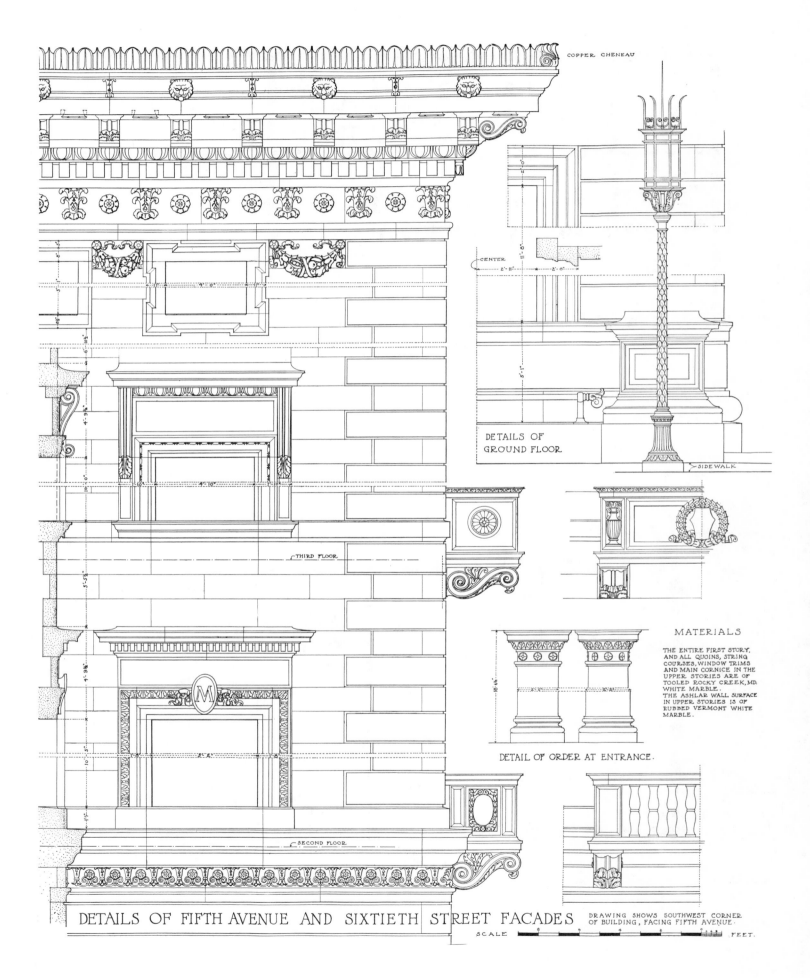

COPPER CHENEAU

DETAILS OF
GROUND FLOOR

SIDEWALK

THIRD FLOOR

MATERIALS

THE ENTIRE FIRST STORY,
AND ALL QUOINS, STRING
COURSES, WINDOW TRIMS
AND MAIN CORNICE IN THE
UPPER STORIES ARE OF
TOOLED ROCKY CREEK, MD.
WHITE MARBLE.
THE ASHLAR WALL SURFACE
IN UPPER STORIES IS OF
RUBBED VERMONT WHITE
MARBLE.

DETAIL OF ORDER AT ENTRANCE.

SECOND FLOOR

DETAILS OF FIFTH AVENUE AND SIXTIETH STREET FACADES

DRAWING SHOWS SOUTHWEST CORNER
OF BUILDING, FACING FIFTH AVENUE.

SCALE   FEET.

METROPOLITAN CLUB, NEW YORK CITY.
1894

ENTRANCE GATEWAY

MAIN HALL

METROPOLITAN CLUB, NEW YORK CITY.
1894

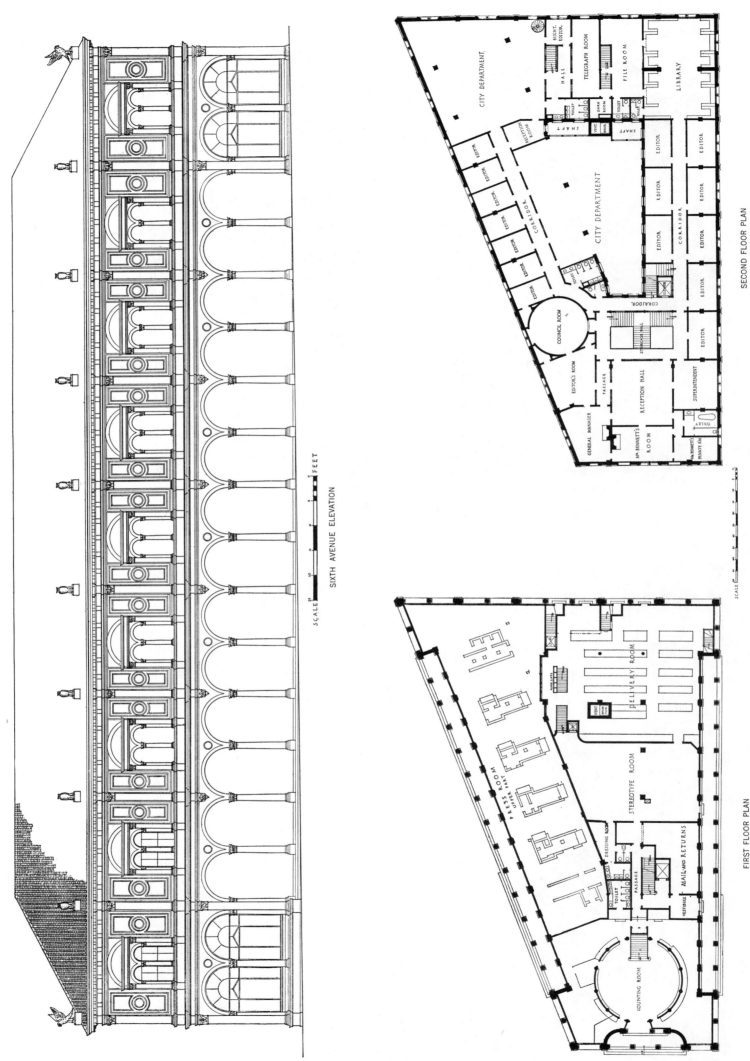

PLATE 62

McKIM, MEAD & WHITE

SIXTH AVENUE ELEVATION

SCALE

FEET

SECOND FLOOR PLAN

CITY DEPARTMENT

NIGHT EDITOR

TELEGRAPH ROOM

FILE ROOM

LIBRARY

HALL

TOILET

DARK ROOM

TOILET

SHAFT

SHAFT

SHAFT

RECEPTION ROOM

EDITOR

EDITOR

EDITOR

EDITOR

EDITOR

EDITOR

EDITOR

EDITOR

EDITOR

EDITOR

EDITOR

EDITOR

EDITOR

EDITOR

CORRIDOR

CORRIDOR

CORRIDOR

CITY DEPARTMENT

COUNCIL ROOM

STAIRCASE HALL

EDITOR'S ROOM

PASSAGE

RECEPTION HALL

SUPERINTENDENT

GENERAL MANAGER

MR. BENNETT'S ROOM

MR. BENNETT'S PRIVATE R.M.

TOILET

TOILET

NEW YORK HERALD BUILDING, NEW YORK CITY.
1894

SCALE

FIRST FLOOR PLAN

PRESS ROOM

PRESS FAST UPPER PART

DELIVERY ROOM

VENT

STEREOTYPE ROOM

DRESSING ROOM

MAIL AND RETURNS

TOILET

PASSAGE

VESTIBULE

COUNTING ROOM

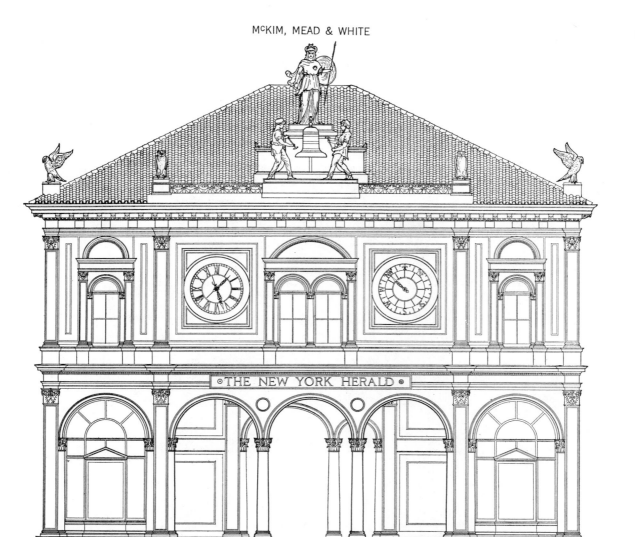

THE NEW YORK HERALD

SOUTH ELEVATION

SCALE [____] FEET

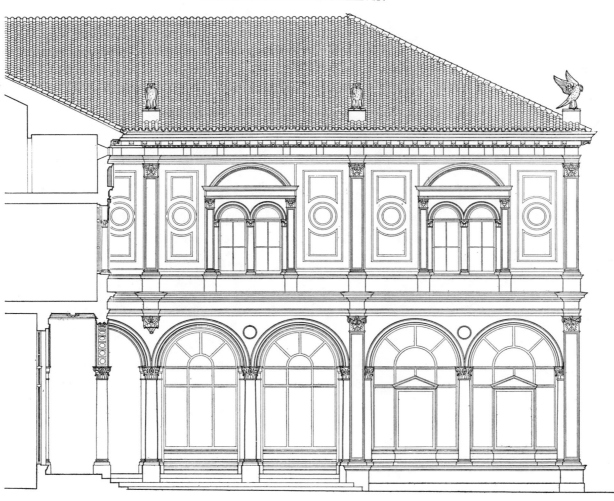

DETAIL OF BROADWAY FACADE
NEW YORK HERALD BUILDING, NEW YORK CITY.
1894

PLATE 64

MCKIM, MEAD & WHITE

NEW YORK HERALD BUILDING, NEW YORK CITY.
1894

McKIM, MEAD & WHITE

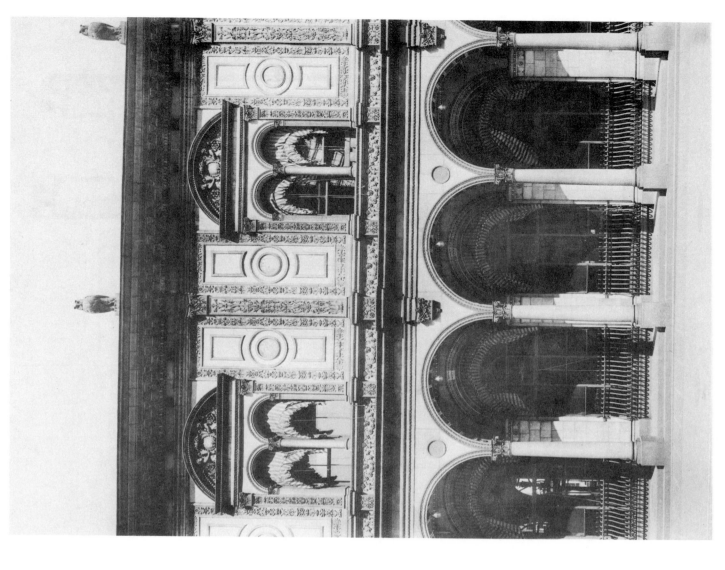

DETAIL OF BROADWAY FACADE

NEW YORK HERALD BUILDING, NEW YORK CITY.
1894

DETAIL OF ENTRANCE

PLATE 66

MCKIM, MEAD & WHITE

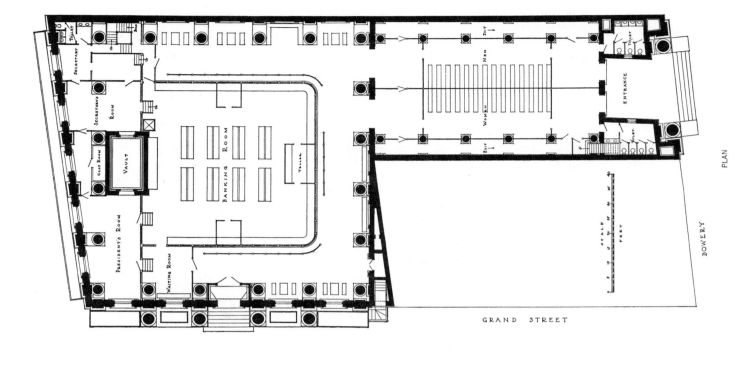

PLAN

GRAND STREET

BOWERY

SCALE FEET

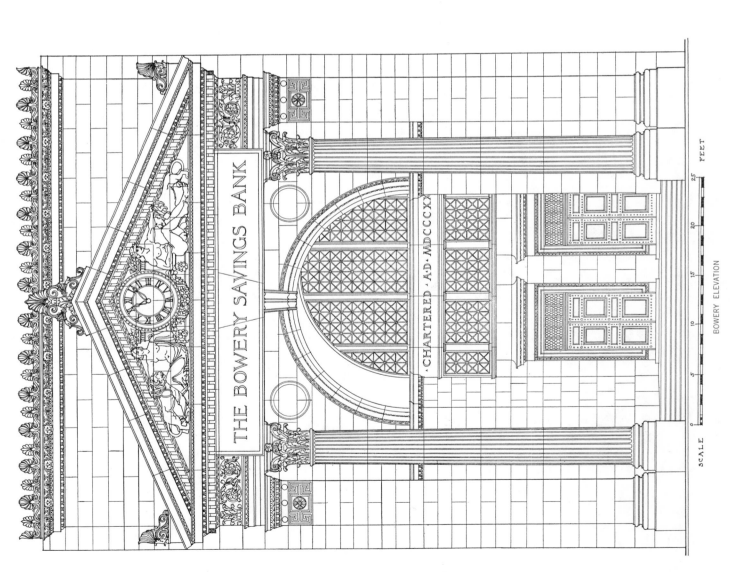

THE BOWERY SAVINGS BANK

CHARTERED · A·D· MDCCCXX

BOWERY ELEVATION

SCALE FEET

THE BOWERY SAVINGS BANK, NEW YORK CITY.
1895

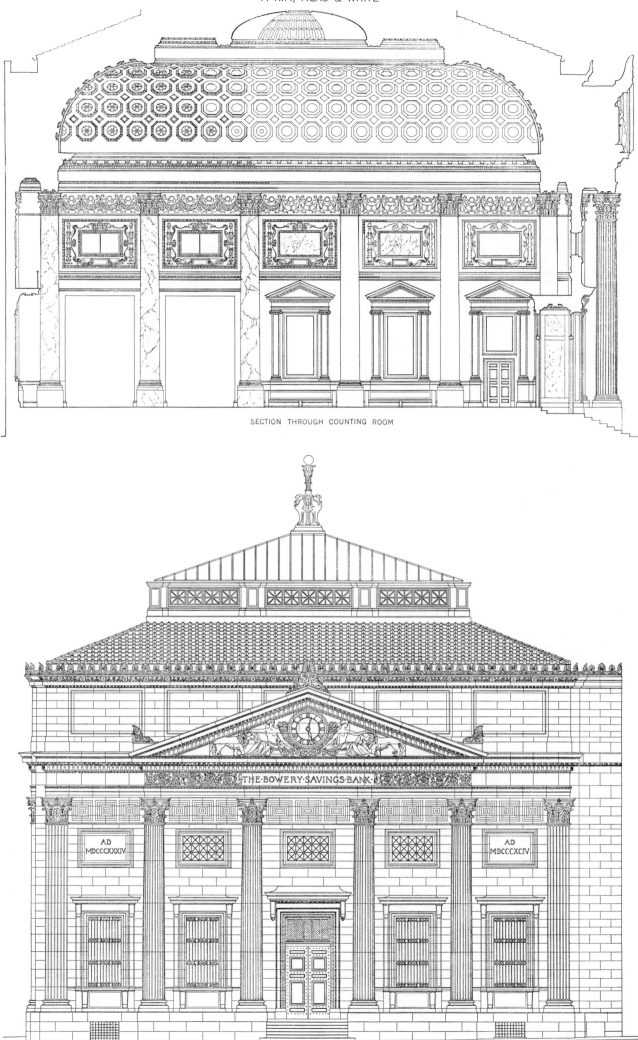

SECTION THROUGH COUNTING ROOM

AD
MDCCCXXXIV

THE·BOWERY·SAVINGS·BANK·

AD
MDCCCXCIV

SCALE

GRAND STREET ELEVATION
THE BOWERY SAVINGS BANK, NEW YORK CITY.
1895

GRAND STREET FACADE

INTERIOR OF BANKING ROOM

THE BOWERY SAVINGS BANK, NEW YORK CITY.
1895

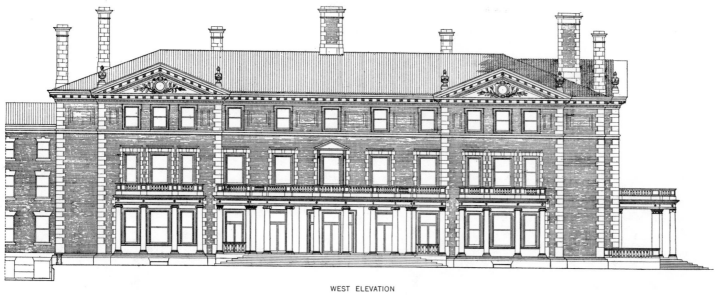

WEST ELEVATION

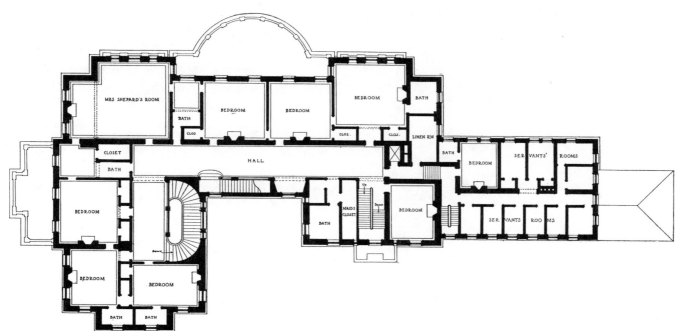

SECOND FLOOR PLAN

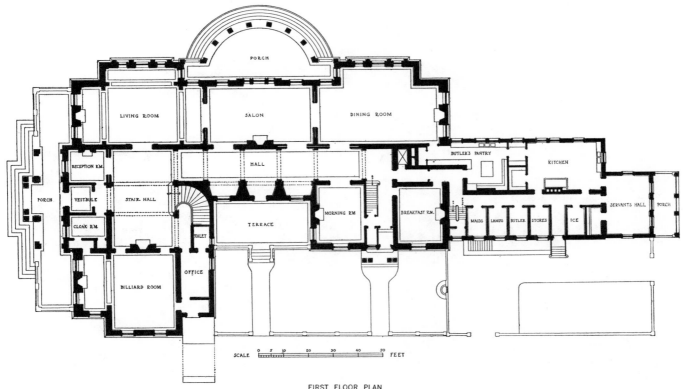

FIRST FLOOR PLAN

ELLIOTT F. SHEPARD RESIDENCE, SCARBOROUGH, N. Y.

1895

GENERAL VIEW FROM NORTHWEST

FACADE TOWARD HUDSON RIVER

ELLIOTT F. SHEPARD RESIDENCE, SCARBOROUGH, N. Y.
1895

PLATE 71

MCKIM, MEAD & WHITE

VIEWS AND DETAILS IN GARDEN

ELLIOTT F. SHEPARD RESIDENCE, SCARBOROUGH, N. Y.
1895

PLATE 72

MCKIM, MEAD & WHITE

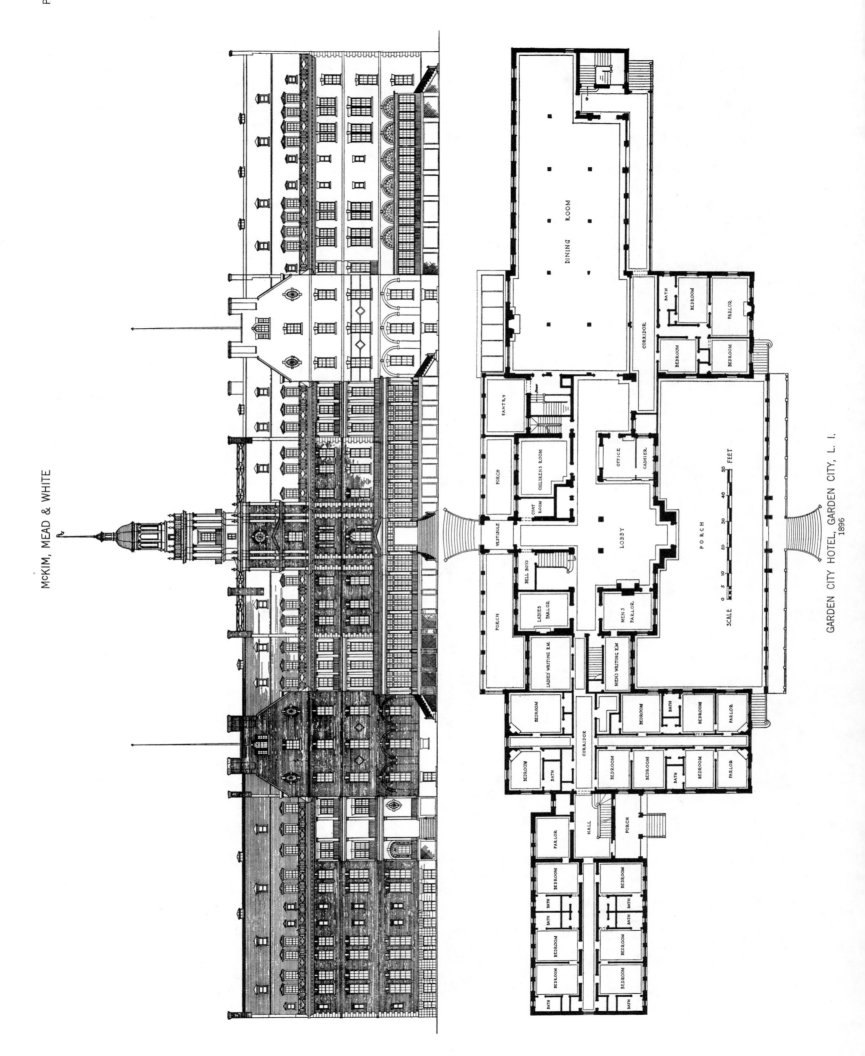

GARDEN CITY HOTEL, GARDEN CITY, L. I.
1896

PLATE 73

MCKIM, MEAD & WHITE

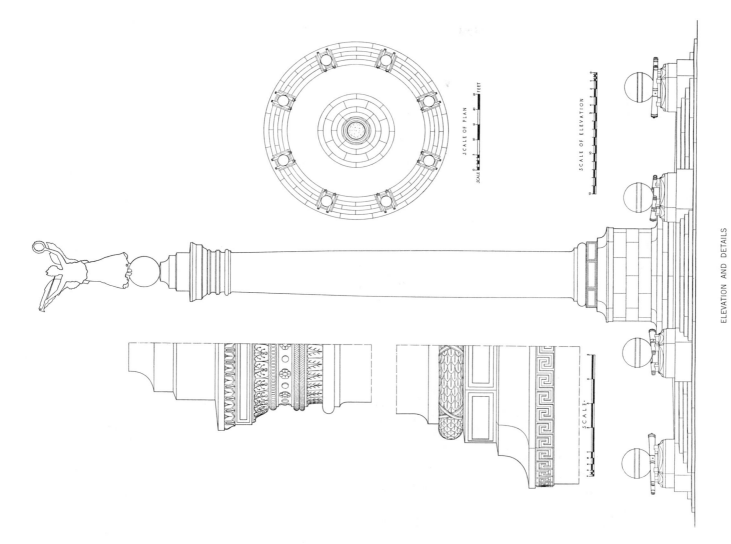

ELEVATION AND DETAILS

SCALE OF PLAN

SCALE OF ELEVATION

SCALE

THE BATTLE MONUMENT, WEST POINT, N. Y.
1896

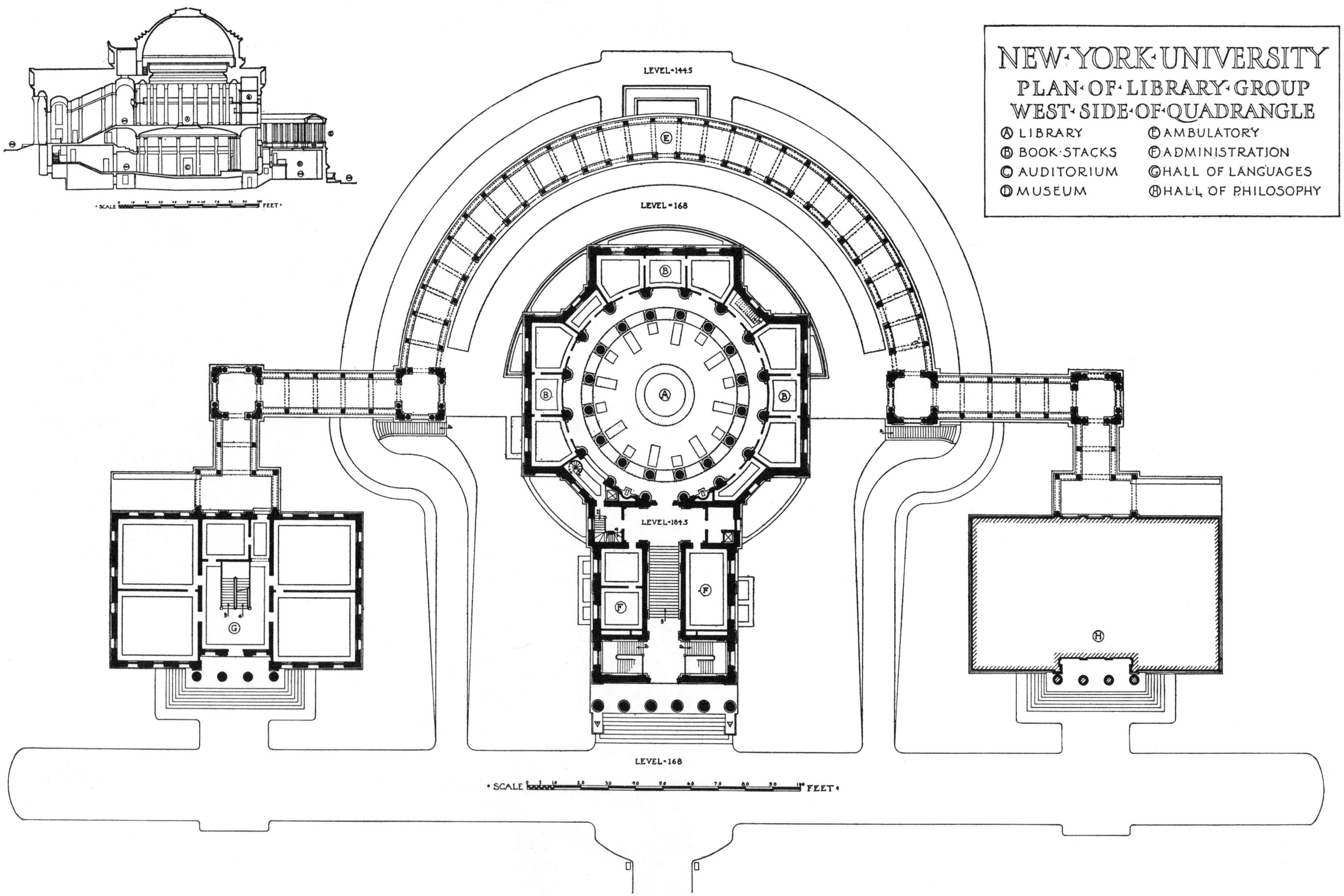

PLATE 74

McKIM, MEAD & WHITE

NEW·YORK·UNIVERSITY
PLAN·OF·LIBRARY·GROUP
WEST·SIDE·OF·QUADRANGLE

Ⓐ LIBRARY   Ⓔ AMBULATORY
Ⓑ BOOK·STACKS   Ⓕ ADMINISTRATION
Ⓒ AUDITORIUM   Ⓖ HALL OF LANGUAGES
Ⓓ MUSEUM   Ⓗ HALL OF PHILOSOPHY

LEVEL·144·5

LEVEL·168

LEVEL·184·5

LEVEL·168

· FEET ·

· SCALE ·

NEW YORK UNIVERSITY, NEW YORK CITY.
1896

PLATE 75

McKIM, MEAD & WHITE

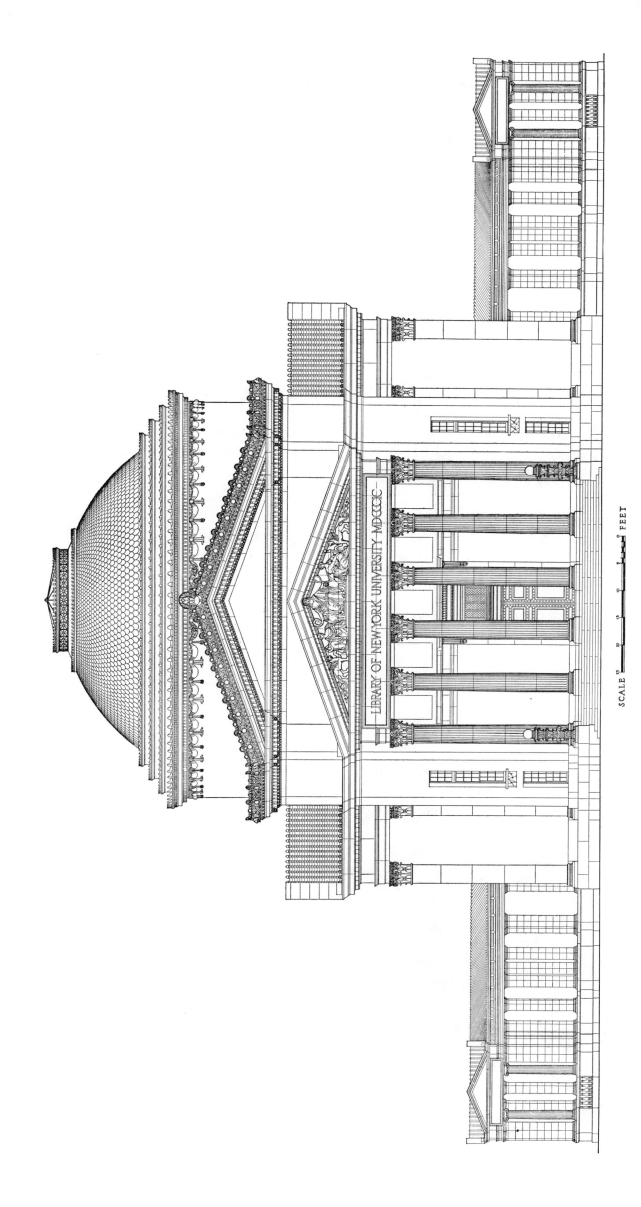

LIBRARY OF NEW YORK UNIVERSITY MDCCCC

SCALE

FEET

NEW YORK UNIVERSITY, NEW YORK CITY.
1896

PLATE 77

McKIM, MEAD & WHITE

PORTICO OF LIBRARY

READING ROOM IN LIBRARY

NEW YORK UNIVERSITY, NEW YORK CITY.
1896

FACADE TOWARD GARDEN

ENTRANCE FRONT

ROBERT W. CUMMING RESIDENCE, NEWARK, N. J.
1896

PLATE 80

MAIN CORNICE DETAIL

SECOND FLOOR PLAN

SERVICE

DINING ROOM

HALL

LIBRARY

DRAWING ROOM

FIRST FLOOR PLAN

SCULLERY

KITCHEN

SERVANTS HALL

HALL

BUTLER

RECEPTION ROOM

MAIN HALL

LAV.

VESTIBULE

DEN

LAV.

GARDEN

SCALE OF PLANS

FEET

McKIM, MEAD & WHITE

MAIN ENTRANCE DETAIL

SCALE

FEET

SOUTH ELEVATION

SCALE

FEET

H. A. C. TAYLOR, RESIDENCE, NEW YORK CITY.

1896

PLATE 81

McKIM, MEAD & WHITE

SECOND STORY HALL

FACADE ON 71ST STREET

H. A. C. TAYLOR RESIDENCE, NEW YORK CITY.
1896

LIBRARY

DINING ROOM

H. A. C. TAYLOR RESIDENCE, NEW YORK CITY.
1896

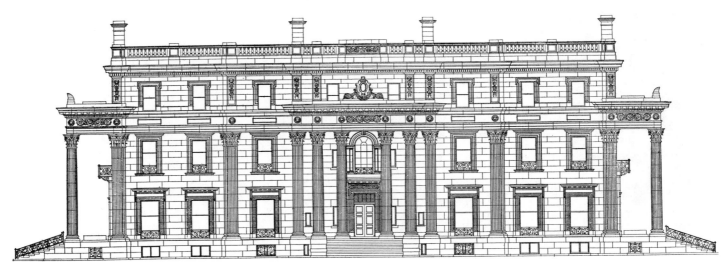

ELEVATION

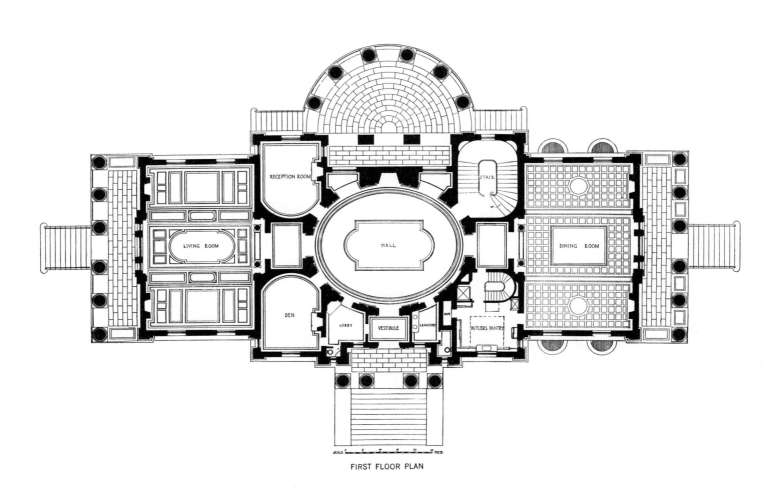

FIRST FLOOR PLAN

FREDERICK W. VANDERBILT RESIDENCE
HYDE PARK, N. Y.
1896

EAST FACADE

VIEW FROM NORTHWEST

F. W. VANDERBILT RESIDENCE, HYDE PARK, N. Y.
1896

PLATE 85

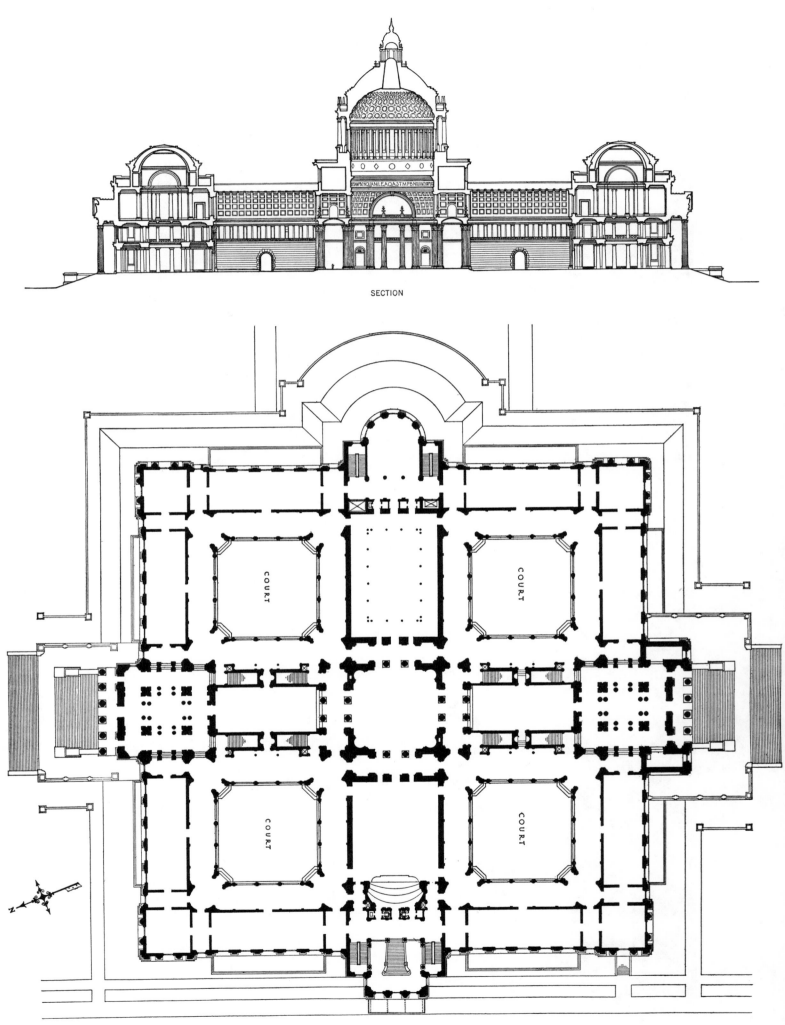

SECTION

·COMPLETE BLOCK PLAN·

SCALE

THE BROOKLYN INSTITUTE OF ARTS AND SCIENCES.
BEGUN 1897

PLATE 86

McKIM, MEAD & WHITE

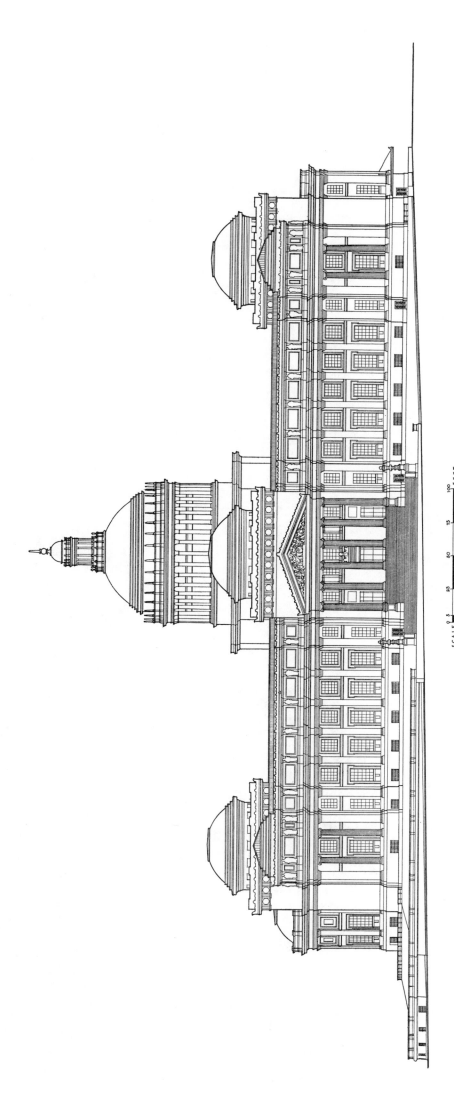

SCALE

NORTH ELEVATION OF COMPLETED SCHEME

BROOKLYN INSTITUTE OF ARTS & SCIENCES.
BEGUN 1897

PLATE 87

McKIM, MEAD & WHITE

NORTH FACADE
THE BROOKLYN INSTITUTE OF ARTS AND SCIENCES.
BEGUN 1897

PLATE 88

McKIM, MEAD & WHITE

DETAIL OF NORTH FACADE

CENTRAL PORTICO, NORTH ELEVATION

THE BROOKLYN INSTITUTE OF ARTS & SCIENCES.
1897

BASE OF DOME

ACROTERION
AT APEX
OF PEDIMENT

UPPER CORNICE
CENTRAL PORTION

SOFFIT OF ABOVE CORNICE

MAIN ENTRANCE
DOORWAY

DETAILS OF
NORTH PORTICO

SCALE

MATERIAL~INDIANA LIMESTONE

BRONZE

GRANITE

EXTERIOR DETAILS
BROOKLYN INSTITUTE OF ARTS & SCIENCES.
1897

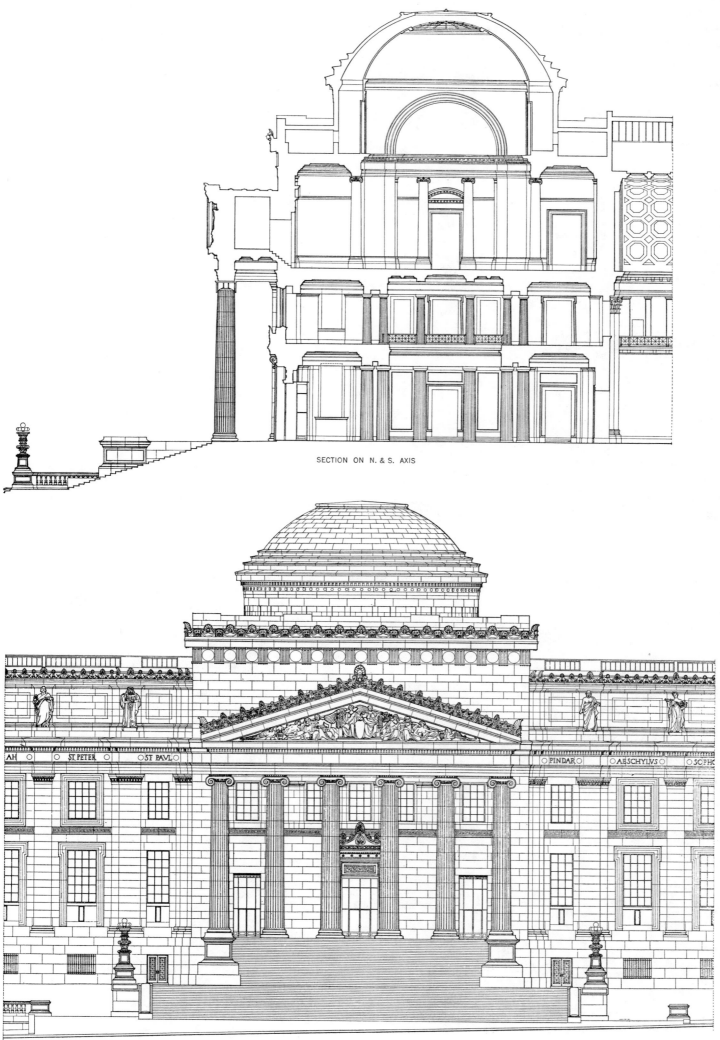

SECTION ON N. & S. AXIS

SCALE ⁵⁰ 40 30 20 10 0 FEET

CENTRAL PORTION, NORTH ELEVATION

THE BROOKLYN INSTITUTE OF ARTS AND SCIENCES.

BEGUN 1897

PLATE 91

McKIM, MEAD & WHITE

HALL OF RENAISSANCE SCULPTURE, THIRD FLOOR

THE BROOKLYN INSTITUTE OF ARTS & SCIENCES.
BEGUN 1897

CORRIDOR OF ANTIQUE SCULPTURE FIRST FLOOR

DIRECTORS' ROOM

BANKING ROOM

NEW YORK LIFE INSURANCE CO., NEW YORK CITY.
1897

PLATE 94

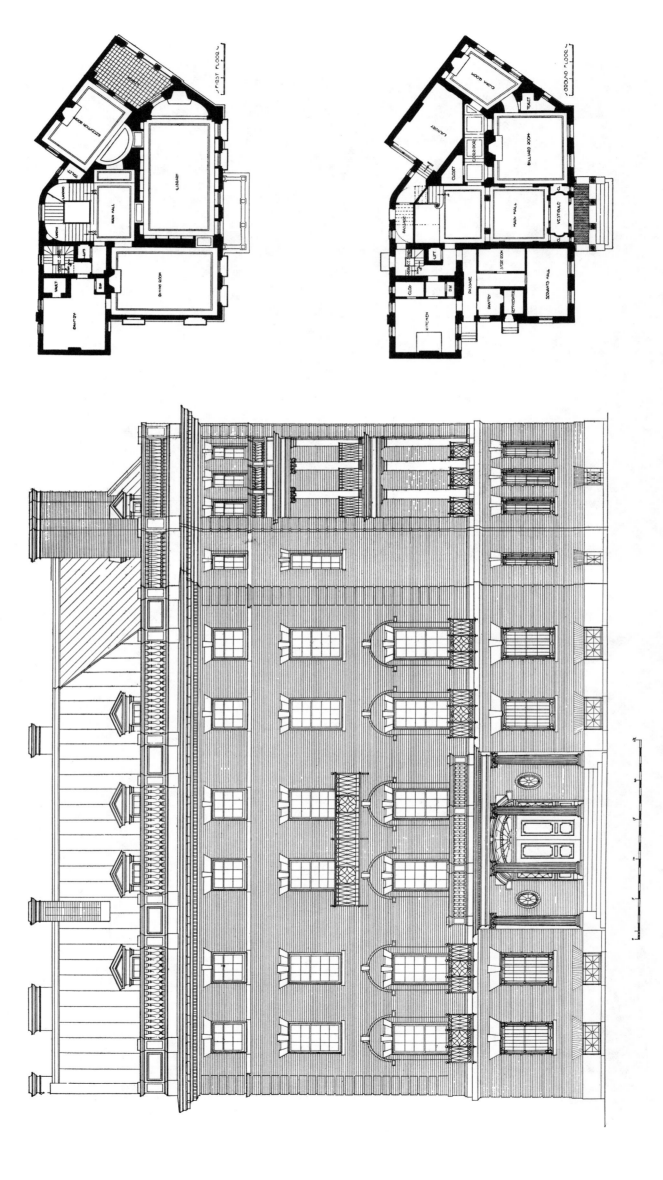

McKIM, MEAD & WHITE

THOMAS NELSON PAGE RESIDENCE, WASHINGTON, D. C.
1897

THOMAS NELSON PAGE, RESIDENCE, WASHINGTON, D. C.
1897

PLATE 96

MCKIM, MEAD & WHITE

1892

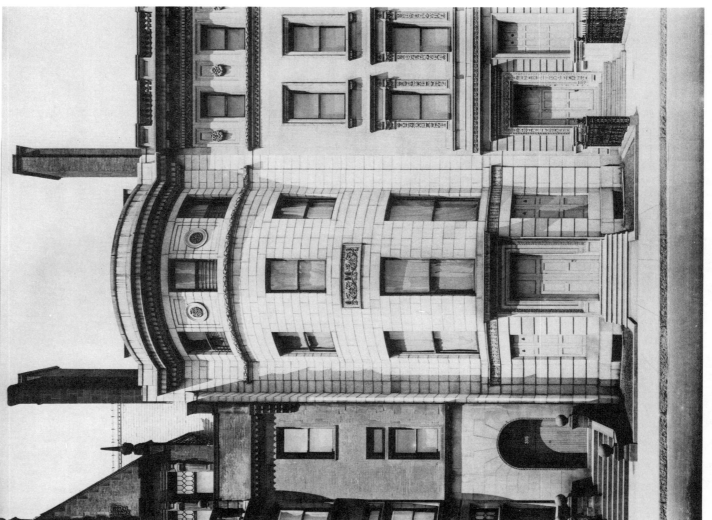

1897

HOUSES ON COMMONWEALTH AVE., BOSTON, MASS.

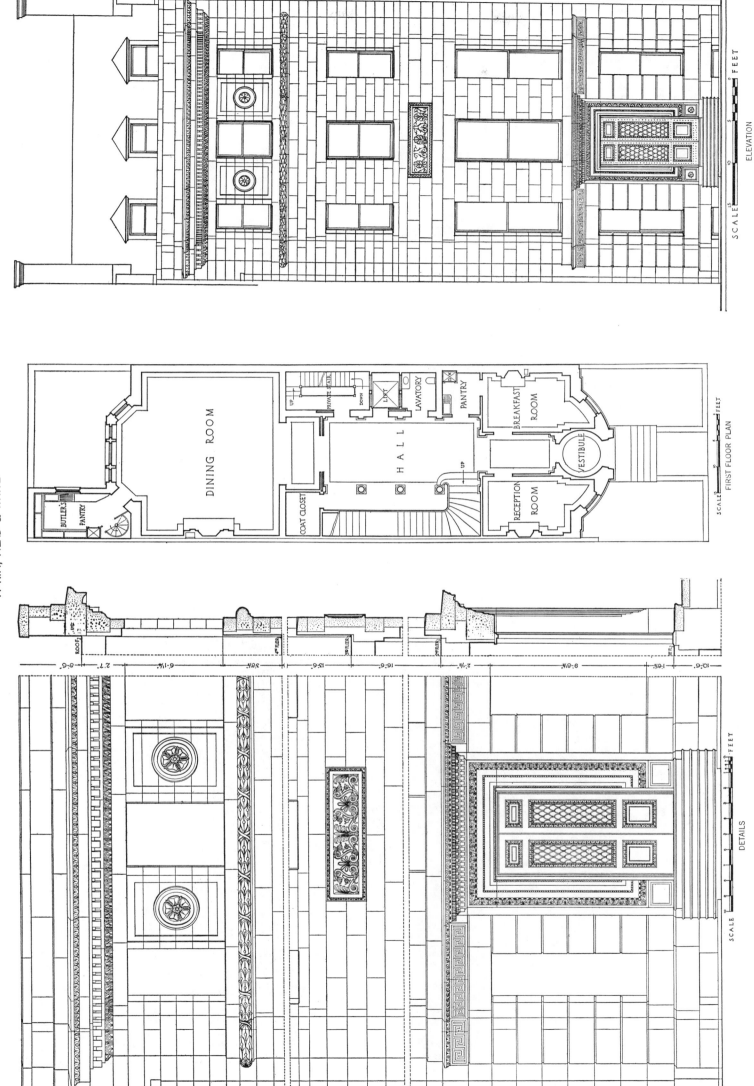

PLATE 97

McKIM, MEAD & WHITE

ELEVATION

SCALE   FEET

FIRST FLOOR PLAN

DINING ROOM

BUTLER'S PANTRY

COAT CLOSET

HALL

UP

PRIVATE STAIR

DOWN

LIFT

LAVATORY

PANTRY

UP

RECEPTION ROOM

BREAKFAST ROOM

VESTIBULE

SCALE   FEET

DETAILS

SCALE   FEET

GEO. A. NICKERSON RESIDENCE, BOSTON, MASS.
1897

PLATE 98

McKIM, MEAD & WHITE

~FIRST FLOOR~

~THIRD FLOOR~

~TYPICAL BED ROOM FLOOR~

SHERRY'S HOTEL, NEW YORK CITY.
1898

PLATE 99

McKIM, MEAD & WHITE

BALL ROOM

DINING ROOM

SHERRY'S HOTEL, NEW YORK CITY.
1898

PLATE 100

McKIM, MEAD & WHITE

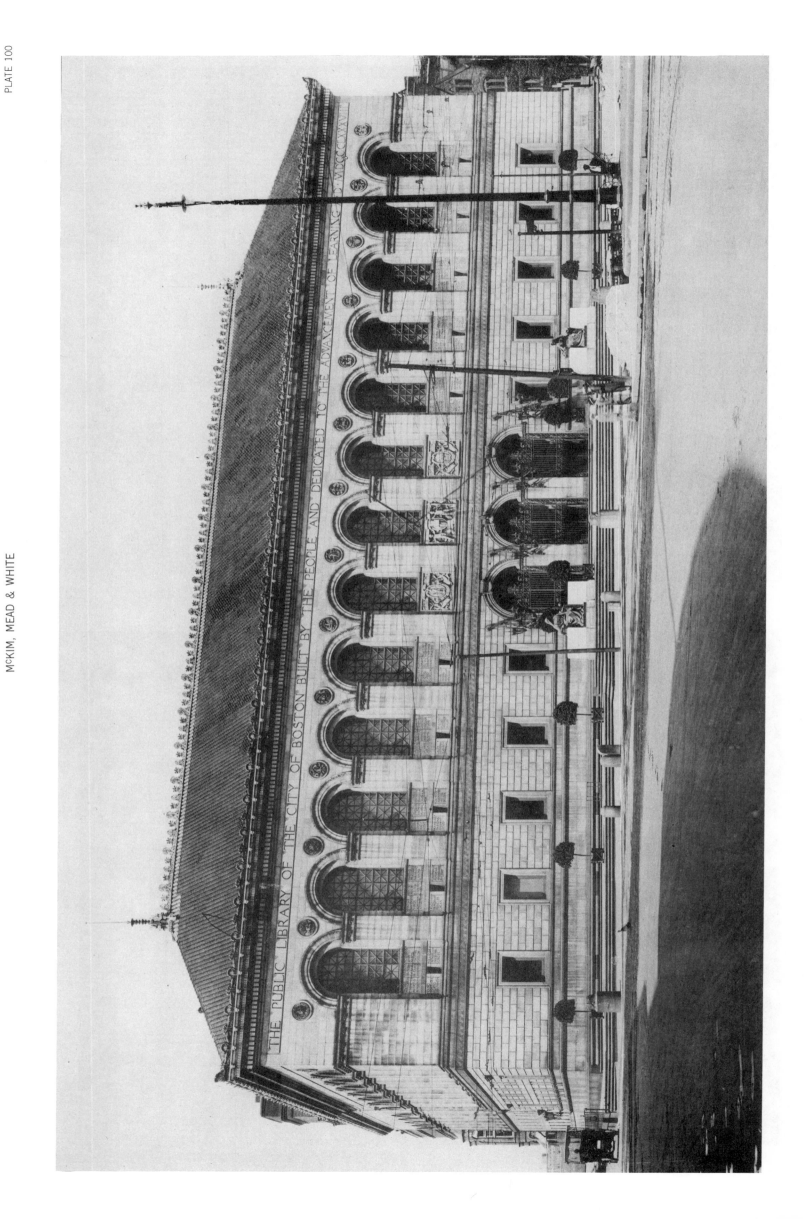

THE BOSTON PUBLIC LIBRARY, BOSTON, MASS.
FACADE FACING COPLEY SQUARE
1898

PLATE 101

MCKIM, MEAD & WHITE

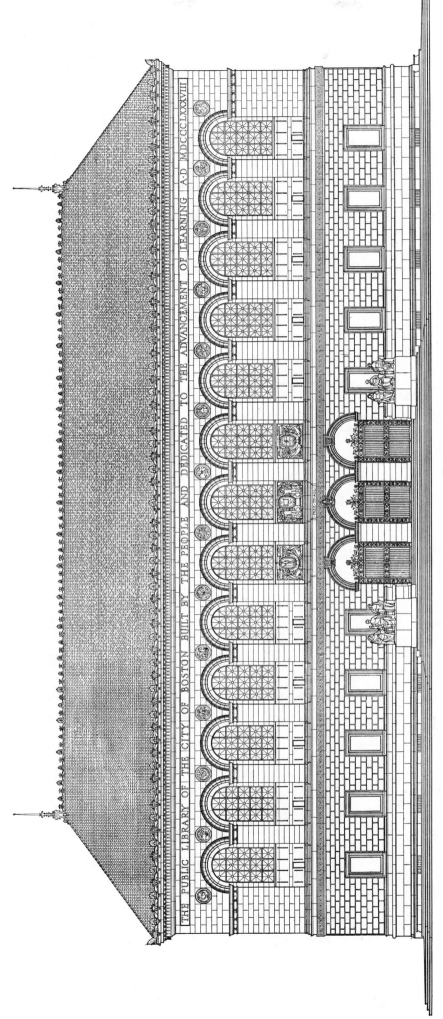

THE PUBLIC LIBRARY OF THE CITY OF BOSTON BUILT BY THE PEOPLE AND DEDICATED TO THE ADVANCEMENT OF LEARNING A·D MDCCCLXXXVIII

SCALE

THE BOSTON PUBLIC LIBRARY, BOSTON, MASS.
DARTMOUTH STREET ELEVATION
1898

PLATE 102

McKIM, MEAD & WHITE

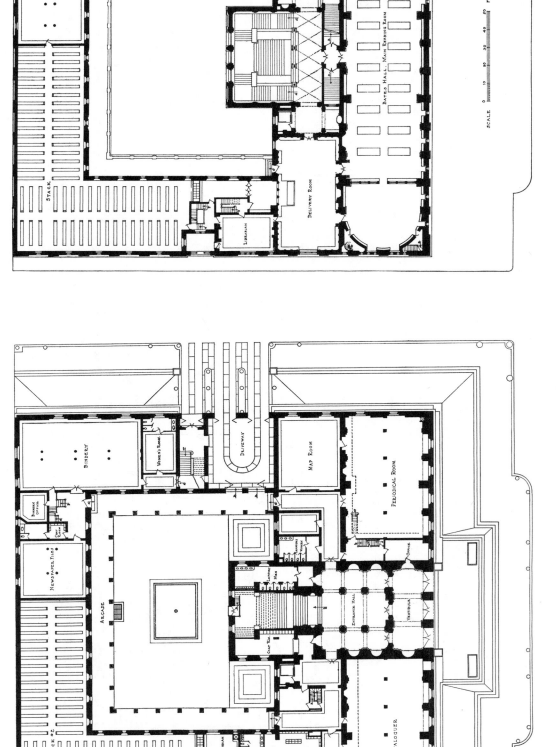

SECOND FLOOR PLAN

FIRST FLOOR PLAN

THE BOSTON PUBLIC LIBRARY, BOSTON, MASS.
1898

PLATE 103

MCKIM, MEAD & WHITE

VIEW IN COURT
BOSTON PUBLIC LIBRARY, BOSTON, MASS.
1898

PLATE 104

McKIM, MEAD & WHITE

START OF MAIN STAIR

STAIR HALL, FROM LANDING

THE BOSTON PUBLIC LIBRARY, BOSTON, MASS.
1898

STAIR HALL WITH DECORATION BY PUVIS DE CHAVAUNES

DELIVERY ROOM WITH FRIEZE BY E. A. ABBEY - THE HOLY GRAIL

THE BOSTON PUBLIC LIBRARY, BOSTON, MASS.
1898

PLATE 106

MCKIM, MEAD & WHITE

DOORWAY IN BATES HALL

BATES HALL, MAIN READING ROOM

BOSTON PUBLIC LIBRARY, BOSTON, MASS.
1898

PLATE 107

McKIM, MEAD & WHITE

DETAIL OF MAIN ENTRANCE

BOSTON PUBLIC LIBRARY, BOSTON, MASS.
1898

DETAIL IN COURT

PLATE 108

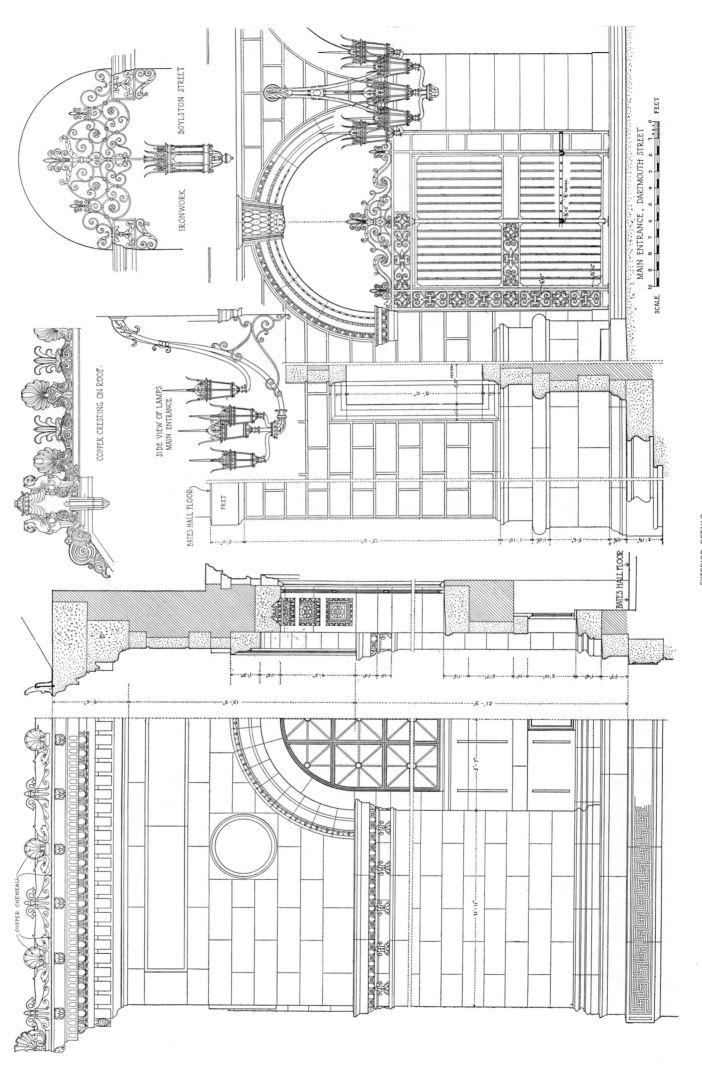

McKIM, MEAD & WHITE

IRONWORK

BOYLSTON STREET

COPPER CRESTING ON ROOF.

SIDE VIEW OF LAMPS
MAIN ENTRANCE

BATES HALL FLOOR.

FRET

CENTER

BATES HALL FLOOR

COPPER CHEMEAUX

MAIN ENTRANCE, DARTMOUTH STREET

SCALE   FEET

EXTERIOR DETAILS

BOSTON PUBLIC LIBRARY, BOSTON, MASS.
1898

PLATE 109

MCKIM, MEAD & WHITE

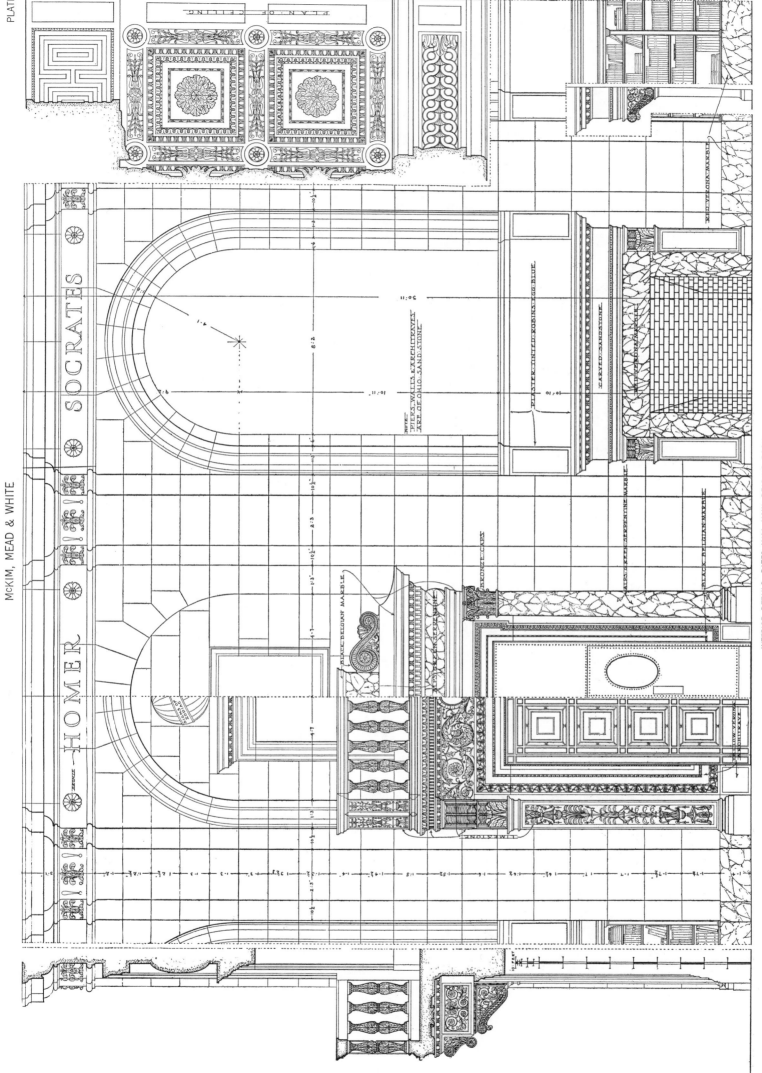

SOCRATES

HOMER

INTERIOR DETAILS, BATES HALL MAIN READING ROOM
BOSTON PUBLIC LIBRARY, BOSTON MASS.
1898

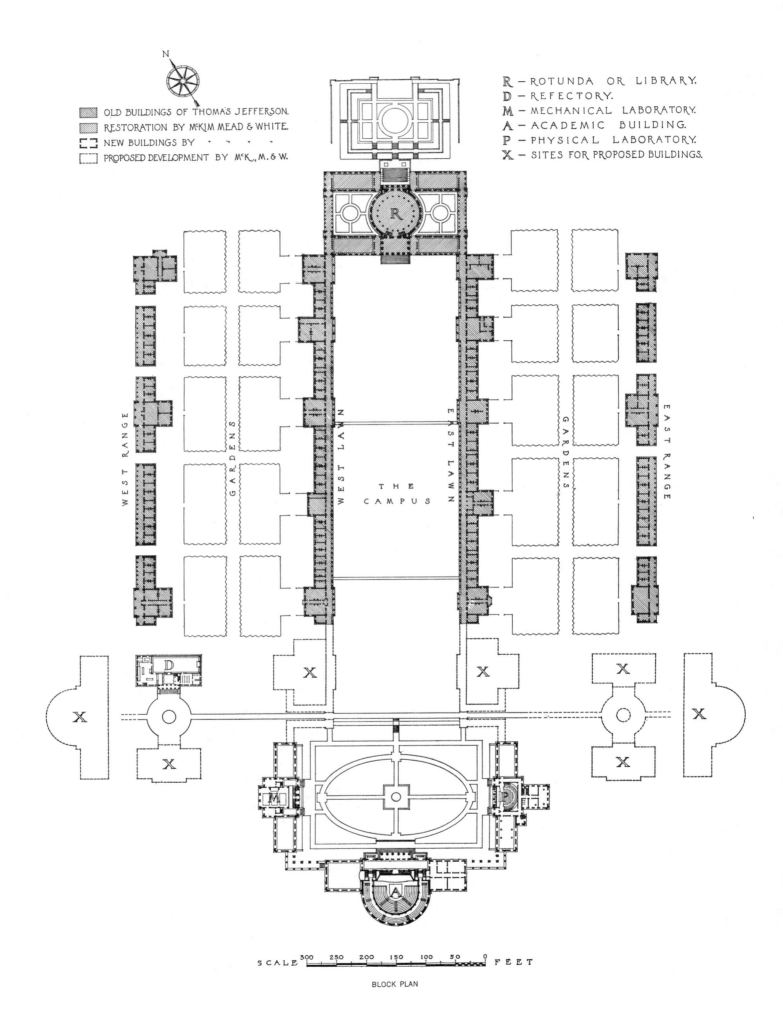

N

OLD BUILDINGS OF THOMAS JEFFERSON.
RESTORATION BY McKIM MEAD & WHITE.
NEW BUILDINGS BY " " " "
PROPOSED DEVELOPMENT BY McK., M. & W.

R — ROTUNDA OR LIBRARY.
D — REFECTORY.
M — MECHANICAL LABORATORY.
A — ACADEMIC BUILDING.
P — PHYSICAL LABORATORY.
X — SITES FOR PROPOSED BUILDINGS.

WEST RANGE

GARDENS

WEST LAWN

THE CAMPUS

EAST LAWN

GARDENS

EAST RANGE

SCALE 300 250 200 150 100 50 0 FEET

BLOCK PLAN

UNIVERSITY OF VIRGINIA, CHARLOTTESVILLE, VA.
1898

MECHANICAL LABORATORY ELEVATION

ACADEMIC BUILDING ELEVATION

MATERIALS, WALLS, RED BRICK; COLUMNS, PILASTERS, CORNICES,
DOOR AND WINDOW TRIMS, PORTLAND CEMENT STUCCO; STEPS, BLUESTONE.

DETAIL CENTRAL PORTION, ACADEMIC BUILDING

UNIVERSITY OF VIRGINIA, CHARLOTTESVILLE, VA.
1898

ACADEMIC BUILDING

MECHANICAL LABORATORY

THE UNIVERSITY OF VIRGINIA, CHARLOTTESVILLE, VA.
1898

RESTORATION OF ROTUNDA & TERRACES ACCORDING TO THE ORIGINAL SCHEME OF THOMAS JEFFERSON, ARCHITECT.

COURT AT SIDE OF ROTUNDA

THE UNIVERSITY OF VIRGINIA, RESTORATIONS & ADDITIONS, CHARLOTTESVILLE, VA.
1898

MAIN FACADE

TENNIS COURT

SWIMMING POOL

CASINO OF JOHN JACOB ASTOR, RHINEBECK, N. Y.
1898

LOUNGING ROOM

SWIMMING POOL

CASINO OF JOHN JACOB ASTOR, RHINEBECK, N. Y.
1898

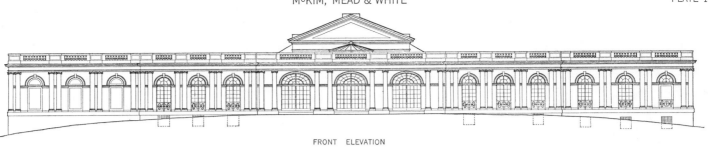

FRONT ELEVATION

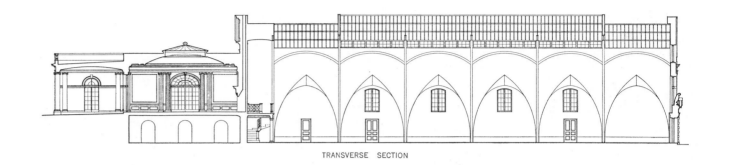

TRANSVERSE SECTION

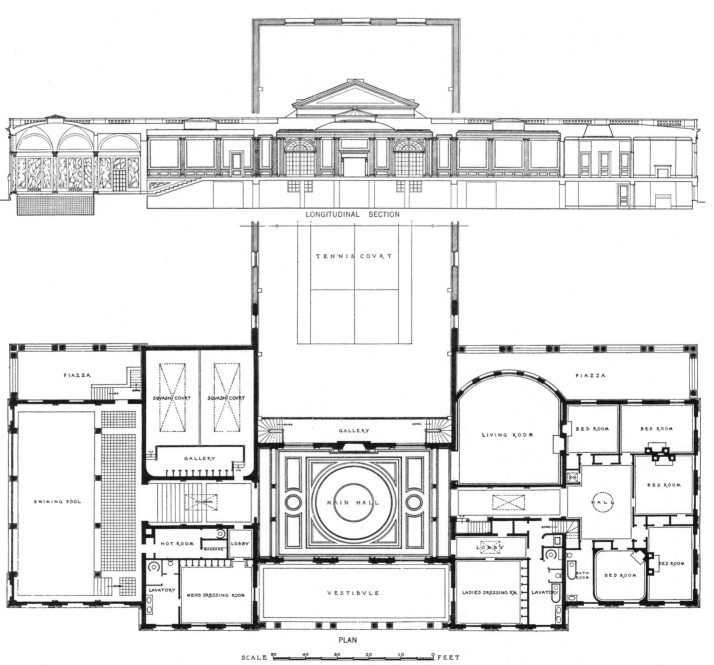

LONGITUDINAL SECTION

TENNIS COURT

PIAZZA

SQUASH COURT

SQUASH COURT

PIAZZA

GALLERY

LIVING ROOM

BED ROOM

BED ROOM

BED ROOM

GALLERY

SWIMING POOL

MAIN HALL

HALL

BED ROOM

HOT ROOM

MASSAGE

LOBBY

LOBBY

BATH ROOM

BED ROOM

LAVATORY

MEN'S DRESSING ROOM

VESTIBULE

LADIES DRESSING RM.

LAVATORY

PLAN

SCALE 50 40 30 20 10 0 FEET

J. J. ASTOR COURTS, RHINEBECK, N. Y.
1898

THE CULLUM MEMORIAL, WEST POINT, N. Y.
1898

ASSEMBLY HALL, SECOND FLOOR

DETAIL OF ASSEMBLY HALL   DETAIL OF ENTRANCE

THE CULLUM MEMORIAL, WEST POINT, N. Y.
1898

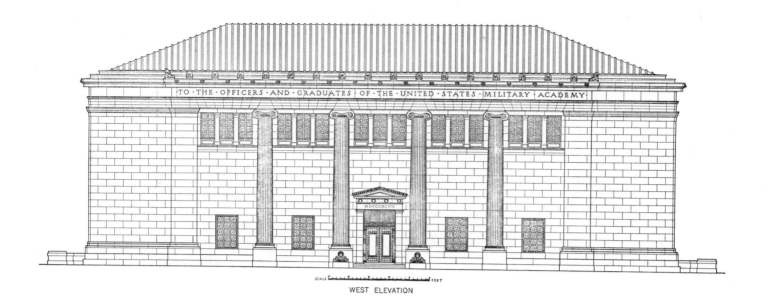

TO·THE·OFFICERS·AND·GRADUATES·OF·THE·UNITED·STATES·MILITARY·ACADEMY

MDCCCXCVIII

SCALE FEET

WEST ELEVATION

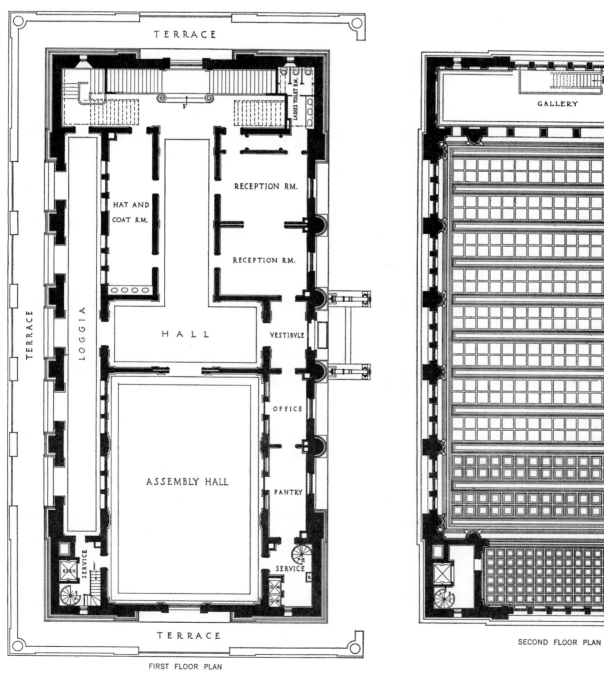

TERRACE

RECEPTION RM.

HAT AND
COAT RM.

LADIES TOILET RM.

RECEPTION RM.

TERRACE

LOGGIA

HALL

VESTIBVLE

OFFICE

ASSEMBLY HALL

PANTRY

SERVICE

SERVICE

TERRACE

FIRST FLOOR PLAN

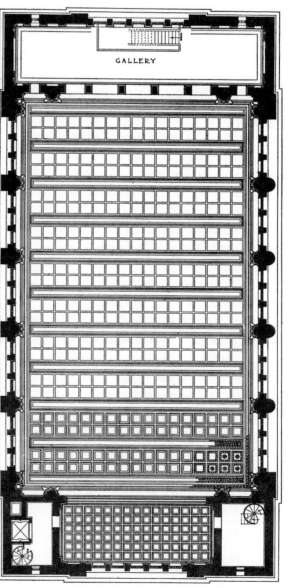

GALLERY

SECOND FLOOR PLAN

CULLUM MEMORIAL, WEST POINT, N. Y.
1898

PLATE 119

McKIM, MEAD & WHITE

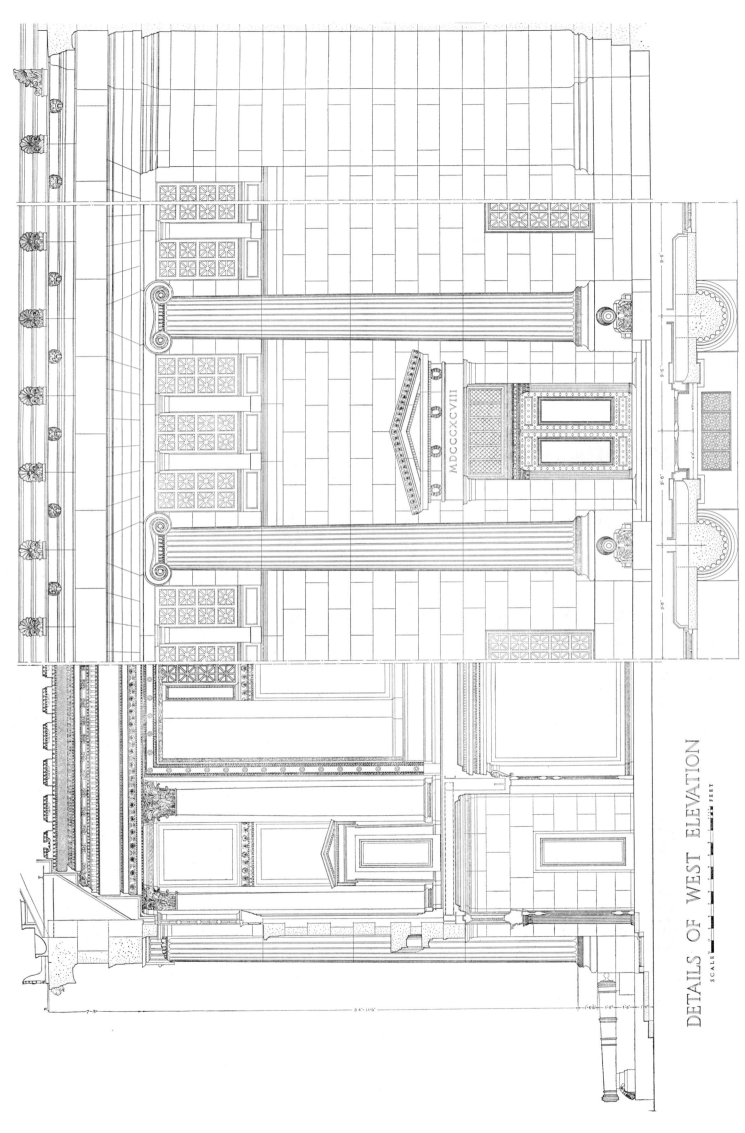

MDCCCXCVIII

DETAILS OF WEST ELEVATION

SCALE

CULLUM MEMORIAL, WEST POINT, N. Y.
1898

SCALE |——————————| FEET
0   5   10   15   20   25

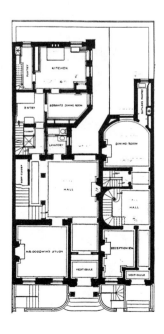

HOUSES FOR JAMES J. GOODWIN, NEW YORK CITY.

PLATE 121

MCKIM, MEAD & WHITE

HOUSES FOR H. A. C. TAYLOR, NEW YORK CITY.
1898

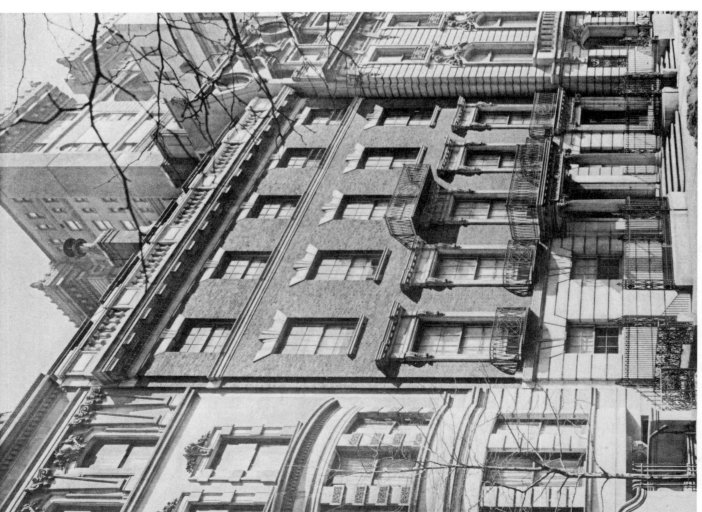

HOUSES FOR JAS. J. GOODWIN, NEW YORK CITY.
1898

FACADE

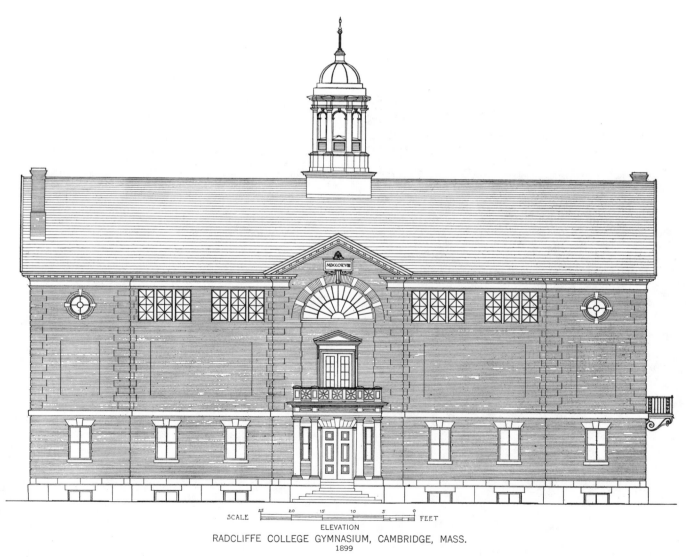

SCALE ⎯⎯⎯⎯⎯ FEET

ELEVATION

RADCLIFFE COLLEGE GYMNASIUM, CAMBRIDGE, MASS.
1899

PLATE 123

McKIM, MEAD & WHITE

SECOND FLOOR PLAN

GYMNASIUM FLOOR.

RUNNING TRACK.

SCALE

FEET

FIRST FLOOR PLAN

LAVATORY

CORRIDOR

ANTHROPOMETRIC DEP.T

BATH ATTENDANT

LOCKER ROOM

HALL

VESTIBULE

CORRIDOR

MEDICAL GYMNASTICS

DIRECTOR'S ROOM

RADCLIFFE COLLEGE GYMNASIUM, CAMBRIDGE, MASS.
1899

DETAIL OF ENTRANCE

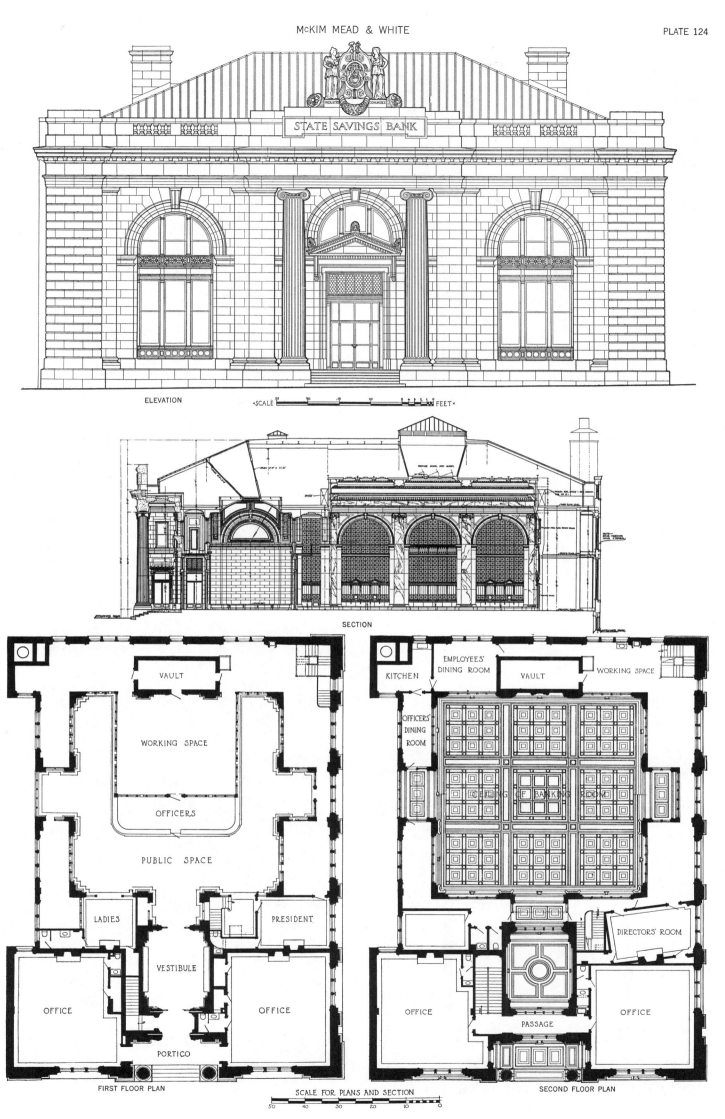

STATE SAVINGS BANK

ELEVATION

·SCALE· FEET·

SECTION

VAULT

WORKING SPACE

OFFICERS

PUBLIC SPACE

LADIES

PRESIDENT

VESTIBULE

OFFICE

OFFICE

PORTICO

FIRST FLOOR PLAN

KITCHEN

EMPLOYEES' DINING ROOM

VAULT

WORKING SPACE

OFFICERS' DINING ROOM

CEILING OF BANKING ROOM

DIRECTORS' ROOM

OFFICE

OFFICE

PASSAGE

SECOND FLOOR PLAN

SCALE FOR PLANS AND SECTION

50   40   30   20   10   0

THE STATE SAVINGS BANK, DETROIT, MICHIGAN
1900

GENERAL VIEW OF EXTERIOR

MAIN ENTRANCE DOORWAY

DETAIL OF COUNTER SCREEN

STATE SAVINGS BANK, DETROIT, MICHIGAN.
NOW THE PEOPLES STATE BANK
1900

INGS BANK

BRONZE

SECTION THRO ENTRANCE
PORTICO SHOWING OFFICE ENTRANCE.

CENTER LINE OF FRONT ELEVATION

BRONZE AND
GLASS DOORS
AND FRAMES

·ONE HALF ELEVATION· CENTRAL PORTION OF FACADE·

BRONZE

PLAN THRO. WINDOW

·ONE HALF BAY WITH WINDOW·

DETAIL OF
UPPER PORTION
OF BANKING
ROOM

CENTER LINE

PLAN OF
CEILING
ENTRANCE
PORTICO

DETAIL OF
COUNTER SCREEN
IN BANKING R'M

RECEIVING TELLER

SCALE FEET

THE STATE SAVINGS BANK, DETROIT, MICH.

EXTERIOR AND INTERIOR DETAILS

1900

THE UNIVERSITY CLUB, NEW YORK CITY.
1900

PLATE 131

McKIM, MEAD & WHITE

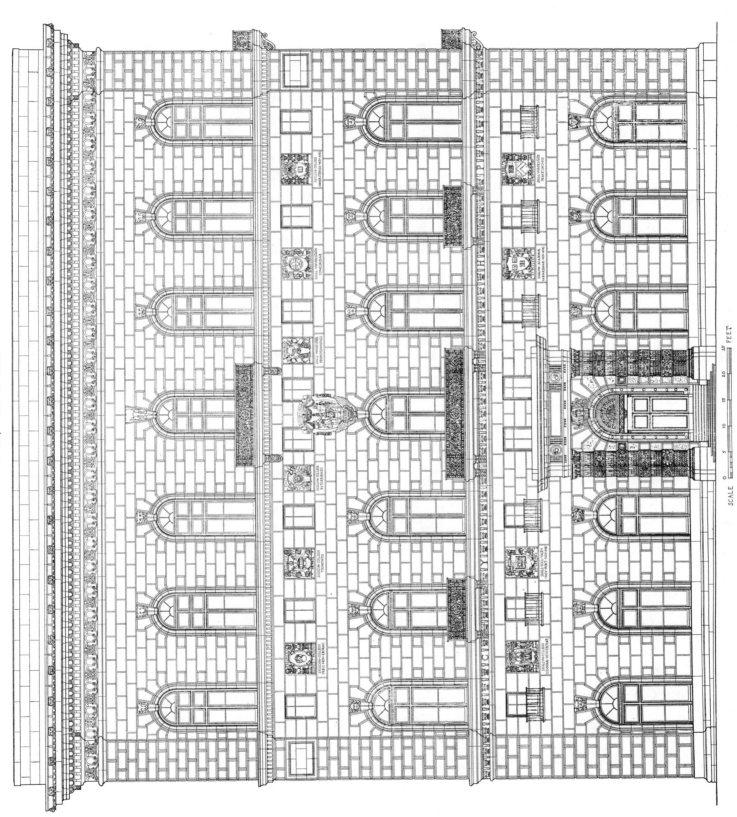

ELEVATION FIFTY-FOURTH STREET
UNIVERSITY CLUB, NEW YORK CITY.
1900

SCALE
FEET

PLATE 132

McKIM, MEAD & WHITE

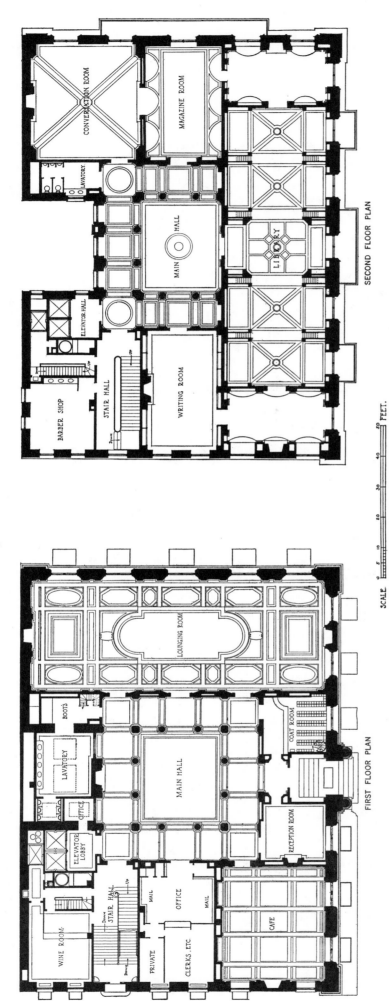

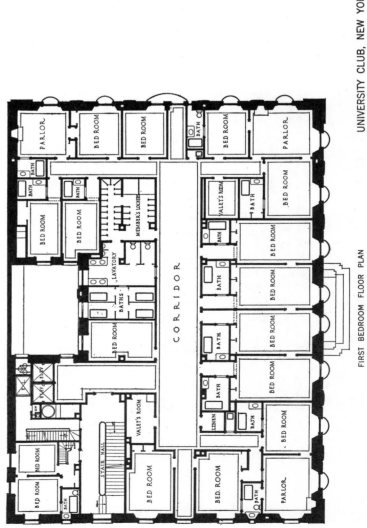

SECOND FLOOR PLAN

FIRST FLOOR PLAN

THIRD FLOOR PLAN

FIRST BEDROOM FLOOR PLAN

UNIVERSITY CLUB, NEW YORK CITY.
1900

SCALE.

FEET.

PLATE 133

McKIM, MEAD & WHITE

DETAIL OF FACADE

UNIVERSITY CLUB, NEW YORK CITY.
1900

ENTRANCE DOORWAY

CHRISTO
VE RI TAS
ET ECCLESIÆ

TERRAS
IRRADIENT

· SECTION THRO' ENTRANCE ·

· PLAN ·

SCALE

· SECTION ·   · FIFTH AVE ELEVATION ·   · MAIN ENTRANCE ·

DETAILS OF EXTERIOR STONEWORK
UNIVERSITY CLUB, NEW YORK CITY.
1900

SECOND FLOOR HALL

FIRST FLOOR HALL

THE UNIVERSITY CLUB, NEW YORK CITY.
1900

MAIN DINING ROOM

LOUNGING ROOM, FIRST FLOOR

THE UNIVERSITY CLUB, NEW YORK CITY.
1900

PLATE 137

MCKIM, MEAD & WHITE

DETAIL OF LIBRARY

GENERAL VIEW OF LIBRARY

UNIVERSITY CLUB, NEW YORK CITY.
DECORATIONS BY H. SIDDONS MOWBRAY, 1904.

PLATE 138

McKIM, MEAD & WHITE

MAGAZINE ROOM

UNIVERSITY CLUB, NEW YORK CITY.
1900

MANTEL IN FIRST STORY HALL

CEILING DECORATION BY H. SIDDONS MOWBRAY

COUNCIL ROOM

UNIVERSITY CLUB, NEW YORK CITY.
1900

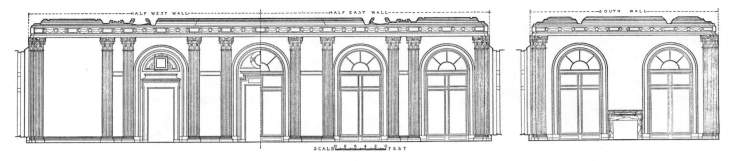

SCALE .... FEET

ELEVATIONS

UPPER CORNICE AND CEILING PLASTER
WITH INSERTS OF MARBLE

WOOD WORK
OF ITALIAN WALNUT
CARVED AND GILDED

HALF ELEVATION
OF WINDOW

HALF ELEVATION
OF DOOR WAY
TO HALL

WALLS
RED VELVET

DOOR WAY ON AXIS
OF MAIN HALL

MARBLE DOOR TRIMS
AND MANTELS
BROWN NUMIDIAN

SECTION THRO.
WINDOW.

PLAN AT WINDOW

PLAN AT DOOR.

PLAN AT DOOR

SCALE 10 9 8 7 6 5 4 3 2 1 0 FEET

DETAIL OF WALL AND ONE FOURTH OF CEILING

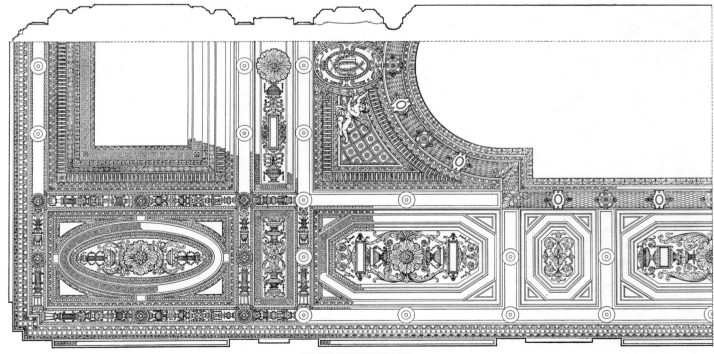

DETAILS OF LOUNGING ROOM
THE UNIVERSITY CLUB, NEW YORK CITY.
1900

SCALE [scale bar] FEET

HALF ELEVATION OF NORTH WALL, AND DETAIL OF PORTION OF CEILING, MAIN DINING ROOM

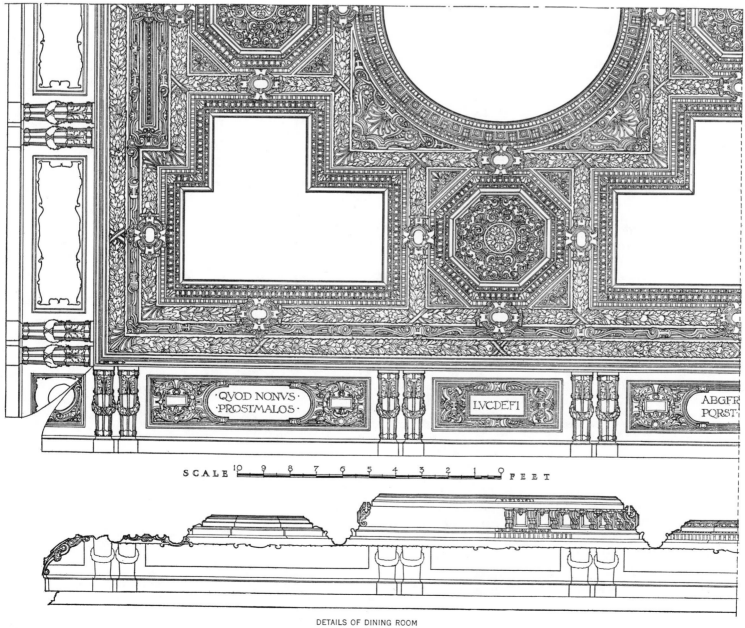

·QVOD NONVS· PROSTMALOS   LVCDEF1   ABGFR PQRST

SCALE 10 9 8 7 6 5 4 3 2 1 0 FEET

DETAILS OF DINING ROOM
THE UNIVERSITY CLUB, NEW YORK CITY.
1900

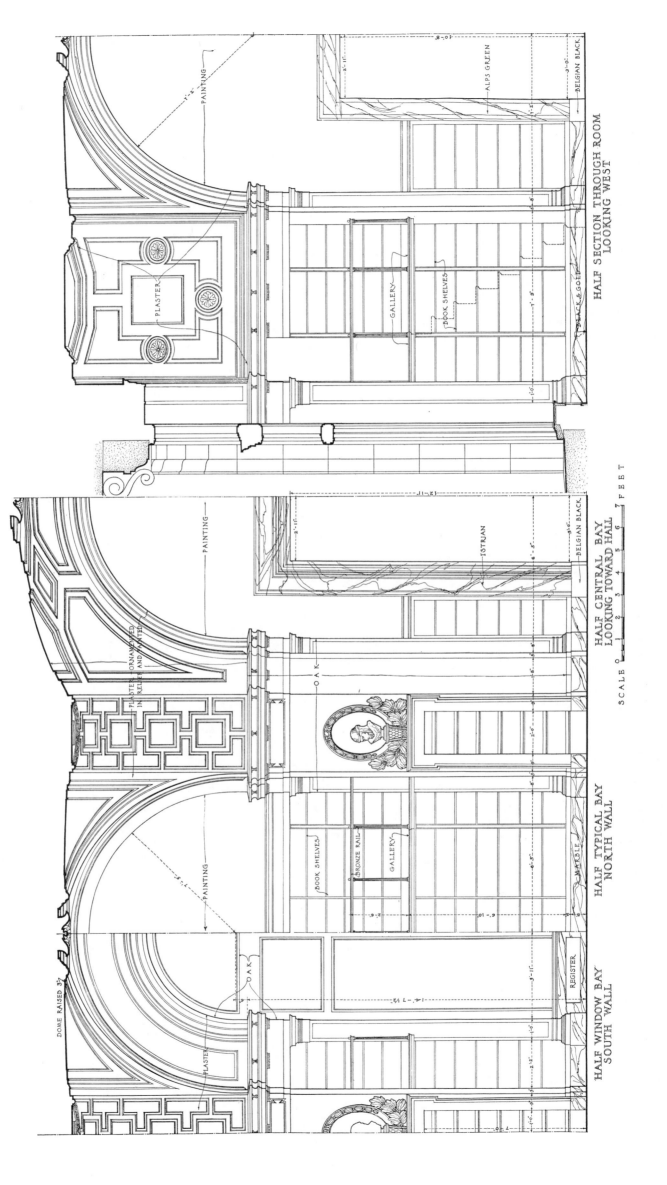

McKIM, MEAD & WHITE

HALF WINDOW BAY
SOUTH WALL

HALF TYPICAL BAY
NORTH WALL

HALF CENTRAL BAY
LOOKING TOWARD HALL

HALF SECTION THROUGH ROOM
LOOKING WEST

SCALE 0 1 2 3 4 5 6 7 FEET

UNIVERSITY CLUB, NEW YORK CITY
DETAILS OF THE LIBRARY
1900

UPPER PART OF CORNICE AND VAULTED CEILING, PLASTER.

WHITE NORWEGIAN MARBLE

BRONZE CAPITALS

TERRAZZO

SIENA MARBLE

TERRAZZO
3-COLORS

WHITE MARBLE INLAY

SHAFTS OF
COLUMNS AND
PILASTERS
CONNEMARA
MARBLE

CARVED PANEL ABOVE
WHITE STATUARY MARBLE

BRICK LINING
ISTRIAN STONE MANTEL

WHITE NORWEGIAN MARBLE

MANTEL IN 1ST STORY HALL

4 3 2 1 0
SCALE

UNIVERSITY CLUB NEW YORK CITY.
1900

EXTERIOR

INTERIOR

THE BOSTON SYMPHONY MUSIC HALL, BOSTON, MASS.
1900

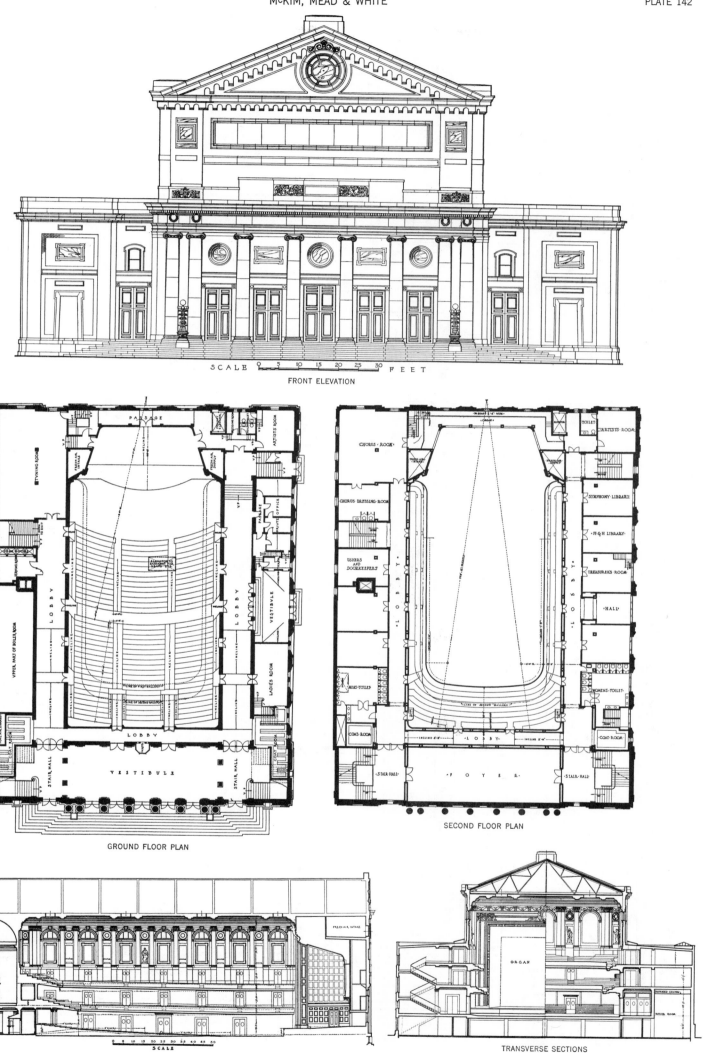

SCALE 0 5 10 15 20 25 30 FEET

FRONT ELEVATION

GROUND FLOOR PLAN

SECOND FLOOR PLAN

SCALE 0 5 10 15 20 25 30 35 40 45 50

LONGITUDINAL SECTION

TRANSVERSE SECTIONS

BOSTON SYMPHONY MUSIC HALL, BOSTON MASS.

1900

CORNER OF CLEAR STORY GABLE

SECTION THROUGH GABLE CORNICE ON LINE B-B'

CENTRAL PORTION OF CLEAR STORY GABLE

SECTION ON LINE A-A' ABOVE

SECTION ON LINE C-C

LEVANTO MARBLE INSERTS

GLASS

GLASS

GLASS

GLASS

CENTER LINE OF FACADE

SECTION ON CENTER LINE

SCALE

THE BOSTON SYMPHONY MUSIC HALL, BOSTON, MASS.
EXTERIOR DETAILS, FRONT ELEVATION
1900

ENTRANCE HALL

STAIR HALL

WM. C. WHITNEY RESIDENCE, NEW YORK CITY.
1900

DINING ROOM

BALL ROOM

WM. C. WHITNEY RESIDENCE, NEW YORK CITY.
1900

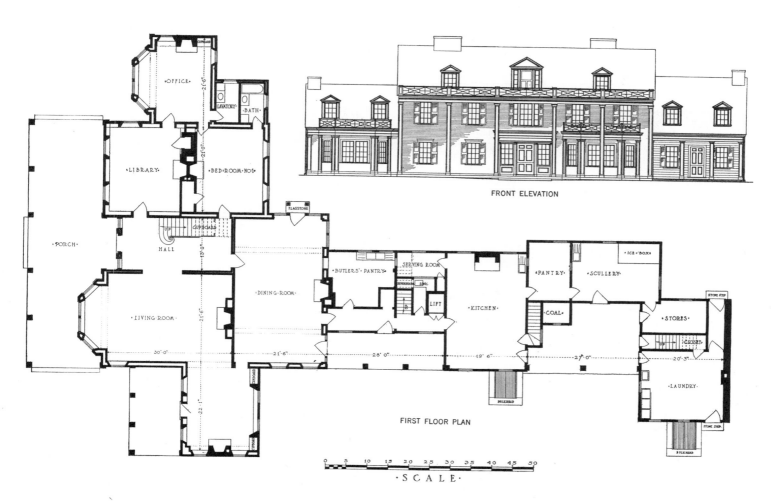

FRONT ELEVATION

FIRST FLOOR PLAN

· S C A L E ·

A. A. POPE RESIDENCE, FARMINGTON, CONN.
1900

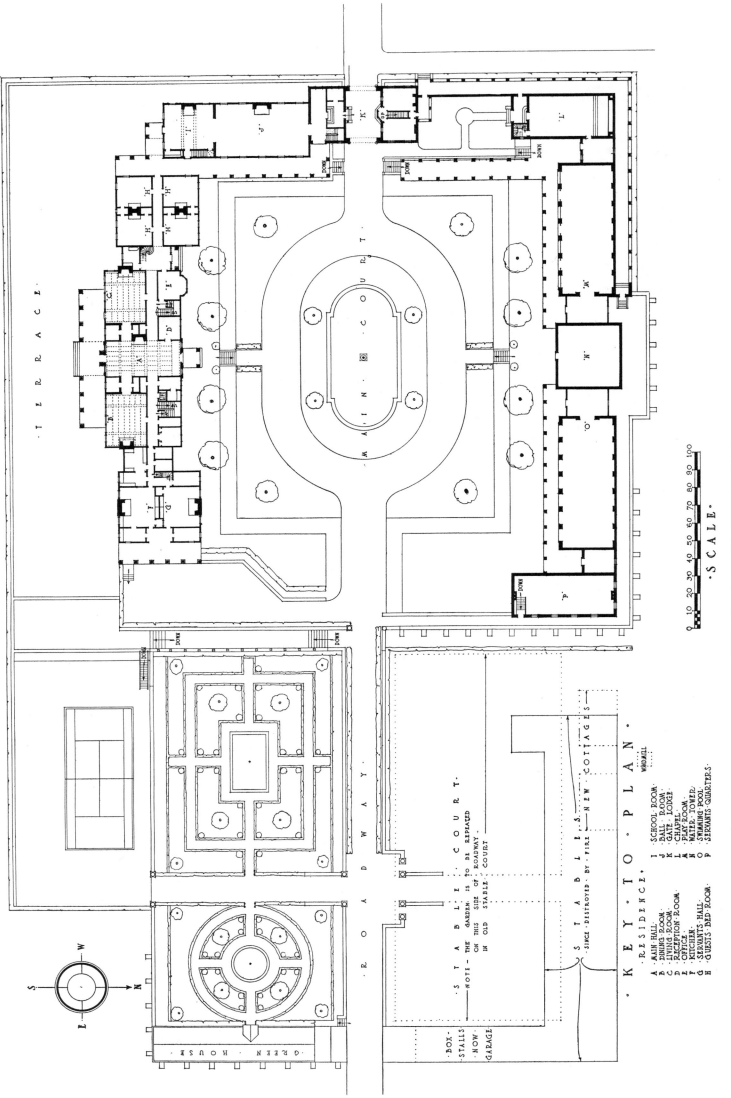

PLATE 147

MCKIM, MEAD & WHITE

· T E R R A C E ·

· R O A D W A Y ·

· M A I N · C O U R T ·

· G R E E N · H O U S E ·

· S C A L E ·

0 10 20 30 40 50 60 70 80 90 100

· K E Y · T O · P L A N ·

· R E S I D E N C E ·

A · MAIN · HALL ·
B · DINING · ROOM ·
C · LIVING · ROOM ·
D · RECEPTION · ROOM ·
E · OFFICE ·
F · KITCHEN ·
G · SERVANTS · HALL ·
H · GUESTS · BED · ROOM ·

I · SCHOOL · ROOM ·
J · BALL · ROOM ·
K · GATE · LODGE ·
L · CHAPEL ·
M · PLAY · ROOM ·
N · WATER · TOWER ·
O · SWIMMING · POOL ·
P · SERVANTS · QUARTERS ·

· STABLE · COURT ·

NOTE — THE · GARDEN · IS · TO · BE · REPLACED
ON · THIS · SIDE · OF · ROADWAY
IN · OLD · STABLE · COURT ·

· STABLES ·

· SINCE · DISTROYED · BY · FIRE ·

· NEW · COTTAGES ·

WINDMILL

· BOX ·
· STALLS ·
· NOW ·
· GARAGE ·

ESTATE OF E. D. MORGAN, WHEATLEY HILLS, L. I.

BEGUN 1900

GENERAL VIEW OF BUILDINGS

VIEW IN GARDEN   ENTRANCE DRIVEWAY

ESTATE OF E. D. MORGAN, WHEATLEY HILLS, L. I.
1901

THE HOUSE

THE CHAPEL   THE WATER TOWER

ESTATE OF E. D. MORGAN, WHEATLEY HILLS, L. I.
1901

ENTRANCE COURT

GENERAL VIEW OF GARDEN

ESTATE OF E. D. MORGAN, WHEATLEY HILLS, L. I.
1901

PLATE 151

MCKIM, MEAD & WHITE

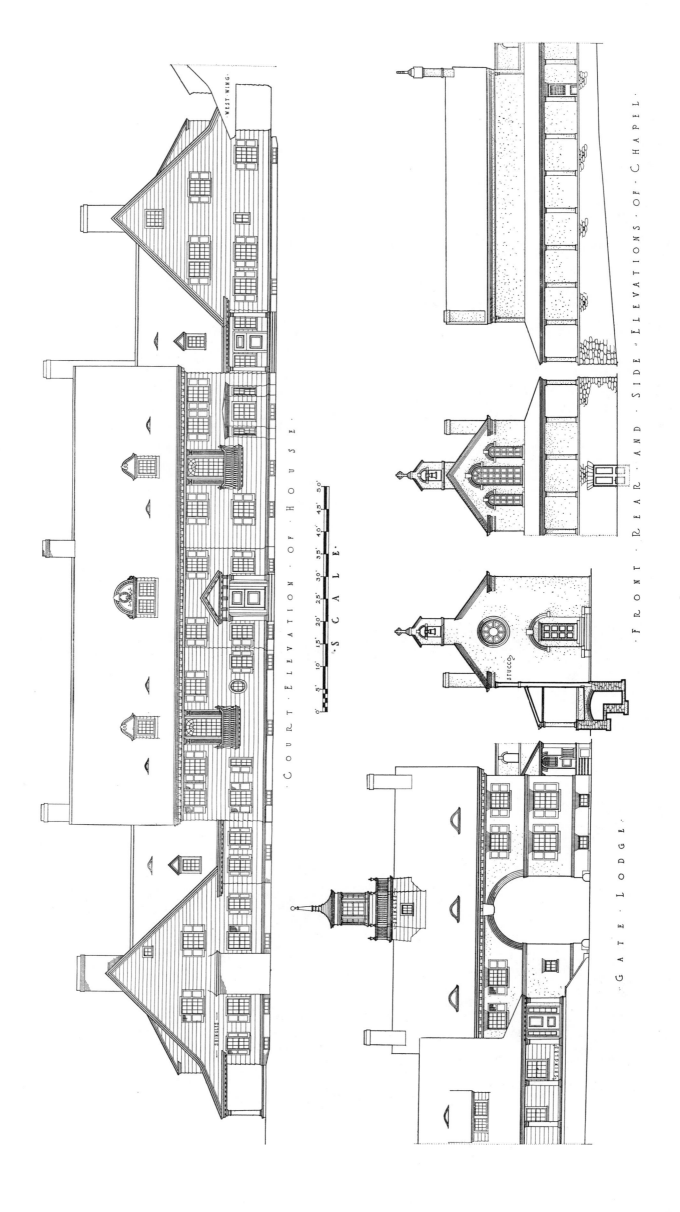

· WEST WING ·

· C O U R T · E L E V A T I O N · O F · H O U S E ·

· S C A L E ·

0' 5' 10' 15' 20' 25' 30' 35' 40' 45' 50'

· SHINGLES ·

STUCCO

· G A T E · L O D G E ·

· F R O N T · R E A R · A N D · S I D E · E L E V A T I O N S · O F · C H A P E L ·

ESTATE OF E. D. MORGAN, WHEATLEY HILLS, L. I.
1901

PLATE 152

McKIM, MEAD & WHITE

THE "PORCELLIAN" GATE OR THE McKEAN MEMORIAL GATE.

CLASS OF 1857

CLASS OF 1875

CLASS OF 1877

MEMORIAL GATEWAYS, HARVARD UNIVERSITY, CAMBRIDGE, MASS.
1900 - 1901

PLATE 153

McKIM, MEAD & WHITE

CLASS OF 1880

CLASS OF 1887-88

CLASS OF 1890

CLASS OF 1870

MEMORIAL GATEWAYS, HARVARD UNIVERSITY, CAMBRIDGE, MASS.
1901 TO 1905

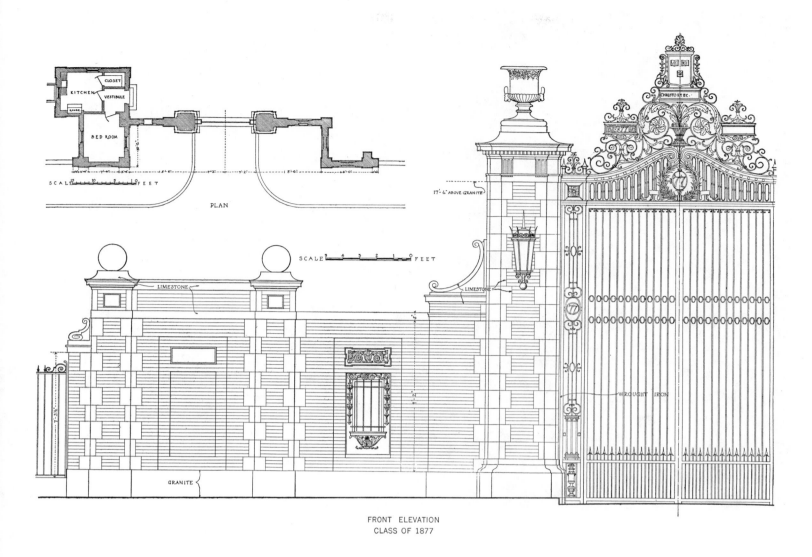

FRONT ELEVATION
CLASS OF 1877

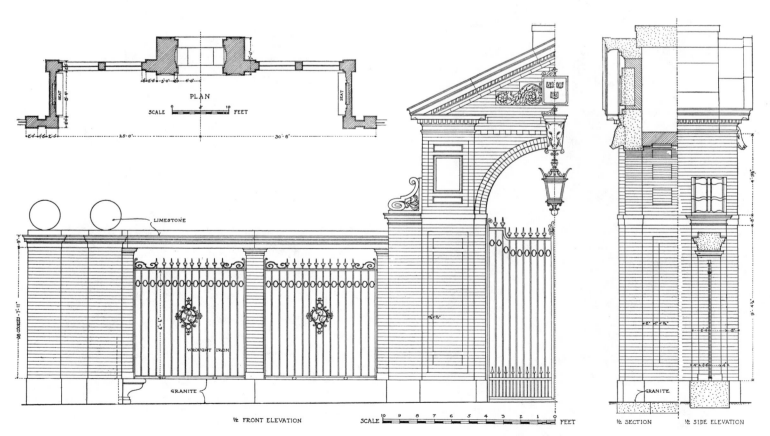

THE "PORCELLIAN" GATE OR THE McKEAN MEMORIAL GATE

MEMORIAL GATEWAYS, HARVARD UNIVERSITY, CAMBRIDGE, MASS.
1900 - 1901

PLATE 155

MCKIM, MEAD & WHITE

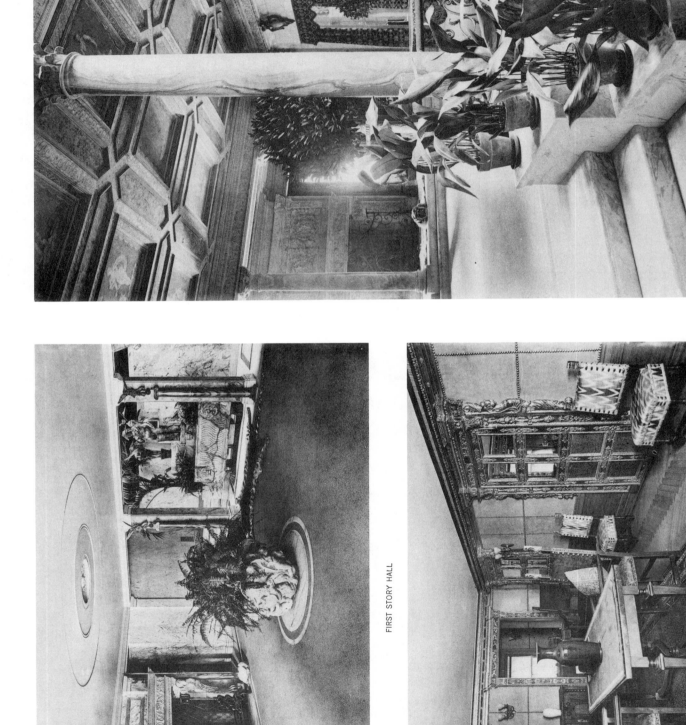

SECOND STORY HALL

FIRST STORY HALL

RECEPTION ROOM

RESIDENCE OF HENRY W. POORE, NEW YORK CITY
1900

LIBRARY

DINING ROOM

RESIDENCE OF HENRY W. POORE, NEW YORK CITY
1900

EXTERIOR VIEW

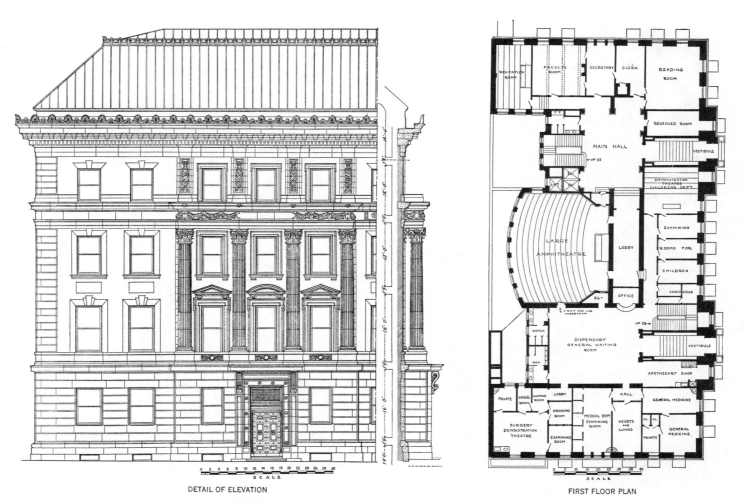

DETAIL OF ELEVATION

FIRST FLOOR PLAN

CORNELL UNIVERSITY MEDICAL SCHOOL, NEW YORK CITY.
1901

THE HARVARD UNION

CLASS OF 1879 MEMORIAL GATEWAY

HARVARD UNIVERSITY, CAMBRIDGE, MASS.

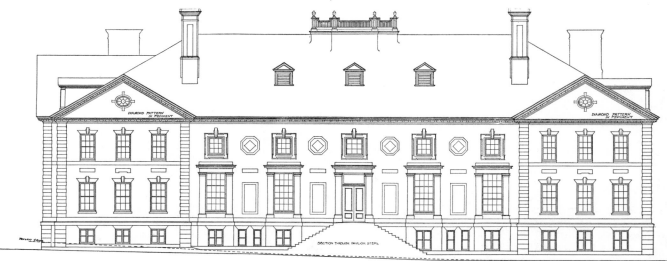

0 5 10 15 20 25 30 35 40 45 50
·SCALE·

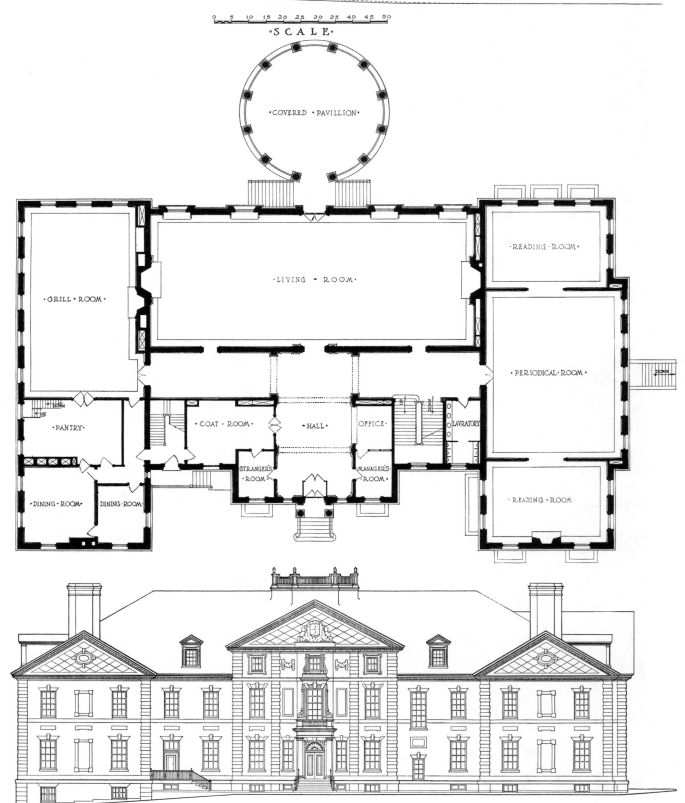

·COVERED·PAVILLION·

·GRILL·ROOM·

·LIVING·ROOM·

·READING·ROOM·

·PERIODICAL·ROOM·

·PANTRY·   ·COAT·ROOM·   ·HALL·   OFFICE   LAVRATORY

·DINING·ROOM·   ·DINING·ROOM·   STRANGER'S ROOM   MANAGER'S ROOM   ·READING·ROOM·

THE HARVARD UNION, CAMBRIDGE, MASS.
1902

PLATE 160

McKIM, MEAD & WHITE

MANTEL IN DINING HALL

DINING HALL

THE HARVARD UNION, CAMBRIDGE, MASS.
1902

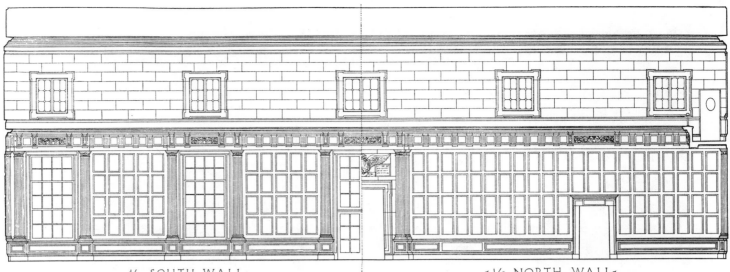

·½ SOUTH WALL·   ·½ NORTH WALL·

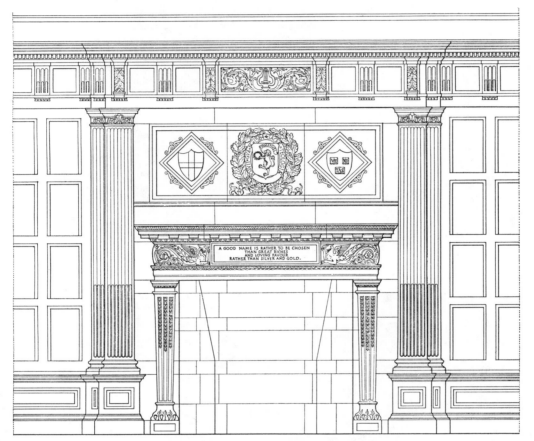

·ELEVATION OF MANTEL ON WEST WALL·

A GOOD NAME IS RATHER TO BE CHOSEN
THAN GREAT RICHES
AND LOVING FAVOUR
RATHER THAN SILVER AND GOLD.

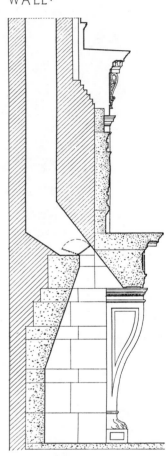

·SECTION·

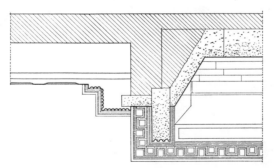

·PLAN OF ABOVE·

SCALE   FOR DETAILS

SCALE   FOR WALLS

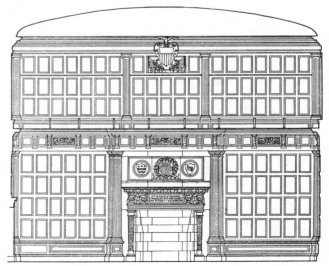

·EAST WALL·

DETAILS OF LIVING ROOM

THE HARVARD UNION, CAMBRIDGE, MASS.

NOTE: FOR "DINING HALL" READ "LIVING ROOM" ON PAGE NO. 160

1902

PLATE 162

MCKIM, MEAD & WHITE

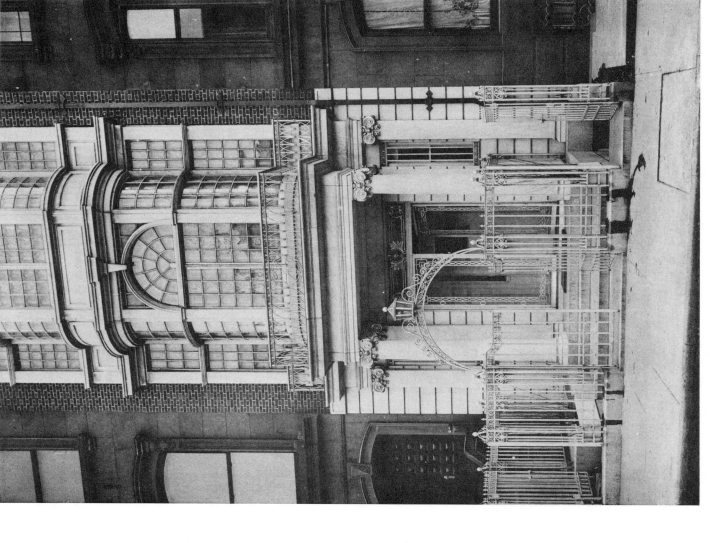

RESIDENCE OF THOMAS B. CLARKE, NEW YORK CITY.
1902

RESIDENCE OF PHILIP A. ROLLINS, NEW YORK CITY.
1902

PLATE 163

McKIM, MEAD & WHITE

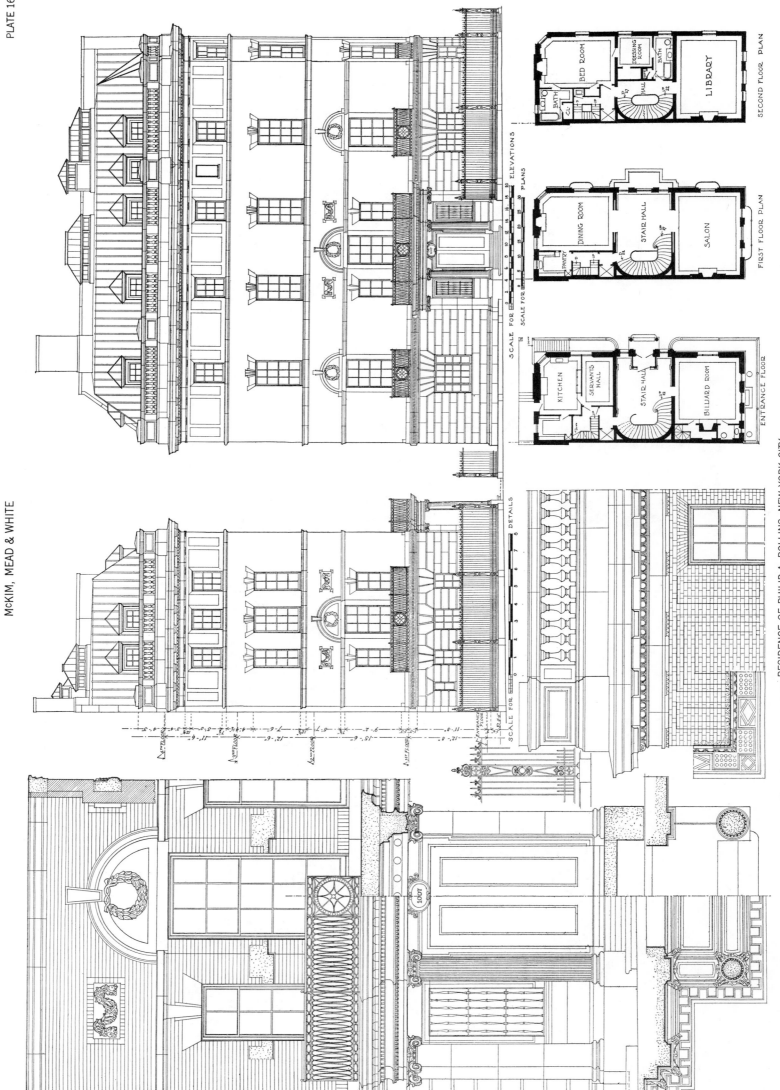

SECOND FLOOR PLAN

BED ROOM

DRESSING ROOM

BATH

LIBRARY

FIRST FLOOR PLAN

DINING ROOM

STAIR HALL

SALON

PANTRY

ENTRANCE FLOOR

KITCHEN

SERVANTS HALL

STAIR HALL

BILLIARD ROOM

SCALE FOR ELEVATIONS

SCALE FOR PLANS

SCALE FOR DETAILS

RESIDENCE OF PHILIP A. ROLLINS, NEW YORK CITY.
1902

PLATE 164

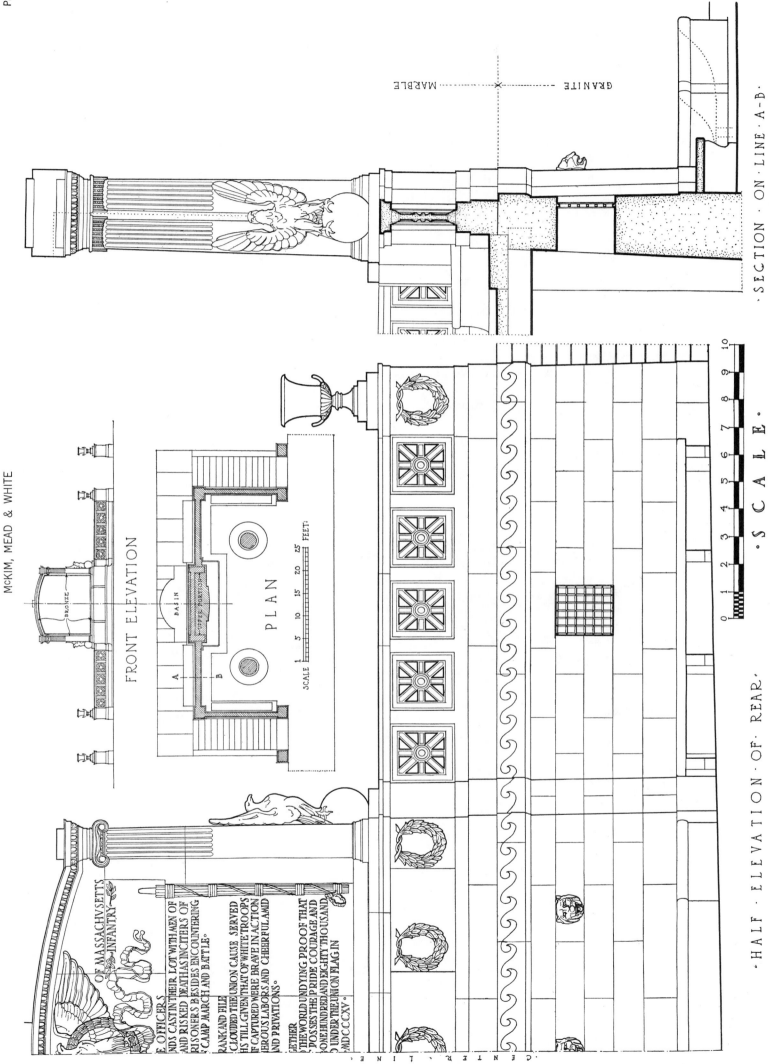

McKIM, MEAD & WHITE

FRONT ELEVATION

PLAN

· SECTION · ON · LINE · A · B ·

MARBLE

GRANITE

· HALF · ELEVATION · OF · REAR ·

· SCALE ·

THE ROBERT GOULD SHAW MEMORIAL, BOSTON, MASS.
1897

FRONT TOWARD STATE HOUSE

REAR TOWARD COMMON

ROBERT GOULD SHAW MEMORIAL, BOSTON, MASS.
1902

ENTRANCE FRONT

TERRACE AT ENTRANCE   DETAIL OF DOORWAY

"HARBOR HILL", C. H. MACKAY RESIDENCE, ROSLYN, L. I.
1902

THE STONE ROOM

DINING ROOM

"HARBOR HILL", C. H. MACKAY RESIDENCE, ROSLYN, L. I.
1902

PLATE 168

McKIM, MEAD & WHITE

ENTRANCE HALL

STAIR HALL

"HARBOR HILL", C. H. MACKAY RESIDENCE, ROSLYN, L. I.
1902

EAST ELEVATION

SOUTH ELEVATION

SITTING·ROOM

ANTE·ROOM

STUDY

BATH·ROOM

CHAMBER

CHAMBER

CHAMBER

ROOF

CHAMBER

BALCONY

UPPER·PART·OF·HALL

BUTLER'S·ROOM

BATH

CHAMBER

ROOF

BATH·ROOM

BATH

GALLERY

CHAMBER

CHAMBER

SECOND FLOOR PLAN

STONE·ROOM

DINING·ROOM

GLASS·ENCLOSED·PIAZZA

SALON

MAIN·HALL

SILVER

PANTRY

PANTRY

SCULLERY

KITCHEN

KITCHEN

CORRIDOR

PIAZZA

LAVATORY

SILVER

PANTRY

MEN'S·DRESSING·RM.

HOUSEKEEPER'S·RM.

STAIR·HALL

ENTRANCE·HALL

BILLIARD·ROOM

SCALE FEET

FIRST FLOOR PLAN

C. H. MACKAY RESIDENCE, ROSLYN, L. I.

1902

ELEVATION
AND SECTION
OF SMALLER
DORMERS

COPPER GUTTER

SLATE ROOF   COPPER GUTTER

SECTION THRO WINDOW
AT SIDE OF CENTRAL DORMER

SECTION THRO
CENTRAL DOOR
ON CENTER LINE

STONE WORK OF
INDIANA BLUE LIMESTONE

ELEVATION OF CENTRAL FEATURE OF FACADE

SCALE ▮▮▮▮▮▮▮▮▮▮▮▮▮▮ FEET

EXTERIOR DETAILS
C. H. MACKAY RESIDENCE, ROSLYN, L. I.
1902

RESIDENCE OF MRS. OELRICHS, NEWPORT, R. I.
1902

LIVING ROOM

STAIR HALL

RESIDENCE OF MRS. OELRICHS, NEWPORT, R. I.
1902

PLATE 173

McKIM, MEAD & WHITE

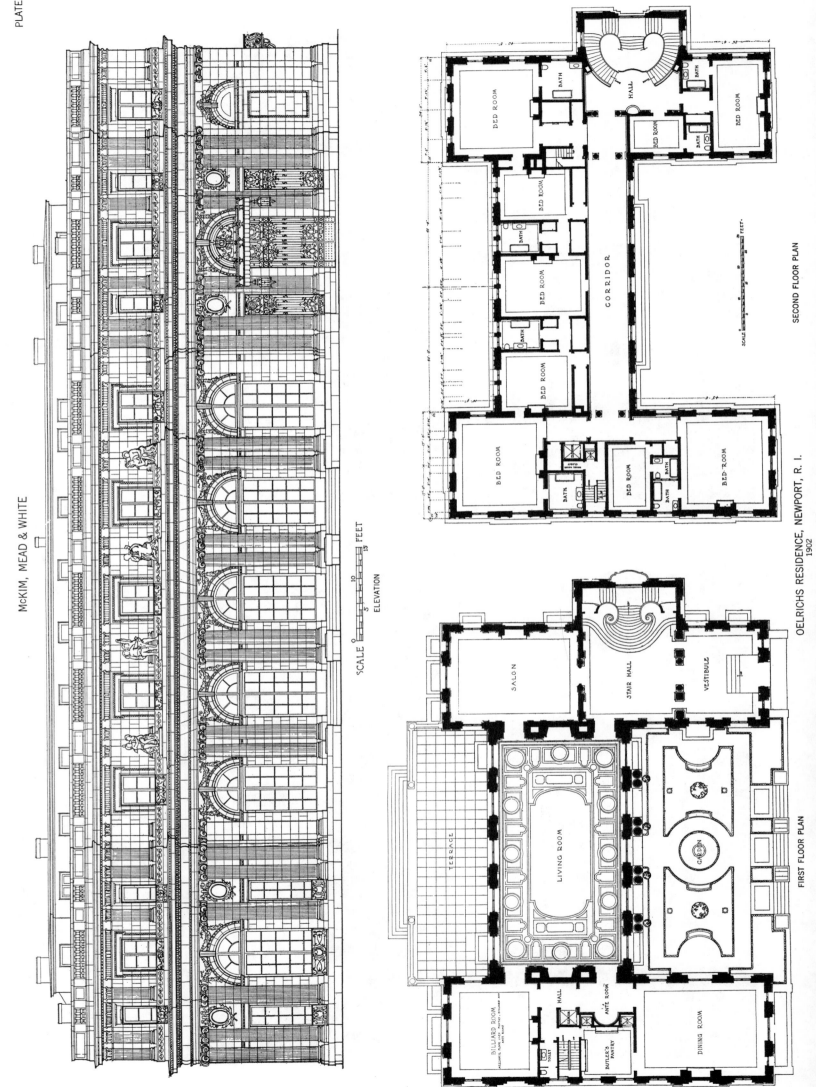

SCALE 0 5 10 15 FEET

ELEVATION

SECOND FLOOR PLAN

FIRST FLOOR PLAN

OELRICHS RESIDENCE, NEWPORT, R. I.
1902

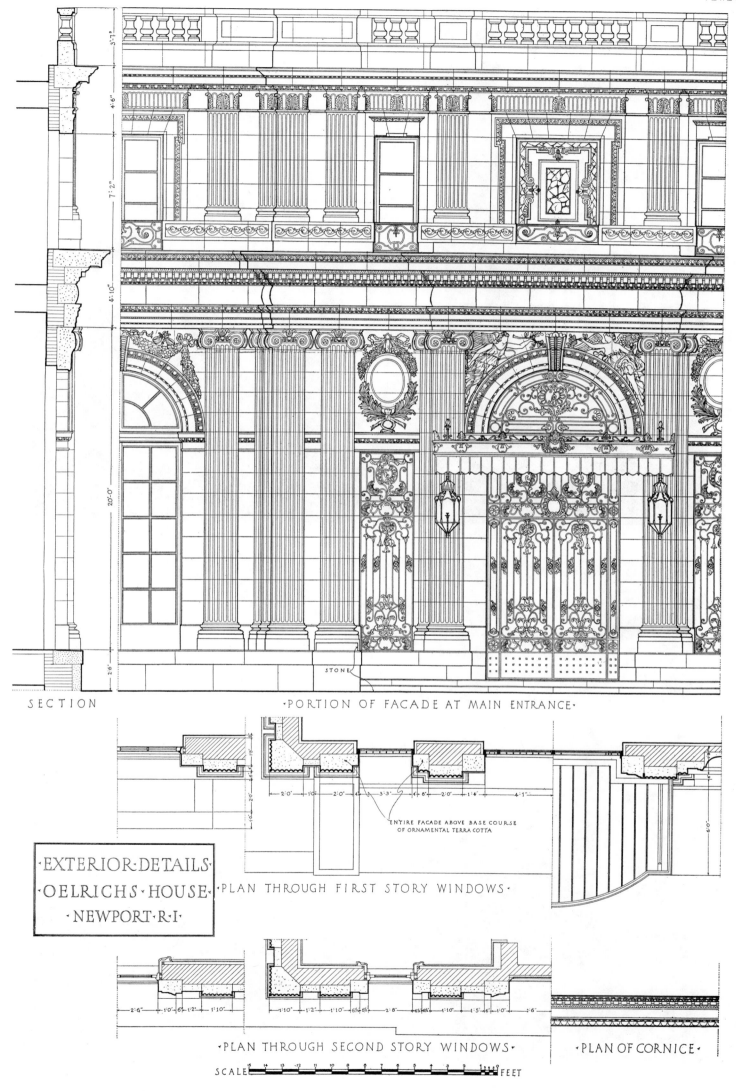

SECTION   ·PORTION OF FACADE AT MAIN ENTRANCE·

STONE

ENTIRE FACADE ABOVE BASE COURSE
OF ORNAMENTAL TERRA COTTA

·EXTERIOR·DETAILS·
·OELRICHS·HOUSE·
·NEWPORT·R·I·

·PLAN THROUGH FIRST STORY WINDOWS·

·PLAN THROUGH SECOND STORY WINDOWS·   ·PLAN OF CORNICE·

SCALE   FEET

ENTRANCE UNDER EAST TERRACE

EAST TERRACE WITH PLAN OF BUILDINGS

THE WHITE HOUSE, WASHINGTON, D. C.
ADDITIONS AND RESTORATIONS
1903

THE BLUE ROOM

ENTRANCE HALL

THE WHITE HOUSE, WASHINGTON, D. C.
RENOVATION OF INTERIOR
1903

DETAILS OF EAST ROOM

DETAILS OF DINING ROOM

0 1 2 3 4 5 6 7 8 9 10
·S C A L E·

ALTERATIONS TO THE WHITE HOUSE, WASHINGTON, D. C.
1903

PLATE 178

MCKIM, MEAD & WHITE

DETAIL OF EAST ROOM

MANTEL IN STATE DINING ROOM

THE WHITE HOUSE, WASHINGTON, D. C.
RENOVATION OF INTERIOR
1903

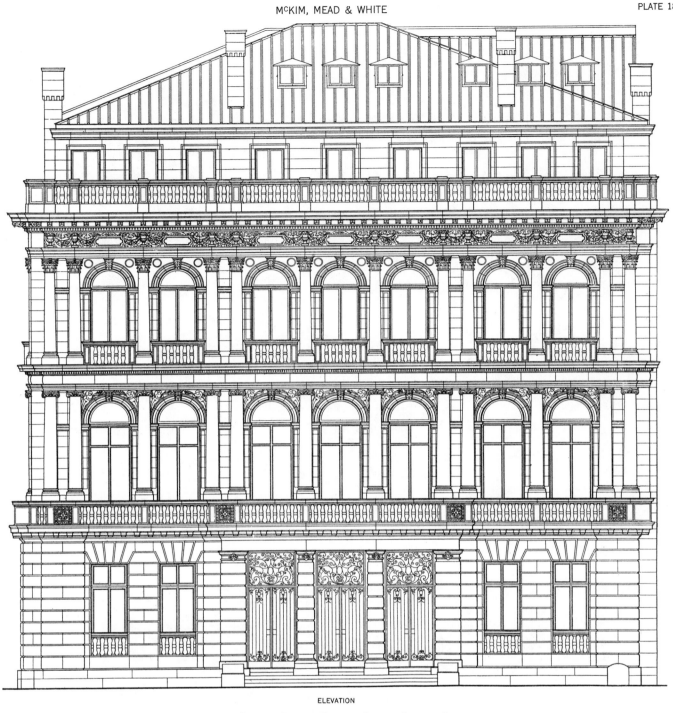

ELEVATION

SCALE 25 20 15 10 5 FEET

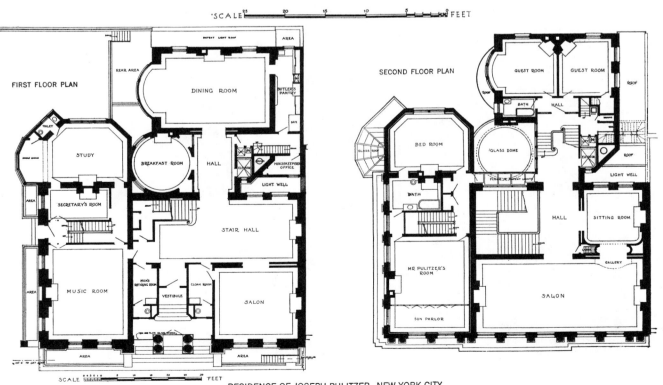

FIRST FLOOR PLAN

SECOND FLOOR PLAN

SCALE FEET

RESIDENCE OF JOSEPH PULITZER, NEW YORK CITY.
1903

PLATE 181

McKIM, MEAD & WHITE

BREAKFAST ROOM

EXTERIOR

RESIDENCE OF JOSEPH PULITZER, NEW YORK CITY
1903

PLATE 182

McKIM, MEAD & WHITE

SECOND STORY HALL

DINING ROOM

RESIDENCE OF JOSEPH PULITZER, NEW YORK CITY.
1903

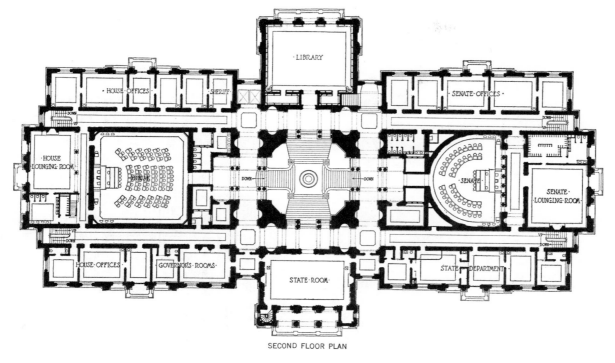

SECOND FLOOR PLAN

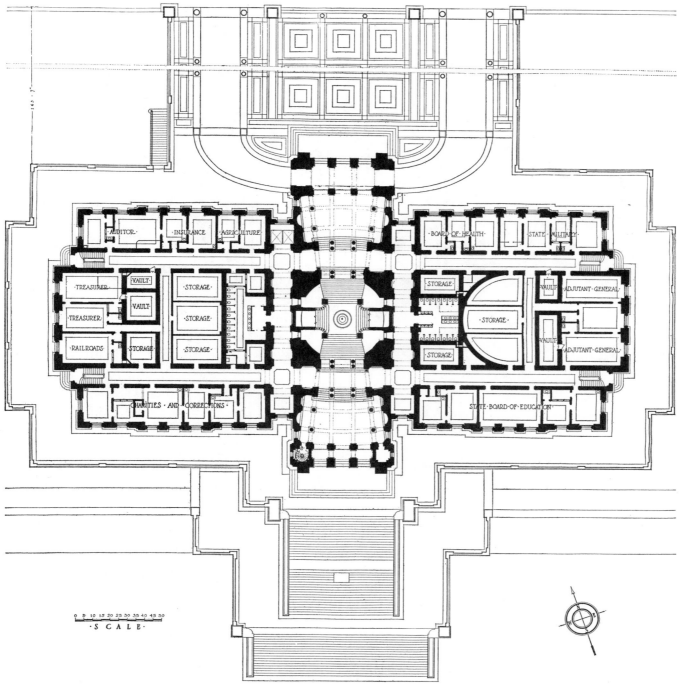

FIRST FLOOR PLAN

RHODE ISLAND STATE CAPITOL, PROVIDENCE, R. I.
BEGUN 1895. COMPLETED 1903.

PLATE 184

MCKIM MEAD & WHITE

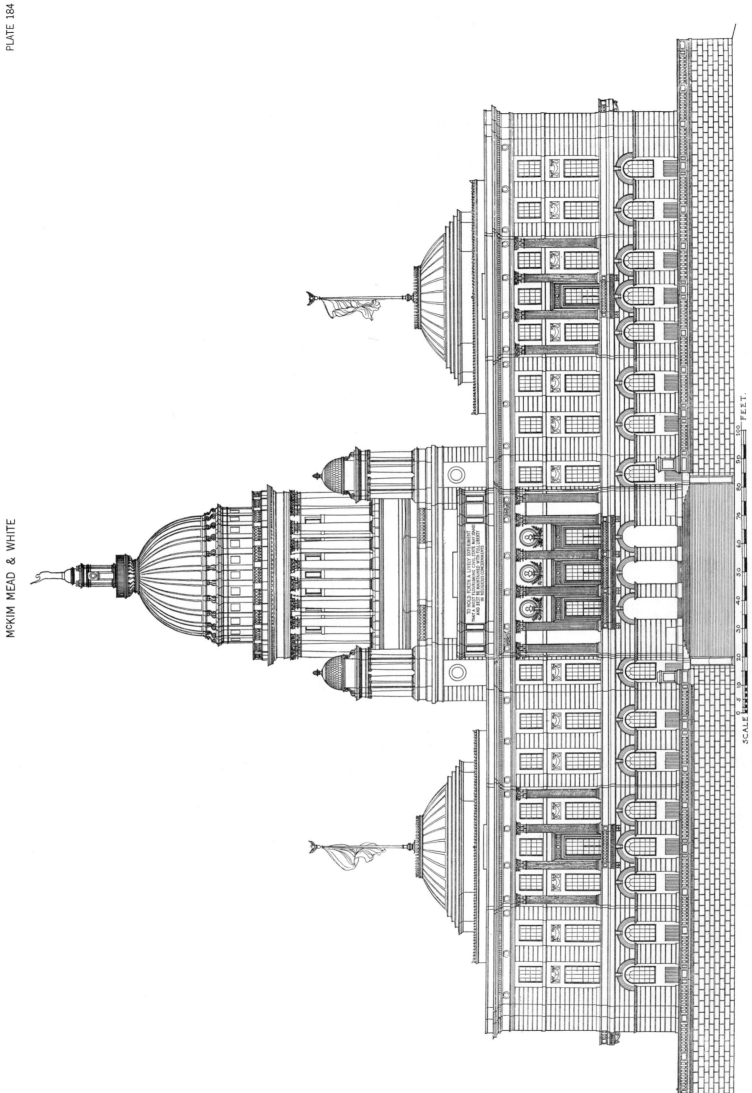

TO HOLD FORTH A LIVELY EXPERIMENT
THAT A MOST FLOURISHING CIVIL STATE MAY STAND
AND BEST BE MAINTAINED WITH FULL LIBERTY
IN RELIGIOUS CONCERNMENTS

SCALE

5 10 20 30 40 50 60 70 80 90 100 FEET.

THE RHODE ISLAND STATE CAPITOL, PROVIDENCE, R. I.

FRONT ELEVATION

BEGUN 1895 · COMPLETED 1903

GLASS

GRILLE

SAME AS BELOW

PAVONAZZI

SAME AS ABOVE

BRONZE

BRICK ARCH

0   5'   10'   15'   20'   25'   30'   35'   40'   45'   50'
· S C A L E ·

THE RHODE ISLAND STATE CAPITOL, PROVIDENCE, R. I.
SECTION THROUGH ROTUNDA
1895 - 1903

PLATE 186

MCKIM, MEAD & WHITE

THE RHODE ISLAND STATE CAPITOL, PROVIDENCE, R. I.
COMPLETED 1903

PLATE 187

MCKIM, MEAD & WHITE

DETAIL OF MAIN ENTRANCE

STAIR IN ROTUNDA

THE RHODE ISLAND STATE CAPITOL, PROVIDENCE, R. I.
1903

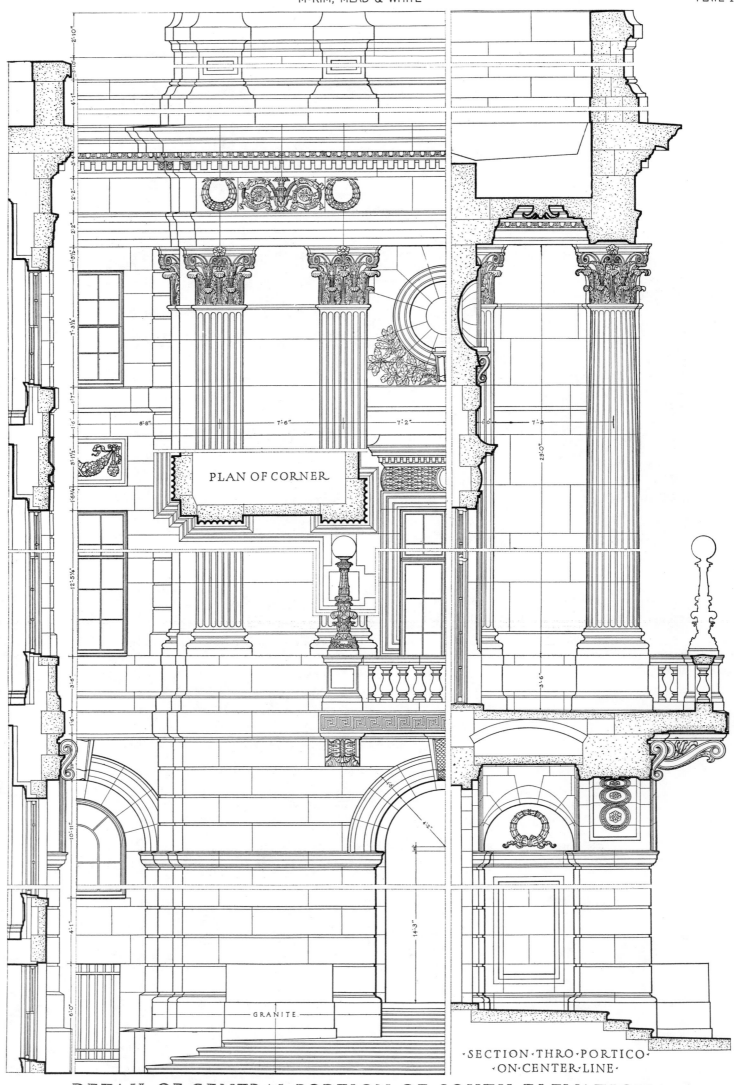

PLAN OF CORNER

SECTION·THRO·PORTICO
·ON·CENTER·LINE·

GRANITE

·DETAIL·OF·CENTRAL·PORTION·OF·SOUTH·ELEVATION·

SCALE   FEET

THE RHODE ISLAND STATE CAPITOL, PROVIDENCE, R. I.
1895 - 1903

HOUSE OF REPRESENTATIVES

GOVERNOR'S RECEPTION ROOM

THE RHODE ISLAND STATE CAPITOL, PROVIDENCE, R. I.
1903

UPPER PART OF ROTUNDA

THE SENATE CHAMBER

THE RHODE ISLAND STATE CAPITOL, PROVIDENCE, R. I.
1895 - 1903

PLATE 191

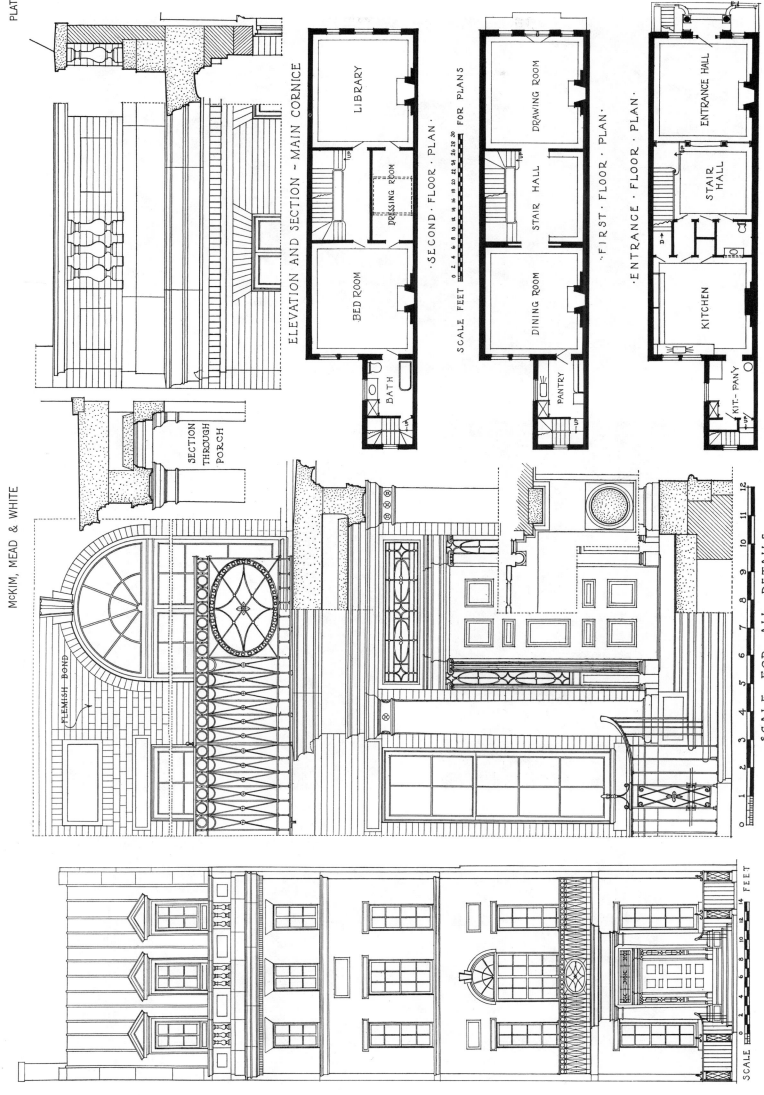

MCKIM, MEAD & WHITE

ELEVATION AND SECTION ~ MAIN CORNICE

SECTION THROUGH PORCH

LIBRARY

DRESSING ROOM

BED ROOM

BATH

·SECOND·FLOOR·PLAN·

SCALE FEET 0 2 4 6 8 10 12 14 16 18 20 22 24 26 28 30 FOR PLANS

DRAWING ROOM

STAIR HALL

DINING ROOM

PANTRY

·FIRST·FLOOR·PLAN·

ENTRANCE HALL

STAIR HALL

KITCHEN

KIT.-PANY

·ENTRANCE·FLOOR·PLAN·

FLEMISH BOND

SCALE FOR ALL DETAILS

0 1 2 3 4 5 6 7 8 9 10 11 12

RESIDENCE OF CHARLES DANA GIBSON, NEW YORK CITY.
1903

SCALE
0 2 4 6 8 10 12 14 FEET

PLATE 192

McKIM, MEAD & WHITE

LIVING ROOM

ENTRANCE HALL

DINING ROOM

RESIDENCE OF C. D. GIBSON, NEW YORK CITY.
1903

EXTERIOR

PLATE 193

MCKIM, MEAD & WHITE

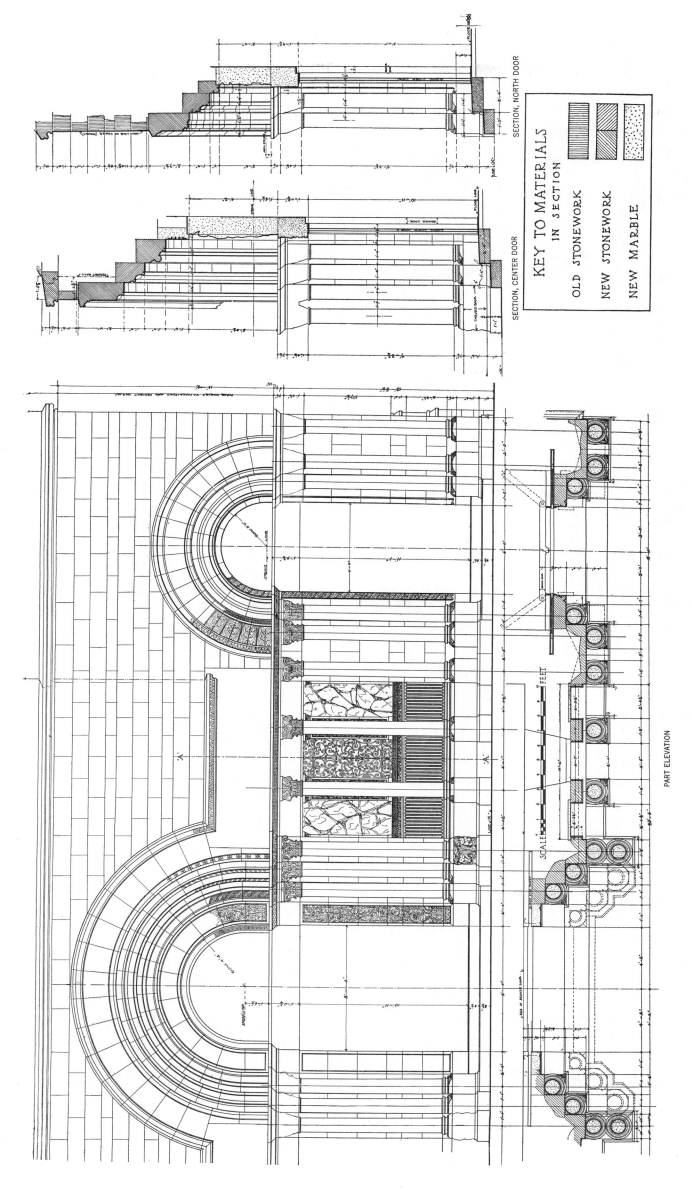

KEY TO MATERIALS
IN SECTION

OLD STONEWORK

NEW STONEWORK

NEW MARBLE

SECTION, NORTH DOOR

SECTION, CENTER DOOR

PART ELEVATION

SCALE

FEET

DOORWAYS TO ST. BARTHOLOMEW'S CHURCH, NEW YORK CITY.
1903

PLATE 194

MCKIM, MEAD & WHITE

EASTERLY DOORWAYS, ST. BARTHOLOMEW'S CHURCH, NEW YORK CITY.
1903

PLATE 195

McKIM, MEAD & WHITE

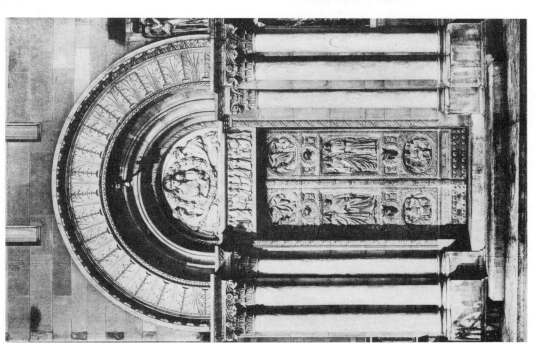

DETAILS OF EAST DOORWAYS
ST. BARTHOLOMEW'S CHURCH, NEW YORK CITY.
1903

PLATE 196

McKIM, MEAD & WHITE

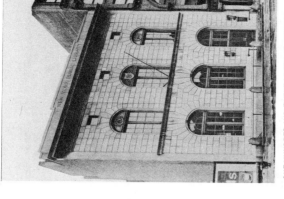

ONE HUNDRED AND TWENTY FIFTH ST. BRANCH
1904

ONE HUNDRED AND FIFTEENTH ST. BRANCH
1907

CHATHAM SQUARE BRANCH
1903

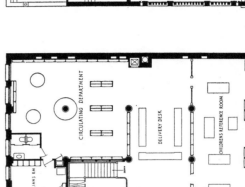

·ROOF READING ROOM PLAN·

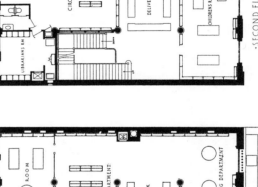

·SECOND FLOOR PLAN·

PLANS OF ST. GABRIEL'S BRANCH

·FIRST FLOOR PLAN·

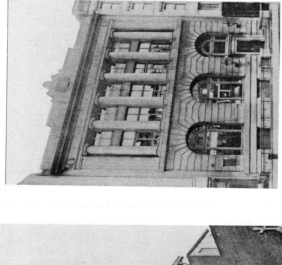

ST. GABRIEL'S BRANCH
1907

NEW YORK PUBLIC LIBRARY, BRANCH BUILDINGS

PLATE 197

McKIM, MEAD & WHITE

NEW YORK PUBLIC LIBRARY

N E W Y O

SECTION

LOGGIA AND ROOF DETAILS

ELEVATION

SECTION
ENTRANCE DOOR

THIRD STORY WINDOW HEAD

CENTER LINE OF WINDOW

BALUSTRADE
FIRST STORY WINDOW

"SCALE"

ENTRANCE DOOR

NEW YORK PUBLIC LIBRARY, ST. GABRIEL'S BRANCH
1906

SCALE

FEET

THOMPKINS SQUARE, 1904

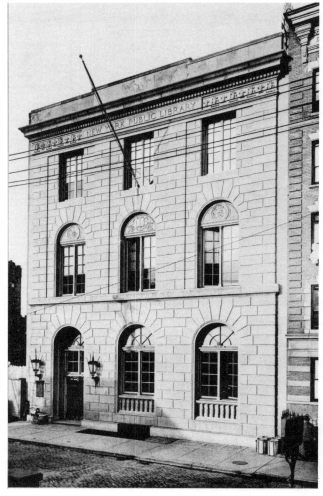

WOODSTOCK, 1913

MT. MORRIS, HARLEM, 1906

HAMILTON GRANGE, 1905

BRANCH BUILDINGS OF THE NEW YORK PUBLIC LIBRARY

PLATE 199

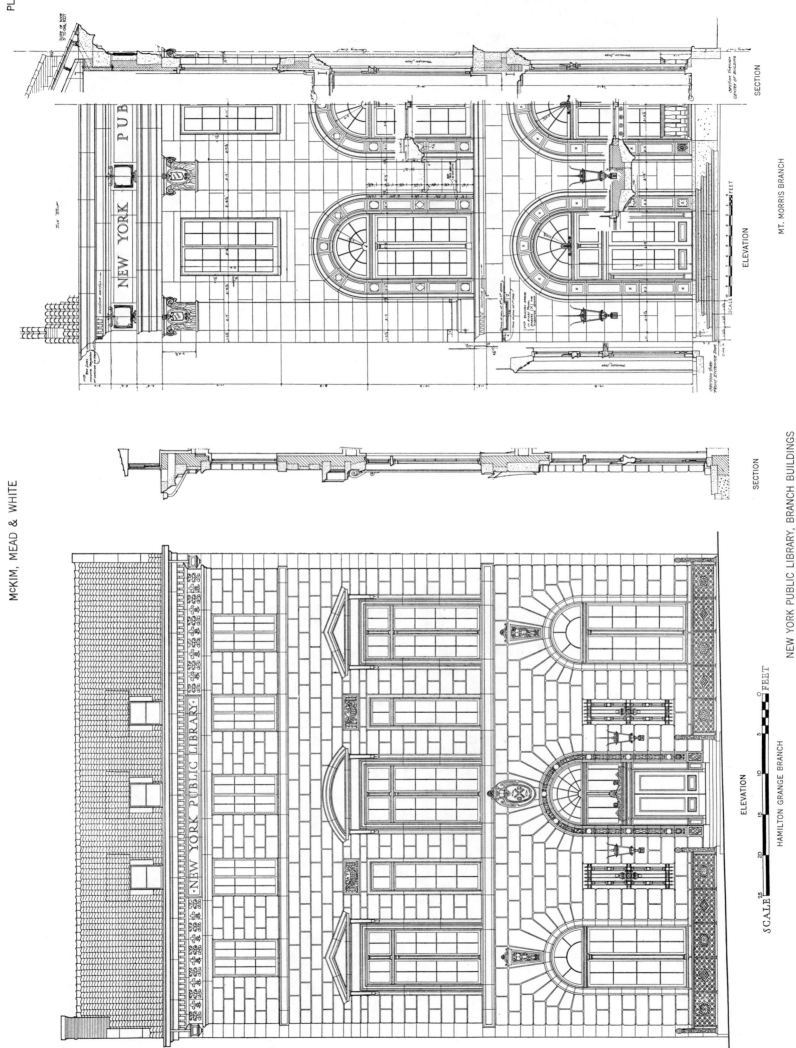

McKIM, MEAD & WHITE

NEW YORK PUB

NEW YORK PUBLIC LIBRARY

SECTION

SECTION

ELEVATION

ELEVATION

MT. MORRIS BRANCH

HAMILTON GRANGE BRANCH

SCALE

FEET

NEW YORK PUBLIC LIBRARY, BRANCH BUILDINGS

PLATE 200

MCKIM, MEAD & WHITE

SOUTH TERRACE WITH COLONNADE OF LIBRARY

EARL HALL · 1901

COLUMBIA UNIVERSITY, NEW YORK CITY.

FURNALD HALL, DORMITORY, 1912

FOUNTAIN IN SOUTH COURT, 1906

COLUMBIA UNIVERSITY, NEW YORK CITY.

PLATE 202

McKIM MEAD & WHITE

AUDITORIUM PLAN

PLATFORM

MAIN HALL

LOBBY

SMALL HALL

REFERENCE LIBRARY

FIRST FLOOR PLAN

SMALL HALL

READING ROOM

HAL

BIBLE STUDY

COMMITTEE ROOM

SECRETARY

RECEPTION R.M.

SCALE

0 10 20 30 40 50 FEET

SECTION

EAST ELEVATION

EARL·HALL·

SCALE

0 5 10 15 20 25 30 35 40 FEET

EARL HALL, COLUMBIA UNIVERSITY, NEW YORK CITY
1902

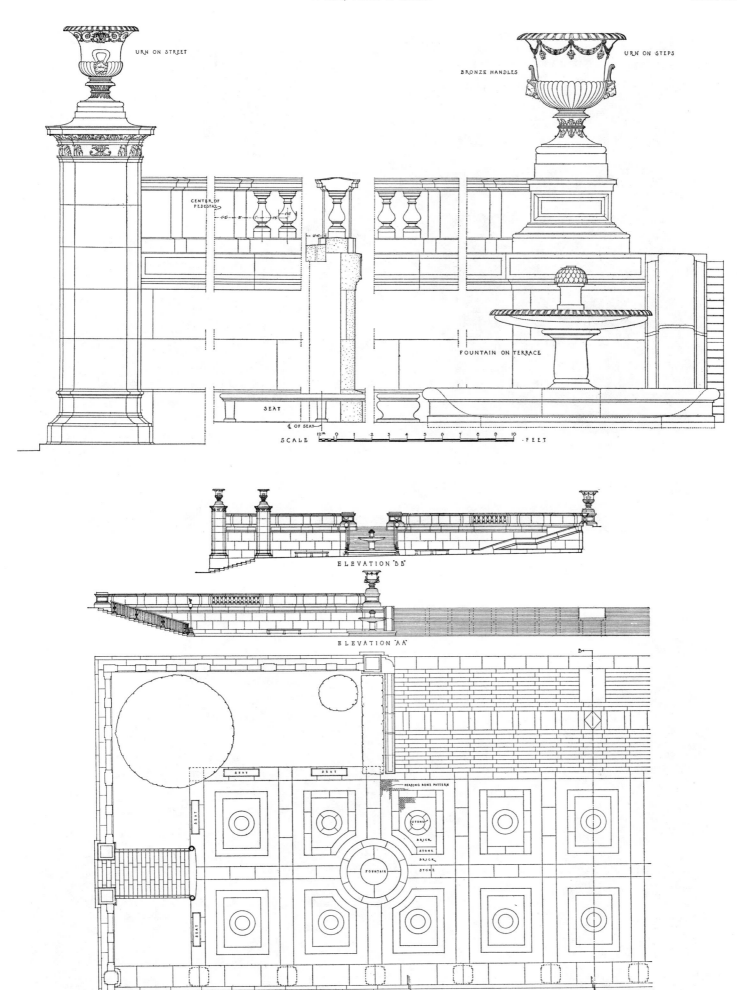

URN ON STREET

URN ON STEPS

BRONZE HANDLES

CENTER OF PEDESTAL

FOUNTAIN ON TERRACE

SEAT

℄ OF SEAT

SCALE · FEET

ELEVATION "BB"

ELEVATION "AA"

HERRING BONE PATTERN

SEAT

SEAT

STONE
BRICK
STONE
BRICK
STONE

FOUNTAIN

SEAT

BUILDING LINE

SCALE FEET

PLAN

DETAILS OF SOUTH COURT, COLUMBIA UNIVERSITY, NEW YORK CITY

ROBINSON HALL, ARCHITECTURAL SCHOOL
1904

MEMORIAL GATEWAY, CLASS 1885

HARVARD UNIVERSITY, CAMBRIDGE, MASS.

PLATE 205

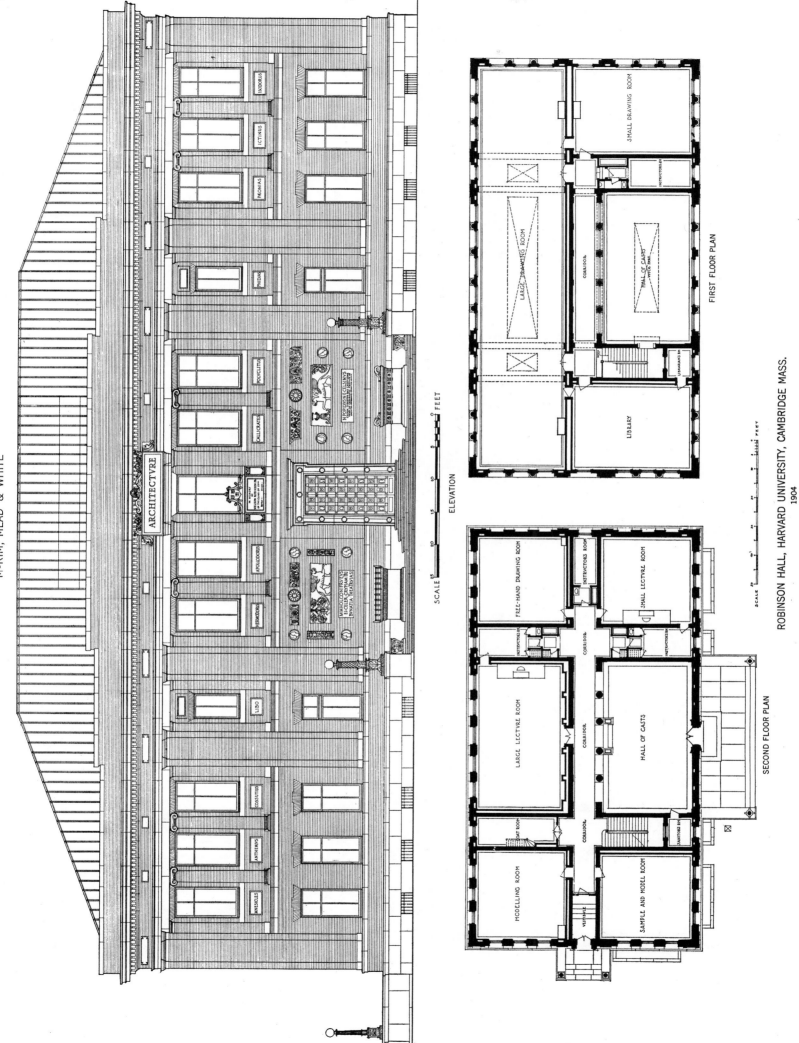

MCKIM, MEAD & WHITE

ARCHITECTVRE

ELEVATION

SCALE

FIRST FLOOR PLAN

SECOND FLOOR PLAN

ROBINSON HALL, HARVARD UNIVERSITY, CAMBRIDGE MASS.
1904

SCALE |⌐⊤⊤⊤⌐| 1 | 2 | 3 | 4 | 5 | FEET

BRONZE ENTRANCE DOORWAY

SCALE 12 11 10 9 8 7 6 5 4 3 2 1 INCHES

ROBINSON HALL SCHOOL OF ARCHITECTURE.
HARVARD UNIVERSITY, CAMBRIDGE, MASS.
1904

INTERBOROUGH RAPID TRANSIT COMPANY, NEW YORK CITY
POWER HOUSE
1903

SCALE 25 20 15 10 5 0 FEET

FIFTH AVENUE ELEVATION

BUILDING FOR THE KNICKERBOCKER TRUST CO., NEW YORK CITY.
1904

THE KNICKERBOCKER TRUST COMPANY, NEW YORK CITY
(NOW COLUMBIA TRUST COMPANY)
1904

PLATE 210

MCKIM, MEAD & WHITE

DETAIL OF ENTABLATURE

DETAIL OF DOORWAY

THE KNICKERBOCKER TRUST COMPANY, NEW YORK CITY
(NOW COLUMBIA TRUST COMPANY)
1904

VIEW OF BANKING ROOM

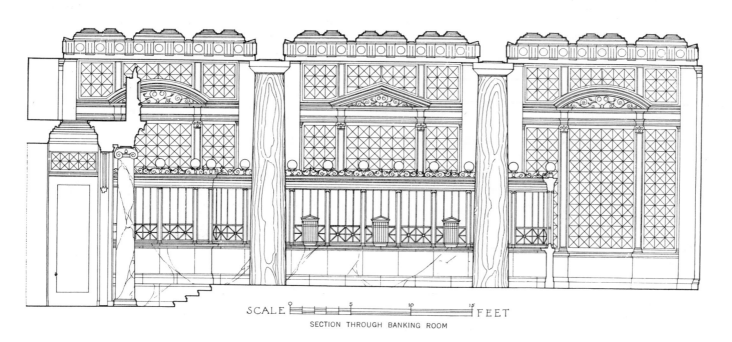

SCALE |———————————| FEET

SECTION THROUGH BANKING ROOM

BUILDING FOR THE KNICKERBOCKER TRUST CO., NEW YORK CITY.
1904

·SECTION·

·ELEVATION·

SCALE 10 9 8 7 6 5 4 3 2 1 0 FEET

·PLAN·

DETAIL OF DOOR

BUILDING FOR THE KNICKERBOCKER TRUST CO., NEW YORK CITY.
BRONZE ENTRANCE DOORS WITH MARBLE TRIM
1904

PLATE 213

MCKIM, MEAD & WHITE

ST. JAMES STREET FACADE

CORRIDOR LOOKING TOWARD MAIN BANKING ROOM

THE BANK OF MONTREAL, MONTREAL, CANADA.

1904

CRAIG STREET ELEVATION

INTERIOR OF MAIN BANKING ROOM

BANK OF MONTREAL, MONTREAL, CANADA.
1904

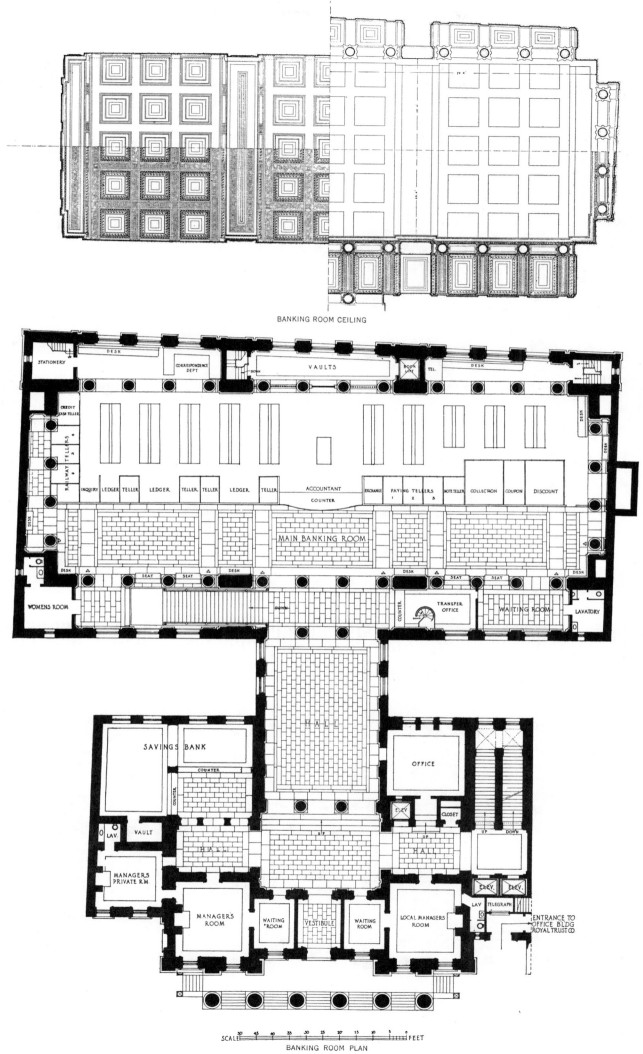

BANKING ROOM CEILING

SCALE FEET

BANKING ROOM PLAN

THE BANK OF MONTREAL, MONTREAL, CANADA.
1904

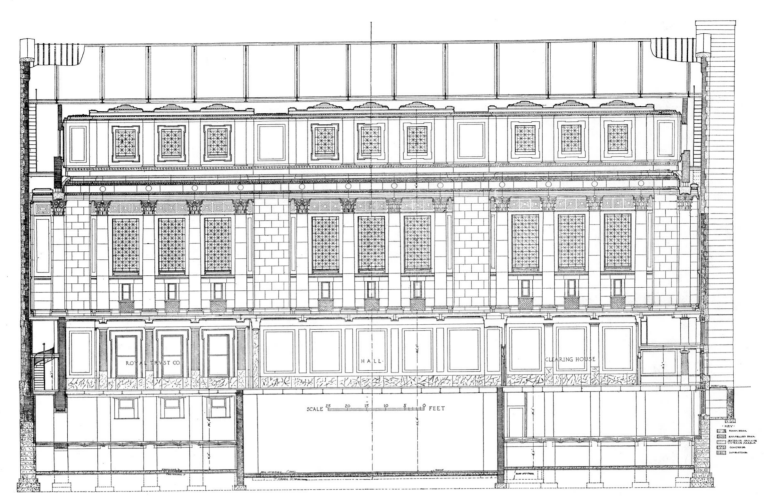

SECTION, MAIN BANKING ROOM

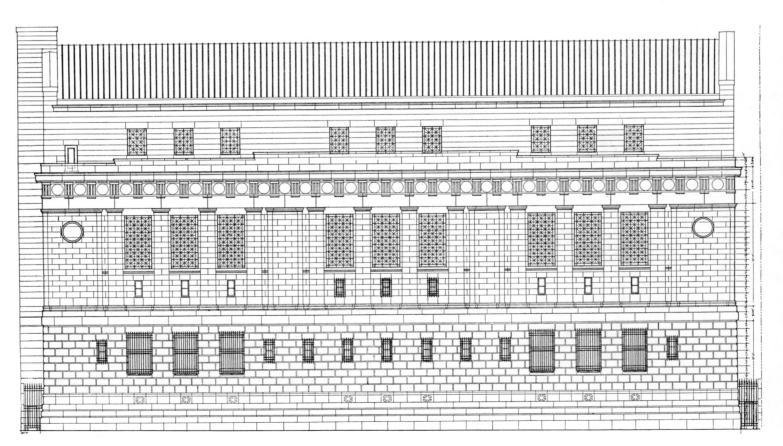

CRAIG STREET ELEVATION

THE BANK OF MONTREAL, MONTREAL, CANADA

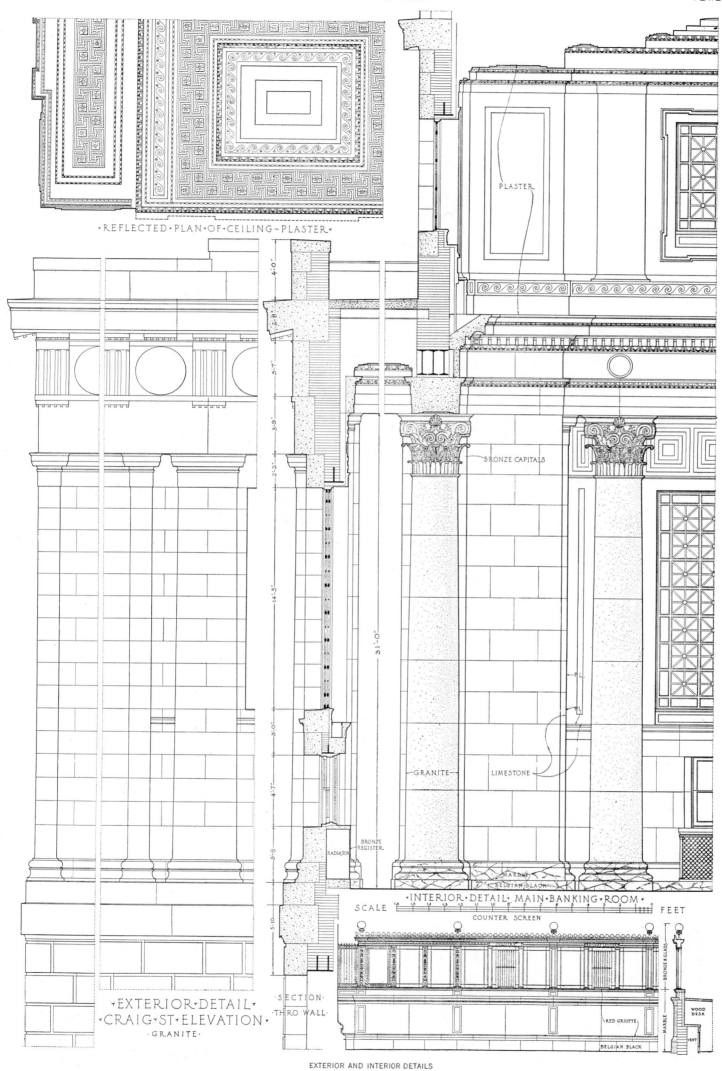

·REFLECTED·PLAN·OF·CEILING·PLASTER·

PLASTER

BRONZE CAPITALS

GRANITE

LIMESTONE

MARBLE
BELGIAN BLACK

·INTERIOR·DETAIL·MAIN·BANKING·ROOM·

SCALE   FEET

COUNTER SCREEN

BRONZE & GLASS

MARBLE

WOOD DESK

RED GRIOTTE

BELGIAN BLACK

VENT

RADIATOR

BRONZE REGISTER

·EXTERIOR·DETAIL·
·CRAIG·ST·ELEVATION·
·GRANITE·

·SECTION·
·THRO·WALL·

EXTERIOR AND INTERIOR DETAILS

THE BANK OF MONTREAL, MONTREAL, CANADA
1904

OSBORN

H. A. C. TAYLOR

GOELET

RUSSELL

WOODLAWN CEMETERY
1900 - 1902

SOUTH ELEVATION

SCALE 0 5 10 15 20 25 30 35 40 45 50 FEET

EAST ELEVATION

MAIN FLOOR PLAN

SCALE 0 5 10 15 20 25 30 35 40 50 FEET

SECOND FLOOR PLAN

NAUGATUCK HIGH SCHOOL, NAUGATUCK, CONN.
1904

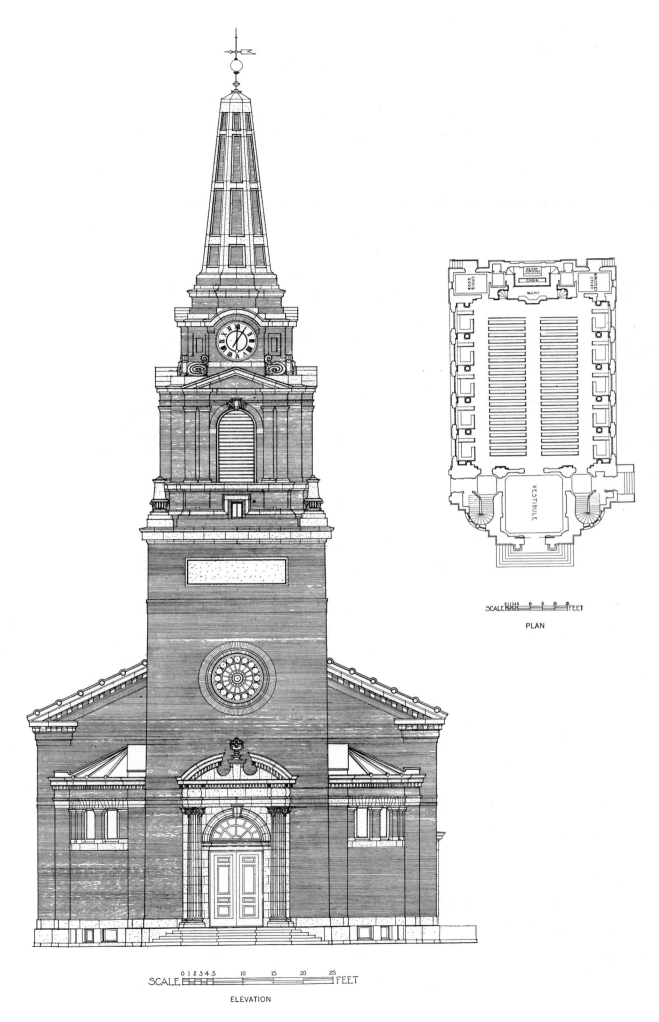

PLAN

ELEVATION

THE CONGREGATIONAL CHURCH, NAUGATUCK, CONN.
1905

PLATE 221

MCKIM, MEAD & WHITE

INTERIOR OF CHURCH

NAUGATUCK, CONNECTICUT.
1903 · 1905

PORTICO OF HIGH SCHOOL · SPIRE OF CHURCH

PLATE 222

McKIM, MEAD & WHITE

LIVING ROOM

DETAIL OF ENTRANCE FRONT

RESIDENCE OF T. JEFFERSON COOLIDGE, JR., MANCHESTER, MASS.
1904

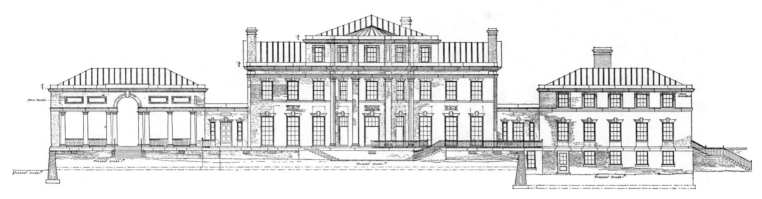

REAR ELEVATION

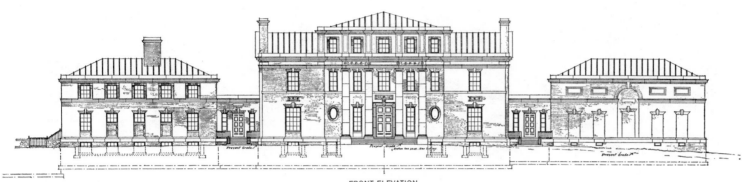

FRONT ELEVATION

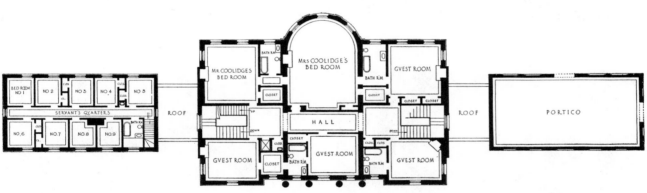

SECOND FLOOR PLAN

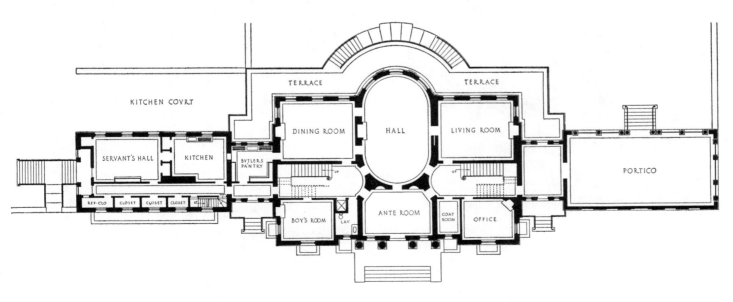

FIRST FLOOR PLAN

RESIDENCE OF T. JEFFERSON COOLIDGE, MANCHESTER, MASS.
1904

THE HALL

MANTEL IN HALL

INTERIOR OF LOGGIA

RESIDENCE OF T. JEFFERSON COOLIDGE, MANCHESTER, MASS.
1904

· SECTION ·

SCALE ⊢⊢⊢⊢⊢⊢⊢⊢⊢⊢⊢⊢⊢⊢⊢⊢⊢⊢ FEET

THE LAMBS' CLUB, NEW YORK CITY.
1906

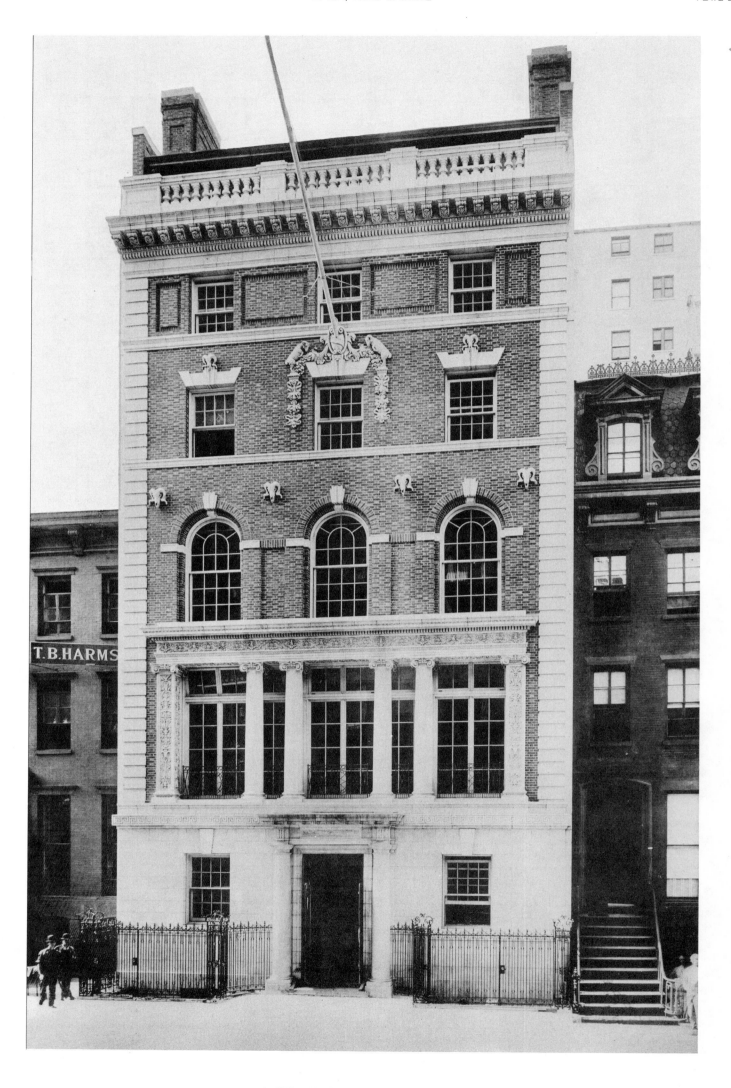

THE LAMBS' CLUB, NEW YORK CITY.
1906

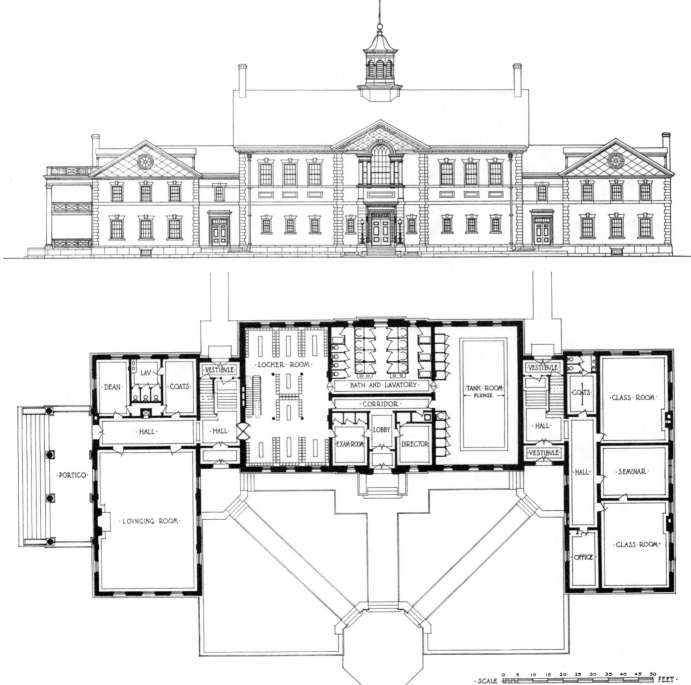

UNIVERSITY OF ILLINOIS, URBANA, ILL.
WOMENS' BUILDING
1905

DETAIL OF UPPER STORIES

DETAIL OF ENTRANCE PORTICO

THE HARMONIE CLUB, NEW YORK CITY.
1906

· S C A L E · FEET·

· P L A N S · O F · G R O V N D · A N D · T H I R D · F L O O R · F R O N T S ·

THE HARMONIE CLUB, NEW YORK CITY.
FRONT ELEVATION.
1906

EXTERIOR

INTERIOR OF BANKING ROOM

BUILDING FOR THE NEW ENGLAND TRUST CO., BOSTON, MASS.
1906

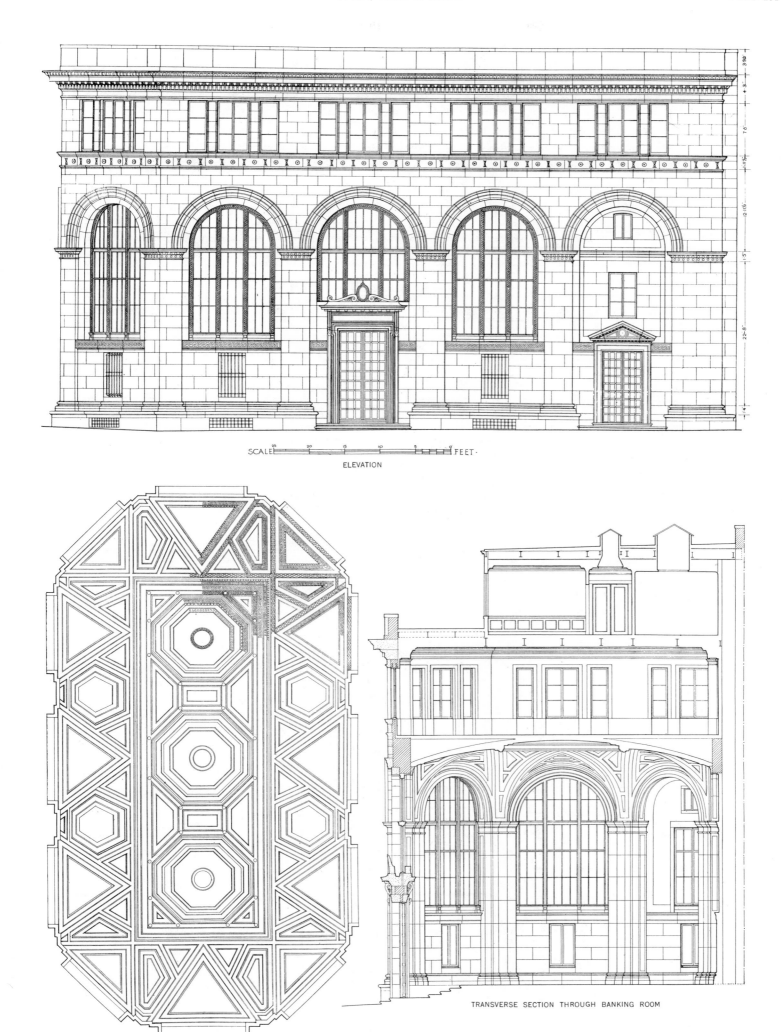

SCALE 25 20 15 10 5 0 FEET

ELEVATION

PLAN OF BANKING ROOM CEILING

TRANSVERSE SECTION THROUGH BANKING ROOM

BUILDING FOR THE NEW ENGLAND TRUST CO., BOSTON, MASS.
1906

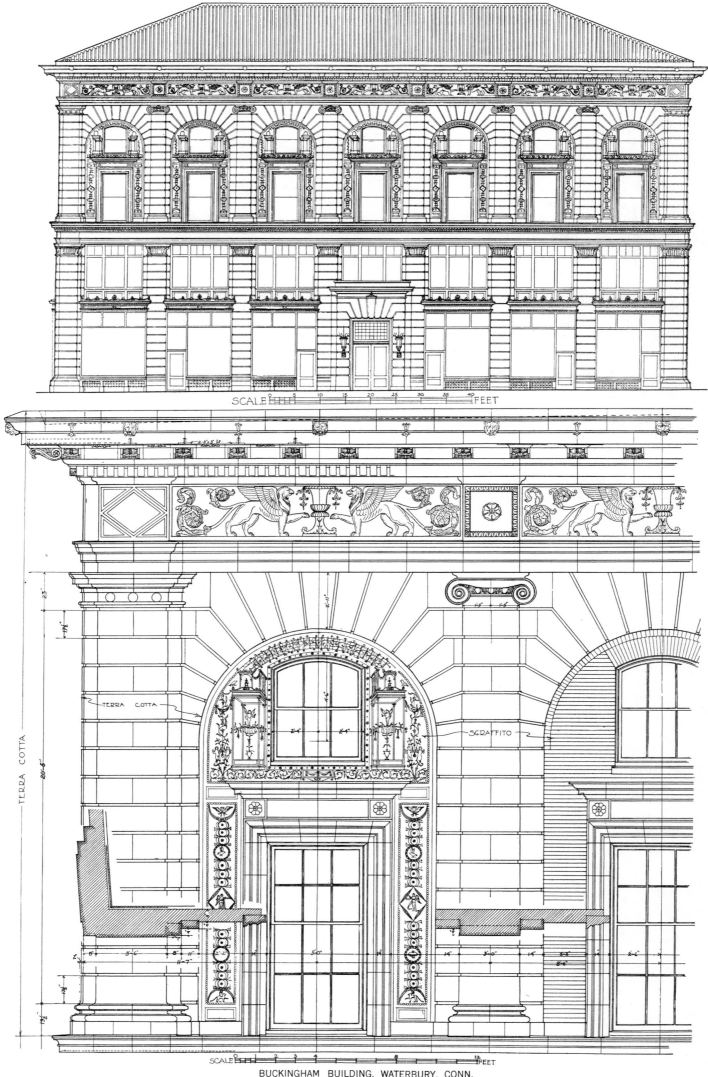

SCALE |⊢⊢⊢⊢⊢⊢⊢⊢ FEET

TERRA COTTA

TERRA COTTA

SGRAFFITO

SCALE |⊢⊢⊢⊢⊢⊢ FEET

BUCKINGHAM BUILDING, WATERBURY, CONN.
ELEVATION AND DETAILS
1906

BUILDING FOR THE GORHAM COMPANY, NEW YORK CITY.
1906

EXTERIOR DETAILS
BUILDING FOR THE GORHAM COMPANY, NEW YORK CITY.
1906

PLATE 236

MCKIM, MEAD & WHITE

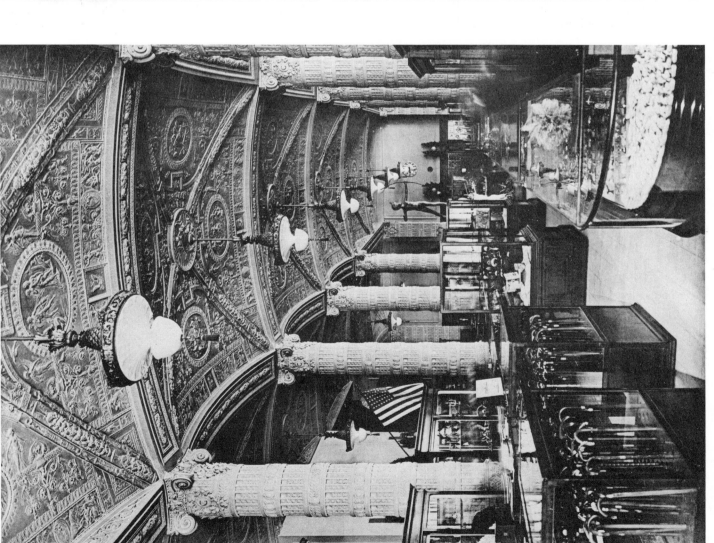

SHOW ROOM, SECOND FLOOR

MAIN STORE, FIRST FLOOR

BUILDING FOR THE GORHAM COMPANY, NEW YORK CITY.

1906

SCALE 0 5 10 15 20 25 30 FEET

SIDE ELEVATION

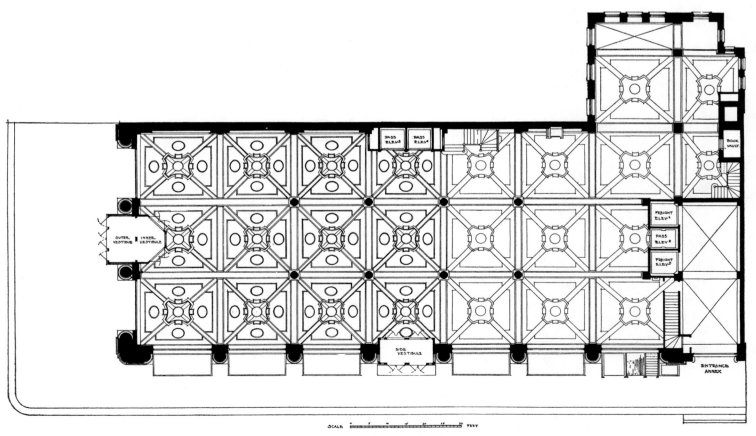

SCALE FEET

FIRST FLOOR PLAN

THE GORHAM BUILDING, NEW YORK CITY
1906

SCALE 0 5 10 15 20 FEET

THE GORHAM BUILDING, NEW YORK CITY
FIFTH AVENUE ELEVATION
1906

APPLIED
BRONZE
ORNAMENT

ENTANCE VESTIBULE SHOWN IN PLAN AND ELEVATION

SECTION THROUGH WALL

FLOOR PLAN   CEILING PLAN

BRONZE BALCONY RAIL

SCALE · OF · FEET ·

GRANITE   LIMESTONE

THE GORHAM BUILDING, NEW YORK CITY
DETAILS OF LOWER STORIES
1906

DETAILS
OF
VPPER
STORIES

SCALE |0 1 2 3 4 5 6 7 8 9 10 11 12 13 14 15| FEET

DETAILS OF UPPER STORIES

BUILDING FOR THE GORHAM CO., NEW YORK CITY.
1906

PLATE 241

MCKIM, MEAD & WHITE

LIBRARY OF J. PIERPONT MORGAN, NEW YORK CITY
1906

PLATE 242

McKIM, MEAD & WHITE

DETAILS OF BRONZE FENCE AND MARBLE POSTS.

DETAIL OF FACADE.

LIBRARY OF J. PIERPONT MORGAN, NEW YORK CITY.

1906

PLATE 242 A

CEILING OF LOGGIA

ENTRANCE DOORWAY

LIBRARY OF J. PIERPONT MORGAN, NEW YORK CITY
1906

PLATE 243

McKIM, MEAD & WHITE

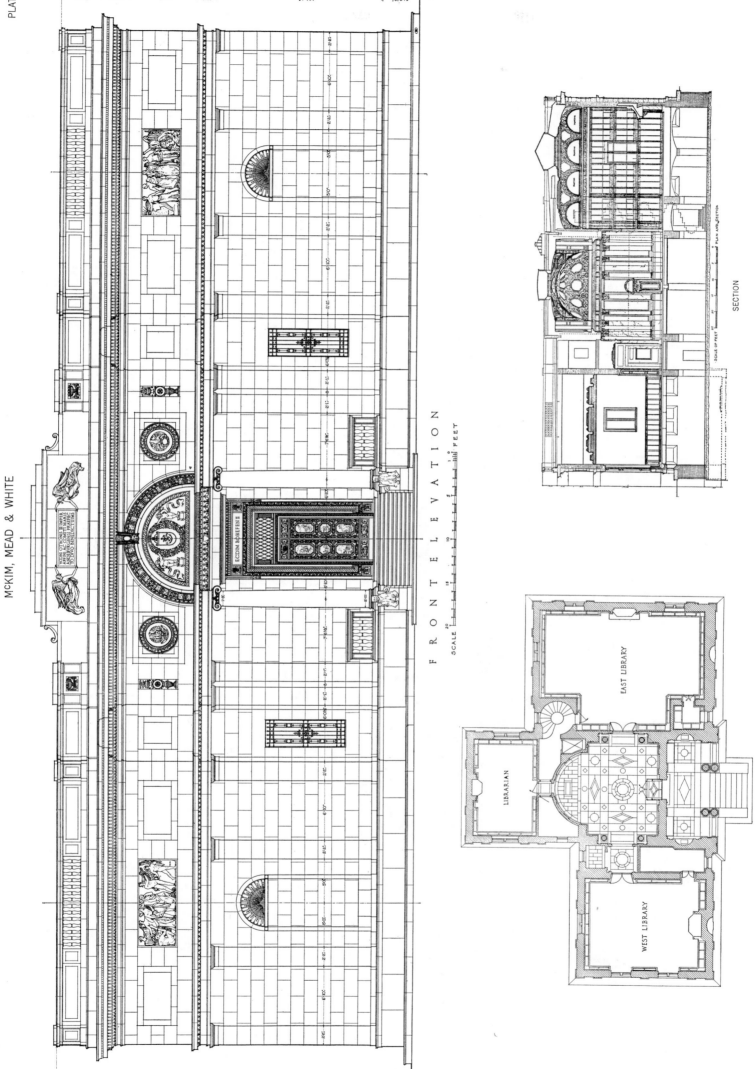

FRONT ELEVATION

SCALE _____ FEET

SECTION

PLAN

LIBRARY OF J. PIERPONT MORGAN, NEW YORK CITY.
1906

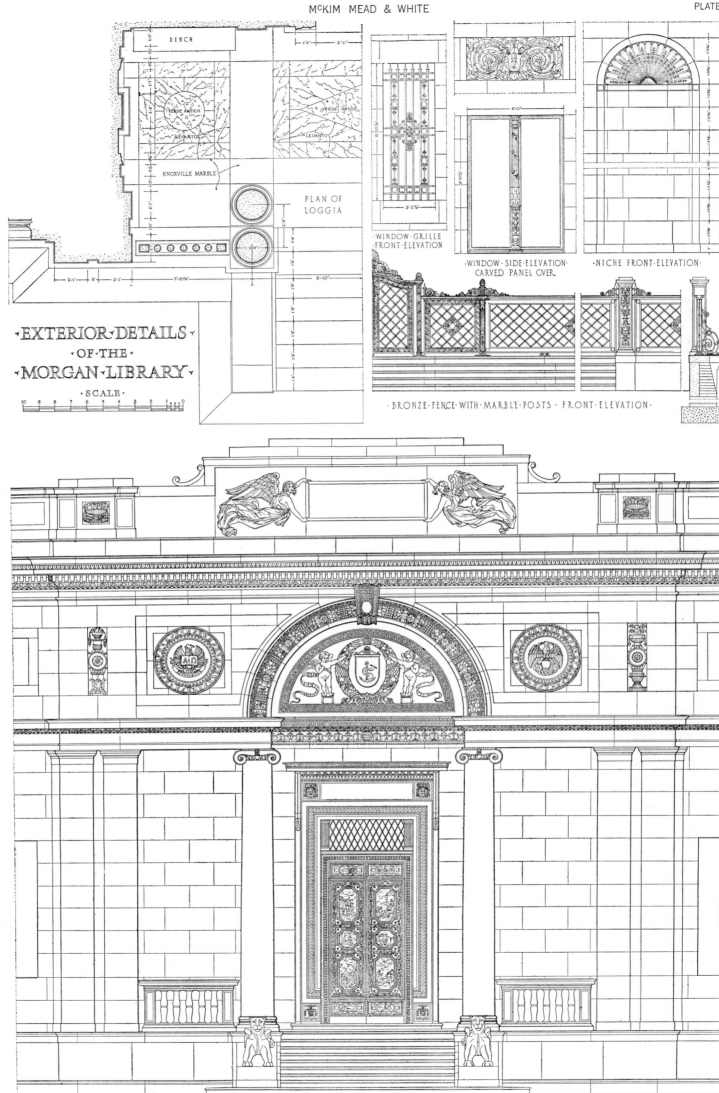

BENCH

VERDE ANTICO

LEVANTO

VERDE ANTICO

LEVANTO

KNOXVILLE MARBLE

PLAN OF LOGGIA

·EXTERIOR·DETAILS·
·OF·THE·
·MORGAN·LIBRARY·

·SCALE·

·WINDOW·GRILLE·
·FRONT·ELEVATION·

·WINDOW·SIDE·ELEVATION·
·CARVED·PANEL·OVER·

·NICHE·FRONT·ELEVATION·

·BRONZE·FENCE·WITH·MARBLE·POSTS·FRONT·ELEVATION·

LIBRARY OF J. PIERPONT MORGAN, NEW YORK CITY
1906

PLATE 245

MCKIM, MEAD & WHITE

GLASS SLAB

DELLA ROBBIA
LUNETTE PANELS

ANTIQUE
DOORWAY

MOSAIC

MOSAIC

SKYROS
MARBLE

CIPPOLINO
MARBLE

MOSAIC

WHITE MARBLE

CIPPOLINO
MARBLE

WHITE

SKYROS

WHITE

SKYROS
MARBLE

WHITE MARBLE

·SCALE·

FEET

LIBRARY OF J. PIERPONT MORGAN, NEW YORK CITY.
TRANSVERSE SECTION THROUGH ENTRANCE LOGGIA AND HALL
1906

PLATE 246

MCKIM, MEAD & WHITE

NICHE IN ENTRANCE HALL

ENTRANCE HALL LOOKING TOWARD EAST ROOM

LIBRARY OF J. PIERPONT MORGAN, NEW YORK CITY.
1906

PLATE 247

MCKIM, MEAD & WHITE

LIBRARY OF J. PIERPONT MORGAN, NEW YORK CITY.
VIEWS OF EAST ROOM
1906

PLATE 248

MCKIM, MEAD & WHITE

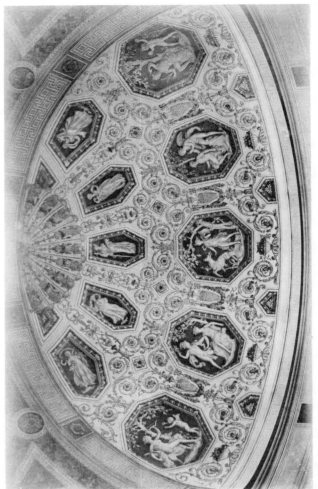

NICHE OPPOSITE ENTRANCE

DETAIL OF EAST ROOM CEILING

CEILING OF ENTRANCE HALL

LIBRARY OF J. PIERPONT MORGAN, NEW YORK CITY.

1906

PLATE 249

MCKIM, MEAD & WHITE

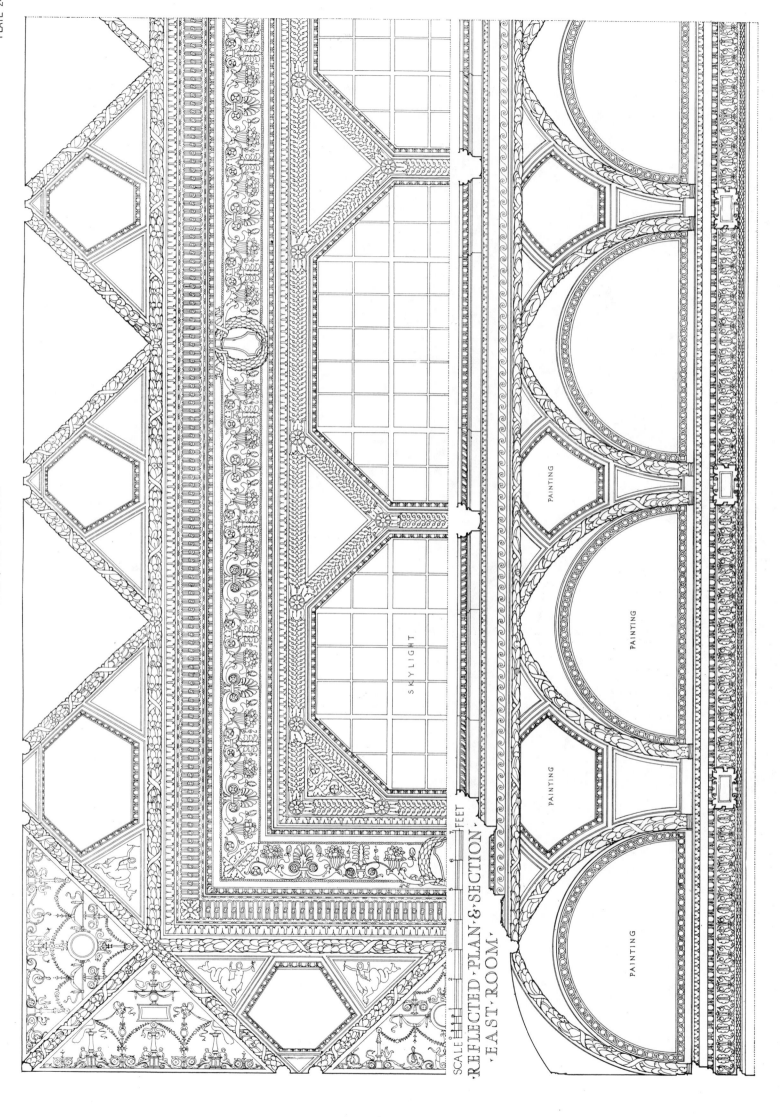

SCALE

FEET

·REFLECTED·PLAN·&·SECTION·

·EAST·ROOM·

SKYLIGHT

PAINTING

PAINTING

PAINTING

PAINTING

PAINTING

LIBRARY OF J. P. MORGAN, NEW YORK CITY.
DETAIL OF CEILING IN EAST ROOM
1906

MADISON SQUARE PRESBYTERIAN CHURCH
NEW YORK CITY
1906

PLATE 252

MCKIM, MEAD & WHITE

MAIN ENTRANCE DOORWAY

MADISON SQUARE PRESBYTERIAN CHURCH, NEW YORK CITY.

1906

DETAILS OF TERRA COTTA AND BRICKWORK

DETAIL SHOWING POLYCHROME TERRA COTTA PEDIMENT
MODELED BY A. A. WEINMAN

DETAIL OF ROUND WINDOW UNDER PORTICO

DETAIL OF UPPER CORNICE

MADISON SQUARE PRESBYTERIAN CHURCH, NEW YORK CITY.
1906

· FRONT ELEVATION ·
· MADISON SQVARE PRESBYTERIAN CHVRCH ·
· SCALE ¼ INCH EQVALS ONE FOOT ·

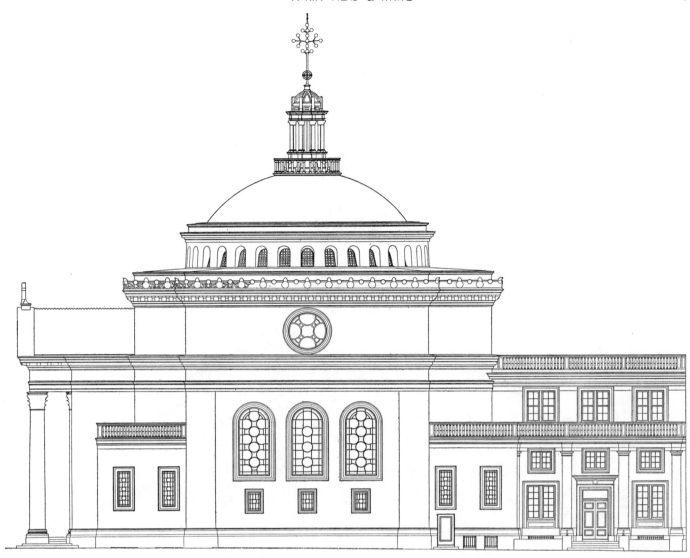

STREET ELEVATION

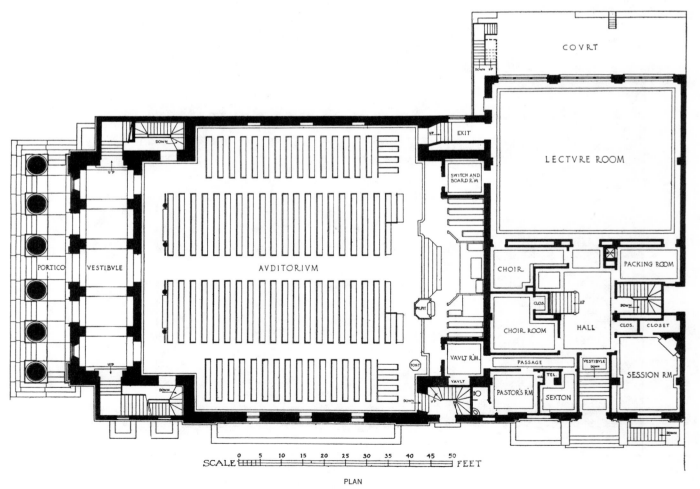

PLAN

MADISON SQUARE PRESBYTERIAN CHURCH, NEW YORK CITY
1906

SCALE | 0 1 2 3 4 5 | FEET

·DETAIL·OF·
·PORTICO·

·BALVSTRADE·

CAPITALS, ENTABLATURE, BALUSTRADE, WINDOW TRIM OF ORNAMENTAL TERRA COTTA, SHAFT OF COLUMN, POLISHED GREEN GRANITE. BASE, WHITE MARBLE. WALLS, LIGHT BRICK.

MADISON SQUARE PRESBYTERIAN CHURCH, NEW YORK CITY.
1906

·VPPER·
·CORNICE·

·MAIN·DOORWAY·

SCALE 0 1 2 3 4 5 FEET

SECTION

MARBLE·JAMB

WALLS, LIGHT BRICK. CORNICES AND DOOR TRIM, ORNAMENTAL TERRA COTTA MARBLE INSERTS, PAVONAZZO. OAK DOORS WITH IRON STUDS.
MADISON SQUARE PRESBYTERIAN CHURCH, NEW YORK CITY.
1906

PLATE 259

McKIM, MEAD & WHITE

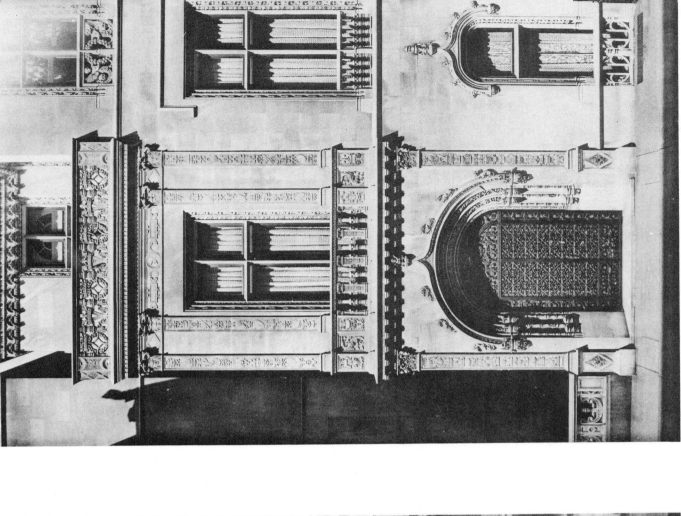

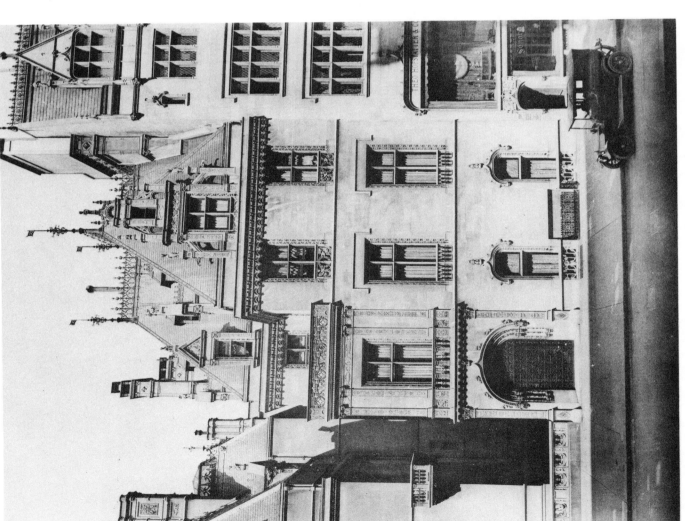

RESIDENCE OF MRS. W. K. VANDERBILT, JR., NEW YORK CITY
1906

PLATE 259

McKIM, MEAD & WHITE

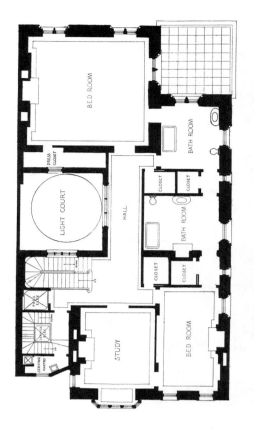

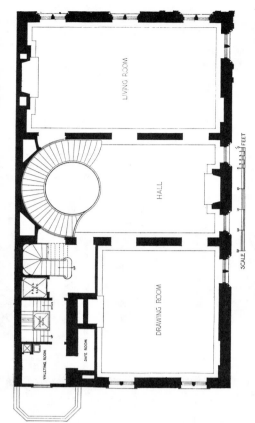

THIRD FLOOR PLAN

SECOND FLOOR PLAN

FIRST FLOOR PLAN

SCALE

FEET

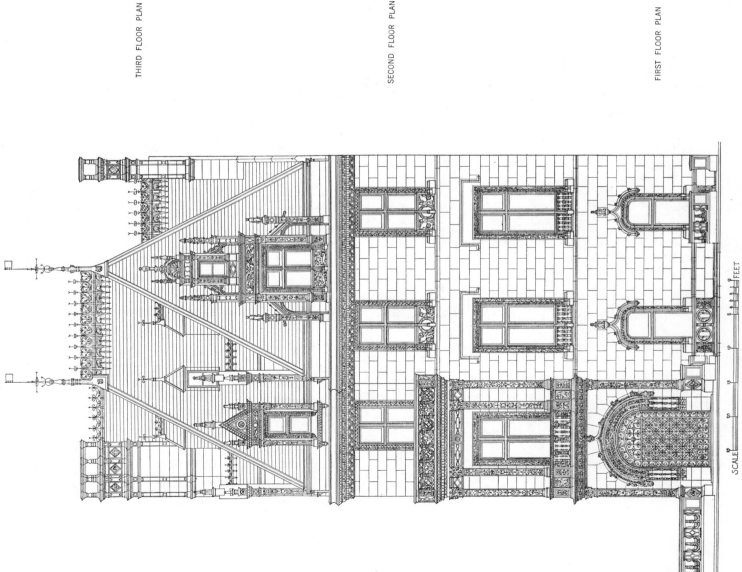

FRONT ELEVATION

SCALE

FEET

RESIDENCE OF MRS. W. K. VANDERBILT, JR., NEW YORK CITY.

1906

PLATE 260

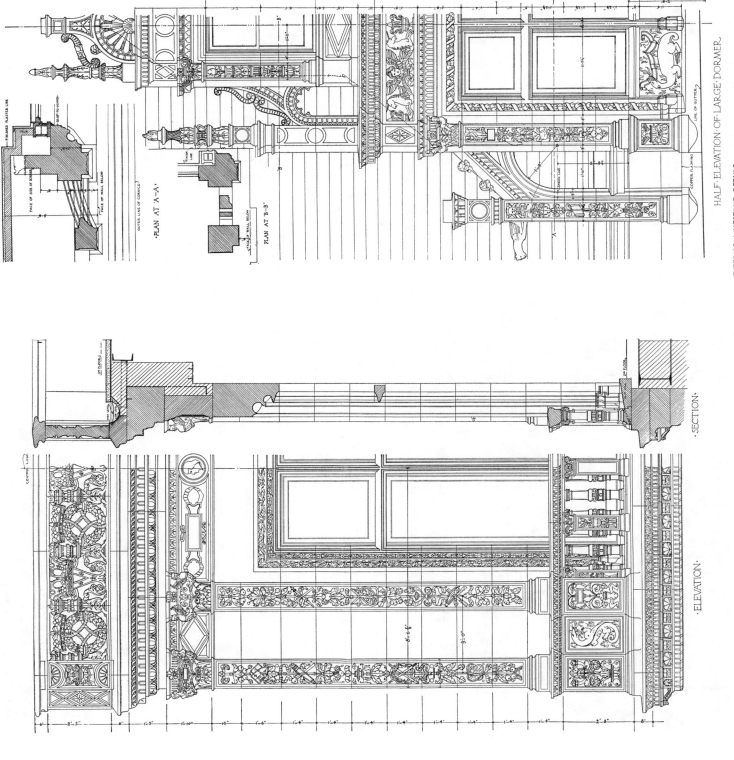

McKIM, MEAD & WHITE

EXTERIOR LIMESTONE DETAILS

RESIDENCE OF MRS. W. K. VANDERBILT, JR., NEW YORK CITY.

1906

BUILDING FOR TIFFANY & CO., NEW YORK CITY.
1906
ADJOINING BUILDING, 391 FIFTH AVENUE
1910

PLATE 262

McKIM, MEAD & WHITE

GENERAL VIEW OF STORE

STAIR AND ELEVATOR ENCLOSURE

BUILDING FOR TIFFANY & CO., NEW YORK CITY.
1906

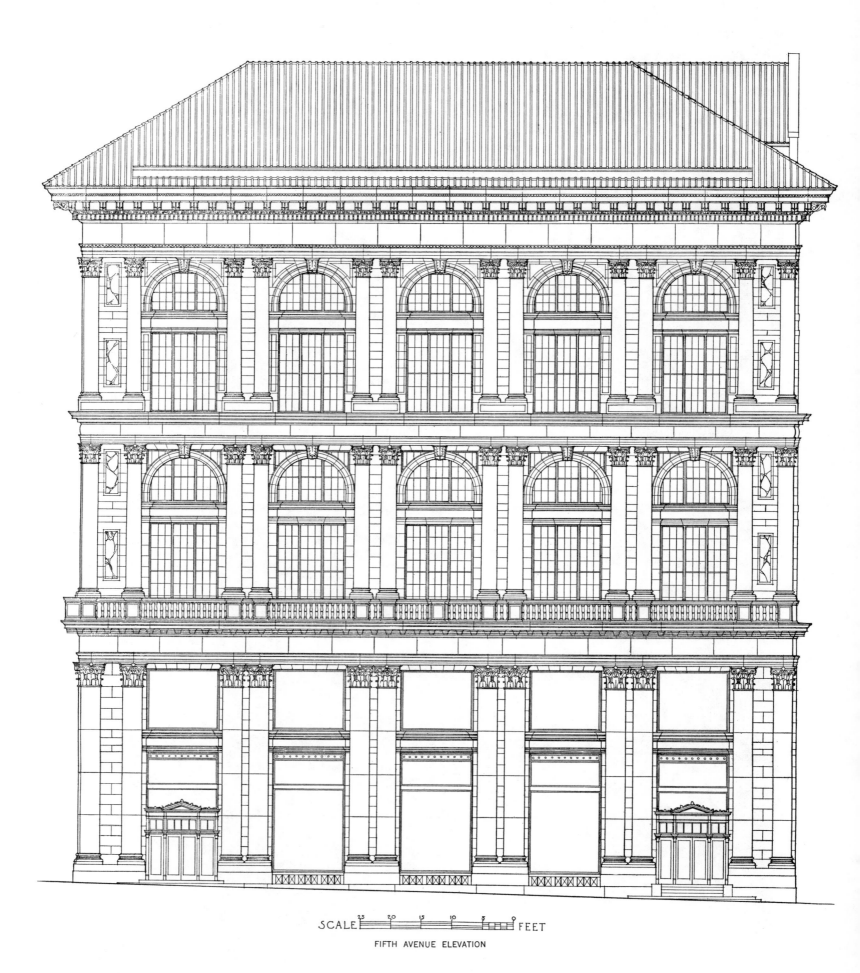

SCALE |⎯⎯⎯| FEET

FIFTH AVENUE ELEVATION

BUILDING FOR TIFFANY & CO., NEW YORK CITY.
1906

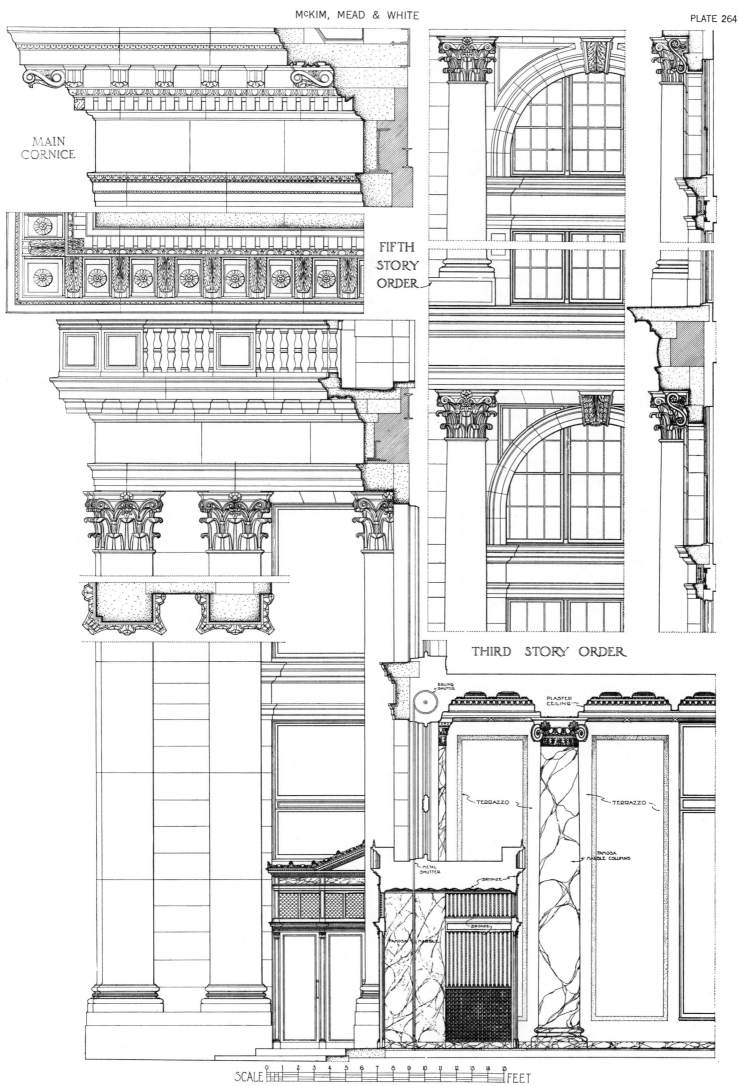

MAIN
CORNICE

FIFTH
STORY
ORDER

THIRD STORY ORDER

ROLLING
SHUTTER

PLASTER
CEILING

TERRAZZO

TERRAZZO

FAMOSA
MARBLE COLUMNS

METAL
SHUTTER

BRONZE

FAMOSA MARBLE

BRONZE

SCALE 0 1 2 3 4 5 6 7 8 9 10 11 12 13 14 15 FEET

EXTERIOR AND INTERIOR DETAILS
BUILDING FOR TIFFANY & CO., NEW YORK CITY.
1906

PLATE 265

McKIM, MEAD & WHITE

ELEVATION OF WAR COLLEGE

SCALE.
0   10   20   30   40   50   60 FEET

· WASHINGTON · HARBOR · POTOMAC · RIVER ·

· J A M E S   C R E E K ·

· C A N A L ·

4½ ST.

P Street

SCALE
0   100   200   300   400   500 FEET

A · WAR COLLEGE·
B · OFFICERS QUARTERS·
C · BOILER HOUSE · TEMPORARY ·
D · OFFICERS · MESS ·
E · BACHELOR · OFFICERS·
F · OFFICERS·
G · FIELD OFFICERS ·
H · NON-COM OFFICERS·

I · OBSERVATORY ·
J · CHAPEL·
K · POST OFFICE & GYMNASIUM·
L · ENGINEER-STORE-HOUSE·
M · ENGINEER· STORE-HOUSE·
N · QUARTER MASTERS 3+4 · COMIS-
       SARY-STORES & OFFICES·
O · MESS · HALLS·

P · HOSPITAL·
Q · ENGINEER· OIL HOUSE·
R · ENGINEER· TIMBER· SHED·
S · QUARTER-MASTERS· COAL·
     & WOOD SHED · SCHOOL·
T · ENGINEER TRADE SCHOOL·
U · ENGINEER· SCHOOL·
V · ENGINEER SCHOOL POWER HOUSE·

W · ADMINISTRATION·
X · POST BAKERY·
Y · QUARTER MASTERS· SHOPS·
     INCLUDING· CARPENTERS·
     PAINTERS·
     PLUMBERS·&
     BLACKSMITHS·
Z · STABLE· GUARD· HOUSE·

AA · QUARTER· MASTERS· WAGON SHED·
BB · BAND· QUARTERS·
CC · ENGINEER· STABLES·
DD · QUARTER· MASTERS· STABLES·
EE · ENGINEER· STABLES·
FF · QUARTER MASTERS OIL HOUSE·
GG · PONTOON SHEDS·
     MAGAZINE·
ERECTED·   PROPOSED·

BLOCK PLAN
1908

ARMY WAR COLLEGE AND ENGINEERS' POST, WASHINGTON, D. C.

PLATE 266

MCKIM, MEAD & WHITE

THE ARMY WAR COLLEGE, WASHINGTON, D. C.
1908

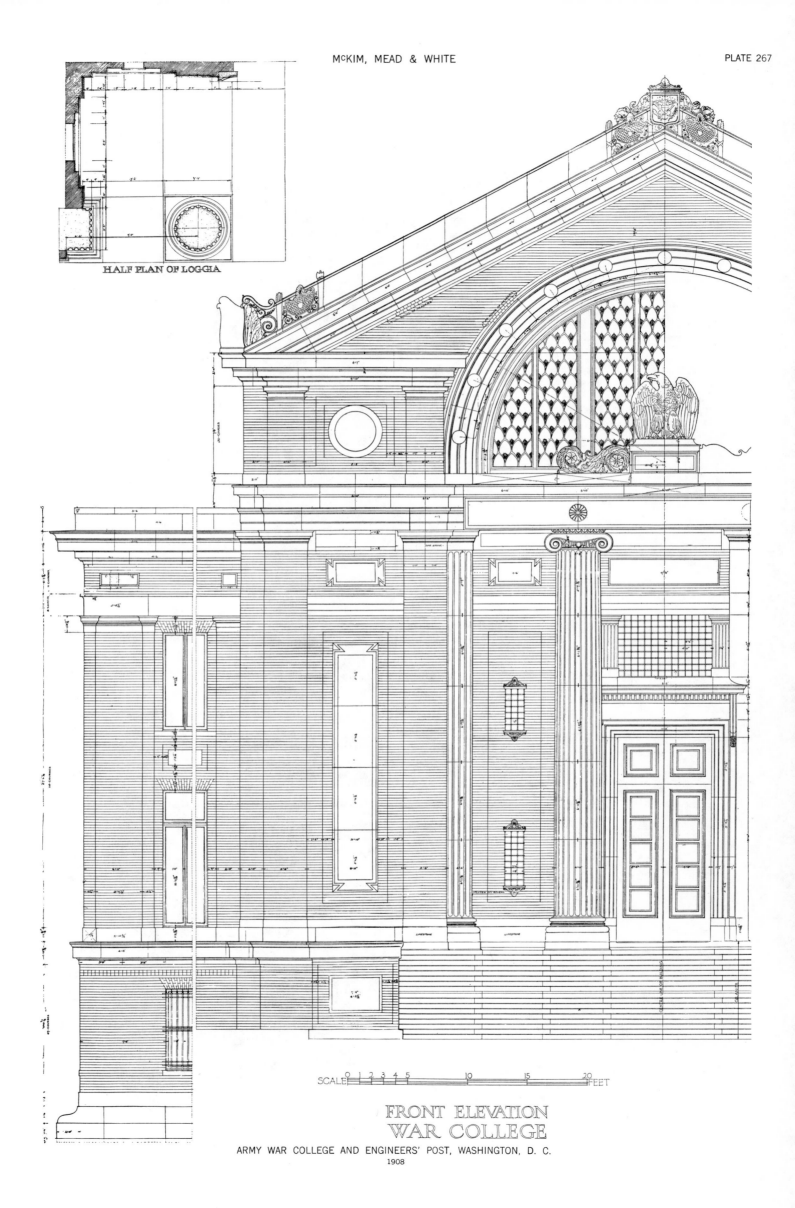

HALF PLAN OF LOGGIA

SCALE 0 1 2 3 4 5   10   15   20 FEET

FRONT ELEVATION
WAR COLLEGE
ARMY WAR COLLEGE AND ENGINEERS' POST, WASHINGTON, D. C.
1908

ENTRANCE FRONT

REAR OF HOUSE WITH GARDEN

RESIDENCE OF JAMES L. BREESE, SOUTHAMPTON, L. I.
1906

PLATE 269

MCKIM, MEAD & WHITE

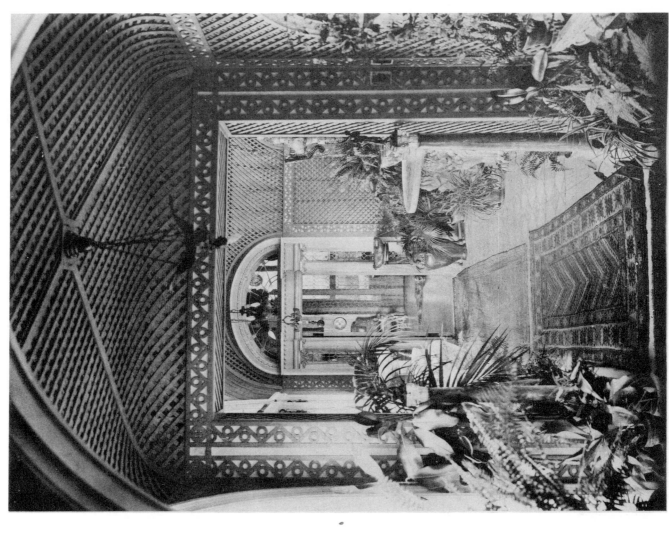

CONSERVATORY

RESIDENCE OF JAMES L. BREESE, SOUTHAMPTON, L. I.
1906

MUSIC ROOM

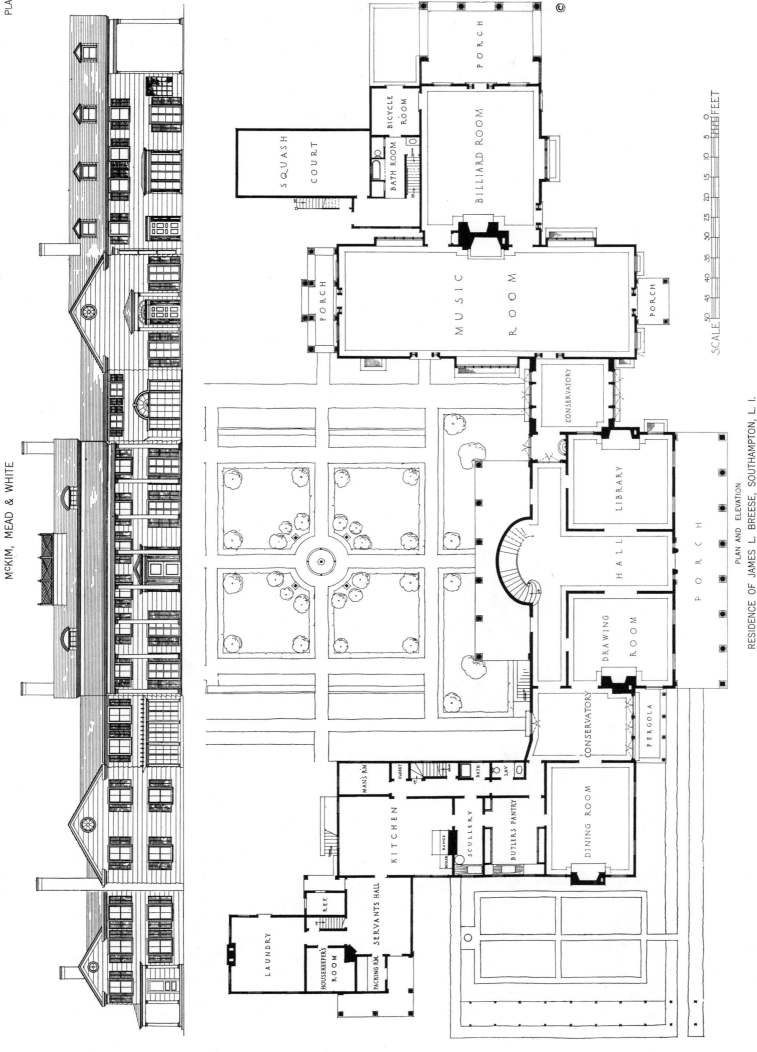

PLATE 270

McKIM, MEAD & WHITE

SQUASH COURT

BICYCLE ROOM

BATH ROOM

BILLIARD ROOM

PORCH

PORCH

MUSIC ROOM

PORCH

CONSERVATORY

LIBRARY

HALL

PORCH

DRAWING ROOM

CONSERVATORY

PERGOLA

MAN'S RM

CLOSET

BATH

LAV

KITCHEN

RANGE

SCULLERY

BUTLER'S PANTRY

DINING ROOM

R.R.F.

SERVANTS HALL

LAUNDRY

HOUSEKEEPER'S ROOM

PACKING RM.

SCALE

FEET

PLAN AND ELEVATION

RESIDENCE OF JAMES L. BREESE, SOUTHAMPTON, L. I.
1906

PLATE 271

MCKIM, MEAD & WHITE

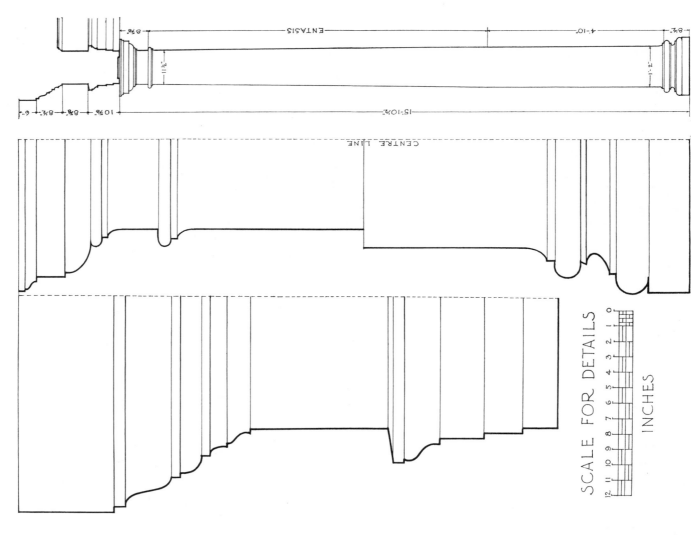

CENTRE LINE

ENTASIS

SCALE FOR DETAILS

INCHES

RESIDENCE OF JAMES L. BREESE, SOUTHAMPTON L. I.
DETAILS OF PORCH, ENTRANCE FRONT
1906

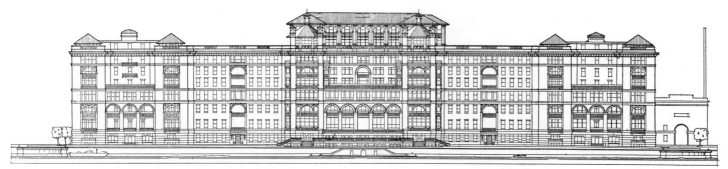

ELEVATION ON EAST RIVER

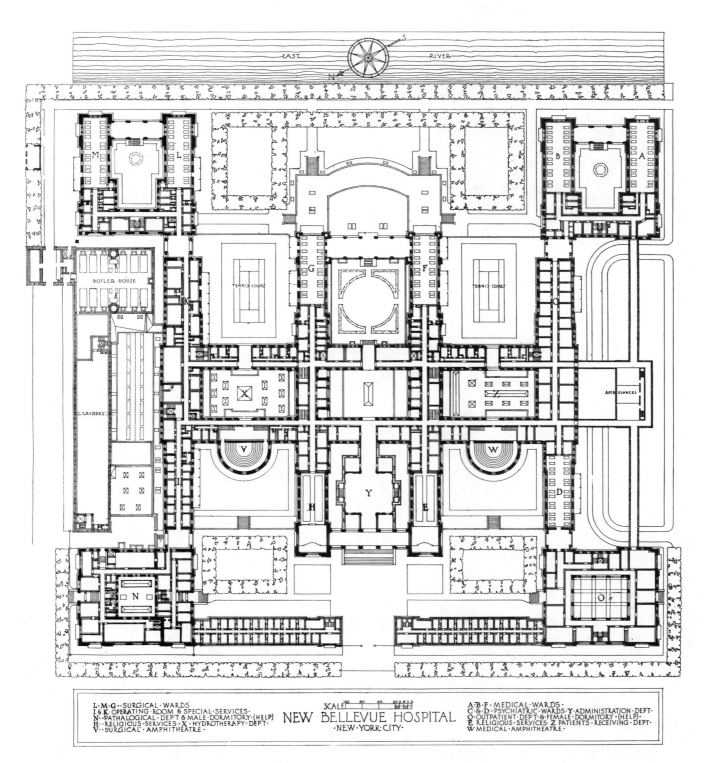

L·M·G·SURGICAL·WARDS
I & K·OPERATING·ROOM & SPECIAL·SERVICES·
N·PATHALOGICAL·DEP'T & MALE·DORMITORY·(HELP)
H·RELIGIOUS·SERVICES·X·HYDROTHERAPY·DEPT·
V·SURGICAL·AMPHITHEATRE·

SCALE

NEW BELLEVUE HOSPITAL
·NEW·YORK·CITY·

A·B·F·MEDICAL·WARDS·
C·&·D·PSYCHIATRIC·WARDS·Y·ADMINISTRATION·DEPT·
O·OUTPATIENT·DEP'T·&·FEMALE·DORMITORY·(HELP)
E·RELIGIOUS·SERVICES·Z·PATIENTS·RECEIVING·DEPT·
W·MEDICAL·AMPHITHEATRE·

BLOCK PLAN

BELLEVUE HOSPITAL, NEW YORK CITY.
1906 - 1916

PATHOLOGICAL DEPARTMENT

PAVILIONS L & M

BELLEVUE HOSPITAL, NEW YORK CITY.
1906 - 1916

ADDITION E

ADDITION H

ADDITIONS TO THE METROPOLITAN MUSEUM OF ART, NEW YORK CITY.
1908 - 1912

PLATE 276

MCKIM, MEAD & WHITE

DETAIL OF LOGGIAS

DETAIL OF PAVILIONS

BELLEVUE HOSPITAL, NEW YORK CITY.
1906-1916

PLATE 277

McKIM, MEAD & WHITE

HALL OF DECORATIVE ARTS · ADDITION F · 1908

LIBRARY · 1910

ADDITIONS TO THE METROPOLITAN MUSEUM OF ART, NEW YORK CITY.

PLATE 278

MCKIM, MEAD & WHITE

ADDITIONS TO THE METROPOLITAN MUSEUM OF ART, NEW YORK CITY.
COURT AND ROOM FOR ARMOR COLLECTION, ADDITION H.
1912

PLATE 279

McKIM, MEAD & WHITE

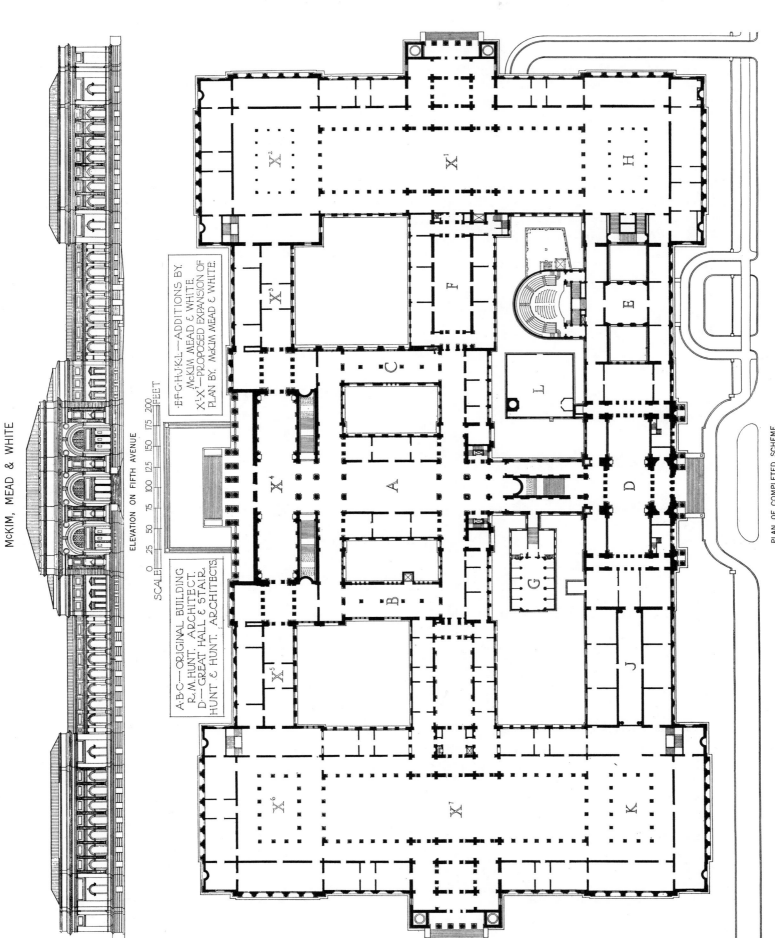

ELEVATION ON FIFTH AVENUE

SCALE 0 25 50 75 100 125 150 175 200 FEET

A·B·C—ORIGINAL BUILDING
R·M·HUNT. ARCHITECT.
D—GREAT HALL & STAIR.
HUNT & HUNT. ARCHITECTS.

·E·F·G·H·J·K·L—ADDITIONS BY.
McKIM MEAD & WHITE.
X¹·X⁷—PROPOSED EXPANSION OF
PLAN BY. McKIM MEAD & WHITE.

PLAN OF COMPLETED SCHEME
THE METROPOLITAN MUSEUM OF ART, NEW YORK CITY.
ADDITIONS, 1908 · 1916

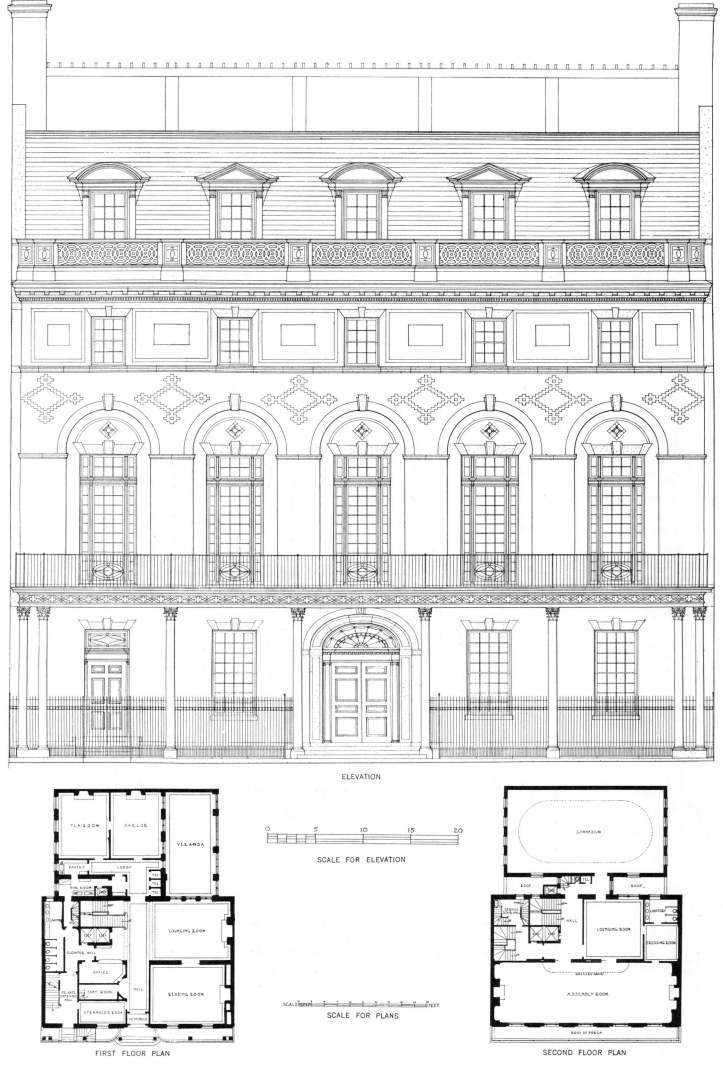

ELEVATION

SCALE FOR ELEVATION

SCALE FOR PLANS

FIRST FLOOR PLAN

SECOND FLOOR PLAN

THE COLONY CLUB, NEW YORK CITY.
1906

THE COLONY CLUB, NEW YORK CITY.
1906

CAST IRON

SECTION

SECTION · THRO
MAIN · DOORWAY

MARBLE   WOOD

PLAN

SCALE   0 1 2 3 4 5 6 7 8 9 10   FEET

EXTERIOR DETAILS
THE COLONY CLUB, NEW YORK CITY.
1906

ATHLETIC FIELD GATES - 1913

MAIN ENTRANCE GATES, NASSAU STREET - 1905

MEMORIAL GATEWAYS, PRINCETON UNIVERSITY.

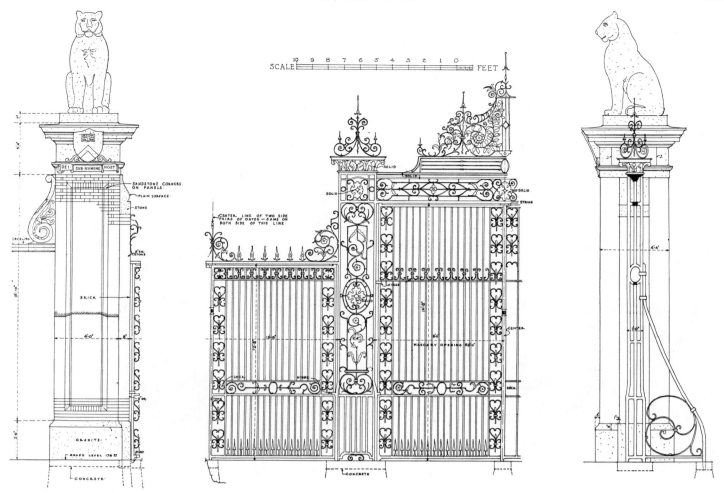

ATHLETIC FIELD GATES, PROSPECT STREET.
1913

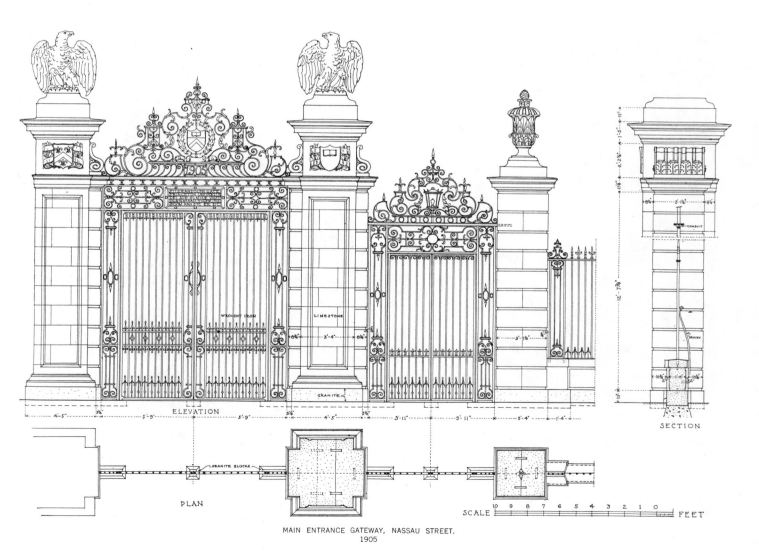

ELEVATION

PLAN

SECTION

MAIN ENTRANCE GATEWAY, NASSAU STREET.
1905

MEMORIAL GATEWAYS, PRINCETON UNIVERSITY.

PLATE 285

MCKIM, MEAD & WHITE

RESIDENCE OF JOHN INNES KANE, NEW YORK CITY.
1907

PLATE 286

MCKIM, MEAD & WHITE

SCALE

FEET

RESIDENCE OF JOHN INNES KANE, NEW YORK CITY.

SOUTH ELEVATION

1906

PLATE 287

McKIM, MEAD & WHITE

MORNING ROOM

DEN

LAVATORY

LOBBY

CLOSET

COATS

LAVATORY

VESTIBVLE

HALL

COVRT

FLOWER

SERVICE
HALL

SERVICE
STAIR

SERVANT'S
DINING ROOM

SCULLERY

R.E.F.

KITCHEN

GARAGE

SCALE FEET

RESIDENCE OF JOHN INNES KANE, NEW YORK CITY.

EXTERIOR DETAILS AND FIRST FLOOR PLAN

1906

· SCALE · FOR · DETAILS ·

VIEWS OF ENTRANCE HALL

RESIDENCE OF JOHN INNES KANE, NEW YORK CITY.
1907

PLATE 289

McKIM, MEAD & WHITE

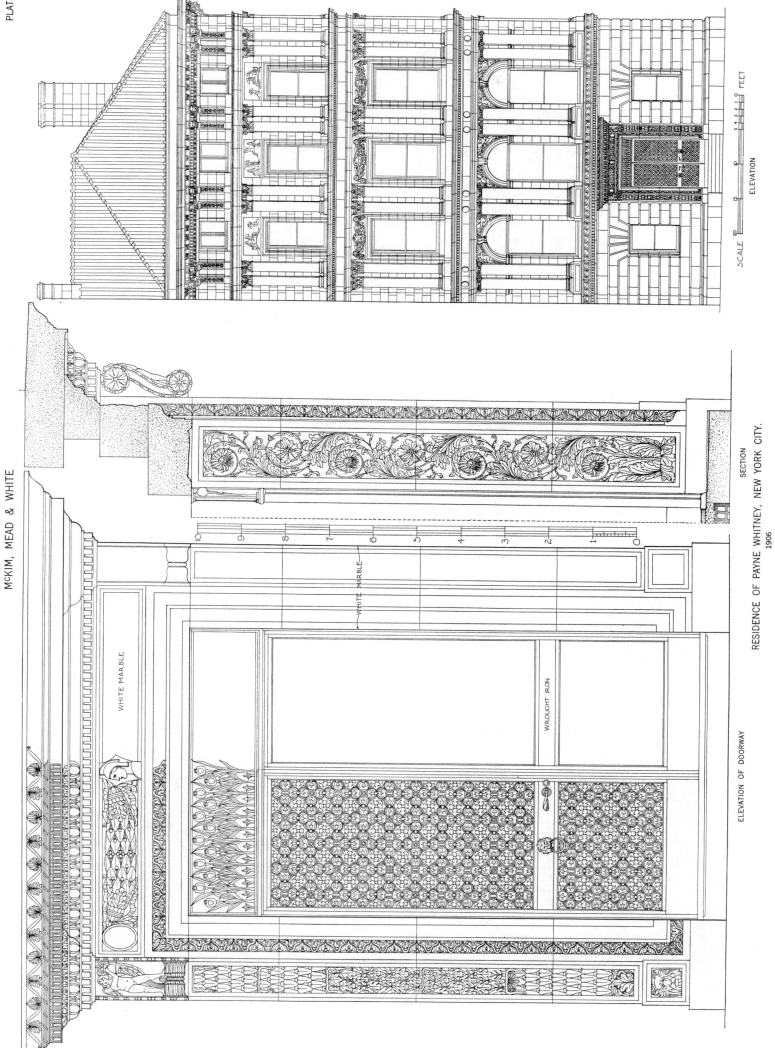

WHITE MARBLE

WHITE MARBLE.

WROUGHT IRON

ELEVATION OF DOORWAY

SCALE

ELEVATION

SECTION

RESIDENCE OF PAYNE WHITNEY, NEW YORK CITY.
1906

VIEW OF EXTERIOR

ENTRANCE HALL

PAYNE WHITNEY RESIDENCE, NEW YORK CITY.
1906

DINING ROOM

LIVING ROOM

PAYNE WHITNEY RESIDENCE, NEW YORK CITY.
1906

STAIR HALL

OFFICE

PAYNE WHITNEY RESIDENCE, NEW YORK CITY.
1906

ENTRANCE FRONT

THE HALL

THE UNIVERSITY COTTAGE CLUB, PRINCETON, N. J.
1906

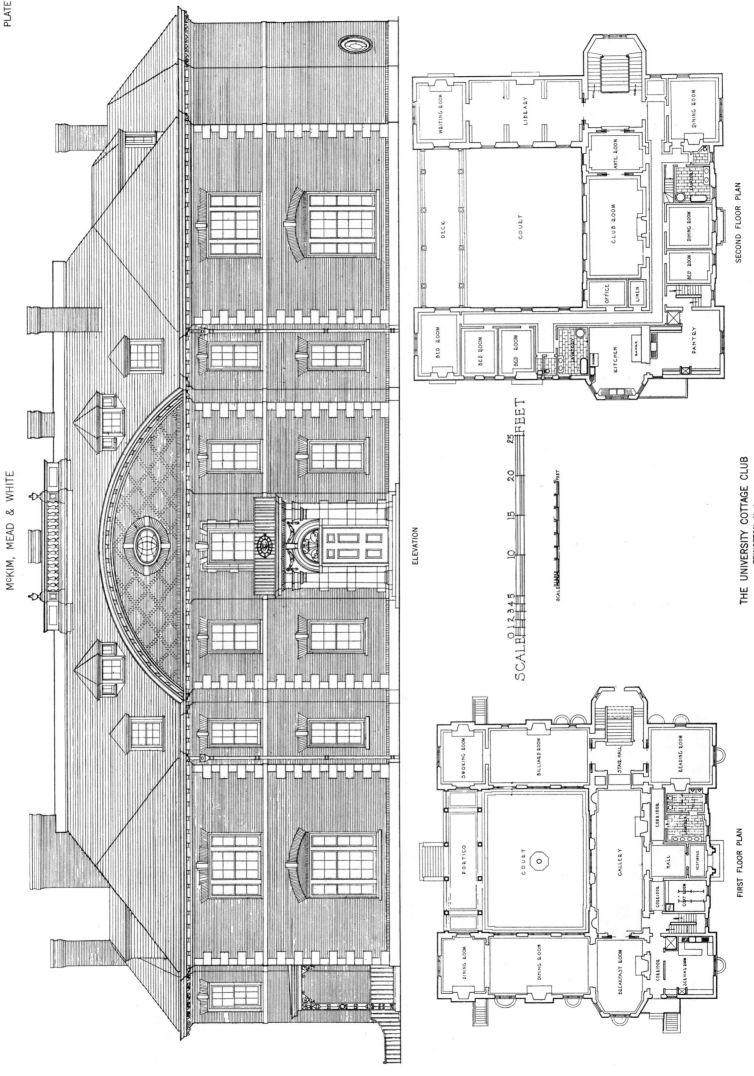

MCKIM, MEAD & WHITE

ELEVATION

SCALE 0 1 2 3 4 5 10 15 20 25 FEET

SCALE FEET

SECOND FLOOR PLAN

WAITING ROOM

LIBRARY

DECK

COURT

ANTE ROOM

CLUB ROOM

OFFICE

LINEN

LAVATORY

BED ROOM

DINING ROOM

PANTRY

KITCHEN

RANGE

BED ROOM

BED ROOM

BED ROOM

DINING ROOM

FIRST FLOOR PLAN

SMOKING ROOM

BILLIARD ROOM

STAIR HALL

PORTICO

COURT

GALLERY

CORRIDOR

HALL

VESTIBULE

COAT ROOM

CORRIDOR

READING ROOM

CORRIDOR

DINING ROOM

DINING ROOM

BREAKFAST ROOM

SERVING ROOM

THE UNIVERSITY COTTAGE CLUB
PRINCETON, N. J.
1906

EXTERIOR

INTERIOR

TRINITY CHURCH, ROSLYN, L. I.
1906

THE NATIONAL CITY BANK, NEW YORK CITY.
BANKING ROOM
1909

PLATE 296

MCKIM, MEAD & WHITE

THE NATIONAL CITY BANK, NEW YORK CITY.
VIEWS IN BANKING ROOM
1909

PRESIDENT'S OFFICE - 1914

DETAIL OF COUNTER SCREEN

CHECK DESK IN PUBLIC SPACE

THE NATIONAL CITY BANK, NEW YORK CITY.
1909

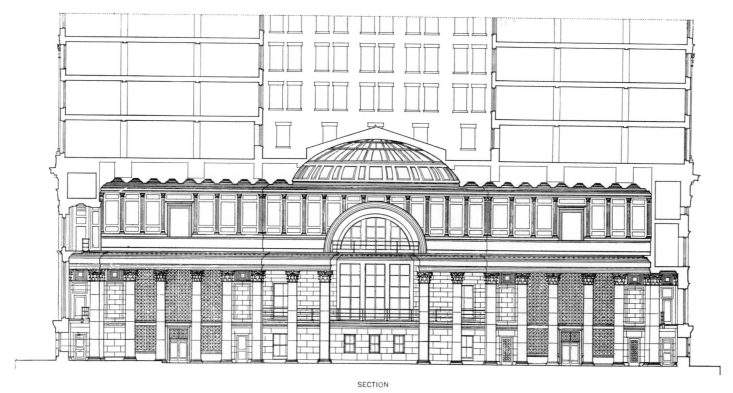

SECTION

PRESIDENT'S ROOM

PRESIDENT'S
COMM ROOM

RECEPTION ROOM

HALL

WAITING ROOM

BOOK-KEEPERS

PUB
ELEV

PUB
ELEV

PUB
ELEV

DOW
ELEV

VAULT
ELEV

PIT

VAULT

PIT

OFFICERS

OFFICERS

BANKING SPACE.

PUBLIC SPACE

HALL

DOW
ELEV

TEL

FLUE

INFORM DESK

FOREIGN DEPT.

VESTIBULE

CLOS.

DUCTS

PUB
ELEV

PUB
ELEV

PUB
ELEV

PORTICO.

ELEVATOR
HALL

BOND DEPT.

SCALE 0 5 10 15 20 25 30 35 40 45 50 FEET

PLAN

THE NATIONAL CITY BANK, NEW YORK CITY.
1909

· SECTION ·
· THROVGH ·
· BANKING ·
· ROOM ·

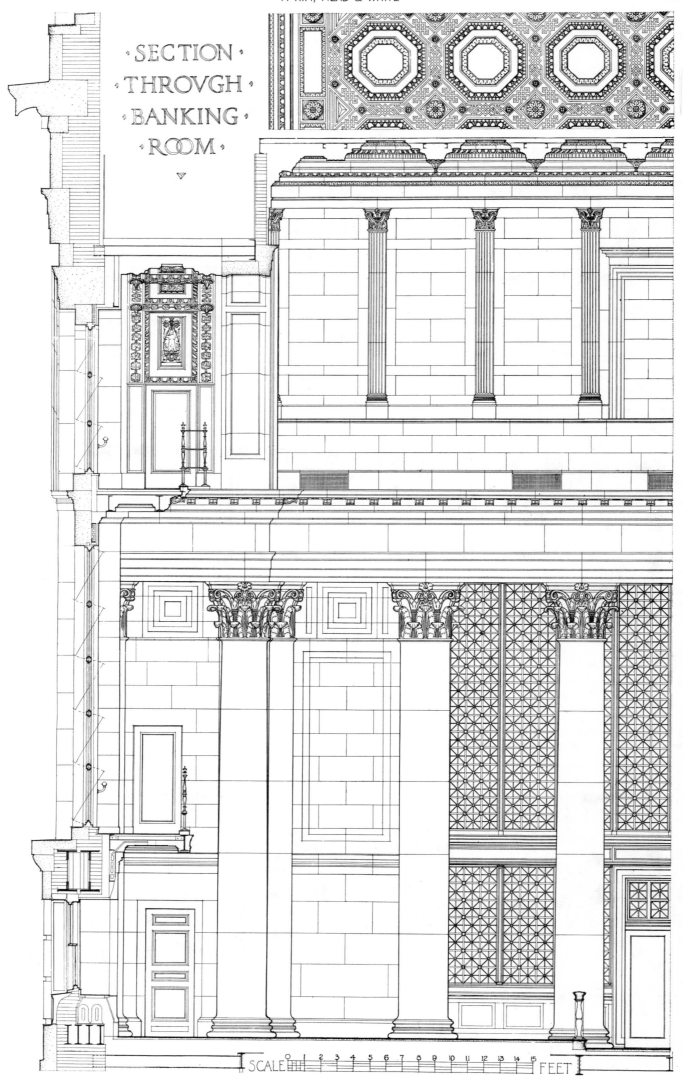

SCALE 0 1 2 3 4 5 6 7 8 9 10 11 12 13 14 15 FEET

THE NATIONAL CITY BANK, NEW YORK CITY.
DETAILS OF BANKING ROOM
1909

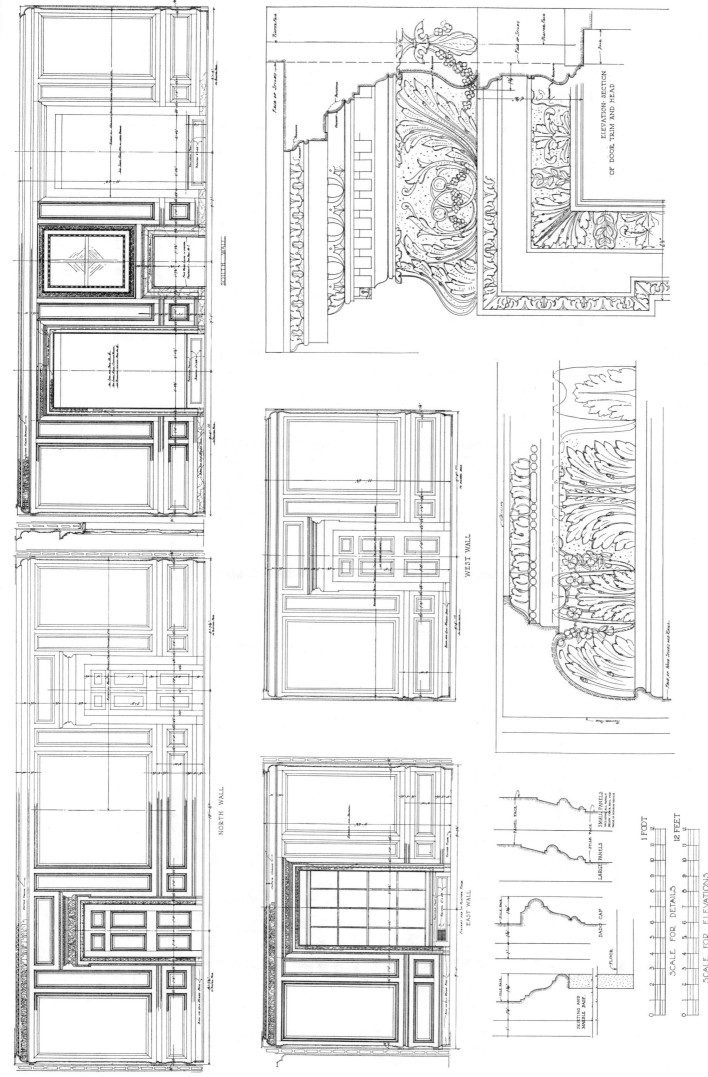

MCKIM, MEAD & WHITE

SOUTH WALL

NORTH WALL

WEST WALL

EAST WALL

ELEVATION-SECTION
OF DOOR TRIM AND HEAD

LARGE PANELS

SMALL PANELS

DADO CAP

SKIRTING AND
MARBLE BASE

PANEL FACE

SCALE FOR DETAILS

SCALE FOR ELEVATIONS

1 FOOT

12 FEET

DETAILS OF PRESIDENT'S ROOM
THE NATIONAL CITY BANK, NEW YORK CITY.
1913

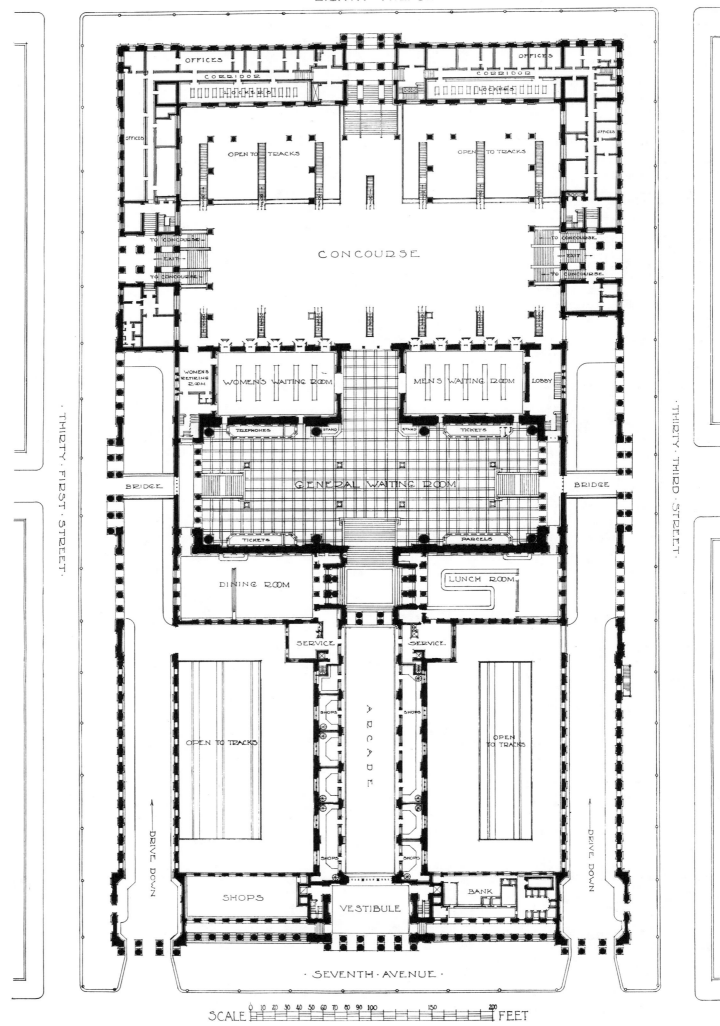

· EIGHTH · AVENUE ·

OFFICES

CORRIDOR

OFFICES

CORRIDOR

LOCKERS

OFFICES

OFFICES

OPEN TO TRACKS

OPEN TO TRACKS

TO CONCOURSE

TO CONCOURSE

TO CONCOURSE

CONCOURSE

TO CONCOURSE

· THIRTY · FIRST · STREET ·

· THIRTY · THIRD · STREET ·

WOMEN'S RETIRING ROOM

WOMEN'S WAITING ROOM

MEN'S WAITING ROOM

LOBBY

TELEPHONES

STAND

STAND

TICKETS

BRIDGE

GENERAL WAITING ROOM

BRIDGE

TICKETS

PARCELS

DINING ROOM

LUNCH ROOM

SERVICE

SERVICE

OPEN TO TRACKS

SHOPS

ARCADE

SHOPS

OPEN TO TRACKS

DRIVE DOWN

DRIVE DOWN

SHOPS

SHOPS

SHOPS

BANK

VESTIBULE

· SEVENTH · AVENUE ·

SCALE ┣━━━━━━━━━━┫ FEET
0 10 20 30 40 50 60 70 80 90 100   150   200

BLOCK PLAN
THE PENNSYLVANIA RAILROAD STATION, NEW YORK CITY.
1906 - 1910

PLATE 301

McKIM, MEAD & WHITE

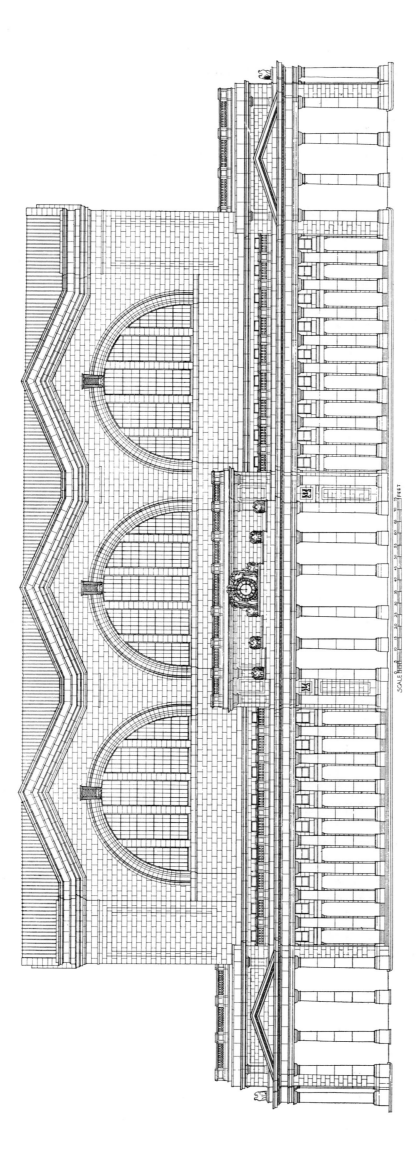

THE PENNSYLVANIA RAILROAD STATION, NEW YORK CITY.
SEVENTH AVENUE ELEVATION
1906 - 1910

PLATE 302

MCKIM, MEAD & WHITE

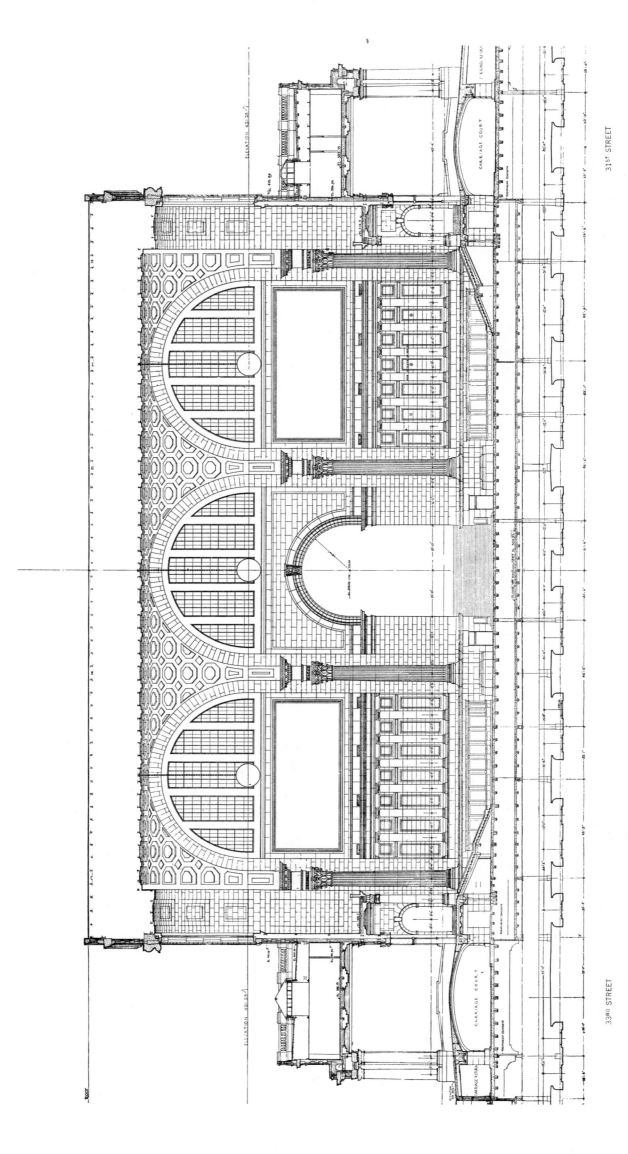

THE PENNSYLVANIA RAILROAD STATION, NEW YORK CITY
SECTION THROUGH MAIN WAITING ROOM
1906 - 1910

PLATE 303

McKIM, MEAD & WHITE

THE PENNSYLVANIA RAILROAD STATION, NEW YORK CITY.
1906 - 1910

PLATE 304

MCKIM, MEAD & WHITE

THE PENNSYLVANIA RAILROAD STATION, NEW YORK CITY.
SEVENTH AVENUE FACADE
1906 - 1910

ARCADE FROM MAIN ENTRANCE TO WAITING ROOM

CARRIAGE DRIVEWAY

THE PENNSYLVANIA RAILROAD STATION, NEW YORK CITY.
1906 - 1910

MAIN WAITING ROOM
THE PENNSYLVANIA RAILROAD STATION, NEW YORK CITY.
1906 - 1910

RESTAURANT

CONCOURSE

THE PENNSYLVANIA RAILROAD STATION, NEW YORK CITY
1906 - 1910

PLATE 308

McKIM MEAD & WHITE

DETAILS OF MAIN WAITING ROOM
THE PENNSYLVANIA RAILROAD STATION, NEW YORK CITY.
1906 - 1910

· DETAILS · OF ·
· SEVENTH · AVENVE ·
· ELEVATION ·

SCALE 0 1 2 3 4 5 6 7 8 9 10   15   20 FEET

THE PENNSYLVANIA RAILROAD STATION, NEW YORK CITY.
1906 - 1910

SPRING LINE

DETAILS
· MAIN ·
WAITING· ROOM

SCALE   0 1 2 3 4 5   10   15   20   25   30   FEET

THE PENNSYLVANIA RAILROAD STATION, NEW YORK CITY
INTERIOR DETAILS
1906 - 1910

PLATE 311

MCKIM, MEAD & WHITE

INTERIOR OF WAITING ROOM

GENERAL VIEW OF EXTERIOR

STATION AT WATERBURY, CONNECTICUT, FOR THE NEW HAVEN RAILWAY
1909

HAMILTON HALL, 1907

SCHOOL OF JOURNALISM, 1913

COLUMBIA UNIVERSITY, NEW YORK CITY.

AVERY BUILDING, SCHOOL OF ARCHITECTURE, 1912

KENT HALL, SCHOOL OF LAW, 1910

COLUMBIA UNIVERSITY, NEW YORK CITY.

PLATE 315

MCKIM, MEAD & WHITE

AVERY LIBRARY 1912

KENT HALL, LAW LIBRARY 1911

COLUMBIA UNIVERSITY, NEW YORK CITY.

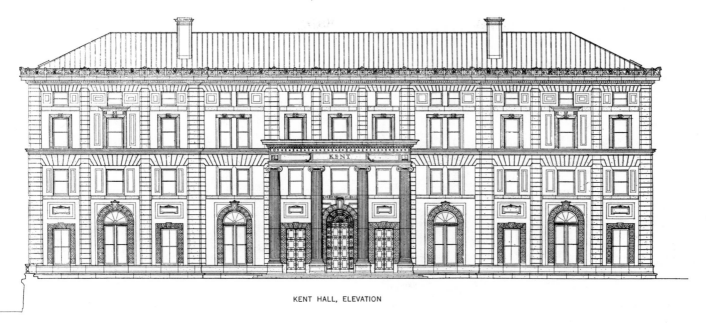

KENT HALL, ELEVATION

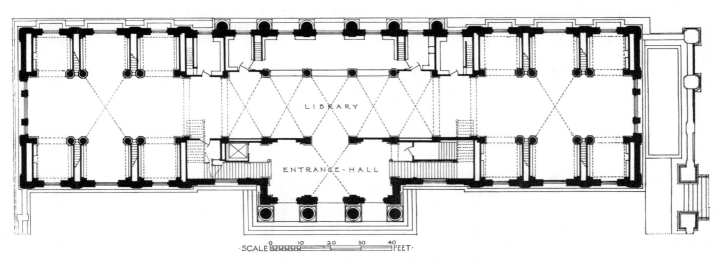

KENT HALL, PLAN OF FIRST FLOOR
1910

SCHOOL OF JOURNALISM, ELEVATION, 1913

COLUMBIA UNIVERSITY, NEW YORK CITY

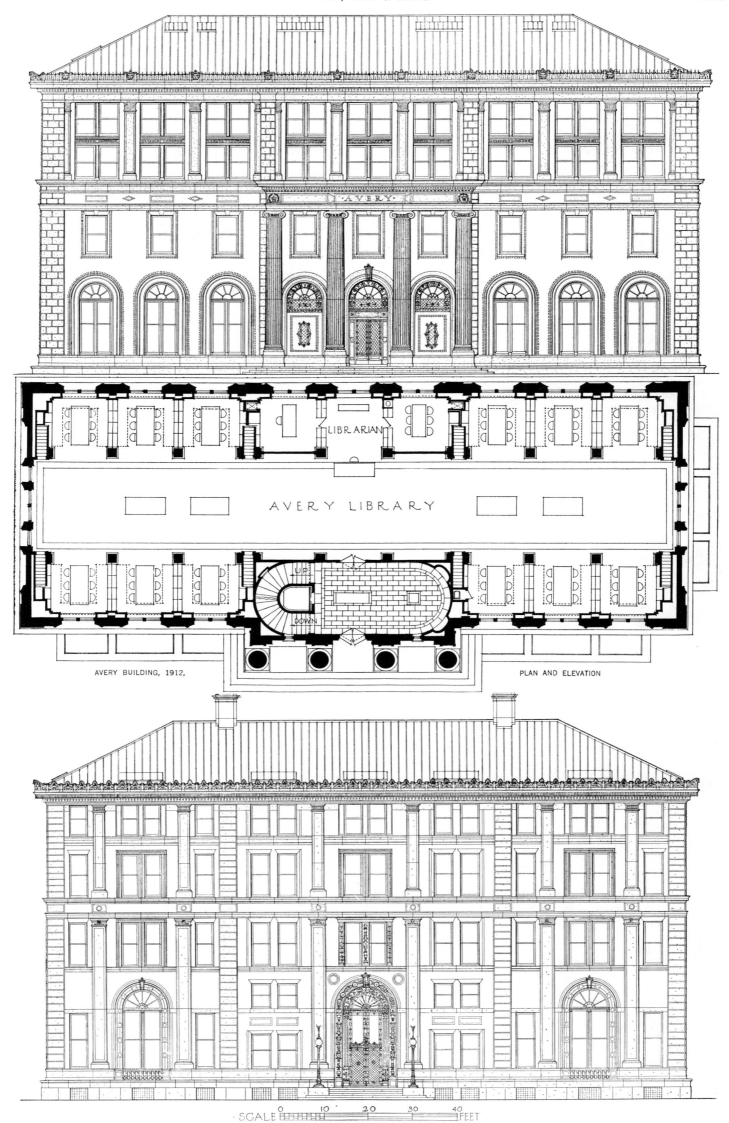

AVERY BUILDING, 1912, PLAN AND ELEVATION

SCALE 0 10 20 30 40 FEET

PHILOSOPHY BUILDING, ELEVATION, 1910
COLUMBIA UNIVERSITY, NEW YORK CITY

PLATE 318

MCKIM MEAD & WHITE

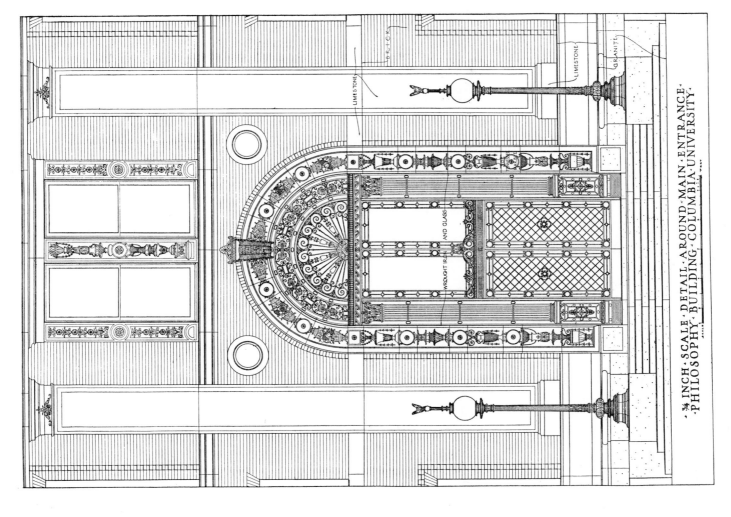

· ¾ · INCH · SCALE · DETAIL · AROUND · MAIN · ENTRANCE ·
· PHILOSOPHY · BUILDING · COLUMBIA · UNIVERSITY ·

ENTRANCE TO PHILOSOPHY BUILDING
COLUMBIA UNIVERSITY, NEW YORK CITY.
1911

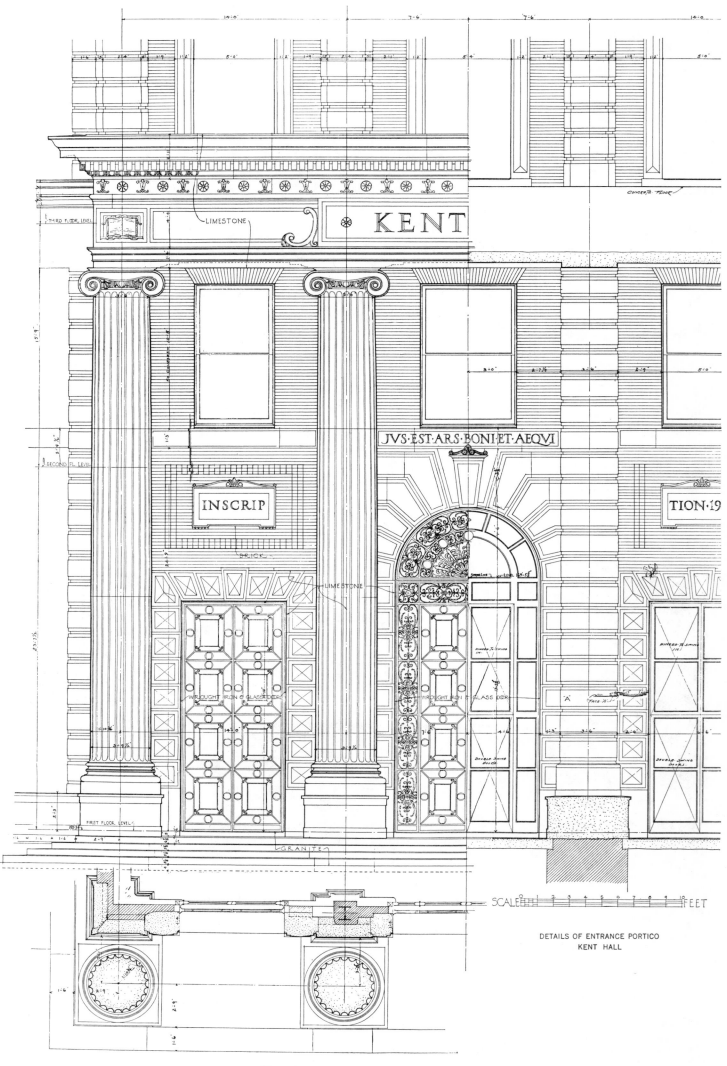

KENT

JVS·EST·ARS·BONI·ET·AEQVI

INSCRIP

TION·19

LIMESTONE

LIMESTONE

BRICK

GRANITE

SCALE FEET

DETAILS OF ENTRANCE PORTICO
KENT HALL

COLUMBIA UNIVERSITY, NEW YORK CITY
1910

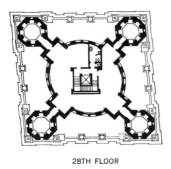

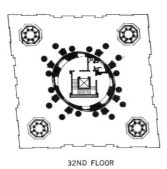

28TH FLOOR   32ND FLOOR   36TH FLOOR

PLANS OF TOWER

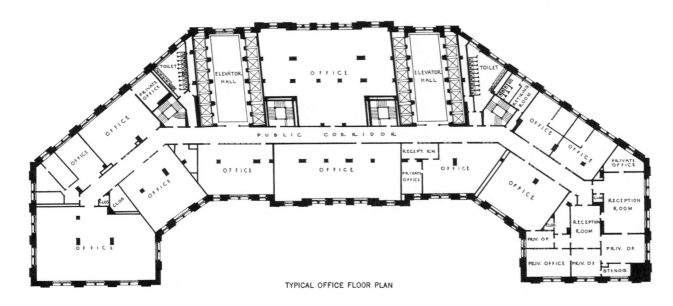

TYPICAL OFFICE FLOOR PLAN

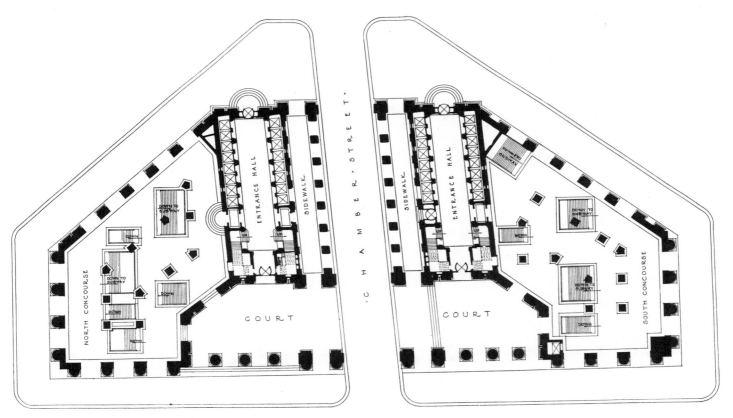

GROUND FLOOR PLAN

·SCALE· FEET·

THE MUNICIPAL BUILDING, NEW YORK CITY
1908

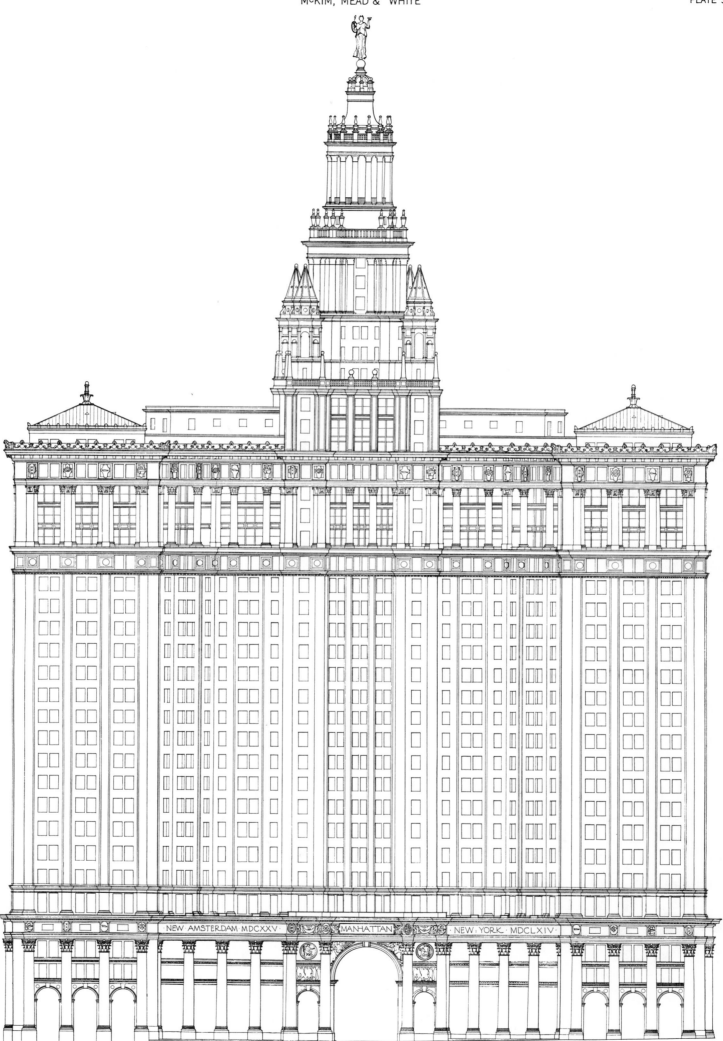

SCALE 0 10 20 30 40 50 60 70 80 90 100 FEET

THE MUNICIPAL BUILDING, NEW YORK CITY
WEST ELEVATION
1908

THE MUNICIPAL BUILDING, NEW YORK CITY
1908 - 1910

PLATE 323

MCKIM, MEAD & WHITE

THE MUNICIPAL BUILDING, NEW YORK CITY.
DETAILS OF COLONNADE AND ARCHWAY AT BASE
1908

DETAIL OF TOWER AND UPPER STORIES

DETAIL OF COLONNADE AT BASE

THE MUNICIPAL BUILDING, NEW YORK CITY.
1908

PLATE 325

MCKIM, MEAD & WHITE

START OF STAIRWAY FIRST FLOOR

ELEVATOR HALL, FIRST FLOOR

THE MUNICIPAL BUILDING, NEW YORK CITY
1908 - 1910

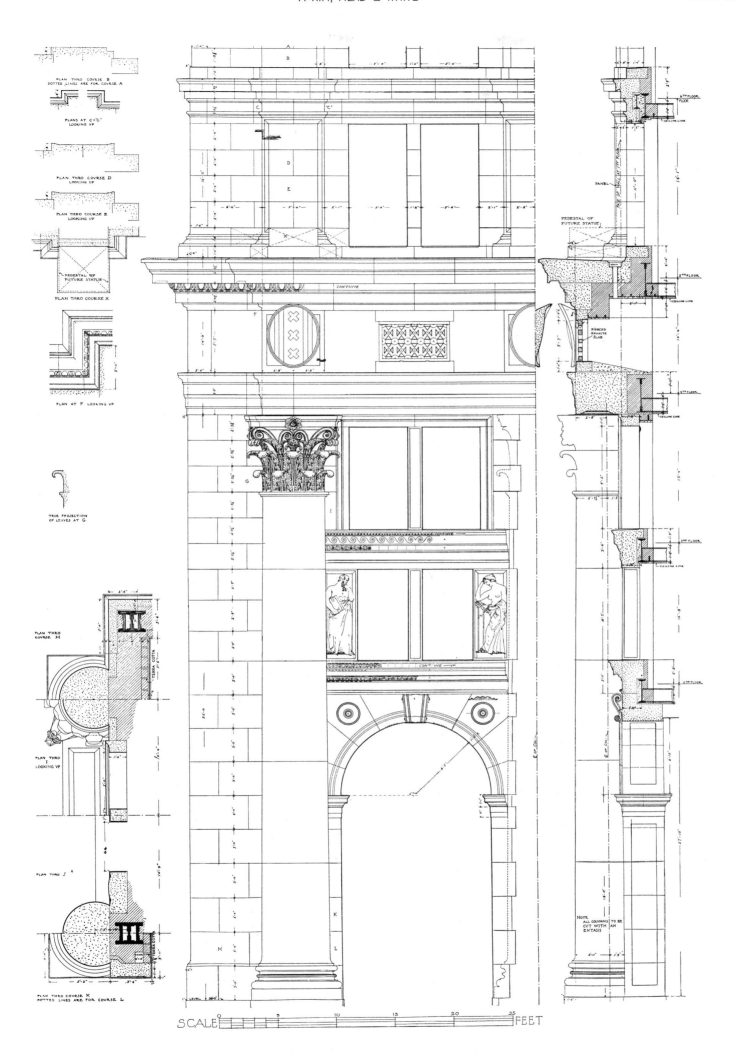

SCALE 0   5   10   15   20   25 FEET

THE MUNICIPAL BUILDING, NEW YORK CITY.
DETAIL OF LOWER STORIES
1908

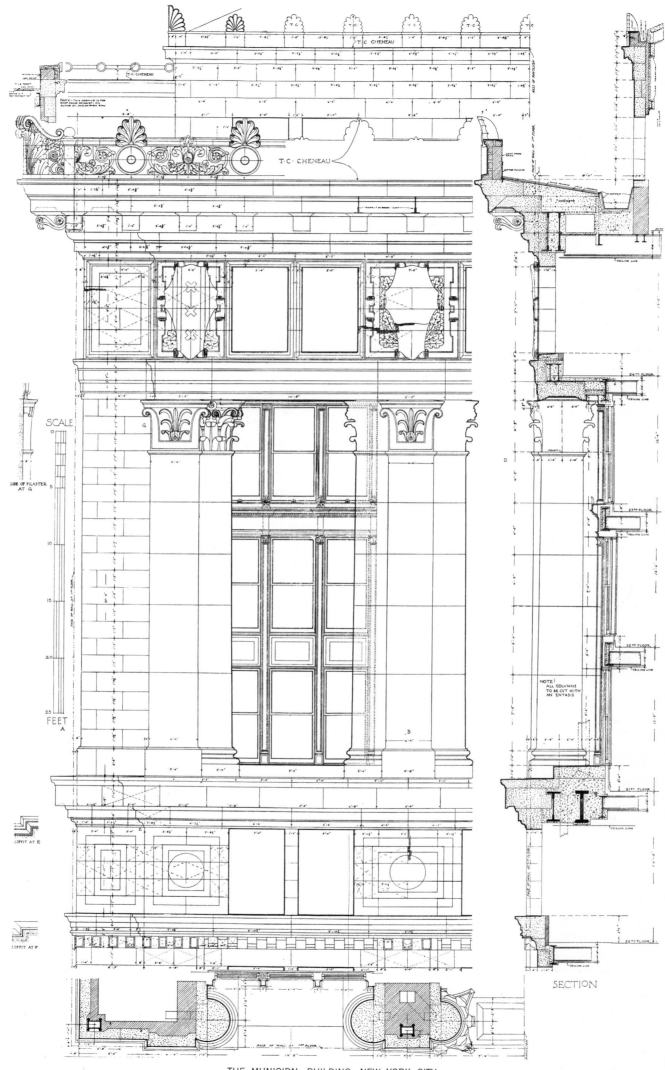

THE MUNICIPAL BUILDING, NEW YORK CITY.
DETAIL OF UPPER STORIES
1908

EXTERIOR

MAIN BANKING ROOM

BUILDING FOR THE GIRARD TRUST CO., PHILADELPHIA, PA.
1908

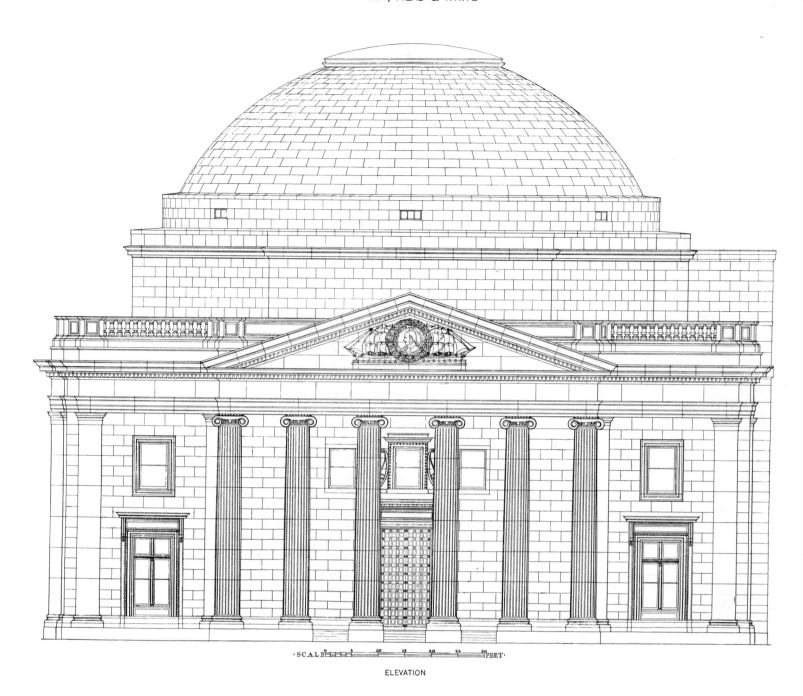

·SCALE· 5 10 15 20 25 30 ·FEET·

ELEVATION

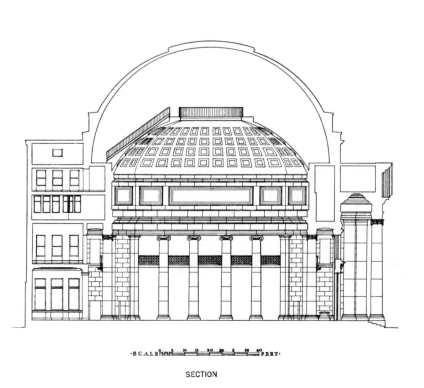

·SCALE· 5 10 20 30 40 ·FEET·

SECTION

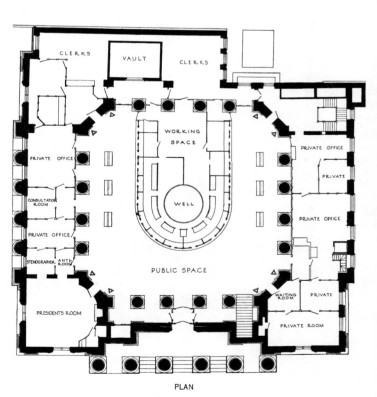

PLAN

THE GIRARD TRUST CO., PHILADELPHIA, PA.
1908

DETAIL·OF·DOORWAY·

DOOR PANEL

·SCALE· |‖‖‖‖‖‖‖‖‖‖‖‖‖‖‖‖‖‖‖‖‖‖‖| FEET·

MATERIALS, WHITE GEORGIA MARBLE AND CAST BRONZE.

BUILDING FOR THE GIRARD TRUST COMPANY, PHILADELPHIA, PA.

1906

PLATE 333

MCKIM, MEAD & WHITE

DETAIL OF LOWER STORIES

GENERAL VIEW

BANK AND OFFICE BUILDING FOR THE COLUMBIA TRUST CO., NEW YORK CITY.
1910

·SCALE· FEET·

DOWNTOWN BUILDING, COLUMBIA TRUST CO., NEW YORK CITY
SIDE ELEVATION
1910

DOWNTOWN BUILDING, COLUMBIA TRUST CO., NEW YORK CITY
EXTERIOR DETAILS,   FRONT ELEVATION
1910

PLATE 336

McKIM, MEAD & WHITE

DETAIL OF ENTRANCE

VIEW FROM LAKE SHORE DRIVE

RESIDENCE OF EDWARD T. BLAIR, CHICAGO, ILL.
1912

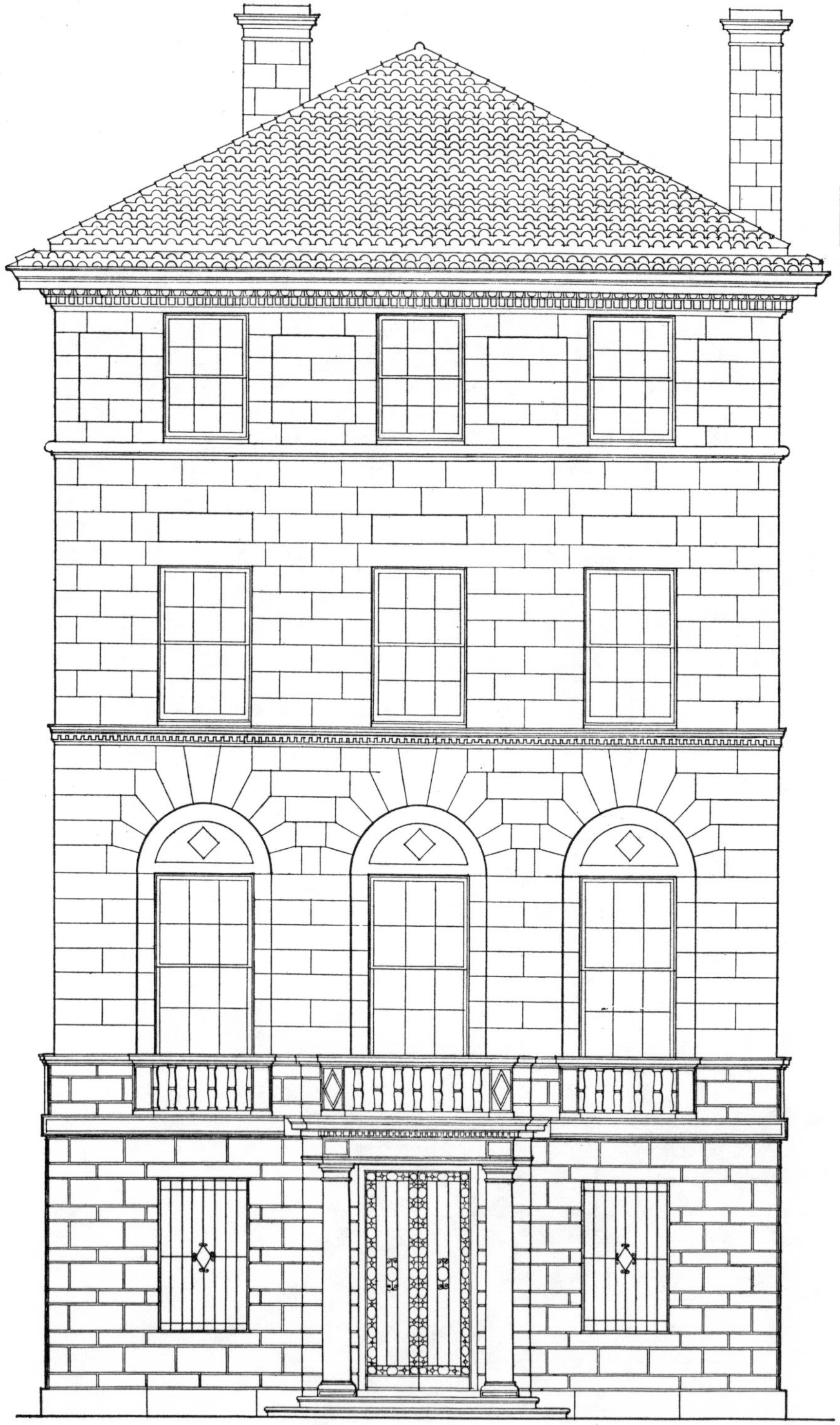

PLATE 337

LIBRARY

LIVING ROOM

DINING ROOM

BUTLER'S PANTRY

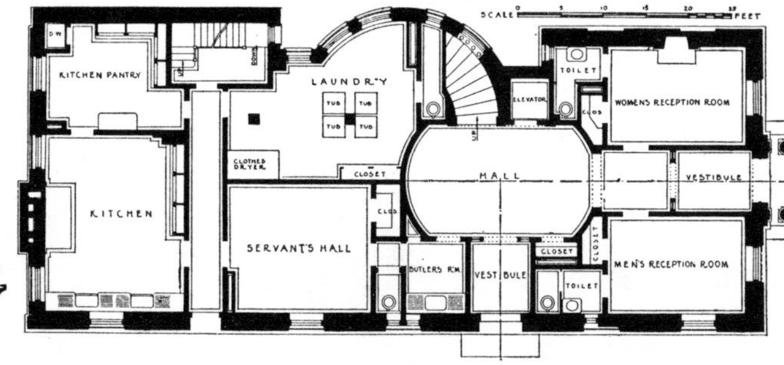

SECOND FLOOR PLAN

McKIM, MEAD & WHITE

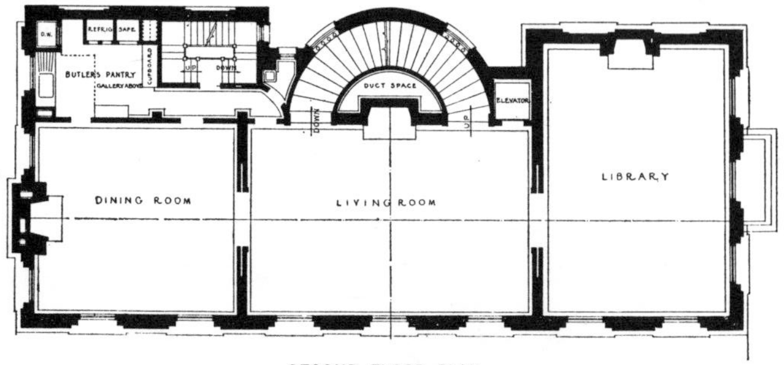

WOMAN'S RECEPTION ROOM

VESTIBULE

MEN'S RECEPTION ROOM

HALL

LAUNDRY

SERVANT'S HALL

KITCHEN PANTRY

KITCHEN

FIRST FLOOR PLAN

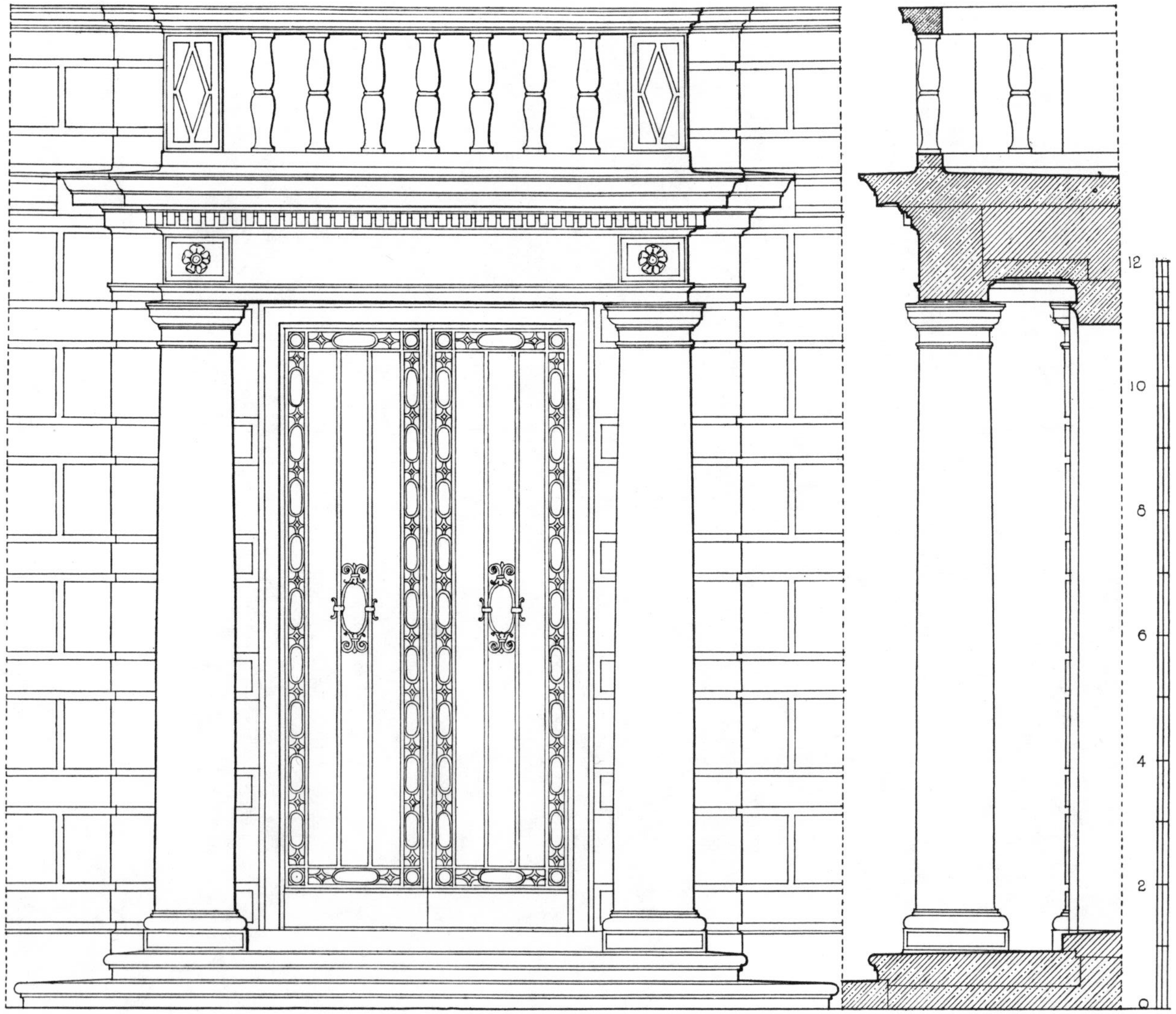

DETAIL OF ENTRANCE

RESIDENCE OF EDWARD T. BLAIR, CHICAGO ILL.
1912

FRONT ELEVATION

SCALE   FEET

PLATE 338

McKIM, MEAD & WHITE

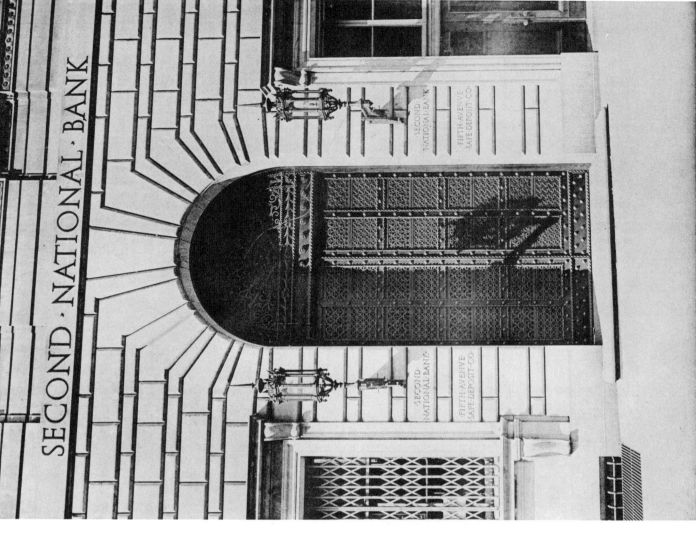

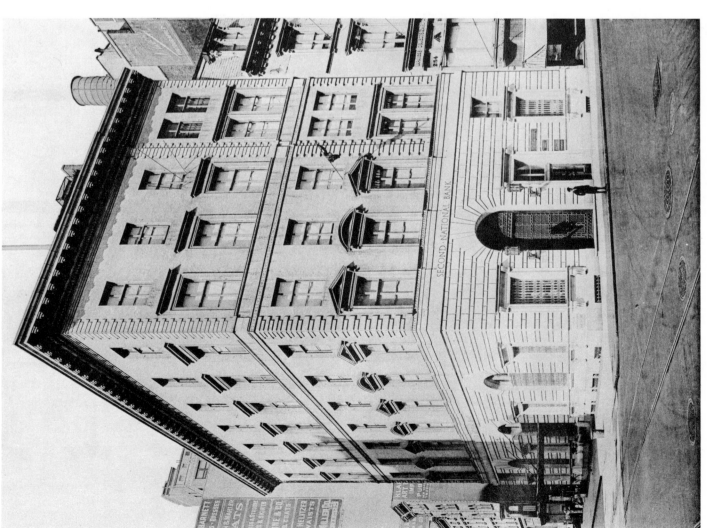

THE SECOND NATIONAL BANK, NEW YORK CITY
1908

SCALE FEET

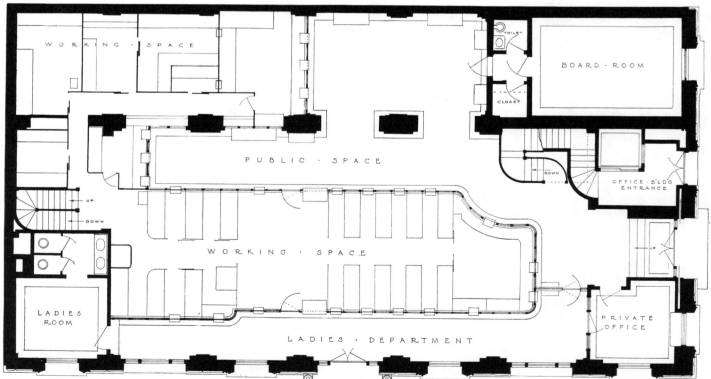

THE SECOND NATIONAL BANK, NEW YORK CITY.
1907

PLATE 340

McKIM MEAD & WHITE

FORTY-FIFTH STREET FACADE

FORTY-FOURTH STREET FACADE

THE HARVARD CLUB OF NEW YORK CITY
1902 - 1915

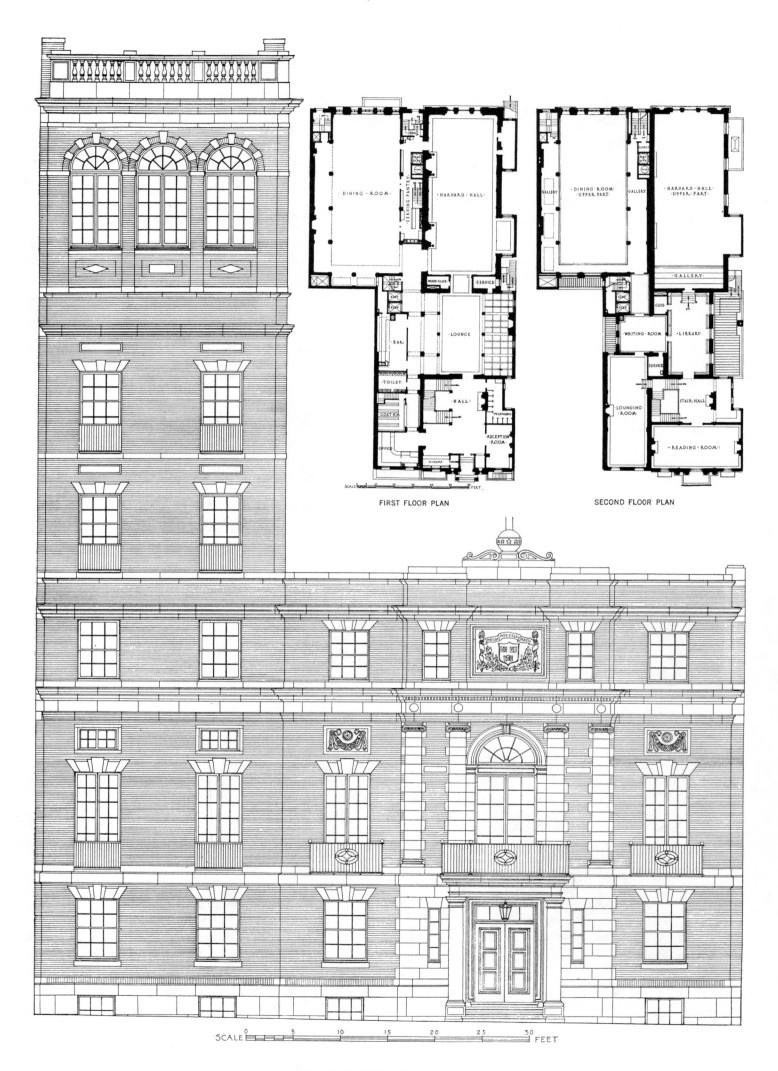

FIRST FLOOR PLAN

SECOND FLOOR PLAN

SCALE 0 5 10 15 20 25 30 FEET

THE HARVARD CLUB, NEW YORK CITY.
ORIGINAL BUILDING ON RIGHT 1902, ADDITION ON LEFT, 1915.

PLATE 343

McKIM MEAD & WHITE

LIBRARY · 1912

HARVARD HALL, LOUNGING ROOM · 1905

THE HARVARD CLUB OF NEW YORK CITY.

PLATE 344

McKIM, MEAD & WHITE

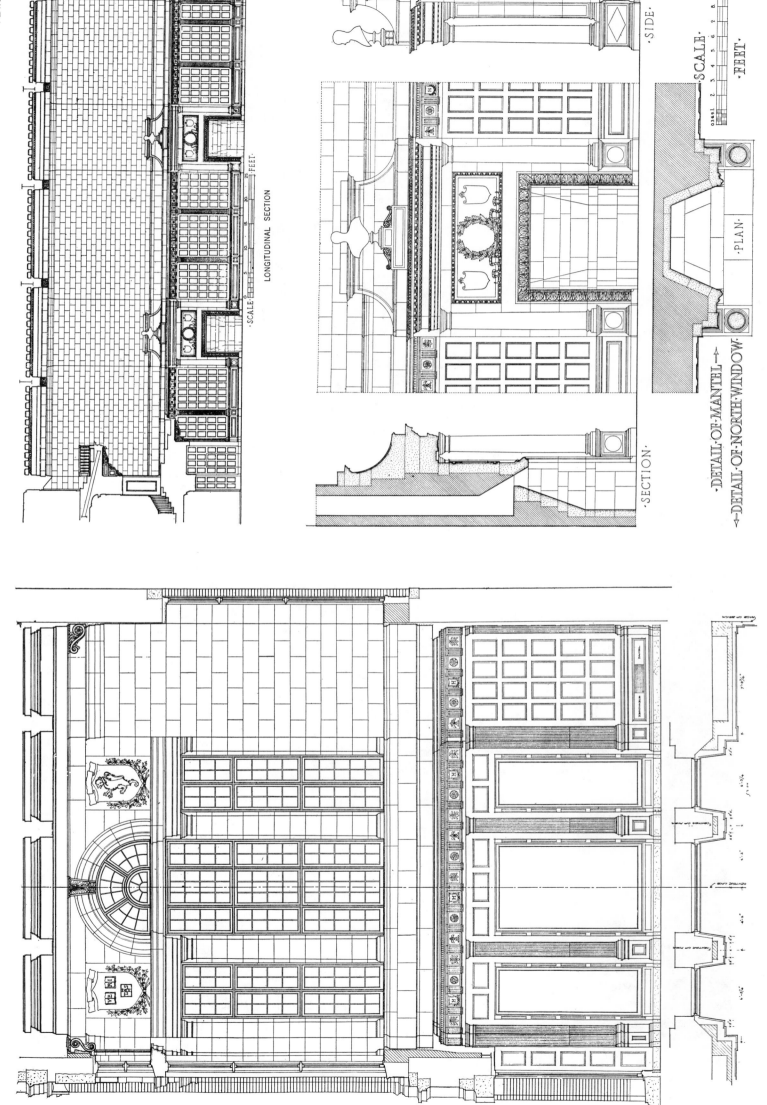

·SCALE· FEET·

LONGITUDINAL SECTION

·SCALE· FEET·

·SECTION·

·SIDE·

·PLAN·

·SCALE·

·FEET·

·DETAIL·OF·MANTEL·→

←·DETAIL·OF·NORTH·WINDOW·

HARVARD HALL, LOUNGING ROOM OF HARVARD CLUB, NEW YORK CITY
1905

PLATE 345

McKIM, MEAD & WHITE

HARVARD HALL · 1905

DINING ROOM · 1914

THE HARVARD CLUB OF NEW YORK

APARTMENT HOUSE, 998 FIFTH AVE., FOR THE CENTURY HOLDING CO.
1911

PLATE 347

MCKIM, MEAD & WHITE

-UPPER FLOOR-

TYPICAL DUPLEX APARTMENT

-LOWER FLOOR-

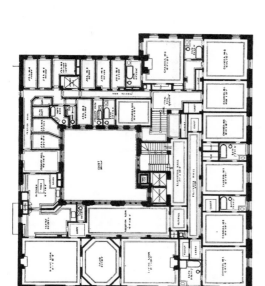

TYPICAL UPPER FLOOR PLAN SHOWING SINGLE APARTMENT
ON LEFT AND PART OF DUPLEX ON RIGHT

FIRST FLOOR PLAN

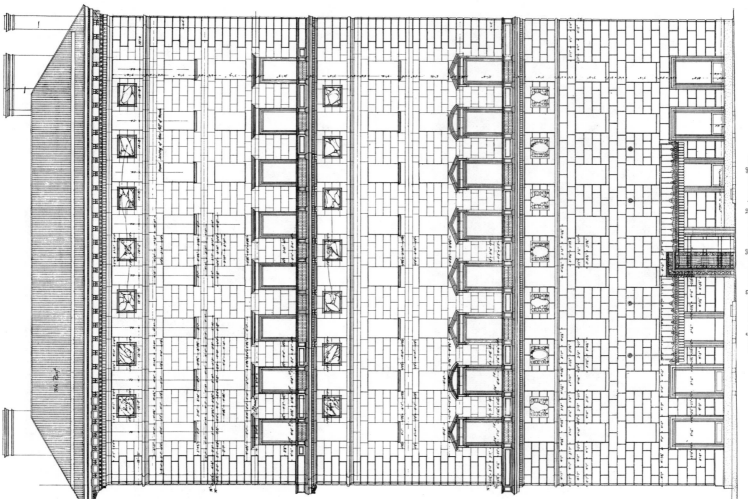

ELEVATION

APARTMENT HOUSE, 998 FIFTH AVENUE, FOR THE CENTURY HOLDING CO.
1911

PLATE 348

MCKIM, MEAD & WHITE

ELEVATION

FIRST FLOOR PLAN

SECOND FLOOR PLAN

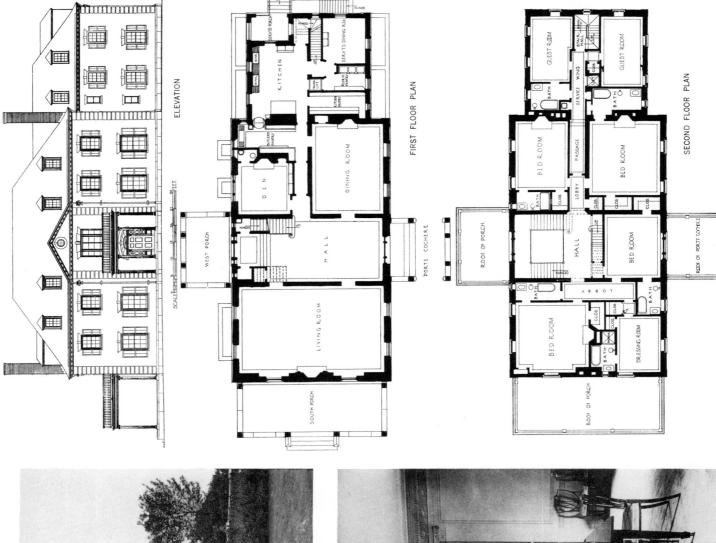

RESIDENCE OF P. H. B. FRELINGHUYSEN, MORRISTOWN, N. J.
1912

SCALE 0 5 10 15 20 25 30 FEET

SCALE 0 10 20 30 40 FEET

SCALE 0 5 10 FEET

RESIDENCE OF PERCY PYNE, ESQ., NEW YORK CITY
ABOVE, SIDE ELEVATION,   BELOW, DETAIL OF ENTRANCE, FIRST AND SECOND FLOOR PLANS
1911

PLATE 350

McKIM, MEAD & WHITE

DETAIL OF ENTRANCE

GENERAL VIEW

RESIDENCE OF PERCY PYNE, ESQ., NEW YORK CITY
1911

PLATE 351

MCKIM, MEAD & WHITE

SALON

LIBRARY

RESIDENCE OF PERCY PYNE, ESQ., NEW YORK CITY
1911

PLATE 351A

MCKIM, MEAD & WHITE

DINING ROOM

SALON

STAIR HALL

RECEPTION ROOM

RESIDENCE OF PERCY PYNE, ESQ., NEW YORK CITY.
1911

FACADE

DETAIL OF ENTRANCE

PRESIDENT'S HOUSE, COLUMBIA UNIVERSITY, NEW YORK CITY.
1912

SCALE 0 5 10 15 20 25 30 35 40 45 50 FEET

ELEVATION

PLAN THRO' BALCONY

DETAIL OF MAIN CORNICE

GLASS ROOF

DETAIL OF MAIN ENTRANCE

SCALE 12 9 6 3 0 1 2 3 4 5 FEET

EXTERIOR DETAILS

THIRD FLOOR PLAN

BED ROOM · BATH ROOM · BED ROOM · BED ROOM · WARDROBE · LOBBY · HALL · LOBBY · WARDROBE · CLO. · ROOF · BED ROOM · BATH RM. · BED ROOM · BED ROOM

SECOND FLOOR PLAN

TILE ROOF · DRAWING ROOM · HALL · MUSIC ROOM · CLO.

FIRST FLOOR PLAN

PAVEMENT · TOILET · SAFE · PANTRY · COAT RM. · CORRIDOR · LIBRARY · DINING ROOM · RECEPTION RM. · VESTIBULE · BREAKFAST RM.

SCALE FEET

PRESIDENT'S HOUSE, COLUMBIA UNIVERSITY, NEW YORK CITY
1912

PLATE 354

MCKIM, MEAD & WHITE

ENTRANCE PORCH

GARDEN FRONT

ALTERATIONS TO HOUSE OF ELON H. HOOKER, GREENWICH, CONN.
1911

EXTERIOR

VIEW OF BANKING ROOM

THE BANK OF MONTREAL, WINNIPEG BRANCH, WINNIPEG, MANITOBA.
1911

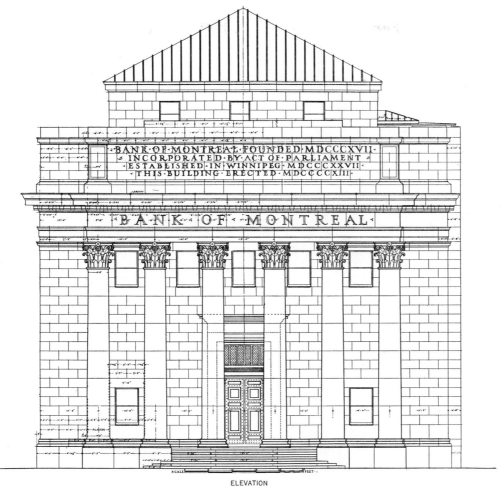

BANK·OF·MONTREAL·FOUNDED·MDCCCXVII·
INCORPORATED·BY·ACT·OF·PARLIAMENT·
ESTABLISHED·IN·WINNIPEG·MDCCCXXVII·
THIS·BUILDING·ERECTED·MDCCCXIII·

BANK OF MONTREAL

ELEVATION

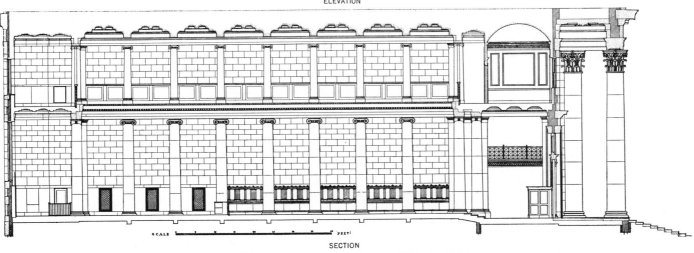

SECTION

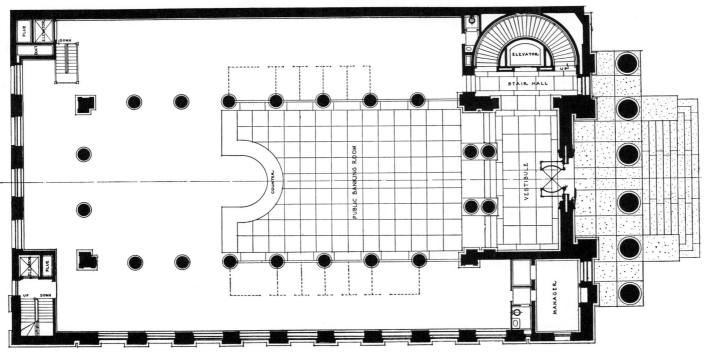

PLAN
THE BANK OF MONTREAL, WINNIPEG BRANCH
1911

PLATE 356-A

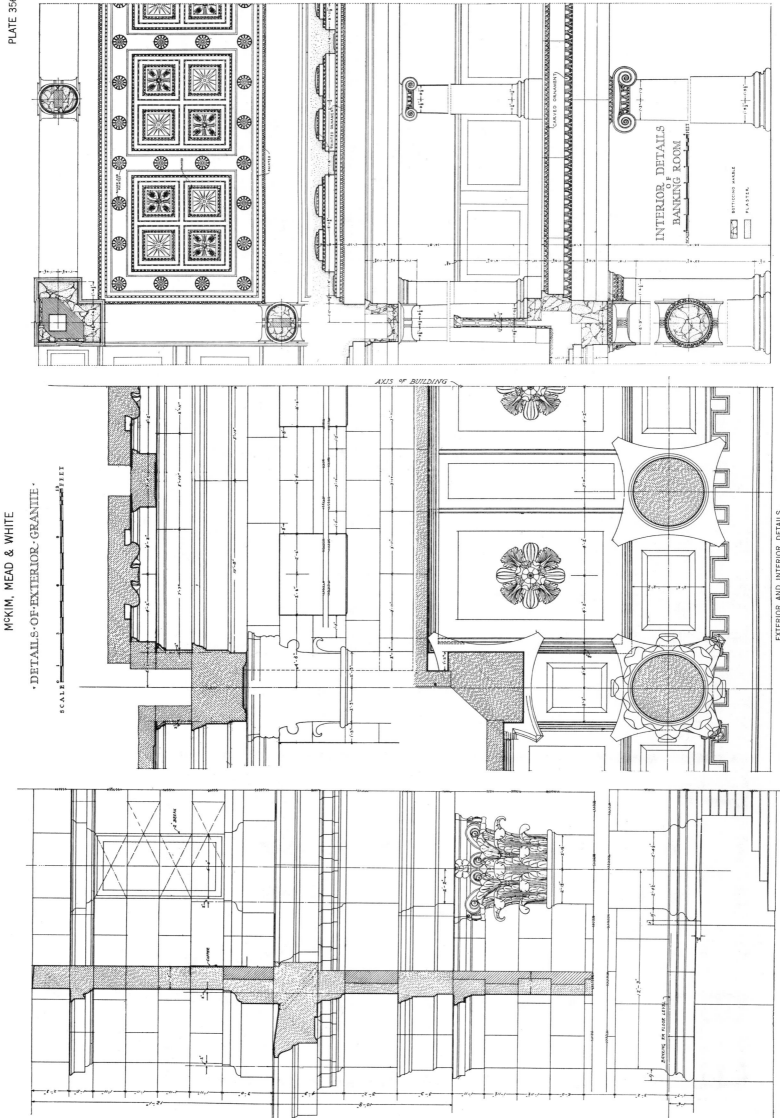

MCKIM, MEAD & WHITE

· DETAILS · OF · EXTERIOR · GRANITE ·

SCALE

INTERIOR DETAILS
OF
BANKING ROOM

EXTERIOR AND INTERIOR DETAILS
THE BANK OF MONTREAL, WINNIPEG BRANCH
1911

AXIS OF BUILDING

PLATE 357

MCKIM, MEAD & WHITE

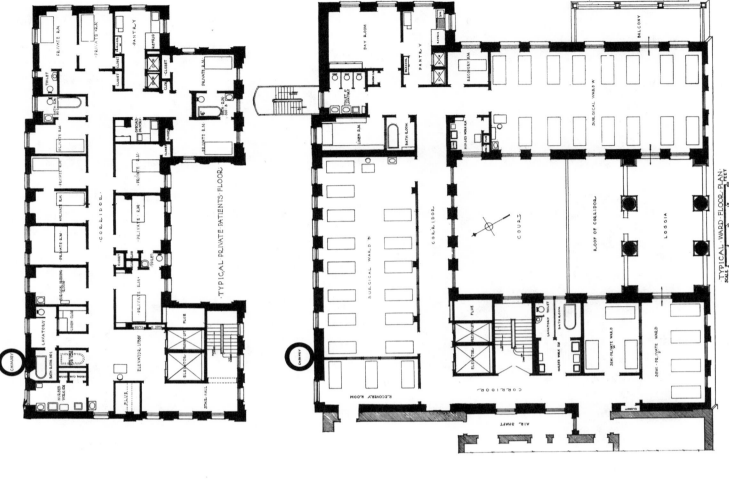

TYPICAL PRIVATE PATIENTS FLOOR.

TYPICAL WARD FLOOR PLAN.
SCALE

ADDITIONS TO THE NEW YORK POST GRADUATE HOSPITAL
NEW YORK CITY
1912

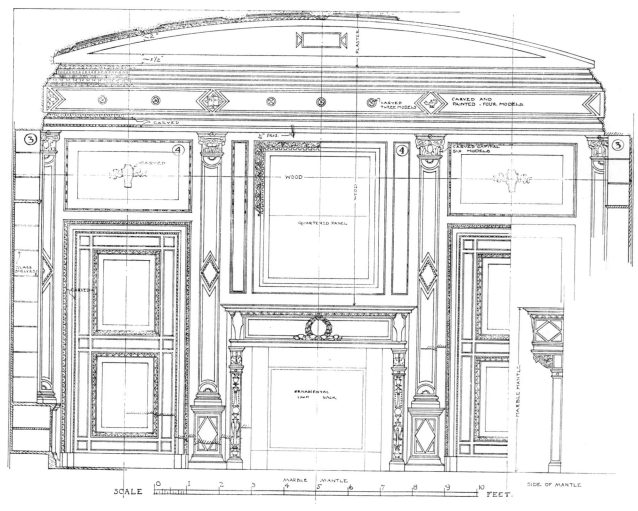

LIBRARY FOR THE HON. WHITELAW REID, NEW YORK CITY.
1910

PLATE 360

MCKIM, MEAD & WHITE

U. S. POST OFFICE, NEW YORK CITY
1913

PLATE 361

McKIM MEAD & WHITE

DETAIL OF FACADE

PUBLIC CORRIDOR

UNITED STATES POST OFFICE, NEW YORK CITY.
1913

PLATE 362 - 362A

McKIM, MEAD & WHITE

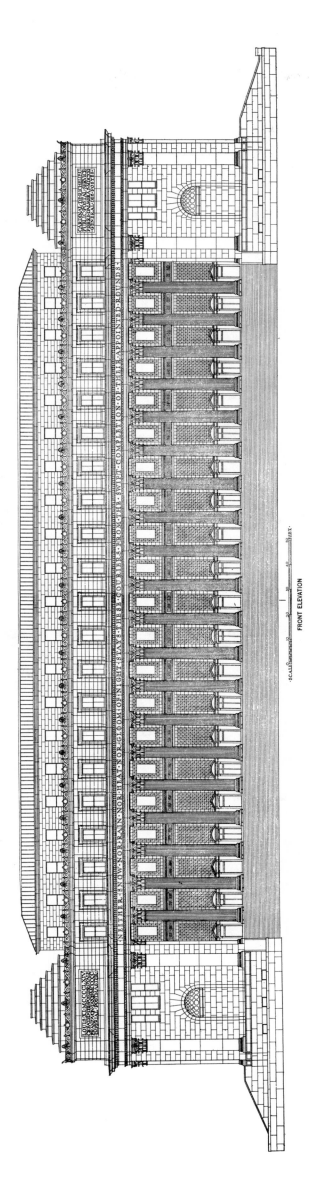

FRONT ELEVATION

UNITED STATES POST OFFICE, NEW YORK CITY

1913

PLATE 362 · 362A

McKIM, MEAD & WHITE

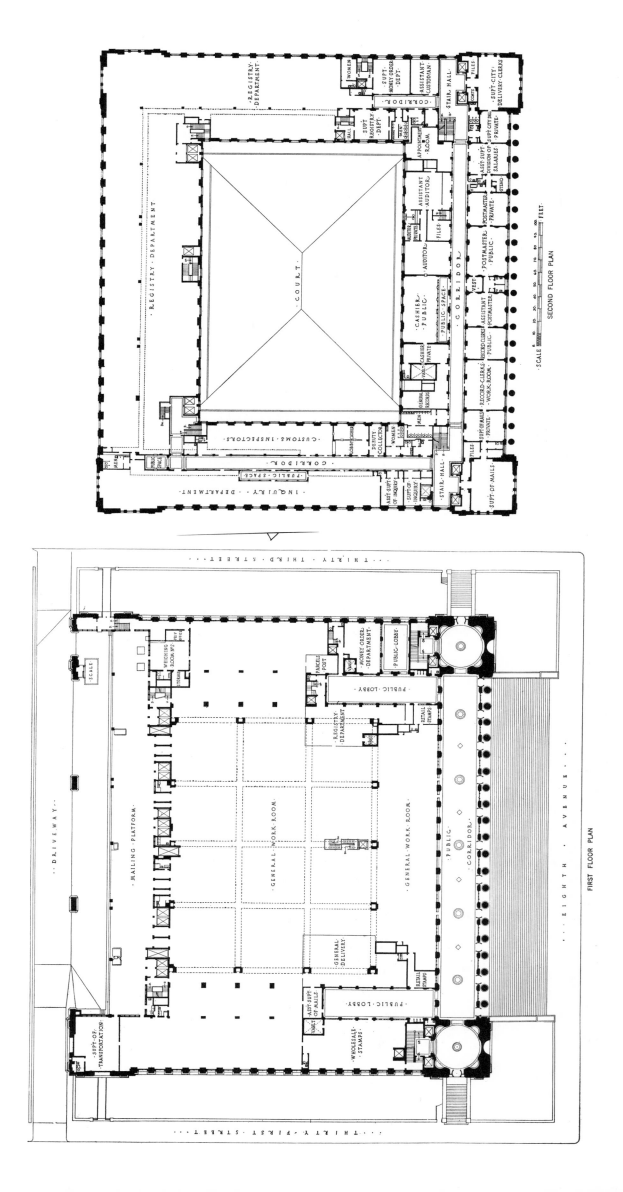

SECOND FLOOR PLAN

FIRST FLOOR PLAN

UNITED STATES POST OFFICE, NEW YORK CITY

1913

DETAILS OF COLUMN AND PILASTER CAPS AND CORNICE - EXTERIOR

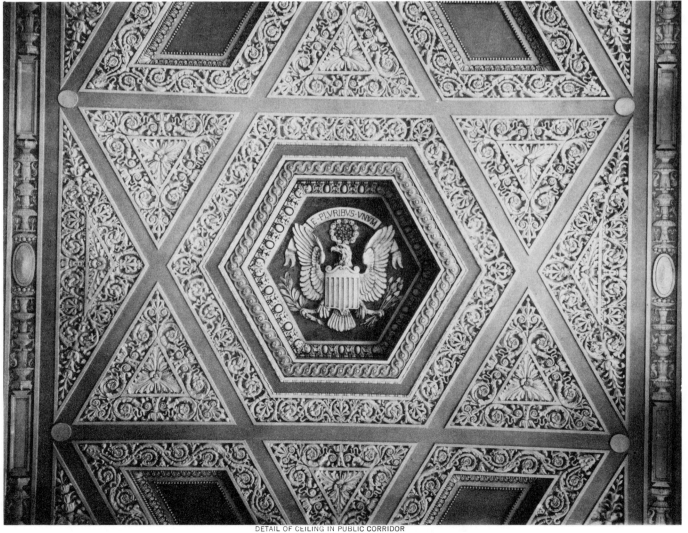

DETAIL OF CEILING IN PUBLIC CORRIDOR

UNITED STATES POST OFFICE, NEW YORK CITY.
1913

· SCALE ·

· TERRA · COTTA · CHENEAU ·

· DETAIL · OF · ATTIC ·

· GRANITE ·

· EXTERIOR ·
· DETAILS ·
· OF · THE ·
· U · S · POST ·
· OFFICE ·
· NEW · YORK · N · Y ·

· GRANITE ·

· DETAIL · OF ·
· ENTRANCES ·
· THIRTY · FIRST · & ·
· THIRTY · THIRD · STS ·

6'-1"   1'-0"   5'-4"

17'-11"

· DETAIL · OF · NICHE ·

· SECTION ·

· CAST · IRON ·

· CAST · IRON ·

45'-0"

· GRANITE ·

· PLAN · THRU · END ·
· OF · COLONNADE ·

4'-0½"   1'-3"   8'-2½"   4'-10"   4'-1¼"

· SECTION · THRU · COLONNADE ·

UNITED STATES POST OFFICE, NEW YORK CITY
1913

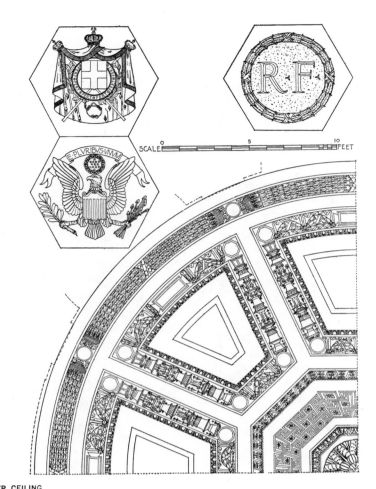

SCALE | 0   5   10 | FEET

DETAILS OF PLASTER CEILING

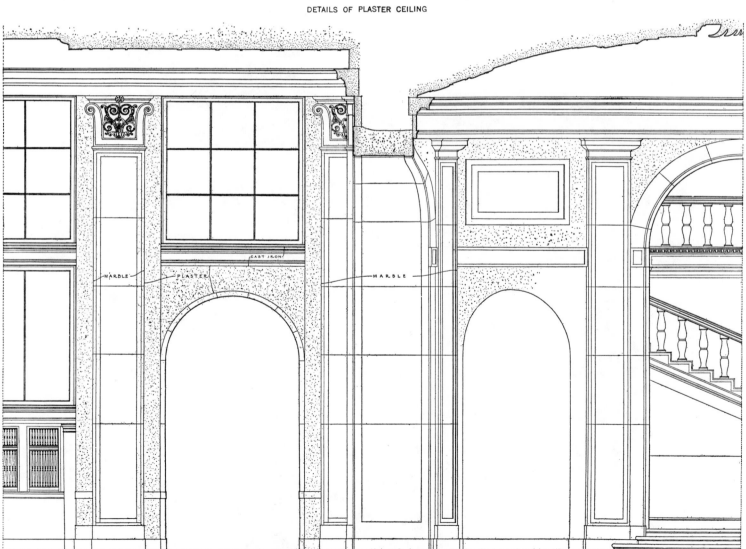

UNITED STATES POST OFFICE, NEW YORK CITY
DETAILS OF PUBLIC CORRIDOR, FIRST FLOOR
1913

PLATE 365

McKIM, MEAD & WHITE

DETAIL OF ENTRANCE

FACADE

BANK AND OFFICE BUILDING FOR THE ROYAL TRUST CO., MONTREAL, CANADA
1912

PLATE 366

McKIM, MEAD & WHITE

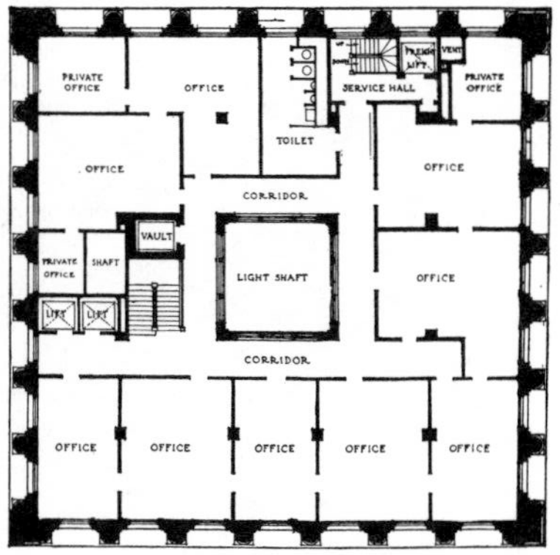

PLAN OF UPPER STORIES

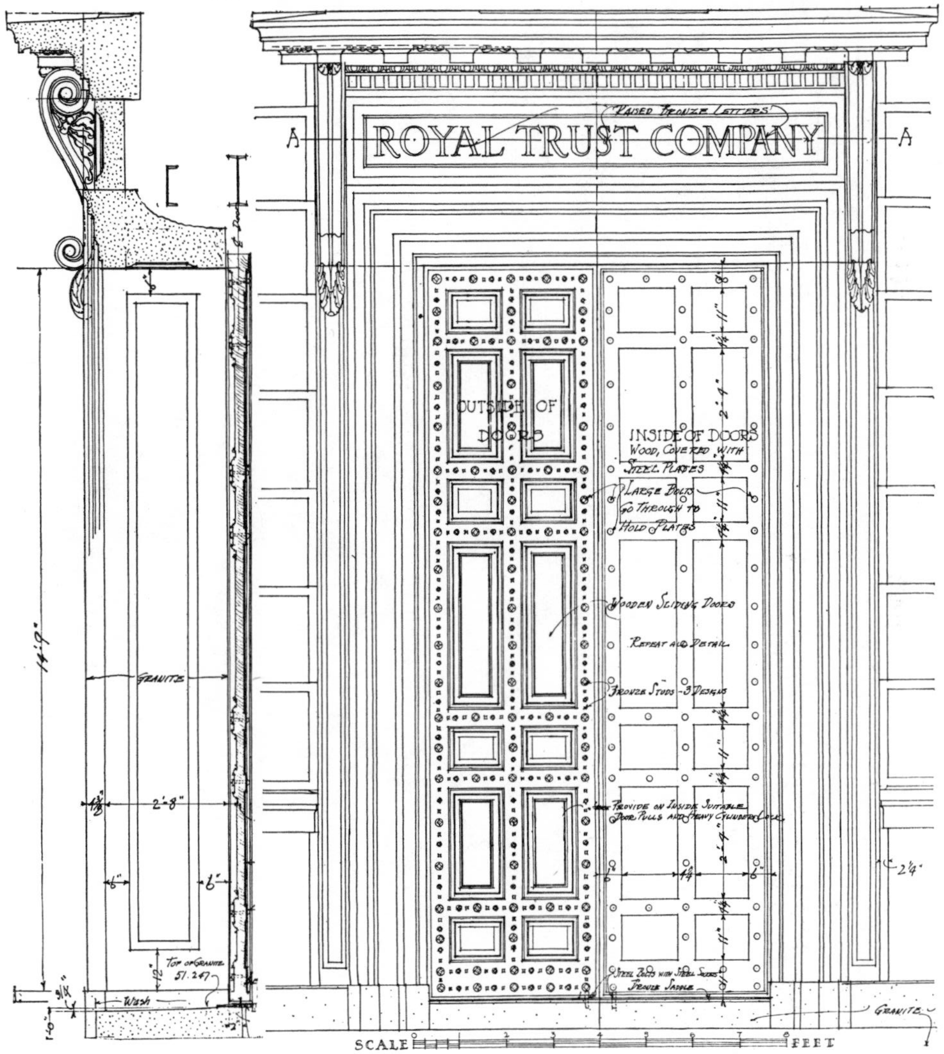

FIRST FLOOR PLAN

DETAIL OF DOORWAY

ELEVATION

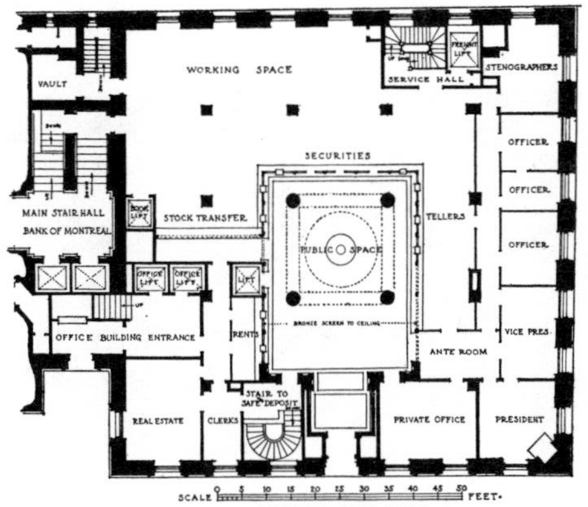

BANK AND OFFICE BUILDING FOR THE ROYAL TRUST COMPANY, MONTREAL, CANADA
1912

ROYAL TRUST COMPANY

PLATE 367

McKIM, MEAD & WHITE

AUDITORIUM BUILDING FOR VASSAR COLLEGE, POUGHKEEPSIE, N. Y.
1913

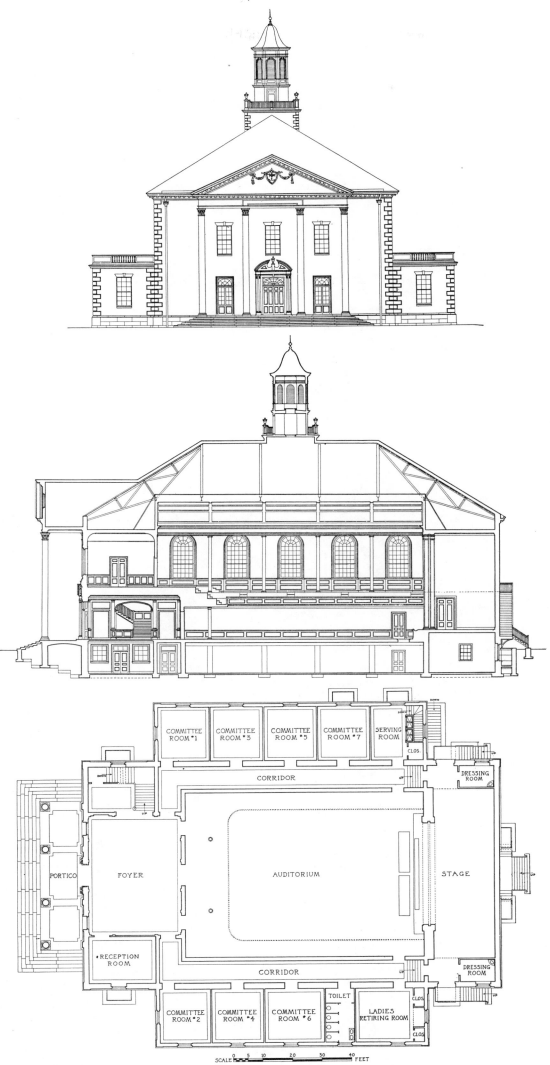

SCALE 0 5 10 20 30 40 FEET

AUDITORIUM FOR VASSAR COLLEGE, POUGHKEEPSIE, N. Y.
1913

PLATE 369

McKIM, MEAD & WHITE

VIEWS OF MAIN ENTRANCE, CORRIDOR AND STAIRWAY

NORTH ELEVATION OF FIRST SECTION

THE MINNEAPOLIS MUSEUM OF FINE ARTS
1914

PLATE 370

MCKIM, MEAD & WHITE

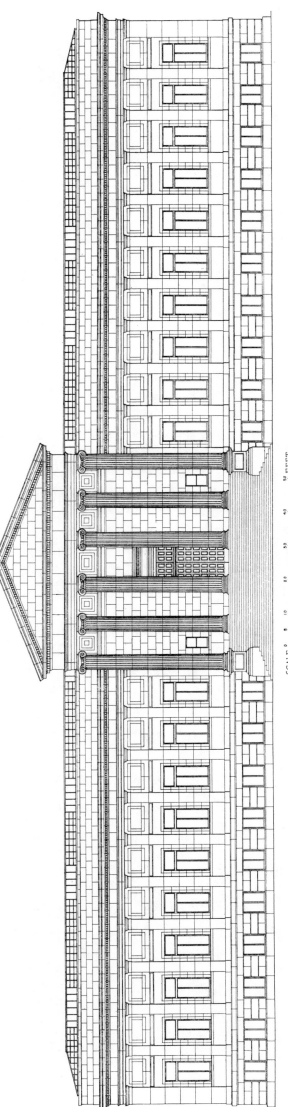

SCALE 0 5 10 20 30 40 50 FEET

ELEVATION OF CENTRAL PORTION NOW BUILT

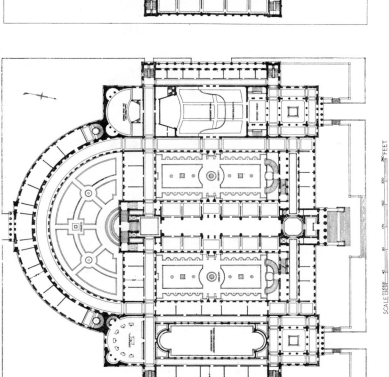

SECOND FLOOR PLAN

MAIN FLOOR PLAN

BASEMENT PLAN

SCALE 0 10 20 40 60 80 100 200 FEET

THE MINNEAPOLIS MUSEUM OF FINE ARTS
MINNEAPOLIS, MINNESOTA.
1912

PLATE 372

MCKIM, MEAD & WHITE

BUILDING FOR THE AMERICAN ACADEMY IN ROME
1913

PLATE 373

MCKIM, MEAD & WHITE

LIBRARY

BUILDING FOR THE AMERICAN ACADEMY IN ROME.
1913

ENTRANCE VESTIBULE

CORRIDOR AROUND COURT

THE COURT

THE AMERICAN ACADEMY IN ROME.
1913

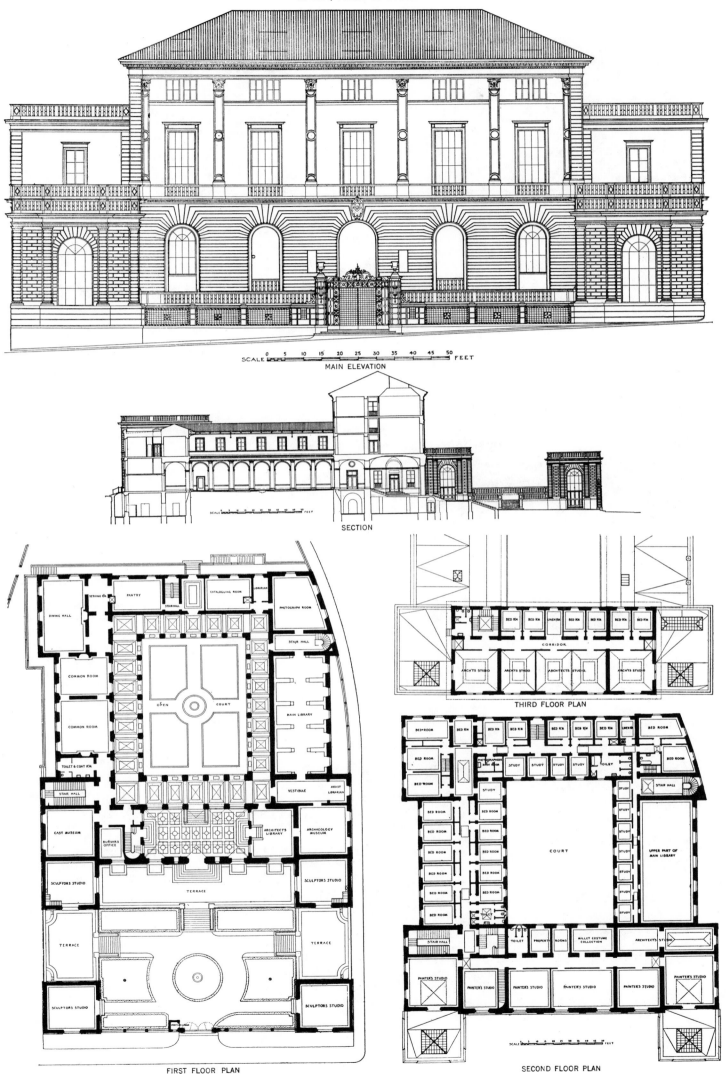

SCALE 0 5 10 15 20 25 30 35 40 45 50 FEET

MAIN ELEVATION

SECTION

FIRST FLOOR PLAN

THIRD FLOOR PLAN

SECOND FLOOR PLAN

THE AMERICAN ACADEMY IN ROME.
1913

FOUNTAIN OF THE GREAT GOD PAN - 1907
SCULPTURE BY GEORGE GRAY BARNARD

CLASS OF 1891, MEMORIAL GATEWAY, 1917.

COLUMBIA UNIVERSITY, NEW YORK CITY.

FACADE TOWARD GARDEN

FACADE TOWARD STREET

BOTANICAL MUSEUM OF THE BROOKLYN INSTITUTE OF ARTS & SCIENCES
1917

PLATE 378

MCKIM MEAD & WHITE

INTERIOR OF CENTRAL PAVILION

DETAIL OF CENTRAL PAVILION

BOTANICAL MUSEUM OF THE BROOKLYN INSTITUTE OF ARTS & SCIENCES
1917

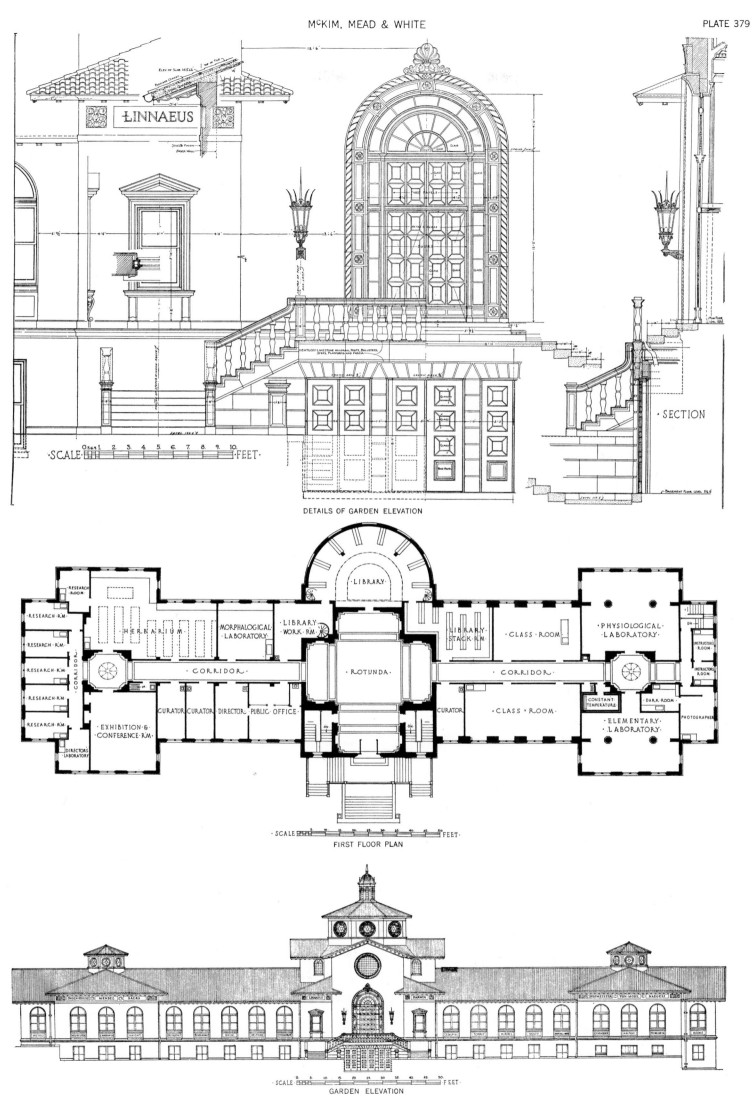

LINNAEUS

·SCALE· 0 1 2. 3. 4. 5 6. 7. 8. 9. 10. FEET·

·SECTION·

DETAILS OF GARDEN ELEVATION

FIRST FLOOR PLAN

·SCALE· FEET·

GARDEN ELEVATION

·SCALE· 0 5 10 15 20 25 30 35 40 45 50 FEET·

BOTANICAL MUSEUM OF THE BROOKLYN INSTITUTE OF ARTS & SCIENCES
1917

PLATE 380

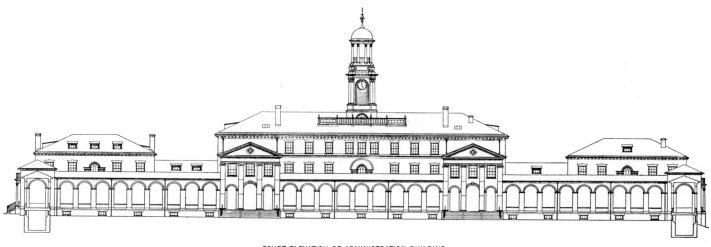

COURT ELEVATION OF ADMINISTRATION BUILDING.

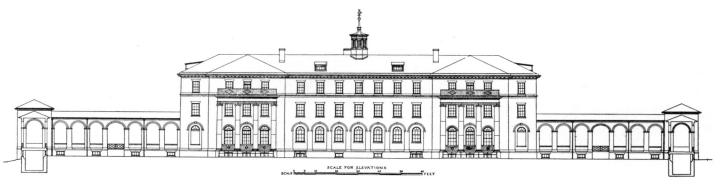

COURT ELEVATION OF DINING HALL BUILDING.

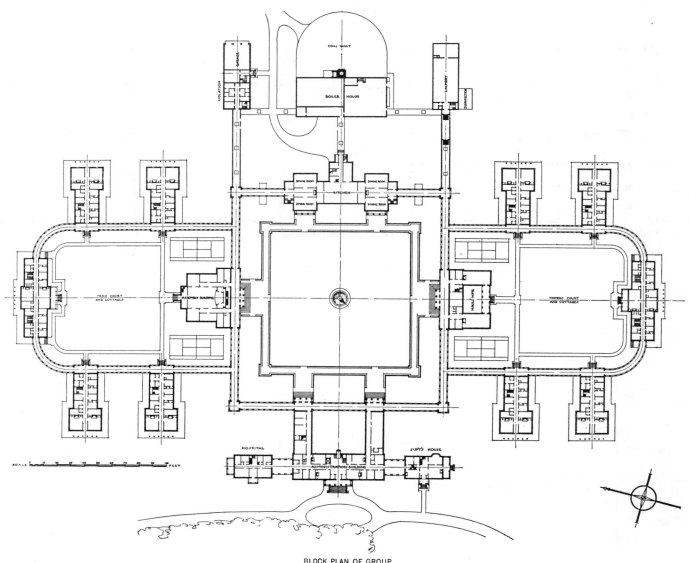

BLOCK PLAN OF GROUP

THE BURKE FOUNDATION HOSPITAL FOR CONVALESCENTS,
WHITE PLAINS, N. Y.
1914

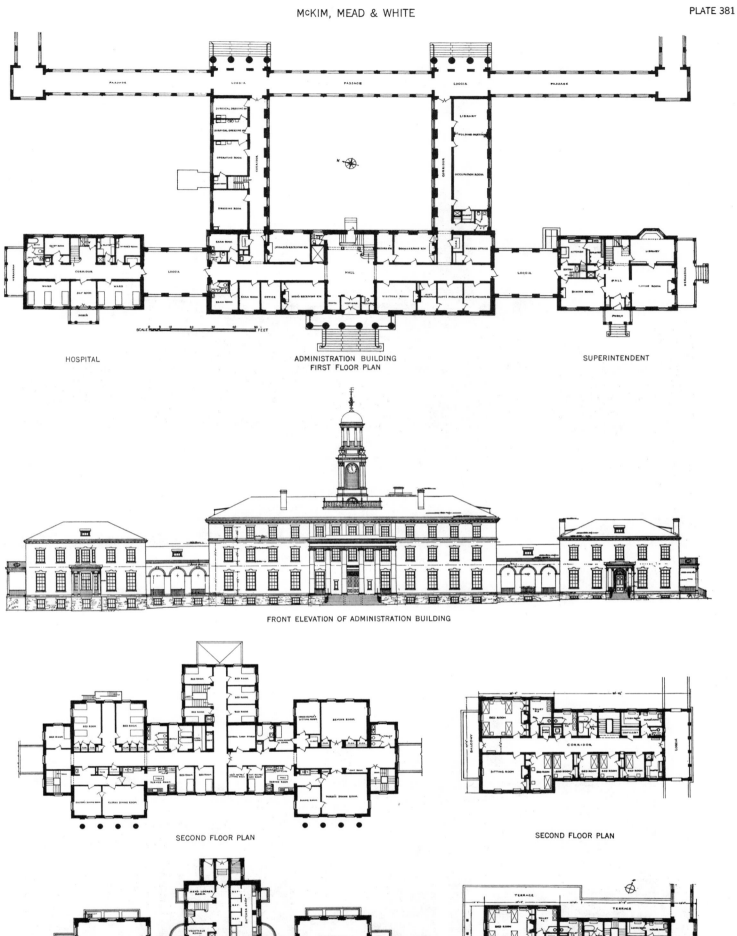

HOSPITAL

ADMINISTRATION BUILDING
FIRST FLOOR PLAN

SUPERINTENDENT

FRONT ELEVATION OF ADMINISTRATION BUILDING

SECOND FLOOR PLAN

SECOND FLOOR PLAN

FIRST FLOOR PLAN
DINING HALL BUILDING

FIRST FLOOR PLAN
TYPICAL COTTAGE

THE BURKE FOUNDATION HOSPITAL FOR CONVALESCENTS,
WHITE PLAINS, N. Y.
1914

MAIN ENTRANCE AND ADMINISTRATION BUILDING

DINING HALL BUILDING FROM QUADRANGLE

THE BURKE FOUNDATION HOSPITAL FOR CONVALESCENTS.
WHITE PLAINS, NEW YORK.
1914

ADMINISTRATION BUILDING, FACADE TOWARD QUADRANGLE

ARCADES CONNECTING BUILDINGS IN QUADRANGLE

THE BURKE FOUNDATION HOSPITAL FOR CONVALESCENTS,
WHITE PLAINS, NEW YORK.
1914

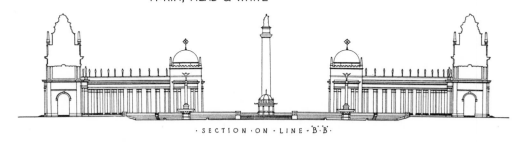

· SECTION · ON · LINE · B·B ·

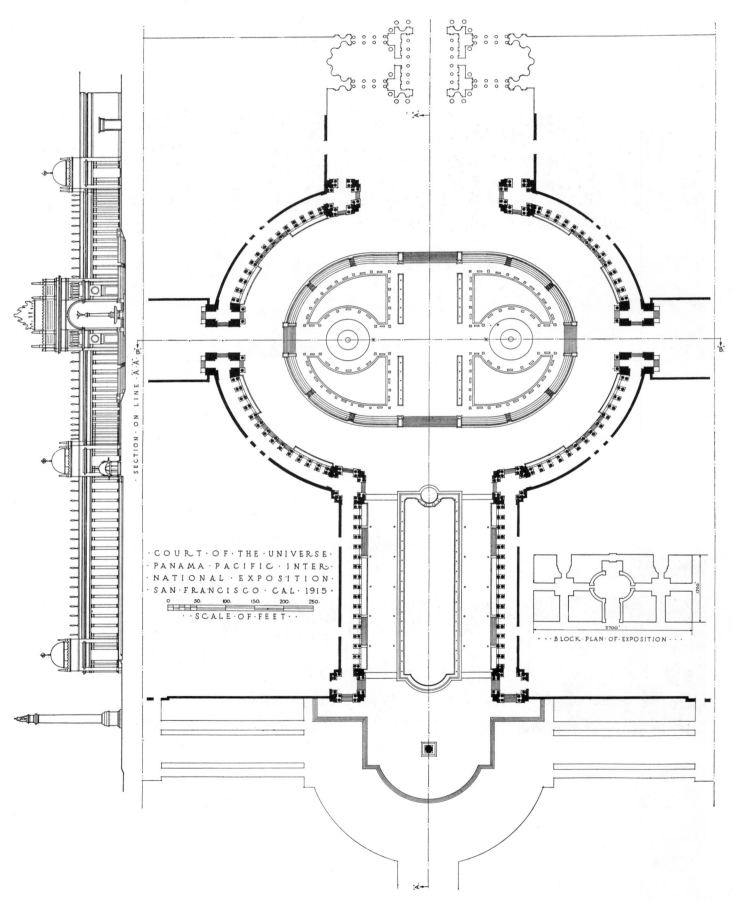

· SECTION · ON · LINE · A·A ·

COURT · OF · THE · UNIVERSE ·
PANAMA · PACIFIC · INTER ·
NATIONAL · EXPOSITION ·
SAN · FRANCISCO · CAL · 1915 ·

0   50.   100.   150.   200.   250.
· SCALE · OF · FEET ·

· · BLOCK · PLAN · OF · EXPOSITION · · ·

THE PANAMA PACIFIC INTERNATIONAL EXPOSITION, SAN FRANCISCO, CAL.
1915

AGRICVLTVRE

DOOR IN COLONNADE

SCALE 0 1 2 3 4 5   10   15   20   25   30 FEET
THIS WORK WAS EXECUTED IN ARTIFICIAL TRAVERTINE, CAST AND PLASTIC, AND DECORATED WITH COLOR.

THE PANAMA PACIFIC INTERNATIONAL EXPOSITION, SAN FRANCISCO, CAL.
DETAIL OF PAVILION AND COLONNADE IN COURT OF THE UNIVERSE.
1915

THE PANAMA - PACIFIC INTERNATIONAL EXPOSITION
SAN FRANCISCO 1915.
VIEWS IN COURT OF THE UNIVERSE

PAVILIONS AND COLONNADE

FOUNTAIN OF THE RISING SUN

COLUMN OF PROGRESS

COURT OF THE UNIVERSE, PANAMA PACIFIC INTERNATIONAL EXPOSITION,
SAN FRANCISCO, 1915.

PLATE 388

McKIM, MEAD & WHITE

THE NATIONAL McKINLEY BIRTHPLACE MEMORIAL, NILES, OHIO
1915

PLATE 389

MCKIM, MEAD & WHITE

THE COURT AND MEMORIAL STATUE

DETAIL OF FACADE

THE NATIONAL MCKINLEY BIRTHPLACE MEMORIAL, NILES, OHIO
1915

ELEVATION

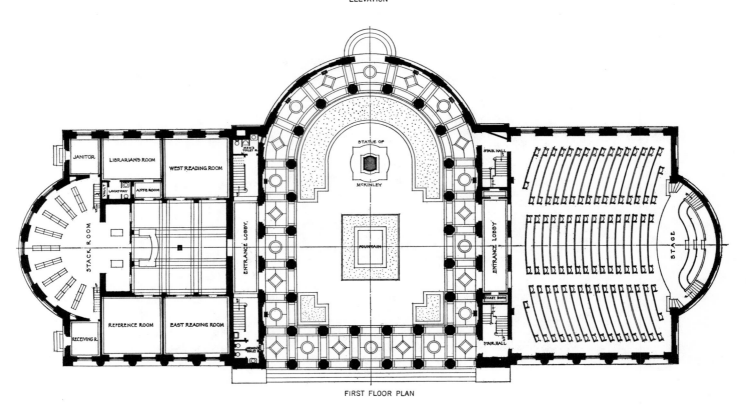

FIRST FLOOR PLAN

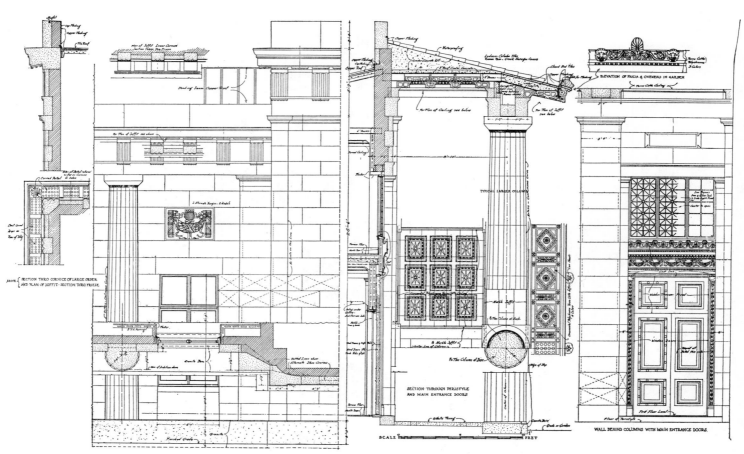

EXTERIOR DETAILS - GRANITE, WHITE GEORGIA MARBLE, POLYCHROME TERRA COTTA, ETC.

THE NATIONAL McKINLEY BIRTHPLACE MEMORIAL, NILES, OHIO.
1915

HOUSES FOR GERALDYN REDMOND ESQ. AND THE COUNTESS DE LAUGIER VILLARS
NEW YORK CITY
1914

FIRST FLOOR PLAN

SECOND FLOOR PLAN

· SCALE · FEET ·

O. 5. 10. 15 20

HOUSES FOR GERALDYN REDMOND ESQ. AND THE COUNTESS DE LAUGIER VILLARS
NEW YORK CITY
1914

PLATE 394

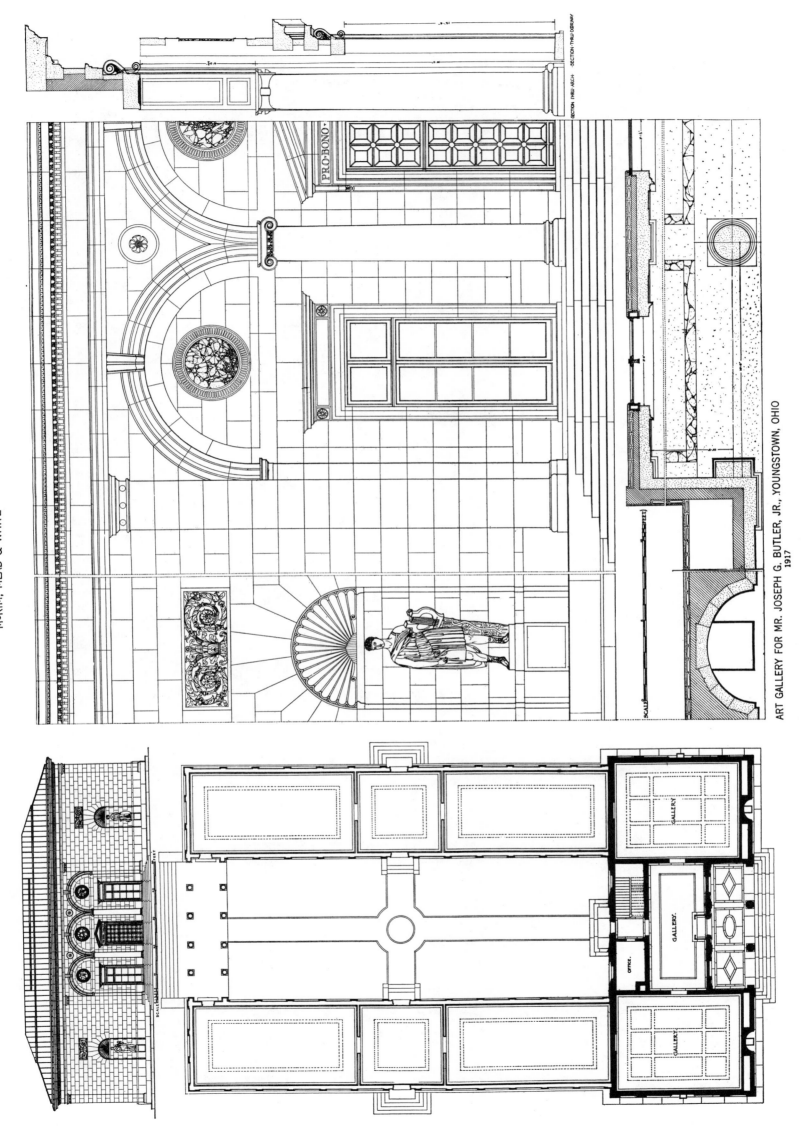

McKIM, MEAD & WHITE

ART GALLERY FOR MR. JOSEPH G. BUTLER, JR., YOUNGSTOWN, OHIO
1917

PRO·BONO·

SECTION THRU ARCH·

SECTION THRU DRIVEWAY

GALLERY

GALLERY.

GALLERY

OFFICE·

PLATE 394-A

McKIM, MEAD & WHITE

ART GALLERY AT YOUNGSTOWN, OHIO, FOR MR. J. G. BUTLER, JR.
1917

FACADE

INTERIOR OF BANKING ROOM

THE FRANKLIN NATIONAL BANK, PHILADELPHIA, PA.
1916

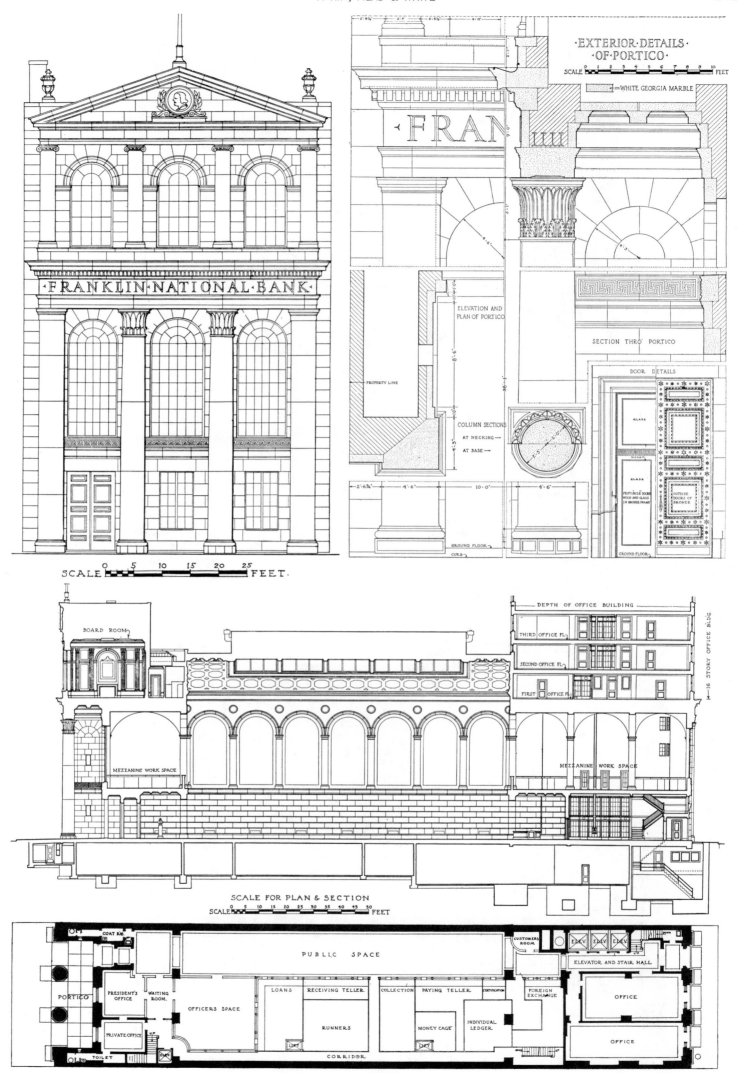

FRANKLIN NATIONAL BANK

·EXTERIOR·DETAILS·
·OF·PORTICO·

SCALE 0 1 2 3 4 5 6 7 8 9 10 FEET

= WHITE GEORGIA MARBLE

FRAN

SECTION THRO' PORTICO

ELEVATION AND
PLAN OF PORTICO

PROPERTY LINE

COLUMN SECTIONS
AT NECKING —
AT BASE —

GROUND FLOOR
CURB

DOOR DETAILS

GLASS

GLASS

VESTIBULE DOORS
WOOD AND GLASS
IN BRONZE FRAME

OUTSIDE
DOORS OF BRONZE

GROUND FLOOR

SCALE 0 5 10 15 20 25 FEET

BOARD ROOM

MEZZANINE WORK SPACE

DEPTH OF OFFICE BUILDING

THIRD OFFICE FL.

SECOND OFFICE FL.

FIRST OFFICE FL.

16 STORY OFFICE BLDG.

MEZZANINE WORK SPACE

SCALE FOR PLAN & SECTION

SCALE 0 5 10 15 20 25 30 35 40 45 50 FEET

COAT RM.

PUBLIC SPACE

CUSTOMERS ROOM

ELEV. ELEV. ELEV.

ELEVATOR AND STAIR HALL

PORTICO

PRESIDENT'S OFFICE

WAITING ROOM

OFFICERS SPACE

PRIVATE OFFICE

TOILET

LOANS

RECEIVING TELLER.

RUNNERS

COLLECTION

PAYING TELLER.

MONEY CAGE

INDIVIDUAL LEDGER.

CERTIFICATION

FOREIGN EXCHANGE

OFFICE

OFFICE

CORRIDOR.

THE FRANKLIN NATIONAL BANK, PHILADELPHIA, PA.
1916

PLATE 397

McKIM, MEAD & WHITE

LIVING ROOM

STAIR HALL, SECOND STORY

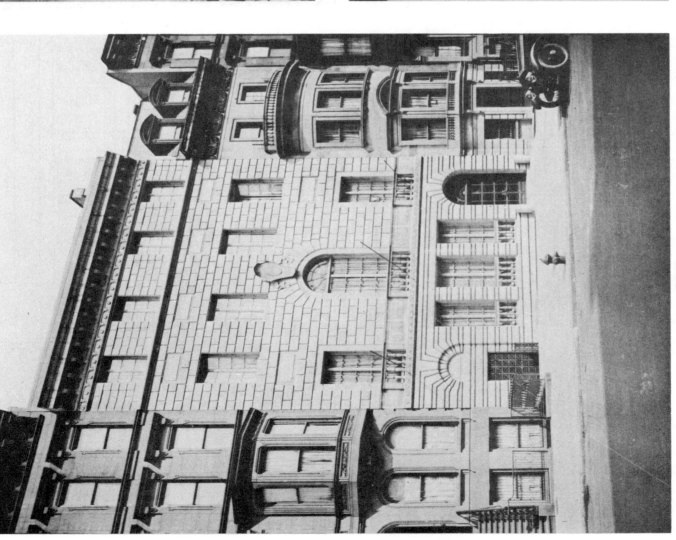

FACADE

RESIDENCE OF THOMAS NEWBOLD, NEW YORK CITY
1917

PLATE 397 A

McKIM, MEAD & WHITE

CEILING
FOURTH FLOOR — 8:0"
THIRD FLOOR — 12:0
SECOND FLOOR — 13:0"
FIRST FLOOR — 16:6"
GROUND FLOOR — 14:0"
EL - 77.18
GRADE AT DOOR EL-74.51

FRONT ELEVATION

SCALE 0 5 10 15 20 FEET

LIVING ROOM
SALON
BOY'S
STAIR HALL

DINING ROOM
HALL
RECEPTION ROOM
STAIR HALL
COAT ROOM
COAT ROOM
PANTRY
MEN'S ROOM

FLOOR PLANS

SCALE 0 5 10 FEET

RESIDENCE OF THOMAS NEWBOLD, NEW YORK CITY
1917

DETAIL OF SERVICE ENTRANCE

SCALE 0 5 10 FEET

LIMESTONE
SILVER GRAY SIENNA
OLD CONVENT SIENNA

DETAIL OF MAIN CORNICE

SECTION
DETAIL OF CARTOUCHE

SECTION
GRANITE
LIMESTONE
DETAIL OF LOWER BALUSTRADE

UPPER PART OF ENTRANCE DOOR

EXTERIOR DETAILS AND DETAIL OF LIVING ROOM

SCALE 0 5 FEET

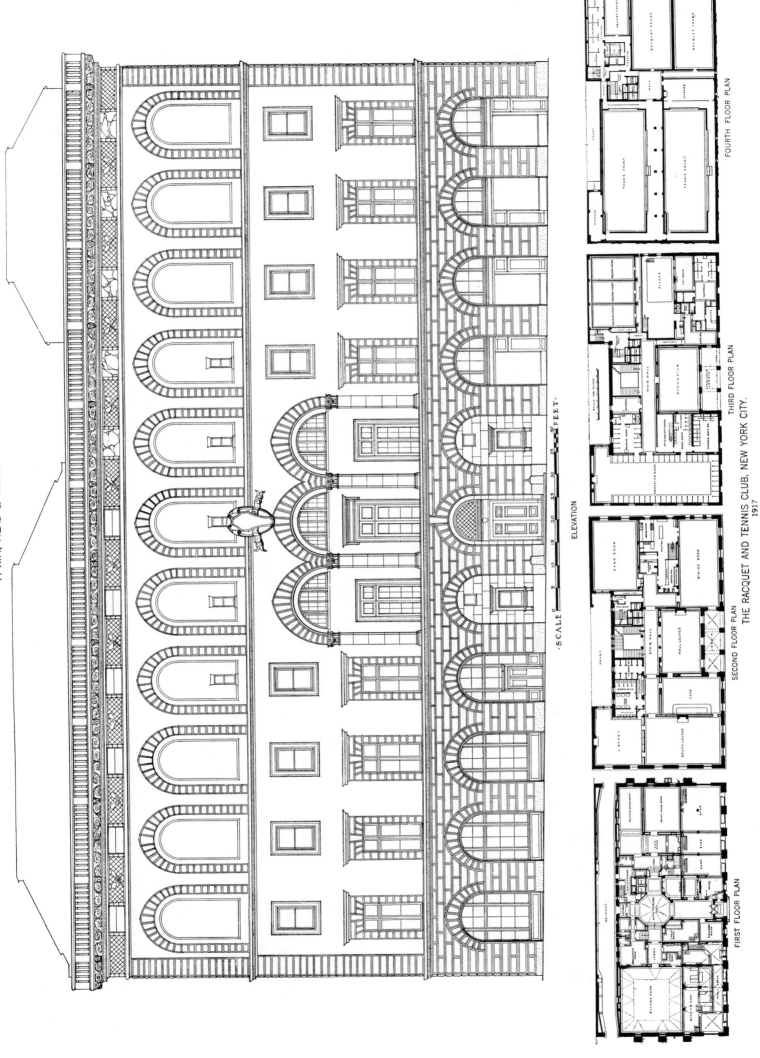

PLATE 398

McKIM, MEAD & WHITE

ELEVATION

·SCALE· 0 5 10 15 20 25 30 35 40 FEET·

FOURTH FLOOR PLAN

THIRD FLOOR PLAN

SECOND FLOOR PLAN

FIRST FLOOR PLAN

THE RACQUET AND TENNIS CLUB, NEW YORK CITY.
1917

FACADE

LOGGIA ON SECOND FLOOR

ENTRANCE HALL

THE RACQUET AND TENNIS CLUB, NEW YORK CITY
1917.

PLATE 399-A

McKIM, MEAD & WHITE

EAST LOUNGE, SECOND FLOOR

HALL LOUNGE, SECOND FLOOR

TENNIS COURT

PLUNGE IN TURKISH BATH

THE RACQUET AND TENNIS CLUB, NEW YORK CITY
1917

INDEX

INDEX

INDEX

INDEX